THE AMAZING ROOSEVELT FAMILY
1613 — 1942

The Amazing Roosevelt Family

1613—1942

KARL SCHRIFTGIESSER

Publishers · New York
WILFRED FUNK, INC.

For Sherwin

Contents

BOOK THREE:
THE RESPECTABLE AGE

BOOK FOUR: PRESIDENTS

A Roosevelt Family Chart

THIS CHART is designed to show the descent of Theodore Roosevelt and Franklin Delano Roosevelt from their first common ancestor to come to America. Only the two branches of the Roosevelt Family leading to the two Presidents are shown. Capitalized names are those of direct antecedents. Italicised names are those of sons who carry on the direct line of the two branches. Dates signify year of birth. Names immediately beneath capitalized names are those of wives. Where more than one is given the order of marriage is followed. Names of wives by whom direct descent is carried on are marked with a star (*).

CLAES MARTENSZEN VAN ROSENVELT.
Jannetje (Samuels) Thomas.

Christaien, 1650; d. inf.
Elsje, 1652.
Anna Margaret, 1654.
Christina, 1656.
Nicholas, 1658.
Anna.

— — — — — — — —

NICHOLAS ROOSEVELT (1658).
Heyltje Jans Kunst.

Jannetje, 1683.
Margaretta.
Nicholas II, 1687.
Johannes, 1689.
Elsie.
Jacobus, 1692.
Sarah.
Rachel, 1699.

— — — — — — — —

JOHANNES ROOSEVELT
(1689).
Heyltje Sjoerts.

Margareta, 1709.
Olphert, 1716.
Maria, 1720.
Jacobus, 1724.
Cornelius, 1731.

JACOBUS ROOSEVELT
(1692).
Catharina Hardenbroock.

Johannes, 1715.
Nicholas III, 1717.
Helena, 1719.
Jacobus, 1721.
Chritoful, 1724.
Isaac, 1726.
Abraham, 1728.
Sarah, 1730.
Peter, 1732.
Adolphus, 1735.
Christopher, 1739.

JACOBUS ROOSEVELT
(1724).
Annetje Bogard.

Anna, 1748.
Johannes, 1751.
Heyltje, 1752.
Margarieta, 1755.
Maria, d. inf.
Jacobus, 1759.
Helena, 1761.
Maria, 1763.
Nicholas, 1767.
Ann (by 2d. marr.)

ISAAC ROOSEVELT
(1726).
Cornelia Hoffman.

Abraham, 1752, d. inf.
Martinue, 1754, d. inf.
Catharine, 1756.
Sarah, 1758.
Jacobus (James), 1760.
Cornelia, 1761, d. inf.
Maria, 1763.
Martin, 1765.
Cornelia, 1767.
Helena, 1768.

JAMES J. ROOSEVELT
(JACOBUS) (1759).
Maria Van Schaack.

Cornelius v S., 1794.
James, 1795.
Nicholas, 1798.
Catherine Angelica, 1803.
William Henry, 1806.
Alfred, 1811.

JAMES ROOSEVELT
(JACOBUS) (1760).
Maria E. Walton*
Catharine Barclay.
Harriet Howland.

Isaac, 1790.
Grace, 1792.
James, 1794.
Walton, 1796.
Edward, 1799.
Richard, 1801.
Hamilton, 1805.
Henry W., 1809.
Susan (by 2d. marr.)
James

– – – – – – – –

CORNELIUS V. S.
ROOSEVELT (1794).
Margaret Barnhill.

Silas Weir, 1823.
James Alfred, 1825.
Cornelius V.X., 1827.
Robert Barnhill, 1829.
Theodore, 1831.
William Wallace, 1834,
(d. inf.)

ISAAC ROOSEVELT II
(1790).
Mary Rebecca Aspinwall.

James, 1828.
John Aspinwall, 1840.

– – – – – – – –

THEODORE ROOSEVELT (1831).
Martha Bullock.

Anna, 1855.
Theodore, 1858.
Elliott, 1860.
Corinne, 1861.

JAMES ROOSEVELT (1828).
Rebecca M. Howland.
Sarah Delano.*

James Roosevelt Roosevelt,
(by 1st marr.)
*Franklin Delano Roosevelt,
1882,* (by 2d marr.)

— — — — — — — — —

THEODORE ROOSEVELT (1858).
Alice Hathaway Lee.
Edith Kermit Carow.

Alice Lee, 1884, (by 1st
marr.)
Theodore, Jr., 1887.
Kermit, 1889.
Ethel Carow, 1891.
Archibald Bullock, 1894.
Quentin, 1897.

FRANKLIN DELANO ROOSEVELT (1882).
Anna Eleanor Roosevelt.

Anna Eleanor, 1906.
James, 1907.
Franklin Delano, 1909,
d. inf.
Elliott, 1910.
Franklin Delano, 1914.
John Aspinwall, 1916.

— — — — — — — — —

Book One

IMMIGRANTS

Against This World

THE BRINGER of the name Roosevelt to America was a shadowy Dutchman about whom extraordinarily little is known. He slips vaguely through the scattered annals of New Amsterdam, hardly more than a footnote to the history of that trading post which became an English colony almost before it was a Dutch town. If we accept the legend that has grown up around him, he was an amazing adventurer, a man of imagination and great courage, who deserves better recognition than he has managed to attain in the 304 years since his name first crept into the records of that outpost of the Old World. But if we seek his biography in the few blotted words that have survived, then he was just another farmer and trader who lived in reasonable honesty and industry from the fruits of a small acreage at the lower end of the island of Manhattan.

The history of his descendants, however, stems from more documented sources than the hazy story of Claes Martenszen van Rosenvelt or Nicholas, the son of Martin, of the Rose Field, as the Dutch progenitor of all the Roosevelts was known in his time. Indeed it does not properly begin with his unrecorded arrival in New Netherland, but in England and with two men of slight contemporary distinction—the one a weaver and the other a tailor—who busied themselves with the affairs of Separatism and the founding of the English colony at Plymouth on Massachusetts Bay. And it quickly includes a dozen or more common people of mixed European extraction who, like the Dutch farmer and the English tradesmen, played their own comparatively inconspicuous parts in the tremendous drama the entire Western World was experiencing as the Seventeenth Century dawned.

Not one of the immigrant antecedents of Theodore and Franklin Delano Roosevelt came closer to greatness than the outermost fringe. They were ordinary folk who were picked up and swept from the accustomed channels of their lives by the surging tide of history that was then changing the face of the world. Great forces beat against them and they reacted to the inescapable, as little people have at all times. Some were charged by a spiritual emotion that caused them to turn like Saint Andrew from home and kindred; others were carried along by the fierce drift of those forces of economic expansion which they could not understand and over which they had no control. All of them—English and Dutch and German and French—eventually reached the New World. And there, through the mysteries of life—through love or the hope of greater fortune—they met and merged. Time and genetics did the rest.

The personal motives which brought to America the men and women who were to form the Roosevelt family, as it has come down to the present time in two straight lines, were as varied as their names. As was the case with all who crossed the seas to settle on these unfriendly shores they were moved to do so by a variety of general reasons that underlay the entire colonization of America, whether English or Dutch or French. As any number of authorities have shown, these were partly religious but primarily economic, and this truism applies as well to those who froze and starved at Plymouth as to those who dodged the Indians along the Hudson or planted corn in Virginia's warmer sun. The sanctification of the codfish as much as any desire for religious freedom made the settling of New England a possibility and the Dutch never denied they were seeking the beaver rather than a place in which to worship God without restraint.

These forces did not break suddenly upon an unsuspecting world. They had been building up slowly, gradually gaining momentum over a long stretch of time. Nor did they cascade without warning upon the shores of the Americas, throwing great armies of builders and toilers into the new land. The infiltration from the Old World was slow and that from England was not part of a conscious plan for empire. As the Sixteenth Century drew into its last quarter some Englishmen and many Scotsmen, it is true, had begun to look across the seas with quizzical and even hungry eyes. But even then the bulk of England's sea dogs were only fishermen. It was not until 1578 that Sir Humphrey Gilbert, who was Sir Walter Raleigh's half-brother, received the first patent from the Crown giving him the right to colonize and rule such lands as he might choose from those he discovered.

There was no cry of *Lebensraum* in those days. Neither England nor Holland was crowded with people restless from the lack of food or work. And so there was no exodus en masse from either country. Indeed, as a colonizer Sir Humphrey was a failure and for several years thereafter colonization was looked upon as a bad investment by the London adventurers who, in the changed economy of their country, were seeking a return for their growing wealth. Feudalism was rapidly disappearing from the island and commercialism was in the ascendancy, based on the fortunes brought back by the privateers who preyed on the ships of Spain. With this new-found wealth there was a demand for luxuries and the London merchants fattened their purses as ship after ship came home, deep-laden with treasure from distant lands.

The war with Spain hastened the tide. A grim financial depression settled over England in the last years of this struggle as the harbors of Spain and Portugal, of Barbary and the Levant were closed to English ships. Even the old, accustomed trade with Germany and Poland and Denmark was cut off. But, when the war ended and the Spanish Armada went to its terrible doom, the pent up forces of trade were unloosed. The Period of Expansion had begun. Holland, too, felt the change, and the noses of English and Dutch ships were poking one after another around strange headlands thousands of salty miles from the harbors where they had fished. The very first year of the new century saw the Dutch East India Company chartered and then, in spaces of two or three years each, English companies were set up for the exploitation of North and South Virginia, Guiana, Newfoundland, Bermuda, New England and Massachusetts. The sea-girt nations of Holland and England were washed by the expanding wave. And every eye at every helm sought the quick passage to the golden East.

They wanted the Orient and they got America. At first it was a hindrance, a barrier in the sea to untold wealth. But one by one the profitable possibilities of American conquest became apparent. In 1607 George Popham was using Sir Humphrey Gilbert's old charter in a disastrous effort to plant a colony at Sagadohoc, as the Kennebec River in Maine was then called. Two years earlier Henry Hudson, working for the Dutch, had given his name to a great river and coasted the shores of North and South Virginia. Mile by mile and inlet by inlet the long coast became familiar as Frenchmen and Dutchmen and Englishmen, seeking the codfish and the pelted beaver, took over the new land. And back in Paris and Amsterdam and London merchants and Adventurers (as investors in stock companies were called)—many of whom never set foot on a ship's deck— supplied the money for ships and immigrants because they knew there would be profits in the end.

History books today print proudly the names of the great navigators and explorers, the governors and chiefs of staff, and even the exploiters, who were leaders of the Age of Expansion, but there is room only in the dull archives of the genealogists and the antiquarians for those thousands of little folk who followed in their wake. Who, reasonably familiar with the history of this country, can recall the parts played by the Cushmans, Allertons, Howlands, Tilleys, Warrens, de la Noyes, Aspinwalls, Bensens, Hoffmans, van Laers, Hardenbroecks, Stobos, Bullocks, and even Roosevelts, in Seventeenth Century America? The names, in many instances, are familiar, but the little acts of these little people, all of whom helped make the Roosevelt Family, are forgotten, for they were then only farmers, trappers, tradesmen, entrepreneurs, now and again the holder of some minor office and immigrants. Their only claim to remembrance is that they helped populate colonial America after the fateful year of 1621. Each added his strain somewhere in the next three hundred years to that of the shadowy Nicholas, son of Martin of Rose Field in Zeeland, who once owned a farm on lower Manhattan and who counts among his descendants two Presidents of the United States.

CHAPTER I

The Dutch Trader

IN THE SUMMER of 1616 Captain Cornelis Hendricks returned to Holland after long adventures in the New World. He had been away three years. Had he been a more imaginative fellow, he might then and there have set down a full account of his wanderings down the coast and up the rivers of the New Netherland. But he was a sea captain, not a poet, and the shrewd men he worked for were interested only in an accounting that was strictly to the point. This he proceeded to make. His version was terse and business-like, which was exactly what Simon Willemszen, Jonas Witsen, Hans Claeszen, and the ten other Amsterdam merchants who had sent him across the sea in the first place, wanted him to give. In so doing this salty fellow created a mystery that has never been solved. Perhaps it never will be.

The summer of 1613 was a busy one in the strange waters of the eastern shores of America. Several small but stout vessels, flying the flag of the Netherlands, were poking about and their captains were busy taking soundings, making notes, and sketching maps, to add to the sum of information which Henry Hudson the Englishman had already brought back to the Amsterdam quays. Captain Pieter Franszen, master of the *Fox*, was one of the curious skippers. Unfortunately he was too curious and one day when he stepped ashore to take the kinks out of his sea legs some unfriendly natives brought his career to a violent end. This left the *Fox* in the command of the unlucky Franszen's mate, Jan De With, who pointed her bow southward towards the Sandy Hook.

There, in the summer calm, the *Fox* met up with two other Dutch vessels. One was the *Tiger,* Adraien Block, master, and the other, a smaller vessel, was the *Fortune,* in the command of Hendrick Christaiensen. The three ship masters talked the situation over and decided that De With should take the *Fox* back to Holland while Captains Block and Christaiensen should continue their coastwise cruise. But before the *Fox* turned towards the horizon, some members of its crew elected to transfer to the other ships.

There is no way of knowing now who these sailors were but it is believed that one was a young fellow who was known to his shipmates as Kleytjen, which simply means "the little one." Whether this was a nickname given in irony because of his strapping size, or whether it was a more apt description we can only guess. If Kleytjen really was the progenitor of all the Roosevelts in America the chances are that he won the title through the simple humor of the forecastle, for none of the Roosevelts has been notoriously short. It is a further legendary belief that his real name was Claes, the son of Martin and Anna, peasants, of the village of Het Rosen Velt (Field of Roses) on the Island of Tholen, near Zeeland, a low island near the mouth of the Rhine. He is supposed to have been about 18 years old in the summer of 1613 when he ran away from home to join the *Fox* in the harbor of Amsterdam.

After Kleytjen of the *Fox* had chosen the *Tiger* as his new ship, Captains Block and Christaiensen headed north from the Sandy Hook. When they came to the mouth of Hudson's River they anchored. From the Manhattoes tribe they got water and food but they were unable to barter for beaver pelts in any quantity. Since the collecting of skins was the real reason for his presence in these waters, Captain Block decided he would sail up the river to try his luck with the tribes farther north. Somewhere, probably near what is now Albany, he anchored the *Tiger,* and decided to wait until he had filled the hold with furs. The crew built a camp and trading post on the shore and the late summer weeks passed. November came and they were still there. One day, while all the crew was ashore, a smouldering log fell from the hearth of the ship's galley. The *Tiger* burned to the water's edge.

Luckily, Captain Block and his men had their camp on the river shore where they had taken their saws and axes to cut fire-wood when the chill winds of autumn had begun to nip. They spent the next three months building a new ship, forty-four feet along the water line, which they named the *Restless,* and in which they planned to go down the river when the ice broke up. That spring they did go down, and around the island of the Manhattoes, through the swirling waters of the Gate of Hell, and far to the eastward in the wake of the *Fortune,* seeking new landmarks and more beaver skins. But Kleytjen was not with them on this trip.

Whether, impelled by an insatiable curiosity concerning the country and its red-skinned natives, he had gone voluntarily into the wilderness, or whether he had been captured by Indians while wandering close to the camp, is not known. But it is recorded that during the next two years two or more Dutchmen were at loose in the northeastern American woods. In his Journal for 1615, Champlain, the explorer who was in America that year, speaks of three such adventurous spirits roaming the forests and shores and hinted that they were tribal prisoners. It is probable that Kleytjen and one or two companions deliberately went into the woods to trap or collect furs, or perhaps they went for the more loftily scientific purpose of making a first-hand report on conditions in the country away from the familiar coastal region, and were eventually taken into a sort of "protective custody" by the Indians.

Late in the summer of 1614 Captain Block left the yacht *Restless* in charge of his mate Cornelis Hendricks, or Hendricksen, and sailed back to Holland with Captain Christaiensen aboard the *Fortune.* The *Restless,* during the next two years, lived up to her name, and her captain was true to his trust. He had been charged by Block to explore particularly the Hudson and the Delaware regions and this he did with a dogged Dutch thoroughness. And so, in the late summer following Captain Block's departure, he was sailing his vessel near the mouth of the Delaware River when he was approached by a group of Minquaa Indians. Through an interpreter the savages asked him how much he would give to ransom three white men who were then living and working at an Indian camp some miles up the river.

If, as seems possible, Kleytjen had left the camp where the *Restless* was being built in the early spring of 1614, he had circled west and south from a point somewhere near Albany, through a country never before penetrated by a white man, until he had come at last to a point on Delaware Bay. Kleytjen evidently had a way with him, for he seems to have got along well throughout the winter with the various Indian tribes in that broad expanse, traveling from the Mohicans in the north to the country of the enemy Mohawks inland and thence down to the Maquaas' stamping ground in the south.

Captain Hendricks ransomed the three white people for a few beads and trinkets, but who they were or what became of them afterwards there seems to be no way of knowing. He himself did not return to Holland until August, 1616. In that month the merchants of Amsterdam who employed him presented a petition to the States-General of Holland for a trading patent covering the territory he had discovered since his master, Captain Block, had left him two summers before. With this petition went a map, drawn in colors on a heavy piece of paper three feet long, and a brief report dictated by Captain Hendricks to Carel van Geldre, a notary. The map delineates in detail the already familiar Hudson River from its wide mouth to its head and shows two other rivers, presumably the Delaware and the Susquehanna. Written on this map is this note:

"Take notice. As to what Kleytjen and his Companions have told me of the situation of the Rivers and the places occupied by the tribes, which they found when going inland away from the Maquaas and along the New river down to the Ogehage, namely, the enemies of the aforesaid northern nations, I cannot at present find anything but two sketches of small maps partly finished.

"And when I think how best to make the one correspond with the rough notes, to the best of my knowledge I find that the dwelling-places of the Sennecas, Gachoos,

Capitannasses and Jottecas ought to have been indicated
rather more to the West." [1]

The annotated map and its accompanying report are the
only documentary evidences concerning the presence of Kleytjen, the fabulous ancestor of all the Roosevelts, that have ever
come to light. He is not mentioned by name in Captain Hendricks' report, however, and so it is only a guess that Kleytjen
and the voluntary prisoner of the Maquaas were the same:

"Report of Captain Cornelis Hendricxz., of Munnickendam,
to the High and Mighty Lords, States-General, of the Free
United Netherland Provinces, made on the 18th of August,
A.D. 1616,—Of the countries, bays and three rivers, situate in
the Latitudes from 38 to 40 degrees, by him discovered and
found for and to the behoof of his Owners and Directors of
New Netherland, by name Gerritt Jacob Witsen, Burgomaster
of Amsterdam, Jonas Witsen, Lambrecht van Tweenhuyszen,
Paulus Pelgrom, and others of their company.

"First, he has discovered for his aforesaid Masters and Directors, certain lands, a bay, and three rivers situate between
38 and 40 degrees.

"And there did trade with the Inhabitants; said Trade con-
sisting of Sables, Furs, Robes and other skins.

"He has found the said country full of trees, to wit:—Oak,
hickory, and pines; which trees were, in some places, covered
with vines.

"He has seen in said country, Bucks and does, turkeys and
partridge.

"He has found the climate of said Country very temperate,
judging it to be as temperate as that of this country, Holland.

"He has also traded with the inhabitants, the Minquaas, and
ransomed from them three persons belonging to this Company, paying for them kettles, coral beads, and merchandise;
which three persons had suffered themselves to be employed
by the Maquaas and the Mahichans."

And so, laconically, the captain told his tale of nearly three
years in the wilderness of Indians, turkeys and does. That, and
nothing more, remains of the adventures of Kleytjen, who per-

[1] Captain Hendricks was correct in his geographical afterthought.

haps was the same Nicholas Martenszen van Rosenvelt, who brought the name Roosevelt to America more than three centuries ago.

Captain Hendricks, in his report to the United Company of the Netherlands, says he ransomed "three persons belonging to this Company," but he does not state what ship they were from or whether he brought them back to Holland or left them somewhere in New Netherland. If Kleytjen had returned with him he undoubtedly would have been available to give detailed information when Captain Hendricks drew his colored map. It is reasonable to assume, therefore, that he stayed behind, but where he lived or how he thrived is a mystery whose answer is lost in time.

The Dutch were a meticulous people. From 1624, when New Amsterdam was settled, until after the English seized the town in 1664, they scrupulously set down the details of their births, their marriages, and their deaths, and many other incidentals of their daily lives. It seems a little strange, then, that there should be no further mention of Kleytjen, or anyone else who might have been the Little One, until twenty-two years after Captain Hendricks noted his name with gratitude on the margin of his map. One explanation for this is that he went to live somewhere in the region of Fort Orange on the west bank of the Hudson or that he lived in one of the tiny Dutch towns that were sprinkled over Long Island. The early records of either region have long since disappeared. Another may be that he continued to live voluntarily with the Indians, as other white men were known to have done.

Wherever the shadowy Little One may have been he seems to have shown up suddenly in 1638. The Council of New Netherland met that year on August twenty-sixth in the Council Chamber of Fort Amsterdam, which was near the present Battery Park at the lower end of Manhattan. Most of the cases which Dr. Jan de Montagne, the Governor's assistant and head of the Council, heard sleepily droned forth in the summer heat concerned derelictions as dull as those usually brought before a police magistrate. But one was a little out of the usual. It consisted of a charge of slander brought by Philip Teyler against

Nicholas Martens, which is just another Dutch way of saying Nicholas, the son of Martin. What Nicholas had said that was so derogatory to Philip as to warrant judicial interference, was not written into the laconic record. The good judge, who could be stern when he wanted to but who had a reputation for judicial fairness, listened to the accusations against the Little One. He then asked the accused what he had to say, and Nicholas Martens, looking a little sheepish, replied that he had "nothing to say" against the plaintiff.

"See that you don't," said the judge, and after a further admonitory word or two he dismissed the complaint and sent the two men on their way.

Nicholas Martens held his tongue for eleven years. Then he began to take on substance. He had now grown to be a man of middle age, but still full of vim and vigor. Wherever he had been during this time, and no one has ever been able to discover, he was back in New Amsterdam in 1649.

On the fourteenth of May that year, just as the warm sun was beginning to turn the meadows green, and the bouweries of the island filled the air with the loamy smell of spring, he bought a farm from one Lambert van Valkenburgh. It covered some forty-eight acres of woods and fields and on it stood a thatched farmhouse, very humble, but still good enough for Claes, the Little One, and Jannetje, his bride. She was the daughter of a Thomas Samuels, that much is known; but where the wedding took place, whether in New Amsterdam or back in the old country, the musty records fail to reveal.

They went at once to live on the farm, and there was work enough for both of them that spring. The farm itself was just a little north of one owned, but not occupied, by peg-legged Peter Stuyvesant, who had arrived from Curaçao as Governor just two years before. Its southernmost corner was at the present juncture of Fourth Avenue and Twenty-ninth street and it stretched easterly to the old, rutted road that led through many a quagmire to the Hell Gate. The farm itself was known as Rose Hill—perhaps Claes gave it that name himself in some moment of nostalgia for the Field of Roses in Zeeland where he was born.

North of the farm was the high hill we know today as Murray Hill. Then it was covered with deep woods and freshened by springs and a stream that ran across Claes's farm. It emptied into a duck pond, near where the old Madison Square Garden used to stand and where the New York Life Insurance building now stands. The house in which lived Claes and his bride, and later his five children, stood not far from the duck pond. On it watered the fat geese and ducks that the Dutchmen loved so well, and on its ice in the winter the Roosevelt children skated.

Rose Hill was in one of the best farming regions of Manhattan Island in those days, set as it was between the flat lands of the lower part of the island and the higher, rocky slopes that began in the present Forties. Claes prospered as a farmer, selling his crops at the market on Maiden Lane down near the old Fort. He kept horses and oxen, plenty of ducks and chickens. His hogs roamed at will all over the place and sometimes strayed as far as the town, four miles to the south.

Claes worked hard on his farm for about ten years and in that time he and Jannetje had six children. The first, whom he named Christaen, died within a few weeks of his birth. The death was duly recorded in the minutes of the Dutch Church on October 23, 1650. The next three children were girls. Then came the much wanted boy, whom Claes named Nicholas, after himself. When, late in the year 1658, the father of this brood was dying, from what cause we do not know, Jannetje was carrying another child. This child, Anna, was not born until after her father's death. Not long thereafter the good wife Jannetje followed Claes.

In the few entries that the Little One left on the records of New Amsterdam he never attained the importance of a name. Always he was referred to by his nickname. Sometimes he was called Klein Klassjie; and at others, Cleyn Claesjen, or even Colyn Claesie. But whatever the spelling it meant Little Claes, or Little Nicholas, or Claus the Little One. Only twice was he given the full resounding name of Claes Martenszen van Rosenvelt, or Nicholas, the son of Martin, of the Rose Field. Even after his death he was still referred to as Claes, the Little Fellow.

The last mention of this stout immigrant couple is a simple statement and the longest. But behind the lines in the old books one may read an indication that Claes was indeed a man of some substance if little prominence when he went to his Dutch fathers.

"Whereas," the old paper in the Dutch Orphans Court records reads, "Janetje Thomas, widow of Cleyn Classie, commonly called so, has lately died, leaving besides some property five minor children, so that it has become necessary to appoint administrators of the estate, therefore the Orphanmasters herewith qualify as such administrators Tomas Hall and Pieter Stotenburgh, who are ordered to make an inventory of the estate, real and personal property, value and debts, due by others, to settle all and make a report to the board for future disposal."

Guardian Tomas Hall, who hailed from Gloucestershire, England, and who had become a citizen of New Amsterdam when he did not find narrow New England to his liking, was a tobacco planter, trader and general speculator. He took his administration seriously, placed a family named Grevenraet, probably relatives of Jannetje, on the farm to keep it cultivated, and named Metje Grevenraet to care for young Nicholas, and perhaps his sisters. In order to settle debts, Hall and Stotenburgh, also a New Amsterdam planter, sold some of the land at once; but the rest, including the farm house, remained a part of the estate for many years. It finally reverted to the city of New York, and still later it was bought by Casper Samler, whose farmhouse was the last of its kind to remain on Madison Avenue.

How large an estate the Little One left is not known, but there was more to it than lands and buildings, for the administrators frequently went to court in efforts to defend its claims, which amounted to several hundred guilders. Inasmuch as a guilder, or florin, as the old Dutch silver coin was sometimes called, was worth a little more than forty cents of our money, Little Claes seems to have amassed a tidy, but hardly spectacular, fortune. Mistress Grevenraet was paid about one hundred dollars a year for the care of little Nicholas. The money probably came from funds belonging to the estate, funds that were loaned out at interest, along with the funds of other orphans, on mortgages to various burghers of the town.

The daughters of the Little Fellow grew up and married. Nicholas, who might well have assumed the name of one or the other of his guardians, as some orphans did, or even of nurse Metje Grevenraet, preferred his father's name. He modified it to Nicholas Roosevelt, thus giving to America a family name that was to grow to greatness within eight generations.

CHAPTER II

The Most Unpuritan of the Puritans

SEVEN YEARS AFTER the Little One went roaming the woods and twenty-eight years before he bought his Manhattan farm a member of the Mayflower group named Isaac Allerton arrived at Plymouth in the New World. In his time he cut his little swath in history but today, nearly three and a quarter centuries later, he is mainly recalled for the very good reason that he was the first maternal immigrant ancestor of Franklin Delano Roosevelt, the thirty-second President of the United States of America.

Isaac Allerton was a Yankee, perhaps the first of the breed. Although he was born in the middle of Queen Elizabeth's long reign and died in 1659, more than a century before the word Yankee was first derisively used, he possessed many of the fundamental characteristics of that lean and salty race, and he handed them down through many generations to his most distinguished descendant. He was bold and independent, self-centered, cranky and driving, and he lived out his three score years and ten with a singleness of purpose that might well have been directed to less selfish aims than those he sought.

At times there was something tight and mean about him yet he was also a man of vision; and in spite of the fact that he lived in the midst of Puritanism he was a tolerant and humorous man. He lived a restless life, for he had a consummate curiosity about the strange new world over which his tireless legs drove him and, even if his neighbors twice exiled him from the homes of his choosing, he lived happily and defiantly throughout the three decades that saw the English and the Dutch build their little towns along the Eastern shore of the new continent.

Among those whom we now hallow with the name of Pilgrim Fathers, but who, at the dawn of the Seventeenth Century, were mostly young men of little consequence in the Anglo-Saxon world, Isaac Allerton stands out. True, he did not hold the "little band of Pilgrims" together with his prayers or his capacity for leadership during the first killing years of the Plantation's existence. That was to be left to the steadier hands of such men as Elder William Brewster, beloved dispenser of the word of God unto them, or Captain Myles Standish, their knight-at-arms, and especially to the scholarly William Bradford, whose godly governing remains to this day an example of benevolent dictatorship. Isaac Allerton's role was that of agent or intermediary, and for several years his calculating mind pacified the uneasy English investors whose money was tied up in the stony fields and rough waters from which the Pilgrims sought to earn their keep. Captain Standish stood off the Indians, but Mr. Allerton calmed down enemies no less dreadful for their lack of warpaint and the existence of a great ocean that lay between.

He was tall and angular and dark. He was never still. The Atlantic held few terrors for him; he knew it in all its brutal aspects from many passages back and forth in ships stinking with beaver skins or the gurry of codfish. He knew, too, the tides and currents of every coastal bay and inlet and his small boats had crashed on rocks that were not marked on Captain John Smith's rough charts. One or another of his vessels was forever slipping in here, or lying at anchor there, while Isaac Allerton busied himself with his eternal and complicated affairs.

Did he keep his books in his head? Or was his grand house on the New Haven creek, or his headquarters in his huge warehouse on the East River? Nobody knew, but everyone was aware that the Dutch Governor of New Amsterdam treated him as an equal; that the great Boston merchants had dealings with him; and that he owned a brewery in London. And if, in his Plymouth days, he did things to offend the Pious it mattered little. The Swedes on the Delaware bought his goods; the Dutch in New Amsterdam asked his advice. He had friends everywhere. Many of them owed him money they never paid. When he died his Harvard-trained son tried vainly to collect his debts. Isaac Allerton was remembered long after he was gone.

This strange mixture of a man was born in London in 1586, the year before Mary, Queen of Scots, was executed in Fotheringay Castle. His family of mixed Saxon and Danish origin had been settled in Southeastern England for many generations. He learned to read and write and was apprenticed to a tailor as a boy. At the time he was growing up, Elizabeth had occupied the throne for more than a quarter of a century, and Robert Browne, the Puritan apostate, had already begun his radical attacks upon the Established Church. Isaac Allerton may have come across one of Browne's scathing books, smuggled into England from Holland where the bishop-baiter was in exile, for Browne's Separatist doctrines appealed deeply to many of Isaac Allerton's class. Tailors, farmers, carpenters, wheelwrights, smiths, made up the bulk of those who took the radical's preachings to heart.

These Separatists were considered a cranky lot. Even to admit a fellow traveler's interest in their unorthodox dream of a free church was to court social ostracism if not physical danger. Reform, of church or state, must come slowly, the cautious said, and why dare queenly rebuke and possible imprisonment for the sake of a chimerical ideal? Had not two of Browne's followers been hanged for their thoughts? And so in Allerton's youth, the "preachment, pratings and pratlings of a swarm of Separatists" fell mainly on deaf ears; although there were many to admit that perhaps, after all, there was something in what those crackpots preached.

Even after Browne, like the Biblical sow, returned from Holland to the Episcopal mire, there were those so struck by his earlier words as to refuse to follow him in his recantation. They were hardly a powerful group and their doctrines did not sweep the countryside. But still, in London and along the post road that led northward to Edinburgh, the sect drew in those who found the comfort of truth in the doctrine of Separatism. And it drew in, too, a number of fanatics who hoped some day for the power to establish their own church, quite as rigorous and unrelenting in its structure as the very ecclesiastical system they would destroy.

Like all movements, large or small, Separatism had its intellectuals. One of them was William Brewster, son of the country gentleman who occupied the stone manor house in Scrooby, an obscure village and hunting lodge in Nottinghamshire and a stopping place for Archbishops and Kings on the great northern post road. The young man had attended Cambridge for a brief time and then had been associated with Sir William Davison, the Secretary of State, as "something better than a valet but a good deal less than a secretary." When the inconstancies of politics put Davison out of grace at court and caused him to be imprisoned in the Tower, thus ending such political ambitions as young Brewster may have entertained, he returned to Scrooby and took over his late father's duties as Post Master. More important, he met John Robinson and William Bradford, both younger than himself by several years, who soon began meeting at the manor house for soul-satisfying discussions on Separatism.

Surrounded by "ignorant and licentious" people, as Cotton Mather later called their misunderstanding and Romanist neighbors, they cogitated the iniquities of the Established Church. It is doubtful if Isaac Allerton, now a young man of about eighteen years, knew anything about the Scrooby group as he plied his needle in a distant London shop. But like everyone else in England he was aware of great changes that were taking place, however hard it was to define them at the time. In 1603 the good Queen Elizabeth, dreaming of joining her old lovers, called the aged Bishop Whitgift to her bedside, and while he prayed and prayed, sank into her last troubled sleep. James Stuart, who had no tolerance for Puritans in any form, ascended the throne.

This change was to affect the farmers and farmhands, those people "used to a plaine countrie life and the innocent trade of husbandry," who dared the rude jibes of their neighbors as they gathered to hear the sweet words of the saintly Robinson

in William Brewster's stone house on the Scrooby road. Five
years later, at the age of twenty-two, Allerton, like many other
Englishmen, was in Holland, safe from the vindictiveness of
"God's silly vassal," who had snarled at the Nonconformists
soon after taking the throne, "I will *make* them conform or I
will harry them out of the land."

As it turned out, neither King James nor Archbishop Ban-
croft "harried" the Pilgrims from Scrooby. As James Truslow
Adams has succinctly put it, in *The Founding of New England,*
"the persecution that the little band underwent . . . was, in the
main, from neither church nor state, but only such as they had
to suffer from the scoffs and jeers of their more easy-going and
more commonplace neighbors and companions." Nevertheless,
the "little band," led by Brewster and Robinson and young
Mr. Bradford, looked enviously at Holland. In 1609, after several brushes with the customs authorities, who treated their
violations of the laws with remarkable leniency in the face of
King James's stern pronouncement, they finally reached Amsterdam, bringing with them their money and their household
goods. There were about one hundred in the group from
Scrooby.

At the time of their arrival, it is interesting to recall, Claes
Martenszen, was a boy of fourteen, bending his shoulders over
his father Martin's plow in the village of Rose Field. He already had dreamed of running away to sea, the desperate act
he was to make four years later, after news of Henry Hudson's
great voyage in the *Half Moon* had spread into the heart of
Zeeland. There was a restlessness everywhere in those dawning
years of the Seventeenth Century, a restlessness that affected
Puritan and plowboy alike as the seas opened and the forces of
expansion began their magnificent push.

Within a year of their arrival at Amsterdam the Pilgrims
moved to Leyden. Economically, perhaps, they were less well
off in this quiet university and wool-manufacturing town than
they might have been if they had stayed in the busier seaport;
but they were nearer to that spiritual peace they so much desired. A clannish lot, they managed to live together "in love
and holiness," attending to their newly acquired trades and

handicrafts, until, by hard work, they "came to raise a competent and comfortable living." Had they not been stubborn folk they might have been absorbed forever into the community where they had cast their lot. But under the tolerant Dutch sky that has always given haven to so many rebellious sects they remained consciously English and grieved that their children were taking on the customs of their benefactors.

Discussion of their lot was constant. Isaac Allerton, Robert Cushman, John Carver, young Mr. Bradford, Elder Brewster, and the saintly John Robinson, we may be sure, were the leaders of this restless talk in their large assembly house on the Kloksteeg. Some, the more religious among them, felt they ought to leave Holland because of the "little good we did or were like to do to the Dutch in reforming the Sabbath." Others cast longing eyes at tropical Guiana, where, so they imagined, "they might grow rich with little labor." This reason found small favor with Messrs. Bradford and Brewster, but it appealed to Mr. Allerton.

Isaac Allerton was already at Leyden when the others of the Scrooby contingent came up from Amsterdam. He quickly joined the Church, and within a short time married a member of the congregation. After the Dutch custom of the day the ceremony took place at the Leyden City Hall, and was witnessed by five other members. His bride was Mary Norris, who had come to Holland from Newbury, England. The date was November 4, 1611. Within the next eight years the Allertons had four children, all born at Leyden. They were named Bartholemew, Remember, Mary, and Sarah.

Isaac prospered reasonably well. He owned his own house, and he worked at his trade of tailoring. He is listed among the members of the congregation who were made honorary citizens of Leyden. But although he was well considered by the others, and by the prudent Dutch, he was not an outstanding leader in their councils. His business sharpness had not yet manifested itself.

No one person has ever been credited with originating the idea of emigration. It was a cumulative and communal idea, hastened on by economic necessity, or at least by a desire for greater comforts, under more nearly English circumstances.

Once the great decision was made, the visionaries and the missionaries among them had to be curbed in their enthusiasm. Few of them understood the barriers that lay between their present sanctuary and whatever haven they might eventually reach. When they began to carry into action their determination to "make a plantation" in the New World they found the way even more difficult than they had anticipated. Their own resources were woefully inadequate for the financing of the daring venture.

Although the Leydenites felt they had been "harried out of the land" by a bitter and cruel King, it was to England that they now turned. They were supremely confident that they would have little trouble in finding money, and even in obtaining royal consent for their emigration. In their patriotism they spurned an offer to be financed in Amsterdam by the Dutch West India Company. Instead they sent John Carver and Robert Cushman (also a Roosevelt ancestor) to London as emissaries. After much scurrying about, talking, beseeching, getting half-promises, these two persistent salesmen eventually made the necessary arrangements. The Reverend Mr. Robinson and the other leaders who remained at Leyden were dissatisfied with the terms insisted upon by those willing to invest their money in the doubtful venture. In the end, however, the leaders at Leyden, among them Isaac Allerton, accepted the contract and the "little group" prepared to move.

To Isaac Allerton fell the task of finding a vessel, an assignment for which neither his trade nor training fitted him. It is his dubious honor to have secured the *Speedwell*. For once, he drove a poor bargain. But he did the best he could under the circumstances. How could a tailor have known that the shipwrights at Delftshaven stepped the masts wrongly and fitted oversized sails to the ship?

When the Pilgrims were at last gathered at Dartmouth Harbor in England, ready to sail for the New World, Allerton chose the *Speedwell* to take himself, his wife Mary, who was again pregnant, and three of his four children. But the *Speedwell* was not destined to get far. Her utter unseaworthiness soon became apparent as the poorly set sails strained the ship's timbers and started its seams. Back it had to put into port.

Allerton crowded his little brood, including a servant boy named John Hooke, onto the *Mayflower*, and, muttering condemnations of the Delftshaven shipwrights, began the long and cruel voyage to the uncharted West.

When the Pilgrims gathered in the cabin of the *Mayflower* on November 11, 1620, in the harbor of Provincetown at Cape Cod, and "solemnly & mutualy in the presence of God, and one of another," did "covenant & combine our selves togeather into a civill body politick," Isaac Allerton's position among the Pilgrims was a high one. His name stood fifth among the signers of the famous compact; just below those of Governor John Carver, William Bradford, Edward Winslow, and Elder William Brewster. His was a bold and dashing signature, written in a firm, determined hand, the largest on the page.

The first winter at Plymouth was grim and cruel. Thirteen of the twenty-four heads of families perished of what is known to-day as tuberculosis. All but four of the wives who had been crowded on the vessel died. One was Mary Norris Allerton, whose fifth child had been delivered still-born during the wintry passage. Even the strong, young men who had come over as members of the ship's crew or as indentured servants, could not stand up against the New England dampness. All but six of the unattached bachelors died, including poor John Hooke. When the hot spring came at last, there were only twenty-one men and six boys left to do the planting!

In April, "whilst they were bussie about their seed," Governor Carver came out of the field one day, stricken by the unseasonable heat. A few days later this godly and well-approved leader died. William Bradford, then about thirty-two years old and the most learned among them, was named in his place. Because Bradford, too, was a sick man at the time, Isaac Allerton was "chosen to be an Asistante unto him." Two men of more nearly opposite temperaments and interests could scarcely have been found. At the start of their association, however, they got along well together; at least nothing occurred that was sufficiently untoward for Mr. Bradford to set it down in his history later on.

Like all the other able bodied men at the plantation, Isaac

Allerton was busy during those first years. There were houses to build, corn to plant, trees to cut and lumber to make, boats to build and codfish and beaver to dress. Like all the others, Isaac had his communal duties, which called for courage. He was among the small group that made peace with King Massasoit and the other savages of the coast in those trying early days when the Pilgrims were establishing friendly relations with the Indian tribes.

When they had become sufficiently settled in their new home they decided that there were about one hundred men and women entitled to a temporary share of the land. Accordingly they measured off about two hundred acres, in 1623, to form the town of Plymouth, which they divided among themselves with some degree of equality. Many received one acre; others were given two; John Howland, who had come over as Governor Carver's manservant, and three others received four acres each; while still others were allotted five and six acres. William Brewster was among those favored with six. But Isaac Allerton, alone of all the planters, got seven acres on "the South side of the brook to the Baywards," where he soon built a house for his motherless children.

Despite the communal nature of the plantation it was difficult for a widower with four growing children to carry on alone; and so after several years of loneliness he married Fear Brewster, the strangely named young daughter of the pious Elder of the Pilgrim Church. She was to be his wife during all his life in Plymouth, and she gave him one son, Isaac Allerton, Jr.

To have married the daughter of one so important in their lives as the senior Elder of the Pilgrim Church added to Mr. Allerton's reputation in Plymouth Plantation. Since the death of Governor Carver, Allerton had been the only officer besides Mr. Bradford. He held the assistant governorship for three years. In the spring of 1625, while all England was excited over the ascension to the throne of Charles I, the little group of men, women and children, who had toiled so hard and prayed so firmly in this cold vineyard of God, were faced with a crisis before which the terrors of the Indians and the New England winters were as nothing. Those, at least, were tangible, physical enemies. The new foe was far away, in London, and it was one with which they were not prepared to cope: the threatened withdrawal of financial aid. John Carver, who had carried on some of the early negotiations with the London Adventurers, as the backers of the Plymouth venture were known, was dead.

Among all the planters there was only one qualified to undertake the task of acting as liaison between the Planters in Plymouth and the Adventurers in London. This was Mr. Allerton. For a year he and Edward Winslow had been the distributing agents empowered to disburse the meagre supplies of food, tools and clothing which Adventurers had sent over to the Plantation in that year. He acquitted himself well at this task and won the confidence of the London holders of the purse strings. Nevertheless the first person the Pilgrims had sent back on a financial errand was Captain Standish. He had returned with much needed funds but he had borrowed them at the high interest rate of 50 per cent. Now they dispatched Mr. Allerton, prayerfully hoping that he would drive a better bargain. In the summer of 1626 he set out aboard a returning fisherman, ready to invade London after more than five years in the New World.

Within two months of his arrival the agile Allerton had rounded up nearly forty of the original investors in Plymouth Plantation, who were willing to listen to his proposals. These stockholders found him neither an easy nor gullible man. He had his strict instructions from the Colonists and was determined to abide by them, and when he was done the results were indeed favorable to the Plantation. The original investors agreed to sell out to Allerton, as agent of the Colony, the entire interest of the London Company in the plantation. Their price was one thousand eight hundred pounds. This fortunate arrangement saved the Plymouth colonists from immediate disaster and gave them an autonomy they had not previously enjoyed. But Isaac was not content with this. In his pocket was a letter empowering him to borrow money for the purchase of supplies. Instead of getting the one hundred pounds the Pilgrims had expected, he borrowed two hundred pounds—at the low rate of 30 per cent interest!

When Allerton returned to Plymouth in the Spring and reported on his London ventures, the planters were greatly

pleased. Even Governor Bradford had to write: "This agreement was well like of, and approved by all the plantation, and
consented unto, though they knew not well how to raise the
payment yet they undertooke it, and 7 or 8 of the cheefe of the
place became joyntly bound for the paimente of this 1800
pounds (in the behalfe of the rest) at the severall days."

Mr. Allerton was sanguine of their ability to pay the debt, for
he became one of the underwriters, or "Undertakers" as they
called themselves, with Governor Bradford, Captain Standish,
Edward Winslow, John Howland, John Alden, Thomas Prence
and the Elder Brewster. Another winter passed. Beaver and
other skins were bought and made ready for shipping, and in
the spring of 1627 Mr. Allerton prepared for a second trip to
London. Before he went, the "7 or 8 of the cheefe of the place"
arrived at a momentous decision. In order to pay off their
£1800 they "resolved to run a high course, and of great adventure . . . which was to hire the trade of the company for
certaine years," or until the debt was paid, when the trade
would be returned to all the colonists. After some agitation this
plan was agreed upon and Mr. Allerton went bravely off to
London to make the deal.

Now once again this "honest & discreete agent"—as James
Shirley, that most arrogant of the Adventurers, called him—
carried out his difficult task. Isaac Allerton was an optimist. He
was certain that the Pilgrims would have no difficulty in ridding
themselves of their debt. In fact, in his dreams, he saw them all
getting rich. And richest of them all would be Mr. Allerton!
Already he had taken steps to this end. On his first voyage he
had carried back to Plymouth "some small quantitie of goods,
upon his own particular, and sould them for his own private
benefite." This "was more than any man had yet hitherto attempted," and it grieved Governor Bradford. But since he was
a man of Christian charity the good Governor forgave the
erring agent. As he wrote:

"But because he had otherwise done them good service, and
also he sould these goods among the people of the plantation, by
which their wants were supplied, and he aleged it was the love
of Mr. Shirley and some other friends that would needs trust

him with some goods, conceiving it might do him some good, and none hurte, it was not much lookt at but past over."

When Isaac returned to Plymouth this second time he brought more goods "upon his own particular." As Bradford complained it was difficult to tell which goods in the hold of the ship that brought him were his and which belonged to the common store. There were shoes and leather, Irish stocking, cloth of all sorts, pitch, tar, ropes and twine, knives, scissors, lead shot, powder, hatchets, axes, hoes, scythes, reap hooks, files, nails, iron pots, drugs and spices in the cargo. And that "what was most vendible, and would yeeld presente pay, usually that was his," sighed Mr. Bradford, sadly. But he was even more disturbed because Mr. Allerton did not confine his trading to the plantation but "began to sell abroad to others of forine places which considering their [the Pilgrims'] common cause they began to dislike. . . .

"Yet because love thinks no evill, nor is susspitious, they took his faire words for excuse, and resolved to send him againe to England; considering how well he had done the former business, and what good acception he hath with their friends ther."

Does one not see here, in this contemporary portrait of Franklin D. Roosevelt's first maternal ancestor to arrive in America, the seeds of certain family traits that have come down to the present time?

Governor Bradford, it is obvious, was beginning even this early to be annoyed with his former assistant and present agent. And yet, although his *History* is filled with querulous accounts of Isaac Allerton's extra-curricular activities, the agent's actual accomplishments were many. During the next few years he made many voyages to England. The moneys he borrowed, at an interest rate that was low for such investments at that time, made it possible for the Pilgrims to keep supplied with goods and cattle, and it ended the extreme poverty of the early years. Also, it was Allerton who arranged for the emigration of the remainder of the Leyden congregation. He got the Plantation a patent that allowed the Pilgrims to extend their fur-trading activities to the Kennebec River on the Maine coast, and before he was through he secured them the so-called Warwick patent of 1630 which at last gave the Pilgrims permanent title to their lands and property. These were among the most important achievements in the history of the colony. Governor Bradford could afford to be charitable.

But, alas, Mr. Allerton had now acquired such an opinion of his own ability, that he was heading for a fall. He had tasted profits and was avid for more. And he was encouraged in his private trading by some of the less scrupulous London backers until he honestly believed he might both "raise himselfe an estate" and bring wealth to his friends in London and to the planters of Plymouth Bay. There were other reasons why he annoyed the righteous but unrealistic Colonists. For one thing, he was a liberal; and for another, he made friends with the wrong people.

When Allerton was in London in 1628 he had a difficult commission to fulfill. The gentle John Robinson had not come with the Pilgrims and so there had been no man of God on the *Mayflower*. Later they had imported a minister named Lyford, but his cuckoldry had upset their pious ways and they had to send him home. Now Allerton was to find a successor. Unfortunately the man he selected and brought over at great expense to the Plantation turned out to a "mazed man," as they said, and quite insane. He too was sent back and Allerton had to stand the gibes of his fellow Pilgrims for not having discovered the man's eccentricities in time.

But they did not hold this misadventure against him quite as much as they did his bringing to Plymouth, as his clerk and secretary, a lustful, young, self-styled lawyer named Thomas Morton. They knew Morton. A year or so earlier, this licentious and convivial young man had been living at a settlement between Plymouth and Boston which bore the quite unpuritan name of Merrymount. There in his ungodly way he had set up, with a maypole as a symbol, what to all intents and purposes was a saloon and bawdy house. This was too much for the Plymouth planters to stand, and so they despatched Captain Standish, who acted as a sort of sheriff in Plymouth, to raid the place. Which he did. Morton was packed off, impenitent, to England. And now here he was back again, under the protection of their own agent!

This enraged the Pilgrims who believed that Allerton had

brought this "unworthy man and instrument of mischiefe" back into their midst just "to nose them." Morton's presence caused such a scandal that Allerton finally had to discharge him. Morton went back to his "old nest in Massachusetts" until he ran afoul of the authorities who again shipped him to England. There, in Exeter Jail, he wrote an exposé of righteous Plymouth that is good, if not accurate, reading to this day.

Mr. Allerton was falling into disrepute. His final dissolution, as far as Plymouth was concerned, came about because of his liberal attitude towards life. Governor Bradford, at least, suspected the existence of what he politely called "a kind of concurrence" between Mr. Allerton and certain of the London adventurers. He felt that some of them paid too much attention to the agent's advice and thus "made him bould to presume above his instructions." And yet, for another, more personal reason, the trusting Pilgrims let him go his way back and forth across the ocean without calling him to account.

"Mr. Allerton," the pious historian explained, "had married the daughter of their Reverend Elder, Mr. Brewster (a man beloved & honored amongst them, and who tooke great paines in teaching and dispenceing the word of God unto them), who they were loath to greeve or any way offend, so as they bore with much in that respecte."

As time went on, however, Mr. Allerton became too sharp for even the most forgiving. By the summer of 1629, the Pilgrims had sent a fur-trading expedition to the Kennebec, and now Mr. Shirley—the most unscrupulous of the London backers— sent a party of his own into the region. In charge was Edward Ashley, "a very profane young man" who, much to the Pilgrims' disgust, had gone naked among the Indians and acquired their lax manners. He now approached the Pilgrims and demanded supplies. They would have refused him if they had dared, but they feared that Ashley and Allerton, "laying their craftie wits together," would get supplies elsewhere and jointly put them out of the Kennebec trade. And so in self defense they provided Ashley with a boat and gave him a supply of beads and trinkets for trade. But, when the rascally young man had got a "good parcel of beaver," he sent it to England—without paying them a farthing!

While all this skullduggery was going on the Pilgrims got word from England that Mr. Allerton, having grown wealthy enough, had bought himself a vessel which he was bringing back. Alarmed, they sent Mr. Winslow over to investigate, and to discharge him as agent if all was "not well." But Mr. Allerton, proud of his new ship, the *White Angel,* sailed back to Plymouth alone, smiling and plausible as ever, and boasting of the profits that were sure to come. Even now the Pilgrims, sure that he was working more for his own profit than for theirs, did not discharge him as their agent. They did, however, demand a financial accounting and the return of the written commission they had given him when he first went to England for them. Alarmed, Allerton stalled for time. He told them it was "amongst his papers" and that he would produce it after he had returned from the eastward where he was bound on a fishing trip. Then they asked for it again as he was about to sail to England. He said he would send it to them as it was with Mr. Shirley. He never did.

Isaac Allerton's time at Plymouth was drawing to a close. Now it was learned that his accounts were in a sorry mess. Indeed, it took the Pilgrims two or three years to audit them, and even then they could "never make them perfecte." He was at least two thousand pounds in debt to the plantation, and, to make matters worse he had "scrued up his poor old father-in-law's account to above two hundred pounds and brought it upon the general account . . . because he knew they would never let it lye on the old man." Even the friendliest historians admit that the indebtedness of the Plymouth colony had more than doubled during these years. The Undertakers, of which he was one, were £5,771 behind in 1631, after having shipped several thousands of pounds of beaver skins to England. The Pilgrims, certain that they had been abused in their simplicity, and sold out by Allerton and his cronies in England, arose in their wrath at last. Even their love for his old father-in-law could not save him now!

Poor Isaac Allerton! Seven times he had crossed the ocean in behalf of his friends in Plymouth, an indefatigable promoter of what, from a financial point of view, was far from a sound risk. That he was aware of the implausibility of Plymouth ever becoming a prosperous plantation we know from statements he made in England to friends who were planning to migrate to Massachusetts Bay. He warned them to go farther south, suggesting that they settle in the region of Hudson's River. There, he said, they would find an incomparable place for a plantation. They did not listen, then, but he was to take his own advice within a few years, and he was to profit thereby!

In 1631 the Plymouth planters informed the merchants in London that they refused to accept any further acts of Mr. Allerton in their behalf. They renounced him altogether as their agent. He apparently left Plymouth at once and made Marblehead on the north shore of Massachusetts Bay his headquarters. Within a year he had established another trading station at Machias on the Kennebec River, which prospered until it was burned down by the French and Indians in 1634.

That year was a disastrous one in his life. He built a large warehouse in Marblehead from which he operated a fleet of eight small fishing vessels. In February this, too, burned down. And during the following December his wife, Fear Brewster Allerton, whom he had left behind in Plymouth, died of the fever. To add to his woes, he was shipwrecked in one of his own pinnaces, which was a total loss.

"With pitie and compassion," Bradford wrote of his former associate, "I may say with the apostle, They that will be rich, fall into many temptations and snares, etc., and perce themselves through with many sorrows; for the love of money is the root of all evill."

Thus Bradford takes his leave of Isaac Allerton, and momentarily, at least, it seems as if his worst forebodings were about to come true. In March, 1635, while living in Marblehead, the General Court of Massachusetts ordered him to depart. The cause of this singular decree is not known. The presence of this man from Plymouth may have been resented by the fishermen of the Bay Colony. Or he may have become too friendly with Roger Williams, the radical preacher, who had been in conflict with the General Court ever since his arrival in Salem in 1633. He had known Williams during the young dissenter's brief stay at the Plantation a few years before.

Whatever the purpose, Mr. Allerton does not appear to have

left at once. He waited until May of that year before he transferred his houses, buildings, and stages for curing fish, to his son-in-law Moses Maverick, who had married his youngest daughter. That August a boat of his, which he had chartered to Rev. Mr. Avery to move his family from Newbury to Plymouth, was lost at Cape Ann. Twenty-one persons perished in the wreck. And the following year Allerton again barely escaped when one of his own boats upset while he was returning from an expedition to Penobscot Bay. But after that his name disappears from the pages of Massachusetts history. Like many a later son of that region he turned his eye to the island of Manhattan as the place where a fortune might be made.

Isaac Allerton left Massachusetts at about the same time that his old friend Roger Williams was banished for disseminating "news and dangerous opinions againt the authority of the magistrates." But he himself never uttered radical political or religious views. He was far more tolerant of other people's opinions than most of his associates at Plymouth. Whatever their many other virtues may have been, tolerance was not one of them. Both the Pilgrims of Plymouth and the Puritans of the Massachusetts Bay Colony must have looked askance at one who professed membership in the Pilgrim Church, yet who gave shelter to the abominable Quakers, and encouragement to Roger Williams and his followers.

Whatever the cause of the General Court's order for his removal from Massachusetts, there was no reason for him to suffer. The New World, in 1635, was a busy place. From north of Boston to south of the Delaware there were already hundreds of scattered traders and settlers—French, English, Dutch, mostly —all striving to grow rich. There was opportunity aplenty for a man of Allerton's talents. The magisterial pressure which forced him to sell out his holdings in Marblehead does not appear to have been so powerful as to rob him of all his property. Some of his vessels, at least, he held onto and sent them here and there under hired captains on trading trips.

Some time within a few years of his departure from the Bay Colony Isaac Allerton qualified as an inhabitant of both Dutch New Netherland and the English colony at New Haven. In New

Amsterdam he maintained a house and quay on the East River, on the south side of present Pearl Street. In New Haven, or Red Hill, as that town was known to the Dutch, he built "a grand house on the Creek, with Four Porches." By establishing these two headquarters he was able to enjoy the advantages of dual citizenship under both the Dutch and the English. This was a considerable benefit to a trader in the wide areas claimed by England and Holland. As a New Netherlander this shrewd Pilgrim had the right to trade on the North, or Hudson River, and on the South, or Delaware River. As a New Havenite the territories claimed by that colony were open to him. It was not long before he had mercantile connections formally established in New England, New Netherland, on the Delaware, in Virginia, Barbados, and Curaçao!

He went to the small waterfront town that was New Amsterdam in about 1638 and for the next twenty years he was to be one of the best known figures there. He was now a man of middle age, well seasoned, and far from provincial, despite his years in Plymouth. The Dutch accepted him as a good neighbor and it was not long before he was taken into their councils. The Dutch had not been as happy in their relations with the Indians as the Pilgrims had been and in the summer of 1643 an ineffectual peace treaty was broken by the depredations of the Wappingers along the Hudson. Director General William Kieft was forced to take action. He asked, although with his tongue in his cheek, that an advisory committee be formed and in September of that year eight men were chosen. Six were Dutch and two were English. Among them were Isaac Allerton, Tomas Hall (Nicholas Roosevelt's guardian) and Abraham Pietersen, a Roosevelt ancestor.

Director General Kieft, a stubborn Dutchman, had no intention of taking the committee's advice seriously. He often "met them with sundry biting and scoffing jests." Nevertheless the Eight Men played a considerable part in the history of New Amsterdam. When the town grew too boisterous they drew up some "good and suitable regulations," forbidding taverns and all other improprieties, and appointing a week's preaching instead. Does one see the hand of the Pilgrim in this? The Eight Men did other valuable work in combating the Indian menace. It was through them that the doughty and cruel Captain John Underhill of New Haven was enlisted to command some fifty men in the ensuing Dutch-Indian war.

But it is neither as a statesman nor Indian fighter that Isaac Allerton distinguished himself. Rather, it was as a merchant. Very soon after his banishment from Massachusetts he formed a commercial partnership with Govert Loockermans. In 1642 he sold this Dutchman a sloop, writing, Yankee-like, into the bill of sale that he should have free passage back to Red Hill! Loockermans was a "bold and enterprising trader" who later was to infuriate the residents of Rhode Island by selling powder to the Indians there. He and Mr. Allerton jointly owned a large tract of land near the East River, which they got from the Director and Council in 1643. But before they made use of it Mr. Allerton had settled down in New Haven.

The "grand house on the Creek, with Four Porches" was to be his real home for the rest of his life. But his business and his inherent restlessness kept him away from it much of the time. Even the presence of his third wife could not keep him there if a penny was to be made elsewhere. Her first name was Johanna, but nothing is known of her before she came to live in New Haven on her husband's two-acre estate between the harbor and the creek. Once she was fined for neglecting to keep her fences in repair during her husband's absence on a trading trip. They were both attendants at the Meeting House, where Isaac had the "second seat of the cross seats at the end." They had no children, but Isaac Allerton, Jr., the son of Isaac and Fear Brewster, came to live with them after his graduation from Harvard in 1650.

In 1647, while his mother country was on the brink of Civil War, Isaac Allerton bought five hundred feet of land along the waterfront of the East River and there he built one of the largest warehouses yet erected in New Amsterdam. He had need for the two-story building, for, by this time he had become deeply interested in the trade with the Netherlands and in dealing directly with the East India Company. Much of the commerce between New Netherland and New England passed through Mr. Allerton's busy hands. The place was crowded with traders from up and down the coast, and with sea captains from Holland and England.

The warehouse was indeed a headquarters for all the New World's businessmen, a sort of exchange for traders. Allerton had to hire a clerk and install a bar for the dispensing of wine and beer, as many strangers applied to him for lodgings. Once, in a slack season, it was rented out to the Burgomaster as a temporary home for some fifty boys and girls who had been sent out from Amsterdam to work on the New Netherland farms. Again, it was ransacked by Indians, who beat up Allerton's servants.

The day the Indians invaded the warehouse Mr. Allerton fortunately was away, down at the Delaware on a trading mission to the Swedes who had settled there. He must have been a welcome visitor, for among the goods he sold the Swedes were millstones, seed barley, and a Dutch bushel measure, all handy provisions for the brewing of beer. Mr. Allerton was at that time one of the best friends the Swedes had. When the Dutch, in 1651, sent a fleet of vessels and a force of men to build a fort and establish a trading post on the Delaware, Allerton went along. The Swedes had a prior claim in the region near Newcastle, but Allerton and his Dutch cronies doublecrossed the Swedes and wheedled a large tract of land from an Indian, on the solemn promise to keep his gun in repair and give him corn whenever he was "empty."

If, as may well have been the case, there was something irregular in this deal, Mr. Allerton made amends a few years later. In 1655 he was again in the region, peddling wine and china goods, hops and butter, shoes and underwear. Later that year the Swedes were greatly disturbed by a rumor that had come to them from the north to the effect that New Haven was about to send three thousand people to the Delaware to start a colony. Perhaps Allerton, who was always playing both ends, had brought the news. The Swedish Governor at once rushed an emissary to New Haven to protest against this invasion of New Sweden's territorial rights. He found that the New Haven authorities were all but ready to begin the migration. The Vice Governor of New Haven, Stephen Goodyear, and the Swedish emissary then met with Isaac Allerton as intermediary to clear the matter up.

The New Havenites, their Governor explained, thought the Swedes were in Delaware merely as traders. Therefore the New Havenites felt they had a right to settle there. Mr. Allerton, however, had seen the Swedish Governor's royal commission, bearing the seal of Sweden, and said so. Governor Goodyear bowed to this ruling of his fellow Englishman and New Haven gave up its idea of transferring the colony to the warmer waters of the Delaware. It was, however, a short-lived victory for New Sweden. The Dutch were not so honorable about royal seals, and later in the very same year Governor Stuyvesant took over the Delaware territory by force. In the end, of course, the English triumphed, for they played the same trick on old Peter Stuyvesant and made New Amsterdam, New York!

Was Isaac Allerton playing the Dutch game all along? We have no evidence that he was, but at least one able historian of the New Haven colony claims that Allerton was "at heart more Dutch than English," and cites an outstanding instance in which he "proved his loyalty to New Netherland." This had happened two years before the Swedish incident. In some way the ubiquitous Allerton, who never seems to have been at loss for the latest news, heard that four British warships had arrived in Boston Harbor. He did not know whether they were to be used against the French or Dutch, "for the instructions had not been opened and were not to be opened until ten days of their arrival." The cause for delay was the impending peace negotiations between the English and the Dutch. But, warned by Allerton, Governor Peter Stuyvesant was able to enlist men, raise money, repair the fort at New Amsterdam, and gain the support of the Dutch towns of Long Island.

Thus Isaac Allerton played his part in the life of the Dutch and English colonies. But he was growing old: too old, now, to go so often to the Delaware with his goods; too old to scurry up the New England coast in a pinnace; too old to dare the voyage to Barbados. He was over seventy when, in 1658, he sold his house and land at Peck Slip, New Amsterdam, and settled down in his grand house on the creek, from which on a clear day he could look across the sound to Long Island. He had done much. He had been everywhere. He had had his fun, helping to run Plymouth, making all those trips to England, dickering with the Dutch, the English, the Swedes, and the hateful Indians. Yes, he had helped run New Amsterdam, too. And now it was time to die. Did he think of Elder Brewster then, that fine old man whose accounts he had screwed up? Or of all the others with whom he had worked and fought and bickered when they first came to this new land nearly thirty years ago?

Early in 1659 this restless Dutch-Yankee ancestor of the Roosevelts died. He who had been the "richest of the Pilgrims" was now a poor man. He left a will, a sorry memorandum of so busy a life. It was really little else than a pathetic list of debts owed him, which he wanted his son, Isaac, and his wife, Johanna, to collect and pay out to his creditors, as far as they would go.

"Account of the debts due at the Dutch," the old document begins, and then goes on:

"700 guilders by Tho. Hall by arbitration of Captain Willett and Augustus Harman, about Captain Scarlett.

"900 guilders from John Peterson the Bore, as by George Woolsey's book will appear.

"18 months rent from Henry Brassen, 3 rooms @ 3 guilders a week.

"Besides all my debts in Delaware Bay and Virginia, which in my books will appear, & in Barbadoes what he can get."

Isaac, Jr., did not tarry long around New Amsterdam or New Haven, but went to Virginia where he founded a line from which President Zachary Taylor descended. The warehouse stood on the river front for several years, a tall, dark and silent tribute to the old trader. Finally it passed into the hands of the Beekmans, a family more prominent in the early days of New York than the Roosevelts. Nobody knows today how the estate was finally settled, or if the debts at the Dutch and Barbados were collected, or if old Isaac's creditors were ever paid. His wife lived in New Haven for many years after his death in the house with four porches which Isaac, Jr. bought for her. Isaac was put to rest in the Burial Ground there. So ends the story of the first English immigrant in the history of the Roosevelts.

CHAPTER III

The Mayflower, Speedwell and the Germ
of the New Deal

IN ANY STORY of the Roosevelt Family the amazing Isaac Allerton must stand out because he was the first maternal ancestor of any Roosevelt to attain historical significance in the New World. But, although he was the most important, he was not the only ancestor of Franklin Delano Roosevelt who arrived at Provincetown on the *Mayflower* in the late Autumn of 1620. His daughter Mary, who was about four years old at the time, came with him on what William Bradford always referred to as "the first ship." Also aboard the vessel was a young serving man named John Howland; a Londoner named Richard Warren; a couple known as John and Elizabeth Tilley and their daughter, Elizabeth; and Degory Priest, Isaac Allerton's brother-in-law. A year later a second contingent came to Plymouth on the ship *Fortune.* Among these second-comers was a lad named Thomas Cushman, who was left at the plantation by his father, Robert Cushman, to grow up under the beneficent wing of Governor Bradford. He was to marry Mary Allerton. Each of these is an ancestor of Franklin D. Roosevelt, a founder of the Roosevelt Family as it is today.

Relationship in this generation to a *Mayflower* passenger is often far too tenuous to have any bearing upon present individual character. Whether or not this ancestry of more than three hundred years has meant much in the development of

Franklin Delano Roosevelt will become apparent later in this book. It is, however, extremely interesting to note at this time that of all the Presidents of the United States only five besides Franklin Delano Roosevelt could claim descent from that group of 102 men, women and children who were "by the blessing of God the first beginers and (in a sort) the foundations of all the Plantations and Colonies in New-England."

Testy John Adams, the second president, and his son, John Quincy Adams, the sixth, had the blood of meek John Alden in their veins. General Zachary Taylor, the twelfth president, was descended from Isaac Allerton and Elder Brewster, through Isaac's and Fear Brewster's only son, who settled in Virginia after his father's death. Ulysses S. Grant, the eighteenth president, claimed descent from Richard Warren, and William Howard Taft from Francis Cooke, one of the longest-lived of the Pilgrims. It remains for Franklin Delano Roosevelt alone to be descended through both his father and mother from *Mayflower* passengers. His distant cousin, Theodore Roosevelt, although like himself a direct descendant of Claes Martenszen van Rosenvelt in exactly the same number of generations, could claim no connection with an ancient Yankee line. His mother's first immigrant antecedent did not land on American shores until most of the Old Comers at Plymouth Plantation had died. And even then his coming was only by the merest chance.

When the *Speedwell* "lay a mending" at Dartmouth Harbor, England, and the *Mayflower* was heading past Land's End towards the open sea, Robert Cushman wrote to his friend Edward Southworth in London a "passionate letter" in which he exclaimed, "Friend, if ever we make a plantation, God works a mirakle . . ."

God and the Pilgrims worked the miracle and the plantation was built, but Robert Cushman was not among them at the time. Nevertheless, he was one of the important leaders who made the venture possible. Fate kept him from crossing the Atlantic and he did not live to see the colony thrive, but his faith in his fellow members of the Pilgrim Church was such that he sent his son to grow up and marry and die on the

Plymouth strand. Although he spent but a few days at Plymouth in 1621 he was, in all justice, a Pilgrim Father.

Robert Cushman was born at Canterbury, England, about 1579 and so was nearly forty years old when he and Deacon John Carver were sent from Leyden by the Reverend John Robinson and the members of his church to find ways and means for the emigration on which the churchmen had set their Christian hearts. He was a wool comber by trade and prospered well enough during his years in Leyden to have bought two houses there. He was married and already the father of a large family at the time he went to Holland. His son, Thomas, was born in England but a few months before the departure from Scrooby. Now, his wife was dead, and he was married to a widow, who had come to Leyden from Sandwich. His fellow church members held him in high regard, a saving, honest man, who could be trusted on the most important of missions.

Deacon Carver and Robert Cushman opened the first negotiations with the Virginia Company, a corporation that had been chartered to finance colonies in America, then often known as Virginia. To Sir Edwin Sandys, a heavy stockholder and a Separatist sympathizer, they presented the Seven Articles which the Pilgrims had drawn up to explain their attitude towards religious conformity and toleration, and in which they promised, if a charter were given, to "practise in our parts all lawful things." Sir Edwin gave them to believe the Articles would be acceptable to the Company and, strangely enough, even to the Puritan-hating king. When Sir Edwin took the matter up with King James, the monarch wanted to know how these innocents expected to support themselves in America. Sir Edwin replied, "By fishing." Whereupon James burst out: "So God have my soul! It is an honest trade! It was the Apostles' own calling!" It appeared momentarily as if the Pilgrims would have the regal blessing to go their Non Conformist way. But King James next instructed them to take the matter up with the Archbishop and Bishop of London. This was too much for the Separatists and they decided to abandon all attempts to have their nonconformity recognized by the Crown.

Deacon Carver and Robert Cushman, the woolcomber, did not obtain their charter from the Virginia Company at once.

The affairs of that corporation were considerably entangled at the time. But when Sir Edwin was elected treasurer, clearer sailing was in sight, and in the early summer of 1619 a charter was forthcoming. It was issued, for purposes of reasonable secrecy, in the name of an obscure "religious gentleman belonging to the Countess of Lincoln." The Pilgrims at Leyden were elated. But Robert Cushman, who was a realist even if his business experience was limited, dashed cold water on their hopes. From London he wrote his "loving friends" in Leyden a most disheartening letter in which he told of the terrible disaster which had befallen Francis Blackwell, a former elder in a Separatist Church at Amsterdam.

Elder Blackwell and part of the congregation of his church, when theological dissension had split the organization, had decided to emigrate to Virginia. Apprehended in London, he had, as Bradford said, "glossed" with the bishops, denied separation from the Established Church, and taken the oaths demanded of him. In a ship so crowded that "they were packed together like herrings," he and his followers had sailed for Virginia. Of the one hundred and eighty who were aboard, one hundred and thirty, including Elder Blackwell and the ship's captain, died. Those who survived returned a year later "with great mutterings and repinings amongst them," Cushman wrote.

No one could have done the Leydenites a greater service than Cushman did when he wrote this informative letter. It brought them to their senses, showing them how insufficient their own resources were. They must find wealthy backers to insure continuity of their proposed plantation, and plan the migration as a profit-making venture. These backers Cushman hopefully set out to find. The year that followed was a difficult one, nor was it made any easier by the attitude of those who were at Leyden,—as may be seen from this excerpt from a letter written by the Reverend Robinson at about this time:

"He [a London merchant approached by Cushman] will not give us a penny although Robert Cushman was sure he was going to get I know not how many hundreds of pounds from him, and from others, I know not whom. Robert Cushman is a good man and of special abilities in some ways, but he is most unfit to deal with other men, by reason of his singularity and his complete indifference to facts. To tell the truth we have had nothing from him for the last three years except rosy hopes and glittering predictions!"

In the meantime the Pilgrims had taken under consideration a Dutch offer to sponsor a plantation in the New World. Thomas Weston, a London merchant with money to invest, scented business, and arrived at Leyden with a scheme of a seven year partnership. During those years, according to his plan, the Pilgrims would trade with the Indians for furs, fish on the Grand Banks, cut lumber and dress it, and collect sassafras and other spices then much in English demand. Those few who did not work at these employments would build houses and make the trading post a permanent plantation. The Adventurers in turn would furnish money, provisions, and goods for trading. At the end of seven years the colony would acquire the houses and the improved lands. The unimproved land and the profits would be divided proportionately, according to money or labor given, among both colonists and investors. The Pilgrims accepted these terms.

Weston then returned to London and told his associates, some of whom had been unearthed by Robert Cushman, of the terms agreed upon. However much faith they may have had in the moral probity of the Leyden group, the Adventurers, being hard-headed businessmen, were not sanguine of great profits from such a venture. It fell to Robert Cushman to persuade them to put up their money, against their plausible objection that the Pilgrims were offering no other collateral than their professed willingness to work hard! The Adventurers, as well they might under the circumstances, imposed terms that seemed extremely harsh. Robert Cushman sent them to Leyden. Immediately great cries of anguish arose in the Pilgrims Assembly House. An angry letter was sent off, finding great fault with poor Cushman's handling of the business in London. The agent, not unreasonably, was annoyed, as may be gathered from this letter he wrote to Deacon Carver:

"Loveing Freind, I have received from you some letters, full of affection and complaints. And what it is that you would have of me I know not; for your crieing out Negligence, negligence,

negligence, negligence, I marvell why so negligente man was used in the business."

Unhappy Robert Cushman, who was, as he said, "fettered with bussines," was having an extremely hard time both at home and abroad, in his vain efforts to bring the Adventurers and the Pilgrims to an agreement. In this he failed. Both he and Weston, who felt the Pilgrims were taking "a heady course," were forced to accept the Company's terms. In Leyden the discontent grew. But the more determined members, Bradford, Brewster, Allerton, among them, continued to prepare. Isaac Allerton went to Delftshaven to purchase and make ready the *Speedwell*. Perhaps they were stung by Cushman's written entreaty: "Entreat our freinds not to be to busy in criticising matters until they know what they are talking about."

Weston, at the last moment, made his peace with Cushman and together they chartered the *Mayflower*. It was now too late to withdraw. Although belatedly, the Pilgrims now sent to Cushman their apologies for their importunate letters. In Leyden and at London preparations for the embarkation went busily on. It looked as if all wounds had been healed. The next month was taken up fitting out the two ships and in the middle of July the Leyden emigrants arrived on the *Speedwell* to join up with their London friends in the great venture. Now Cushman's troubles began anew. In the cramped cabin of the *Speedwell* he presented the merchants' amended articles for signature, but these the principal members of the congregation from Leyden refused to sign. A heated argument ensued. Weston went off to London in a huff, leaving them to pay their own way out of the harbor. The articles were still unsigned when the two ships sailed.

In charge of the smaller group aboard the *Speedwell* was Robert Cushman. When the master put the leaking and ill-fitted vessel back to port for safety's sake, many of those under Cushman's care crowded with their belongings aboard the *Mayflower*. Robert Cushman elected to remain behind. That his decision was tied up with the rejection of the amended articles of agreement is certain. But, although he sailed back to London on the crippled *Speedwell*, he did not lose interest in those who went off to help God work his miracle and continued to act as their agent.

During the first year that the Plantation was in the making Robert Cushman arranged for the emigration of the second group of Pilgrims who went out in the summer of 1621 aboard the *Fortune,* the first ship to visit Plymouth after the *Mayflower.* When this ship sailed he was aboard, and in his pocket were the amended articles. After considerable debate and wrangling they were finally accepted. Thus when Cushman returned the Pilgrims had contracted to work a whole week in the interests of the Adventurers throughout the entire seven years the contract was to run. Although he probably did not suspect it, Isaac Allerton's work was cut out for him the day the articles were signed. The Pilgrims then loaded the *Fortune* with a cargo of clapboards they had hewn by hand and such furs as they had collected. Before he sailed, leaving his thirteen-year-old son Thomas behind with Governor Bradford, the patient Cushman spoke to them all these words:

"Now, brethren, you have given your names and promises one to another, and covenanted here to cleave together—what then must you do?

"May you live as retired hermits? and look after nobody? Nay, you must still seek the welfare of one another; and enquire, How liveth such a man? How is he clad? How is he fed? He is my brother, my associate; we *venture* our lives here together, and had a hard brunt of it, and we are in league together. Is his labor harder than mine? Surely I will ease him. Hath he no bed to lie on? Why I have two suits, I'll give him one. Eats he coarse fare, bread and water, and I have better? Why surely we will part stakes. He is as good a man as I and we are bound each to other, so that his wants must be my wants, his sorrows my sorrows, his sickness my sickness, and his welfare my welfare.

"Great matters have been brought to pass where men have cheerfully, as with one heart, hand and shoulder, gone about it; both in wars, buildings, and plantations; but where every man seeks to himself, all cometh to nothing. The country is yet raw, the lands untilled, the cities not builded, the cattle not *settled,* we are compassed with a helpless and idle people, the natives of the country, which cannot in comely or comfortable manner help themselves, much less us. *Is this then a time for men to begin to seek for themselves?* It is here but the first days and (as it were) the dawning of this new world; *it is now therefore no time for men to look to get* riches, brave clothes, dainty fare; but to look to present necessities; it is now no time to pamper the flesh, live at ease, snatch, catch, scrape and pill, and hoard up; but rather to open the doors, the chest and the vessels, and say, Brother, neighbor, freind, what want ye? Anything that I have, make bold with it; it is yours to command, to do you good, to comfort and cherish you. . . ."

Here in these words of this pious man may, perhaps, be found the germ of the New Deal of his descendant, Franklin Delano Roosevelt.

Robert Cushman's return from his only visit to the Plantation he had helped to build at Plymouth was not a pleasant journey. The *Fortune* was captured by a French privateer and the first fruits of the sweat and toil of the Pilgrims never reached the London markets where the disgruntled Adventurers impatiently awaited at least an indication that their money had not been invested in a vain and foolish venture. Their lagging spirits were buoyed up, however, when Cushman finally arrived, and if the ship's hold were empty his report on what it had contained before the privateer hove in sight sweetened the dispositions of many who were growing sour on the project. Also encouraging was his "Reasons and Considerations touching the Lawfulness of Removing from England into the Parts of America," which he published in 1622, the first printed account of the Plymouth Plantation. For the next three years Cushman continued to act as the Pilgrims' ambassador in London, but he was in failing health. He was only forty-six years old when in 1625, dreaming of someday returning forever to Plymouth, he died.

William Bradford was singularly aware of the interest which posterity was to take in the First-Comers to Plymouth, but, being an honest historian he made no concessions to the vanity of those who might descend from the men and women who peopled his tale. John Howland was, as he states, one of the two manservants John Carver brought with him in the cramped confines of the *Mayflower*. From the outset, despite his lowly beginnings, John Howland showed himself to be a brave and able adventurer; and when he died, after more than half a century on the Plymouth shore, he was among the wealthiest of those who had tilled the thin soil of that godly outpost.

The little *Mayflower* ran into many storms on its way across the Atlantic. More than once the ship had to be stripped of sail and lie for days at a time with the wind whistling through the halyards as the great waves tossed her to and fro. During these grim intervals most of the Pilgrims huddled in the cabin that reeked of their seasickness. One day Howland decided some fresh air would do him good and, despite the storm, went on deck. He missed his footing when the ship lurched and was swept into the sea as the waves poured across the deck. Luckily for him the sailors had not made fast all the lines and a top sail halyard hung overboard. The "lusty young man" grabbed the rope and shouted for all he was worth until some unremembered sailor heard him and pulled him up with a boat hook. He was shaken by the ordeal, but when the ship had run for shelter behind the hook of land that formed Provincetown Harbor he had recovered.

After the ordeals of the voyage, during which the sailors had scornfully treated the passengers, the leaders of the expedition feared dissension might break up the sea-weary group of men and women. To forestall this John Carver, the governor, and some others drew up a "compact," or agreement of mutual cooperation. Then they called the group into the cabin. The governor solemnly read to them the words of the now famous agreement and one by one the men stepped forward and signed the paper.

THE MAYFLOWER COMPACT

In ye name of God Amen. We whose names are underwritten, the loyall subjects of our dread soveraigne lord King James, by ye grace of God, of great Britaine, France, & Ireland king, defender of ye faith, etc.

Haveing undertaken, for ye glorie of God, and advancemente of ye christian faith and honour of our king & countrie, a voyage to plant ye first colonie in ye Northerne parts of Virginia. Doe by these presents solemnly & mutualy in ye presence of God, and one of another; covenant, & combine our selves togeather into a civill body politick; for our better ordering, & preservation & furtherance of ye ends aforesaid; and by vertue hearof to enacte, constitute, and frame shuch just & equall lawes, ordinances, Acts, constitutions, & offices, from time to time, as shall be thought most meete & convenient for ye generall good of ye Colonie: unto which we promise all due submission and obedience. In witnes whereof we have hereunder subscribed our names at Cap-Codd ye .11. of November, in ye year of ye raigne of our soveraigne lord king James of England, France, & Ireland ye eighteenth, and of Scotland ye fiftie fourth. Ano: Dom. 1620.

John Carver	Sampel Fuller	Edward Tilley
William Bradford	Christopher Martin	John Tilley
Edward Winslow	William Mullins	Francis Cooke
William Brewster	William White	Thomas Rogers
Isaac Allerton	Richard Warren	Thomas Tinker
Myles Standish	John Howland	John Ridgdale
John Alden	Stephen Hopkins	Edward Fuller
John Turner	Degory Priest	Richard Clarke
Francis Eaton	Thomas Williams	Richard Gardiner
James Chilton	Gilbert Winslow	John Allerton
John Crackston	Edmund Margeson	Thomas English
John Billington	Peter Brown	Edward Doty
Moses Fletcher	Richard Britteridge	Edward Leister
John Goodman	George Soule	

Although he was but an indentured servant John Howland signed and from then on he stood on equal footing with all the rest aboard the shaken ship.

At this time John Howland was twenty-seven years old and a bachelor. Having proved his strength and quickness of mind he was a natural choice to go forth in the shallop from the *Mayflower* with nine other Pilgrims and some seamen on the third desperate attempt to find a suitable place for the plantation. John Carver, already chosen Governor, led the expedition.

The weather was fearfully cold as the men sailed eastward and the spray froze onto their clothing "like unto iron." It was an unfriendly if hardly rockbound coast they followed. On the second morning away from the comparative safety of the *Mayflower* they were attacked by Indians at what is now called Eastham, at Cape Cod, Massachusetts, but which they laconically named First Encounter. That evening their small sailing boat lost mast and rudder in a heavy rain squall and was all but wrecked in the breakers. But they escaped and made the lee of an island. All were drenched to the skin and weak with exposure, but they got ashore and started a fire. The next morning the sun shone and they explored the harbor which they found deep enough for the *Mayflower*. Going ashore they discovered brooks and ponds and cornfields, abandoned by the Pequots, who had been nearly wiped out in an epidemic two years before. "At least" this place "was the best they could find, and the season, and their present necessitie, made them glad to accepte of it."

Returning to Provincetown they told the others of the place they had seen, and in due time the *Mayflower* weighed anchor and sailed to Plymouth. The story of the first year that followed this is now too well known to call for elaboration here, except to say that it was not, as is generally believed, an extremely cold winter. The terrific death toll was caused not so much by the cold weather as by the drenchings received by the men in their daily trips to and from the *Mayflower,* across the broad mudflats of the harbor. They lived on the vessel while they were making the first houses ready. An epidemic of some sort of cold, or "galloping consumption," beset them and, as already noted, all but a handful of those who had come on the ship died. Among the early victims were John Tilley and his wife. Their daughter Elizabeth, then about fourteen years old, managed to survive.

After the death of his master, Governor Carver, in the first spring, John Howland was accepted as one of the substantial men of the Plantation. His advancement in the estimation of his fellow colonists was rapid. In 1627, he was listed as one of the eight men who undertook to pay off the Colony's debt to the Adventurers, as arranged by Isaac Allerton. And later, in 1633, when the Colony was well established and advancing towards its eventual freedom from debt, he was named an Assistant Governor. He held this post for three years.

By this time he was married. There were not many young women at Plymouth from among whom the bachelors might make a choice. Undoubtedly there is more poetry than truth in the story of John Alden's wooing of Priscilla Mullins, the only love story of the Pilgrims that has survived. Mr. Bradford was not interested in love (although his own love story is not without interest) and so we have no knowledge of how John Howland, that lusty young man, wooed the orphaned Elizabeth, daughter of his companion in the shallop. Mr. Bradford's concern with the romance is restricted to these words:

". . . John Howland maried the doughter of John Tillie, Elizabeth, and they are now both living, and have 10 children, now all living; and their eldest daughter hath 4 children. And their second daughter hath 1, all living; and other of their children mariagable. So 15 are come of them."

So much for love and romance in Plymouth, as its historian saw it in those days.

John Howland must have liked the life of the Colony, which was indeed a land of opportunity for one so lately a servant. His two brothers, Henry and Arthur, came over a few years later, but unlike John, they did not subscribe to the tenets of the Pilgrim Church. Instead, they became Quakers, that argumentatively peaceful sect towards which the Pilgrims never showed any noticeable tolerance. But John remained faithful to the Pilgrim Church to the end.

In the later years of his life John Howland was a farmer but he was a trader when he became involved in the first murder in New England.

The Pilgrims were engaged in many ventures, but the fur trade was the most lucrative. In 1634 they sent John Howland to the Kennebec in charge of the trading post they had established there. The post was in a country rich in furs where some of the men spent the winter hunting and trapping and waiting for the arrival of the pelt-laden Indians in the spring. In

April of that year John Alden appeared in the river aboard a pinnace with supplies. One morning another bark appeared and anchored nearby. Since the Pilgrims alone had a patent entitling them to the use of the territory, the group at the trading post were surprised and angry.

The master of the newcomer was John Hocking, a free-lance trader with whom the Pilgrims had previously had trouble. He was from the Massachusetts Colony, which had no permission from the British crown to trade in the country of the Kennebec. John Howland now rowed out into the stream and told John Hocking to leave at once. The poacher refused to hoist anchor. Words were passed. Howland told Hocking that the year previous, the Pilgrims had investigated his claims and found them false, that he had no license in these waters. Hocking mockingly dared the Plymouth agent to drive him out by force.

Howland's men rallied around him now on the deck of John Alden's vessel and asserted that they would stand with him in whatever he did. Howland thereupon ordered three men into a canoe with axes and told them to go alongside Hocking's ship and cut his anchor lines. They managed to hack through one of the hawses, but the swift current swept them away before they could sever the second. Howland then ordered them back to the boat and to take their most expert canoeman, Moses Talbot, aboard. Moses, a veteran woodsman, clambered in and dexterously brought the canoe up to the cable. All this time Hocking has been grimly watching. He now dashed into the cabin and got his gun, which he brought to bear on the bow man in the canoe.

When Howland saw what the poacher was doing he shouted that his men were acting only on his orders and if Hocking must shoot any one, to shoot him. The angry poacher ignored this and took aim. The canoe was directly under the bow. Talbot swung his axe and cut the second cable. The roar of a gun echoed against the fir-lined shores of the Kennebec. Talbot, his head shattered by the close range of the shot, fell dead in the canoe's bow. Another shot rang out, this time from the gun of one of Talbot's companions. It killed Hocking on the deck of his ship. The pinnace, cut loose from its moorings, swept down on the spring tide of the river, out of control.

Hocking's men soon made sail, however, and streaked for the open sea. When they reached Massachusetts they told their own version of the double murder—omitting to mention the first death of Talbot, and insisting that the attack had been un-provoked!

A short time later John Alden was arrested in Boston town, despite the fact that the Massachusetts Bay authorities had no jurisdiction in the matter. Letters demanding his release were at once sent to Boston. One of these Governor Thomas Dudley tried to suppress, and might have, if Captain Myles Standish had not required "an answer thereof publickly in the courte." Alden was released, but Standish had to appear in court to prove the Pilgrims' right to the Kennebec. This he readily did; but it was not until Edward Winslow and William Bradford came up from Plymouth and faced Governors Dudley and Winthrop that a true version of the encounter was sent to Eng-land. The high-handed action of the Massachusetts authorities was long resented in the colonies, but the Pilgrims' rights on the Kennebec were not again disputed.

Shortly after this John Howland settled down on his Plym-outh farm to raise his ten children and increase his wealth. He stayed in Plymouth the rest of his life. Others who had come over in the first ship sooner or later moved away to other towns nearby. But not John Howland. He and William Bradford stayed at the first settlement always. When he died, in 1673, at the ripe age of eighty years, his children shared an estate valued at £157, much more than most Pilgrims left behind. This included three horses, seventeen cows and oxen, thirteen swine, forty-five sheep, and nearly two whole pounds in ready money, an unusually high amount for those times.

During the years that Isaac Allerton was traversing the At-lantic on his many errands, Robert Cushman dreaming of spending his last days at Plymouth, and John Howland trad-ing with the Maine Indians, young Thomas Cushman was growing into manhood. He was thirteen when he heard his father preach against avarice to the Pilgrims, after their first winter of self-sacrifice in the strange land where the Indians ran wild like animals and neither toiled nor spun. Neither saw each other again. But William Bradford, however stern he may appear from the pages of his *History,* did his best to be a good father to the lonely boy.

Governor Bradford himself knew what loneliness could mean. While living in Leyden he had married Dorothy May, the daughter of a member of an English church in Amsterdam. Their son John did not come with them on the *Mayflower,* and thus was spared the witnessing of his father's grief when his mother slipped overboard and was drowned. Thus bereft, Bradford had gone through the first winter. But he was not to be lonely for long. In Leyden he had known Alice Carpenter Southworth, a widow and the mother of two boys. When the *Mayflower* left in the Spring it carried William Bradford's first love letter from these shores. Others followed and in July, 1623, Alice and her two sons came ashore from the *Anne* at Plymouth. The next month she and Governor Bradford were married. Although they were to have a daughter and two sons, and although she had brought her own two boys with her, Alice Bradford accepted young Thomas Cushman as one of her own.

Tutored by his foster-father, the boy grew up at Plymouth, doing his full share of the work. When he was twenty-two or twenty-three years old he duly fell in love. And he married Isaac Allerton's daughter, Mary. She was about twenty years old at the time. Later, their son, Eleazar, was to marry Elizabeth Coombs, the grand-daugher of Isaac Allerton's sister Sarah, in one of the series of marital unions that was to lead to Franklin Delano Roosevelt in six more generations.

Thomas Cushman was a solid, god-fearing Pilgrim. From his strain came many persons notable in the life of America, including Charlotte Cushman, who was once considered the greatest of American-born actresses. But his own life in Plymouth was uneventful. It was more closely associated with the Church than with any of the meaner aspects of the Plantation's life. As we have already seen, his father-in-law had, as one of his earliest commissions, the finding of a suitable Minister for the Colony. His choice was regrettable, although forgiven. It was not for several years that they had a minister anywhere near to their liking. During these years several preachers came to the Plantation, including Roger Williams, but for various reasons of theology all were soon found wanting.

By now Thomas Cushman was approaching middle age, and for five years had been ruling elder of the Church. He ran the church and preached the sermons to the satisfaction of all for the next thirteen years, when a new Minister took over his duties. By that time the original colony had been pretty well dispersed. But he remained at Plymouth until death took him in his eighty-fourth year. His wife Mary lived eight years longer than he, dying in 1699, the last survivor of the *Mayflower*.

Richard Warren, the first immigrant ancestor of Franklin D. Roosevelt's mother, was a Londoner, a grave man, who took his religion seriously. Although he was not a member of the Church at Leyden he was aboard the *Mayflower* when it sailed, as were some others who were related in one way or another with the Adventurers. He signed the Compact, and he was with the company on the adventurous coastal exploration that resulted in the settlement at Plymouth.

One other ancestor of Franklin Delano Roosevelt on the *Mayflower* was Degory Priest, who had married Isaac Allerton's sister, Sarah. He signed his name in a halting hand to the Compact and died in the first winter. His widow married again and one of her daughters married a Frenchman named John Coombs. Their daughter, Elizabeth, married Eleazar Cushman, Thomas Cushman's son, thus getting on the Roosevelt genealogical chart.

During the decade spent in Leyden, the Pilgrims had many kindly friends who were not members of their church. Some, of course, were Dutch; others, like themselves, had settled in the town because of oppression of one kind or another in their native lands. Among the latter was a family of French origin named de la Noye. The mother of this brood, which had joined the Walloon Church, seems to have been on especially good terms with the English. Her son, Philippe, who was born in 1603, grew up with the children of the English expatriates. He learned their language and manners, but when they evacuated the old university town of Leyden he stayed behind. The next year, however, he made his way to England, and that summer, when Robert Cushman shepherded the thirty-five newcomers aboard the *Fortune* young Philippe, then just eighteen years old and sturdy, was one of them.

In 1637, three years after he had married a girl named Hester Dewsbury, who had come from England with her parents to Duxbury, Massachusetts, Philippe answered the call of the Connecticut General Court for volunteers to fight the Pequot Indians. Some ninety men were called from Plymouth, Massachusetts and New Haven, to serve under Captain John Mason and Captain John Underhill. Accompanied by several hundred warriors from the Narraganset tribe, these doughty Englishmen set out for the Pequot village near Narraganset Bay. The Indians deserted before they reached the Pequot town, but the English made a surprise attack at dawn, and set fire to the village. In the early May morning, as a high wind sent the flames shooting through the huts and wigwams, some 500 men, women and children were slowly burned to death.

After his return from that ghastly mission Philippe de la Noye settled on his farm at Duxbury, but he also spent much time going throughout the Colony as a surveyor. Under the influence of the English colonists with whom he associated, his name soon lost its French spelling and became Delano. His son, Jonathan Delano, was born at Duxbury in 1647, and was reared there and in Bridgewater, Massachusetts, both settlements near Cape Cod, to which Philippe later moved. From his father Jonathan seems to have inherited a liking for Indian fighting. In the summer of 1675 began the depredations of King Philip, chief of the Massasoit Indians, and within a year nearly a thousand white lives were lost, thirteen towns were destroyed, and six hundred buildings burned by Indian fire. The men of the Colony were called upon to defeat the Indian chief and his men. They raised a force of eighteen white men and twenty-two friendly Indians and ended the war with the capture of King Philip. One of the men on this historic expedition was Jonathan Delano.

Two years after he had done with Indian fighting the young soldier received rights to eight hundred acres of land at Dartmouth near New Bedford which became the world famous whaling port where the Delano family fortune was made. He went there to live, taking with him his bride, Mercy Warren, the daughter of Nathaniel Warren and the granddaughter of Richard Warren. She was then a girl of twenty years. There in 1704 a son was born to them, among other children, whom they named Thomas, and the line of descent to Franklin Delano Roosevelt was begun.

From these men and women of Plymouth and the south shore of Massachusetts Bay, who sprang from the most humble origins in England and France and who were of but slight contemporary distinction in the struggle to make America a vast colony of the English Crown, there have descended several families whose names have survived for nearly three and a quarter centuries. Had testy President John Adams had his way and established an aristocracy of titled office holders in this country these families might have contributed their share to that caste. But fortunately John Adams had to bow to the democracy that he never trusted. It was not for many years after the arrival of the first Allerton and Cushman and Howland and Delano that this English strain was joined with the blood of certain Dutch and German and Swedish immigrants who had settled on the Island of Manhattan and in the fertile valley of the Hudson River. Three hundred years later the most famous descendant of these little people, looking back upon them not without fondness and thinking of the great years of history that lay between, said proudly:

"Remember always that all of us are descended from immigrants!"

CHAPTER IV

New Amsterdam and the Future Pavements of New York

IN 1623, A LITTLE MORE than a decade after Claes the Little One had gone prowling in the strange forests along the shores of the Hudson, a Dutch engineer arrived on Manhattan Island with a set of blue prints in his pocket and a gang of seasoned workmen at his heels. His name was Kryn Frederikszen and he was under assignment from his masters, the shrewd burghers of Amsterdam and Directors of the Dutch West India Company, that far-flung and sometimes profitable commercial agency of the Dutch Republic.

After scouting the wooded water fronts where the East and the Hudson rivers joined their flood, and after many arguments with his fellow travelers on the ship, *Arms of Amsterdam*, Kryn pointed to the tip end of the Manhattan Island and ordered the shipmaster to drop anchor there. He went ashore in a small boat, and landed on a rock at what is now the foot of State Street in New York City, for in those days the land which forms the present end of Manhattan was all under water. After making a rough survey of the territory he staked off a sizable plot located about where the steamship agencies now have their offices on lower Bowling Green. Then he put his men to work.

Kryn's plans, drawn up in Holland, called for four stout stone houses and a fort. But when poor Kryn began looking around for materials for the masons he had brought, he was in a quandary. There were plenty of trees for lumber but mighty little stone fit for building fine structures of the kind they had in old Holland. The first thing he did was to dig out some holes in the ground, what Hendrik van Loon has called "inverted igloos," for temporary dwellings. Then he set out to build his fort, but the best he could do, with the materials on hand, was to throw up a crude blockhouse and surround it with cedar palings and sodded earthworks.

Soon, however, the resourceful engineer became somewhat acclimated to the strange country, so different from his flat Holland, and within a year thirty small log houses with tree-bark roofs had been built in a close huddle around the fort. But even with this good start the Dutch investors had no intention of establishing a colony, in the accepted sense of the word. All they wanted was a safe harbor for their vessels and an easily defended post where the trappers and traders might bring the pelts of beaver and fox for transshipment to the European markets. Those who came to Manhattan, to live in the crude huts around the rough blockhouse, were not adventurers like the Englishmen in Virginia, nor politicians and religious fanatics like those in Massachusetts or Plymouth. They were traders, out for a profit and nothing else. Few of them thought of staying long on the island. To them it was an outpost of commerce; it was not a new Zion.

The first thing they did after they had their fort was to put up a counting house. This, the keystone of the colony, they built with walls strongly made of stone. The church, which was not built for some time, was a poor affair of wood, but it served the purposes of the rough and ready traders and seamen that crowded the tiny port. New Amsterdam, which was, officially, the capital of all New Netherland, as the Dutch called the vague territory they claimed, was under the charge of Peter Minuit at the beginning. Old Peter was an able enough administrator of that primitive place. Although some of his servants had killed and robbed an Indian soon after his arrival, he had no serious Indian troubles on his hands. England and Holland were at peace and a gift of sugar and Holland cheese to Governor Bradford of Plymouth served to settle such difficulties as arose between them over trading rights.

None of the people at New Amsterdam were in any way distinguished. Old Peter himself is remembered mainly because,
with typical Dutch thoroughness, he insisted upon a deed to
the land and gave the Indians twenty-six dollars worth of
trinkets in return for a piece of paper. The first minister, old
Jonal Michaelius, a zealous missionary if ever there was one,
hoped to make the little port a real colony, but the Directors
at home scoffed at such an idea. And so, for twelve years, New
Amsterdam remained a scabby outpost, peopled by unimaginative traders and shopkeepers. The untidy settlement was a
long time in taking on the air of permanence which Plymouth
had before the first summer was past.

The Dutch West India Company from the beginning was a
mismanaged affair. There were others besides the Reverend
Michaelius who urged colonization, both at New Amsterdam
and elsewhere in the larger territory that was New Netherland,
but the quicker profits in pelts kept this from occurring for
several years. But after awhile the Company discovered that
there could be profits in settlements. Although the European
world was changing, feudalism had not yet disappeared, and
there was still something in that system to appeal to man's vanity—if one could be a lord. Recognizing this, the West India
Company's directors began the creation of lordships. They were
known as patroons.

A patroon was, in reality, little more than a feudal chieftain.
He was a semi-independent monarch "who could make laws and
dispense justice and force subjects to grind their corn in his
mills; a man in whom were vested all the fishing rights of the
broad acres and wide estuaries he called his; a Lord of the
Manor who appointed clergymen and dismissed school teachers
as the spirit moved him; in short a petty sovereign who was
responsible to no one but his own conscience and the government of the Dutch Republic."

Anyone who could afford it could be a patroon. He might be
a dull, penny-pinching shop-keeper, but if he could buy stock
in the West India Company and finance the sending of at least
fifty emigrants (entirely at his own expense) to New Netherland, then he might be lord of sixteen miles of river front and
as much of the adjacent interior as he cared to claim. For this

privilege he was taxed five per cent on all exports. The Company felt that through this system it could fill New Netherland (roughly the present State of New York) with "desirable" people and safeguard miles and miles of territory on which the English, their legendary enemies, were already beginning to encroach.

Unfortunately it did not work out as well as expected. Instead of bringing people who would advance the company's interests, it brought those whose aims and ambitions were at variance with the directors' dreams of profits. By the time the patroon was settled with his serfs his authority went to his head and he thumbed his nose at all outside authority. As soon as there were enough patroons, they began to dominate the directorship of the Company. An independent Director General of New Netherland, like old Peter Minuit, quickly found this out. It was not long before the trading post of New Amsterdam, which was also the capital, if it could be called that, of New Netherland, was surrounded by semi-independent states resentful of any dictation by the Director General. To add to the confusion, the majority of the patroons preferred to live in old Amsterdam, thus creating the chaotic condition of absentee landlordism.

Kiliaen van Rensselaer, diamond merchant whose surname still ranks high in New York society, was the first and greatest patroon. His patroonship of Rensselaerswick, on both sides of the Hudson near Albany and Troy, lasted one hundred and fifty years longer than the Dutch West India Company itself. He sent over his first shiploads of farmers and mechanics in 1630. But what was more important for the time being, he procured for his besotted nephew, Wouter van Twiller, the Director Generalship of New Netherland. Van Twiller's regime was a sorry one. He spent most of his time in the tavern and the rest of it fighting with the Reverend Everhardus Bogardus, whose fondness for gin was equal to his own. As David Pieterszen de Vries, an experienced old sea dog who invested his savings in a patroonship, said of van Twiller and his gang: "They know nothing but how to spend their time carousing . . . in the East Indies they would not be allowed to hold down a job as second assistant, let alone director or treasurer."

Van Twiller and his friends and relatives grabbed off most of
the best lands and, while he neglected the affairs of the Company, New Amsterdam degenerated into a sailor's town of the
worst order. The complaints against van Twiller grew. It was
said that he was drunk even in church, and his personal quarrels with Bogardus became so ridiculous that the Company at
last had to remove him, even if he was van Rensselaer's nephew.
In 1638 William Kieft became Director General. He found the
town in a deplorable condition. The muddy streets were
peopled by a riotous crowd of drunkards, thieves and whores.
Homicides were frequent. The Fort, which van Twiller had
taken two years to rebuild at the cost of about $1700, was a
scandal. Although he had replaced the old blockhouse with a
stone quadrangle 300 feet in length and 250 in breadth, with
a bastion at each corner, it still was a mess. The Colony was on
the verge of bankruptcy.

Van Kieft, himself an undischarged bankrupt, was a stubborn
dictatorial fellow, quite without the gift of running a colony.
He made the great mistake of disliking the Indians. They recip-
rocated. As a result he won the enmity of eleven tribes, who
turned in concert against the Dutch. The Dutch-Indian wars,
in which Isaac Allerton played his minor part, were all but disastrous. They so weakened New Netherland financially and in
population that Kieft also had to be removed. Nor was his
political reign much better than his military. As was the case
with van Twiller, he had his silly quarrels with his neighbors
and associates. He spurned the advice of the men, including
Isaac Allerton, chosen to advise him, and went his stubborn
way.

By 1645 all New Netherland was in a sorry state. Its population had declined. Many had gone back to Holland to escape
the Indian menace; there was little, if any, new immigration;
trade, which depended on the Indian trappers, had fallen off;
farms had been abandoned, the cattle destroyed. Five years of
warfare had caused suffering among the Indians, too. Their
corn was gone, their cornfields unattended. Peace was made at
last. But it came too late to save Kieft. He was called back to
Holland, along with his drinking companion, the Reverend
Bogardus, both under charges preferred by the colonists. Un-

fortunately their ship, the *Princess*, took the wrong channel and was dashed to pieces off the coast of Wales. The Director-General and the minister were drowned.

Claes Martenszen van Rosenvelt did not buy his farm, or bowery, until two years after Kieft was superseded but, if he was in New Amsterdam in 1647, he along with most of the settlers, was glad to see the dictatorial, quarrelsome Kieft depart. When the settlers heard who was to take his place they exulted. Old Peter Stuyvesant was known to all Dutchmen as a statesman and soldier of great ability. He had been governor of Curaçao, that little island off the northern coast of South America, and the loss of his leg at the siege of St. Martins, when the Dutch tried to drive out the Portuguese, had established his claim as a soldier. Everyone in New Amsterdam—except the worst drunks and water-front villains—expected this two-fisted and hard-bitten warrior to work a miracle in the Colony.

Everyone in the region, on Manhattan and up the Hudson, came clattering to town on the May Day that the fleet bearing the new governor, his lady and their suite cast anchor in the Bay. Perhaps a thousand people—there were seven-hundred living in New Amsterdam—thronged to the shore below the gaily decorated fort, and cheered when the seldom-used guns pounded their salute. The four ships of war responded with equally deafening blasts. When Stuyvesant came ashore, in his regimental coat decorated with brass buttons from chin to waist-band, the skirts turned up at the corner to set off his brimstone-colored breeches, his wooden leg set boldly in advance, his hair standing out stiff with pomatum, and one hand holding his gold headed cane while the other grasped his broad sword; every Dutchman in the port roared himself hoarse. That night there was great revelry in the forty or more taverns, "blind tigers" and other resorts of the water front village. Perhaps Claes, his cows mooing mournfully for their forgotten supper, was as drunk as the rest?

Old Petrus, as Stuyvesant was called, was governor for eighteen years. During those years he had his troubles. The little town, with its 150 thatch roofed houses, its two or three roughly cobbled streets leading to the water front, was populated with a heterogeneous group. Being a port, many of the residents were a rough lot. There was so much drunkenness that Old Petrus had to clamp down and enforce the first prohibition act in America placed on the statute books by Isaac Allerton and the other Eight Men under William Kieft. The three weeks after Christmas were one long sodden celebration. Day or night the soldiers of the Fort could be found carousing about the town.

There were, of course, among the traders and merchants many who were disgusted at the licentious and liquorous antics of their more loutish neighbors. Despite the West India Company's indifference, they tried to make a decent town out of New Amsterdam. On the Company's rolls there were always listed a minister, who was paid $576 a year to administer to the inhabitants, a schoolmaster, and a sexton for the Stone church that was built in 1642 to replace the first "mean barn." Vanity, not piety, was the motive for building the church within the fort, a sort of civic pride in answer to the fine churches that were built first in every New England town.

Drunkenness and reform were not the only problems that peg-legged Peter had to face. He did his best. It is due to his ability that the Dutch directors in Holland decided, in 1653, to make the village of New Amsterdam into a city, thus signifying their intention of maintaining the place not merely as trading post, but as the seat of a colony. In the next few years Peter had his troubles with the Swedes and the Indians, and he was called upon to take action against the hogs that roamed the streets, destroying the earthen walls of the fort with their snouts. This was a more serious matter than it seems, for the fort was fast falling to pieces. And as early as 1664 there were rumors of war. If herdsmen and fences could not rid the city of hogs, perhaps the guns of British men-of-war would.

Shortly after the restoration of England's Charles II, that monarch issued "the most despotic instrument recorded in the colonial archives of England"—the charter conveying to his brother, the Duke of York, all the land between Saint Croix and Pemaquid and the tract between the Connecticut and the Delaware Rivers, with all adjacent islands, thus completely wiping out Dutch ownership of New Netherland. The Duke, without warning, sent four warships under Richard Nicolls, chosen as his deputy governor of the colony. The day the news of the fleet's arrival in Boston reached the port of New Amsterdam, old Peter was up at Fort Orange (Albany) straightening out some trouble with the Indians. He hurried back. The fleet anchored in Gravesend Bay on August twenty-eight. There wasn't much Stuyvesant could do against the four warships, with his rusty guns and crumbling fort, now hastily repaired, so he resorted to diplomacy. His pleadings failed. The old Governor, proud and defiant to the last, surrendered and three years later the treaty of Breda was signed, confirming England's possession of New Amsterdam, now called New York.

For nine years British officers sunned their red coats on the bastions of Fort James, as the British renamed the old garrison. Then England and Holland were once more at war. One July day in 1673 a Dutch fleet came up the Bay. As usual the fort was in a sad state of disrepair and the Dutch easily recaptured the city, which they renamed New Orange. They held it, under martial law, for nearly a year, but in 1674 it was returned to England by treaty. The old fort, useless in war, worse than useless in peace, rotted away before the march of commerce, as New York, under British hands, began to thrive as it never had under the inept management of the Dutch.

The city was still Dutch, however, when the children of the Little One were born on his farm on Rose Hill. They spent their earliest years there, away from the contaminating influences of the noisy village at the island's end. The country there was not flat as it was nearer the village. It was high and hilly, but neither as high nor such a tall hill as the one that is now known as Murray Hill to the north. Because of the Indians who still lurked outside the village, it is doubtful if little Nicholas's sisters ever roamed far from the wooden thatched-roofed farmhouse, but they could coast on the hills and skate on the duck pond.

The Little One was an able farmer who, as we have seen, prospered from the produce that he laboriously carted in to sell at the market on Maiden Lane. But farming did not appeal to his son, Nicholas, who was only one year old when Claes died. The nurse provided by the estate cared well for Nicholas's physical well-being but neglected his education. Probably she lived too far away to see that he went to the deplorable little school then kept in the barnlike church within the confines of the Fort. He never learned to write his own name.

Young Nick's sisters, Elsje, Anna-Margaret, and Christina, were all older than he, and what became of them after the death of the Little One does not appear in the records of the old Orphans Court of New Amsterdam. Presumably they, too, were parcelled out to occupants of other farms or boweries, or perhaps they lived in the town. But wherever they lived they all managed to grow up and marry in the church near the Fort.

Elsje, the oldest, married Hendrick Jillesh Meyer, a cordwainer, as cobblers were called in those old Dutch days. His father was a craftsman of some importance, often called upon by Governor Kieft to patch up the old Fort and do other work on the buildings and mills of the West India Company. Young Meyer and his wife lived and had their cobbler shop near the waterfront on what later became Pearl Street. In his old age Meyer had risen to the prominence of an assistant alderman for the south ward of the city, after it had long been under British rule.

Anna-Margaret also married, but her husband, Alderste Roosa, seems never to have done anything important enough to get his name on the records. Her younger sister, Christina, however, married young Nicasius de Montagne while she was in her teens. Nicasius's father was a man of considerable prominence. He had the title of Doctor and he was a French Protestant who had fled to Holland. He had come over as an assistant to the irascible Governor Kieft and indeed was one of the few people to whom the Governor ever turned willingly for advice. He was the public school teacher, presiding over a small, crowded room in the Stadt Huys, or City Hall, on a green lane that is today known as Coenties Slip. There he taught his charges, who included his own son Nicasius and little Christina and often subjected them to whippings when they did not know the catechism and ciphering. Sometimes Dr. de Montagne sat as judge in court and it was he who had heard the charge of slander brought against the Little One many years before. Another member of the de Montagne family was sexton of the church and later the local undertaker.

Of Anna, the child who was born after her father's death, no record remains.

In her *History of New York in the Seventeenth Century* Mrs. Schuyler van Rensselaer rather patronizingly remarks that "at no pre-Revolutionary period was the Roosevelt family conspicuous nor did any member of it attain distinction." It is not quite true that no bearer of the name of Roosevelt attained distinction before the Revolution, for at least two grandsons of the Little Fellow had their fingers in many New Amsterdam pies, along with others quite as irreproachable as the Schuylers or the Van Rensselaers, but Nicholas did not. Of that there can be no refutation.

Nicholas grew to be a strapping young man with ambition. The life of the waterfront town did not lure him. Instead he turned his blond head northward into the woods. By canoe he traveled up the Hudson to the little trading village, then known as Esopus, later as Kingston. In this river-front town he built his home, married, and raised most of his eight children. He was a fur trapper, happiest when he was off in the woods, following some creek in his canoe, or bartering with his Indian friends at some forest rendezvous for the skins they had gathered. He knew every inch of the Hudson, from Fort Orange to Fort Amsterdam. More than once he set his traps on the forbidden acres of Rensselaerswick, the patroonship that lay on either side of the Hudson, as far as Albany. He became a prosperous trader, trapping for himself, buying from the Indians and from the patroons themselves who were legally forbidden to deal in pelts in competition with the West India Company.

When Nicholas was twenty-four years old he married an estimable young lady, fair like himself, of Dutch and German extraction. There is evidence that she was more German than Dutch. She was Heyltje Jans Kunst, the daughter of Jan Barentsen Kunst, who, in turn, was the son of Barent Jansen, a German who probably went from Germany to Holland before migrating to Esopus. In that town Jan Kunst earned his living as a house carpenter. He had the reputation of being a tight fisted fellow, who more than once had a neighbor brought to court for failing to pay him his bill. At one time he owned a house in New Amsterdam, where he probably was in the employ of the Company, but he sold it when he moved to Esopus, where he bought a large acreage near the present Kingston churchyard.

Heyltje was nineteen when she married the fur trapper. For the next eight years Nick ran his trap lines and bargained in sign language with the tribesmen, but in 1690 he suddenly tired of the arduous life of the river and woods, sold his canoe and traps, and with his growing family went down to New Amsterdam. There he settled in business. Just where were his home and shop is not now known. Some say he opened a dry goods store on Pearl Street, but this appears to be one of those myths that arise from misunderstanding. It is doubtful if he ever sold a bolt of calico in all his life but it is quite likely that he had a small mill for grinding corn somewhere near the waterfront. He was rarely mentioned in the old records, but when he was, he was listed as a bolter, which meant miller. One of his sons also was a mill owner.

Nicholas was at least a man of minor substance. He took an interest in politics. Back in Esopus he spoke out against the policies of Jacob Leisler, the German-born official of the West India Company who seized the old fort at New Amsterdam in the name of William and Mary when the Glorious Revolution broke out in England in 1689. Indeed, Leisler was acting as Governor when Nick moved to New York, but Nicholas would have no part of his aristocratic ways. As soon as Henry Sloughter arrived from England and Leisler was tried for treason, Nicholas swore allegiance to the English King. In 1700 and 1701 he served the city as an alderman, a lowly but often profitable post, thus becoming the first Roosevelt to hold a public office.

This first male native born Roosevelt had five daughters and three sons to carry on the name. The first child, Jannetje, married Johannes van der Heul, part owner of a privateer, the *Hunter,* and a trader along the Atlantic coast. Margaretta, the second born, died in her youth. The third child was a boy and the joyful father named him Nicholas after the Little One and himself. The second son was born at Esopus in 1689. He was named Johannes and it was he who was the ancestor of Theodore Roosevelt, the twenty-sixth President of the United States. The third son was Jacobus. He was born in New York in 1692 and it is from him, in six generations also, that Franklin Delano Roosevelt, the thirty-second President of the United States, was descended. The other children were Sarah, who married a member of the prominent Schuyler family, and Rachel, who married Cornelius Loeuw, a farmer of Eospus.

There were also "at the Dutch" in the Seventeenth Century other families who, within one or two generations were to become mingled with the Roosevelts. Sometime before 1662 one Adolph Hardenbroeck came over from Elberfeld, a small town on the Wipper River near Düsseldorf in Rhenish Prussia, and settled at Bergen, on the west shore of the Hudson. His son, Johannes Hardenbroeck, came a few years later. They were landowners. Johannes had a sister, Margaret, who had married Pieter Rodolph de Vries, an Amsterdam merchant of means. He soon died, however, leaving her wealthy. She then married Frederick Philipse, whose family had fled to Holland from Bohemia for religious reasons. Margaret Hardenbroeck de Vries Philipse was a shrewd woman who knew how to make her more than widow's mite increase. Her house in New Amsterdam was one of the finest, and the "castle" which she built on the Hudson at what is now Tarrytown was the grandest for miles around. Frederick called himself Lord of Philipse Manor, and his two sons, Frederick and Adolph, also became Lords, as it were. The Philipses lived for several generations in a grand style.

Other members of the Hardenbroeck family came over soon after the first arrival. One was Abel, who brought his wife, child and servant in 1662 on the *Hope*. He was the brother of Johannes and Margaret. The two boys lived side by side on Prince Graft (Beaver Street) and were shopkeepers of one kind or another. Johannes' son, Jon, was, in 1700, a member of a Foot Company, or infantry, and several years later, a member of the General Assembly of the Province of New York. In 1686 he married Sarah van Laer, the daughter of Stoffel van Laer, from Münster, Germany, and a prosperous dealer in wheat, butter, furs, rum, tobacco and other commodities on Broad Street. Old Stoffel knew where his bread was best buttered, and, although he had given 200 florins to help fortify the city against the English in 1664, as soon as old Peter Stuyvesant surrendered he was on hand to swear allegiance to the English Crown. Abel and Johannes Hardenbroeck, also, lost no time in becoming British subjects. Jon and Sarah had a daughter whom they named Catharina, after Sarah's mother, the former Catharina Jans, a native of The Hague. In 1713 Catharina married Jacobus Roosevelt, the son of Nicholas I and forebear of Franklin Delano Roosevelt.

During the regime of Peter Stuyvesant, when the British were edging in closer and closer to the old trading post, there arrived a young man of about thirty-two, who had been born at Revel on the southern shore of the Gulf of Finland. He claimed, without giving proof, that his father was an officer in the army of Gustavus Adolphus, the King of Sweden. But Martinus Hoffman himself was a lowly saddler by trade. He did not tarry long at New Amsterdam, but went up the river to Esopus. A fiery young man, whom the Indian-hating Kieft would have liked, he was always getting into trouble. The year after his arrival the soldiers in the garrison were ordered to fight the Indians only if attacked. Martinus was impatient, as were others of the settlers, and took things in his own hands. He went on the warpath against the Indians, and although the authorities saw fit to reprimand him for his rash act, he was a hero in the eyes of the town.

A restless fellow, Martinus lived for a time at Esopus, later at Albany and for a time in New Amsterdam. He owned a small vessel which he used to sail up and down the Hudson. In 1664 he married Emmerentje de With, the sister of Tjerck de With from whom stems the once noted De Witt family of New York. She was a native of Esens, near the North Sea, in East Friesland, Germany. Their son Nicholas Hoffman was born in 1680. When he was twenty-seven years old he bought land at Esopus on which he built a stone fort, which the British were to cannonade and burn in 1777. He, too, was a warlike young man, and served as a captain in the Ulster Militia which he led in several forays against the Indians. He married, in 1704 Jannetje Crispel, daughter of a French Huguenot, who had owned a farm in the rich lowlands near Esopus since 1660 and who remained there, ignoring the other Huguenots who migrated to New Paltz in 1677.

Martin Hoffman, the son of Captain Hoffman and Jannetje Crispel, was born in 1707. When he was of age he moved across the river into Dutchess County to occupy land his father had owned for some time. He eventually became a large landowner. In 1755 he had ten negro slaves, more than any other person in that region. He married Tryntje Benson, the grand-daughter of a Swedish carpenter who had arrived in 1648 to work for the patroon of Beverwyck (later Albany).

This grandson of a Swedish saddler, who now owned slaves and many acres of rich lowlands, was to all intents and purposes a patroon, and a man of some importance in his community. Like his predecessors he liked the military and rose to the rank of colonel in the Dutchess County Militia. It is said that many soldiers of the Revolution were trained under him. He also held some minor civil offices and for several years was a judge. His daughter, Cornelia Hoffman—who married Isaac Roosevelt in 1752—was the first to bring that name to Dutchess County. Isaac Roosevelt, of course, was the son of James Roosevelt II, and Franklin Roosevelt's own great-great-grandfather.

And so, through these Dutch and French and Swedish and German immigrants, all settled at or around what Isaac Allerton so succinctly called "the Dutch," the descendants of the Little Fellow were tied to the future pavements of New York, the broad acres of Ulster and Dutchess County, and the long history of the United States.

CHAPTER V

Panama Adventure

AS THE SEVENTEENTH CENTURY drew towards its close all Scotland was excited by a magnificent scheme of colonization that had originated in William Paterson's fertile mind. Word of it spread throughout the land and rich and poor alike had visions of gaining wealth. From the great lairds and the lesser gentry money poured in to Mr. Paterson's coffers to finance the company this wizard had formed. After all, there was nothing to fear, no great chances to take, under the direction of one so skillful as he. Wasn't Mr. Paterson a famous Scot, one of the founders of the Bank of England? That was how hundreds of people looked at the matter in 1698. Young Archibald Stobo, a newly ordained minister, saw it that way, with the rest.

Mr. Paterson's proposal was simple enough and it seemed perfectly sound to hundreds of canny Scotsmen. It was, too, a dream born of experience. Mr. Paterson knew the strange lands beyond the sea, for he had been to them and lived in them. It was, indeed, while residing at the Bahamas that the idea of a Great Colony in Central America had first entered his mind. His plan of empire might have resulted in another India for Britain, if all had gone well. The government of James II, however, did not look favorably upon the idea, and the merchants of Amsterdam and Hamburg and Berlin, whom he approached, rejected his proposals. Undeterred, he returned to London, put his golden hopes temporarily aside, and built up his own fortune by other means. But he never forgot, and all the time he planned someday to make the rich Isthmus of Panama, although then a Spanish outpost, another place upon which the British sun would never set. Standing there between two continents and two oceans it could rule the Western World.

England was growing rich, so rich that some reform in its economic pattern was imminent. To William Paterson came the idea of a national bank, supported by subscription, which would lend money to the nation. The debt thus incurred would become the bank's stock. It was an ingenious theory, and in 1694 it was adopted. Paterson became one of the original directors of this Bank of England, but it was not long before he differed with his colleagues as to its management. He was forced to withdraw. When he tried to start a rival bank he was quickly frozen out. By then he had had enough of England. He went to Edinburgh, where he was welcomed heartily.

Scotland was avid for some of England's wealth. William Paterson, undoubtedly one of the keenest economists of his time, set out to show Scotland the way. It was to be through trade. After listening to his reasonable proposals the Scottish Parliament passed an act whereby was created "The Company of Scotland Trading in Africa and the Indies." William Paterson became its guiding light and thousands of little folk were attracted by the brilliance of the great who opened their purses to buy its stock. That he had no intention of trading either in Africa or in the Indies made no difference. Darien, on the Isthmus of Panama, was his goal, and he cared not that for two centuries Spain had dominated this strip of land. Spain had done nothing with it. Scotland would.

To Darien, halfway between Porto Bello and Cartagena, he would go, bringing men and women with him, and there he would establish a free trade route to the Pacific, "Whereby to Britain would be secured the Key to the Universe, enabling their possessors to give laws to both oceans and to become the arbiters of a commercial world." He would build a great harbor there, where the ships of all nations could gather. And each would pay its small tribute to the Company, until Scotland and the Scottish investors had grown rich. The vision of empire had changed since the Pilgrims haggled with the Adventurers for a little corner of the New World! Wealth such as Isaac Allerton in his most expansive moments never dreamed of awaited those Scotsmen who would go and take it!

There were plenty to share this dream. Within a year of his arrival at Edinburgh nearly two million dollars in shares in the Company of Scotland had been sold. No wonder the East India Company, which controlled the Indian and Chinese trade, looked coldly at Paterson and his associates. But the East India Company could not restrain Paterson from settling at Darien, even if such a venture was in direct defiance of the long-claimed rights of Spain. And so he went ahead, and all Scotland was excited. He had no difficulty in finding recruits for his colony. When the summer of 1698 came on, one thousand two hundred souls or enough people to fill five vessels, were clamoring to be on their way. But William Paterson, having differed with the other directors as to the arrangements was no longer in charge.

The departure of the first five boats, *Caledonia, St. Andrew, Unicorn, Endeavor* and *Dolphin,* was far different from the departure from Southampton earlier in the century of those two smaller ships, the *Mayflower* and the *Speedwell.* Thousands lined the waterfront at Leith as the ships went down the Firth of Forth and they made a noisy holiday of it. Many of those who were going to Panama had to be carried aboard, so arduous was the celebration. The ships were filled with a rough and ready lot. This was no religious pilgrimage. This was the start of a voyage that was to end in a land of milk and honey, where gold could be picked from the meadows, perhaps even from trees!

Young blue-eyed Archibald Stobo was one of the many who were enamored of the great adventure. He was very young and very serious and his motives were mixed. He wanted to go for the very human reason that he thought he would thereby better his lot; and he also wanted to go because, as a newly ordained minister, he might further God's word in that land of heathens, five thousand miles away. But he did not sail with the first ships. Instead, he waited a year for the next vessels to leave.

If he had known the fate of those who went before him, he might have changed his mind without a twinge of his Christian conscience. But he did not know. No one in Scotland knew that.

And so, in his innocence, he waited impatiently. He was in love, and before the next summer came along he had married. He and his bride, who had been Elizabeth Park, bravely determined that they would face the unknown together, and when the *Rising Sun* made sail in September, 1699, they stood on its deck, their hands clasped, taking their last look at Scotland. A brave, light-hearted pair, standing unafraid, fortified by their love of each other, and by their faith in their God.

William Paterson, although without title or authority, had sailed with the first. His early reports to Scotland were encouraging. When the vessels put into Madeira he wrote with enthusiasm: "A good harmonie between us; and none of the whole fleet dead but two—one Drunk Dead, with Brandy. . . . All the English here are very kinde—we shall not find a Dog to move his Tongue Against Us . . ." The good luck did not hold. By the time the fleet had left the West Indies about 150 men had died of some tropical sickness. Later one of the vessels was nearly lost at Barnado, near Cartagena. By adroit seamanship she was snagged, and limped back to Jamaica. The rest kept on, despite the pestilential heat, and at last reached the Gulf of Darien. Their first view of this jungle paradise made them optimistic, and the returning ships carried back gay, brave letters, urging others to come out. They named their anchorage Caledonia Bay.

Had the settlement at New Caledonia owned a leader with the capacities of a William Bradford, and had the settlers been imbued with some of the religious spirit of those who had gone to New Plymouth, disaster might not have come as quickly as it did. The settlers had an excellent site, and one easy to defend. Their first enemies, however, were neither Indians nor Spaniards. Sickness quickly overcame these roistering Scotsmen, none of whom was used to the intense heat. Provisions, too, were scarce. Because they had no great leader, anarchy soon split their ranks. William Paterson might have risen to the occasion, but he was stricken with the fever. His wife and child died, and as he lay on his pallet in one of the rude huts they had built on the beach, looking more like a skeleton than a man, he saw his "golden dream" fade before his sunken eyes. Nevertheless, he protested to the last against abandoning the venture. It was of no avail. They had to carry him aboard the ship when at last they decided to give up and go home.

Somewhere on the broad oceans between Darien and Scotland the bedraggled vessels of the first comers and the spick and span ships of the brave new adventurers must have passed in the darkness. They did not speak. And so, all unaware of what lay ahead, the *Rising Sun,* carrying Archibald Stobo and his bride, sailed on. It dropped anchor in Darien Bay on the last day of November. There was no welcome from the shore. No fires gleamed, no boats put out to greet them. The abandoned huts were already weed-grown. There was only silence, and the jungle and the equatorial heat.

Aboard the *Rising Sun* there were two other clergymen besides the Reverend Archibald Stobo. Some six weeks later one of them, a Mr. Shields, wrote this revealing account:

"When we came to Cape Tiburon, on this side of the Gulf of Darien, there came on board of us some Indians who talked of Caledonia and named some Captains they had seen here and called them their Bon-Camerads. Only it grieved me to hear them parrotting the language of our Countrymen in cursing and swearing, which were the only words they had of our language. . . .

"But when we arrived we found the colony was deserted. . . . I need not tell you how we were affected, to find a waste howling in the wilderness instead of a Colony, and how our grief was increased when we were informed by the captains of two sloops which we found in the bay, which were from New York and New England, of the cause of the desertion. And by others that have been well entertained all this time among the Indians we were told what befell Jameson's ship, that was burnt while Jameson and his mate were cutting each other's throat for a whore. . . .

"The Lord is truly contending with us in a raging contagious sickness which very few have escaped and whereby many were cut off.

"A few days ago one of our Rascalls in the night time ran away with our pinnace, and for several nights together some, keeping Guard ashore, on the ground of the forest, have deserted; as we suppose, entyced by an Irishman that lives here among the Indians, on a design to form a society to live by Rapine.

"When we arrived here, Mr. Borland (another minister), Mr. Stobo and I, meeting in the woods, judged it necessary duty to propose a day to be kept for thanksgiving and humiliation together. But the Councill delayed the appointing of the day until the Huts be all built, and all the men go a shoar to possess them, for as yet we lie all on board the Shipps, except a few that keep guard ashoar.

"We have little hope of doing any good among these people, those with whom we came. As for the Indians, we have as little hope of doing any good among them. We find them indeed an Affectionate Innocent and Simple People and inclined to Peacableness with all men; and (contrary to what we heard in Scotland) entertaining peace actually both with Spaniards and French and everybody that comes. But they have been both much abused and injured by our Rascalls' cheating and stealing from them, and Scandalized and stumbled by seeing the profanity of our people, teaching them to lie and curse and Swear. . . ."

The three ministers had signed to do a year's missionary duty at Darien and were determined to carry out their contract. This was to be no easy or happy task. Soon after their arrival the entire party was put on rations in order to make the meagre ships' supplies do. Not only was food scarce, but the presence of the "Rascalls" among them, the sickness that swept through the camp, and the general dissoluteness of all but a few aboard, made life hard indeed for these men of the cloth. There were but a few women at Darien. Elizabeth Stobo was one. She was, as Mr. Shields wrote, "very uneasy," and one can easily see why. The homesick bride longed to return to Scotland and wanted her husband to go with her in the next ship. The other ministers would not agree to this.

"We cannot, for the time, yeeld to this, but would fain encourage one another to wrestle out the difficulties of the first years . . ."

In the first weeks in this tropical wilderness fully 150 persons died of fever, and the horrible screams of the delirious mingled with the raucous shouts of the drunken Highlanders, were familiar sounds in the bay. As had been the case with the first comers, disappointment and discouragement swept among them. "Our murmurings still continue and increase among all sorts," Mr. Shields lamented, "having formed in their minds too big Ideas of mountains of Gold, and Nicaraguawood growing on them, and no preconception of sweating, and working, with the pinching allowance of a Little Stinking Saltbeef and rotten meal, &c, and finding themselves confoundedly disappointed, this makes many of them desperate."

Several ran away to the Spaniards and became slaves. Nine ruffians decamped with one of the boats. Those who stayed caused the three ministers many uneasy moments. Too many of them were "perverse men" and the rest were "wild Highlanders," who were "more barbarous than the Indians and no more understand our language than they." The complaints of Elizabeth Stobo, who must have lived in nightly terror, increased and she again asked to be sent back. But the other men of God repeated that Mr. Stobo would have to put in his full year as a missioner. When she saw that he was determined to stay, she resigned herself to her fate, and agreed to remain with her husband. Brave though her decision was, there really was nothing else she could do!

In February a small vessel arrived from Scotland with provisions. They were badly needed. For the first time in weeks those who remained on the ships had a fortifying meal. As they ate they talked about the hated Spaniards who were encamped at Tubacanti, on the Santa Maria River, a few miles south. The wilder spirits among them, presumably the "wild Highlanders," urged an immediate attack, despite the fact that the Spaniards were better armed and outnumbered the Scots two to one. Saner counsel failed to prevail at the general meeting that followed. The Scots, who might well have saved their strength for the more prosaic work of colonizing, set out under the command of one Captain Alexander Campbell of Fonab, to do the Spaniards in. A terrific battle ensued. The Highlanders, screaming their uncouth war cries, swept over the breastworks that guarded the river encampment and scattered their adversaries through the jungle. They lost nine of their own men in the senseless skirmish. And they sealed their own fate.

Probably the Spaniards would not long have tolerated the Scotch invasion of their long-held, if uncultivated, terrain, at Darien, and would have come eventually to drive the hapless colonizers out. Within less than a week a large fleet of ten or eleven ships showed up off Golden Island in the Bay. The Scots prepared for an attack. Several minor brushes took place along the shores of the bay. But the major attack did not come. The Spaniards were playing a more cruel game, the game of waiting.

Meanwhile the Scots threw up a hastily built fort on the peninsula to which the entire company, those who were well and the sick and the dying, all moved. In the cramped and fetid quarters the fever spread rapidly. The Reverend Mr. Stobo and the other ministers were busy reading the burial service over a daily average of sixteen dead. Within a fortnight the harried company was ready and eager to quit Darien forever. After a parley the Spaniards agreed that if they would leave the place they might depart in peace. Ten days later all who had survived crowded aboard the *Rising Sun* and sailed from the harbor of their woes.

The long journey was a voyage of horror. The ship was a fever ship, crowded with sick and dying men. When it sailed it had left behind buried on the narrow isthmus, more than three hundred dead. Now, on the passage to the north, some two hundred and fifty more died, and were buried at sea. At last the ship made Jamaica, and there it stayed for three months. In that port nearly one hundred more died before the *Rising Sun* set sail again. And then, off the coast of Florida, the ship nearly foundered in a terrific storm. Wrenched and leaking, the vessel made for Charleston, that harbor newly settled by the English on the Carolina coast. Water and provisions, too, were badly needed.

The ship had been lying at anchor off Charleston for a little more than a week when a skiff came alongside and the boatman asked if there were a Scotch clergyman aboard. At least, that is the legend. The Reverend Archibald Stobo answered the call, saying that he was and asking if he could be of service. The boatman answered that there was a young Scotch couple in the port who would like to be married by a minister of their creed and kind. Glad of an excuse to leave the ship that had brought him nothing but trouble, the Reverend Mr. Stobo said he would come with the skiff. When he started down the ladder, Mrs. Stobo was with him.

After the wedding service Mr. and Mrs. Stobo were asked to spend the night ashore. It was a stroke of good fortune that they accepted the kind invitation for, with the dawn, a hurricane struck without warning. Trees fell in the wind, houses were blown asunder, heavy seas pounded over the sand bar. Fighting their way, and praying as they fought, they got to the waterfront in time to see the *Rising Sun* picked up by a tidal wave and dashed to destruction. Not a soul aboard was saved.

Not long thereafter Archibald Stobo wrote to a friend who had been with him at Panama. "I doubt not but you have heard how narrowly I escaped the judgment that came upon the *Rising Sun,*" he said, "I and my wife were scarce well gone from her, when wrath seized upon her; we were the last that came from her; and after our departure the storm came so sudden that none could find their way to her. It was the Lord's remarkable mercy that we were not consumed in the stroke, with the rest. They were such a rude company, that I believe Sodom never declared such impudence in sinning as they; any observant eye might see that they were running the way they went; hell and judgment were to be seen upon them, and in them, before the time. You saw them bad, but I saw them worse; their cup was full, they could hold no more; they were ripe, they must be cut down with the sickle of His wrath. Here I lost my books, and all; and have only my life for a prey, with my skin, as it were, between my teeth."

Scotland was far away, many watery, dangerous miles away. Archibald Stobo and his wife looked at the sea, and knew they had had enough. They decided to stay in Charleston. There, ten years later, a daughter, whom they named Jean, was born to them. When she was nineteen she married the Reverend James Bulloch, another young minister recently arrived from Scotland. And their great-granddaughter, whose name was Martha Bulloch, married Theodore Roosevelt, the First. Her son became President of the United States and her grand-daughter the wife of the second Roosevelt to hold that office.

Book Two

REVOLUTIONARIES AND TORIES

Little Old New York

THE EIGHTEENTH CENTURY, which was to give democracy to the world, knew an America that was in almost every way different from the primitive country over which the Little Fellow and Isaac Allerton had roamed. Plymouth Plantation had long since been deserted by the sons and daughters of its settlers, who had gone elsewhere in search of broader acres and better land. By the year 1700 New Amsterdam had been New York for more than thirty years and already the Dutch influences were being overwhelmed by English manners and customs. Indeed, as early as 1677 Johannes de Peyster, an old Dutch merchant and politician, had refused the office of Mayor because of his imperfect knowledge of the English language.

The port was growing. Soon it would have a population of twenty thousand, greater than that of busier Boston, nearly as great as that of Philadelphia, and the time was fast approaching when the wind of freedom would sweep through the streets that were spreading willy nilly at the island's tip. New York was about to play its part in the great economic and political drama that was to reach its climax in bloody revolution.

The children of Nicholas Roosevelt I, who was already settled in New York as a shopkeeper when the new century dawned, were to see even greater changes than he had witnessed in the years that had passed since his birth on the Little One's farm. Their children, in turn, were to take an active part in the confused life of the century that centered around 1776. During this period the Roosevelt Family, in all its many branches, attained the wealth and social standing that was to give most of its members some degree of comfort and security for generations to come. If Mrs. van Rensselaer sniffed because, in her rather aloof estimation, no Roosevelt achieved distinction before the Revolution, during and after it they were, on the whole, people of substance. And the families with which the Roosevelts became allied through marriage also made their mark in the predominantly commercial world of the Eighteenth Century.

New York and the Hudson Valley were to know the Roosevelts and their allies well, but the changing city of New York was to know them best. There they founded their fortunes and took their place in Society. Some became extremely wealthy, in the light of their own times, and their homes became the center of good living and right thoughts. In pre-Revolutionary New York the pattern of their lives was formed, and it was a pattern that did not materially change until the echoes of the Civil War had ceased to sound. The ledger-minded city of New York, with its docks and markets and counting houses, its shops, taverns, coffee houses, and its fine homes, where the dying burghers smoked their last pipes and the Yankees aped the London way, was the place into which they sank their tenacious roots and the soil in which they flourished.

Even at the beginning of the century New York was becoming a cosmopolitan and picturesque city. It has been said that, except for Rio de Janeiro and possibly Quebec, no place equalled it outside of Europe. It had already over-run the bounds of the squalid Dutch trading post where Isaac Allerton had built his Yankee warehouse on the muddy river banks; the Bowery had become an important thoroughfare; Wall Street no longer marked the town's end; Broadway had been given its immortal name; and soon new houses would be built above First Street on the East Side. Beyond were prosperous farms and stately country seats. It had, however, taken a full century to grow this much. Even in mid-century, what we now call City Hall Park was still The Fields, and it was used for the same purpose as the Common in Boston: cows grazed on it in peaceful times, rioters filled it in times of strife.

Although New Netherland had been under the British flag

ever since the Duke of York's navy made him a present of its
rich terrain, the regions to the north had changed less than the
clustered town itself. Patroonships still occupied the choicer
territories all the way up the Hudson to Albany, and many a
self-made Dutch lord, or his descendants, still lived in grand
style on these holdings. Westchester, which pugnacious Governor Kieft had so vainly tried to keep from the English, was
being peopled by Connecticut farmers. Long Island was thickly
dotted with New Englandish towns.

The city itself counted many new citizens among its people:
Scotch, Irish, Germans, Jews. The wealthier families all had
their Negro slaves (indeed, at one time, there were so many
that they became a menace to their owners and were placed
under strict surveillance by the authorities). All this had come
about slowly. New York was no boom town. But it was nevertheless on its way to becoming the commercial capital of the
New World. When Isaac Roosevelt—the Little Fellow's great-
grandson who was to be a founder of the city's first bank—was
growing up, New York was the port of entry and the outlet for
half of New Jersey, half of Connecticut, all of western Massachusetts, and the rich Hudson Valley.

With Albany it divided the juicy profits of the fur trade that
was soon to attract the acquisitive John Jacob Astor's shrewd attention. Its own warehouses, larger than Isaac Allerton had ever
needed for his business "at the Dutch," were crammed with
hogsheads of rum and molasses, sacks of sugar and indigo from
the West Indies. Its magnificent harbor that seldom froze, surrounded as it was on three sides by deep water and yet protected
from the sea by many islands, made the city a natural port. The
great Hudson gave access to the as yet untapped interior.

It was only natural that New York, whose merchants were in
constant contact with the capitals of the Old World, should be
a lively place. Its shipyards hummed. Over the magnificent
houses of the merchants and the wooden shacks of the slums
hung an aura of commercialism. Trade dominated its people
and their way of life. "Hospitable, even lavish in its entertainment," as one historian has said, "it seemed 'unintellectual,'
even 'over material' to a Bostonian, somewhat 'pushing' to a
Southerner."

We know how lawyer John Adams, coming down from his cold Boston corner on the eve of the Revolution, was unfavorably impressed:

"With all the opulence and splendor of this city," this Harvard-trained son of a Braintree farmer said, somewhat petulantly, "there is little good breeding to be found. . . . At their entertainment there is no conversation that is agreeable; there is no modesty, no attention to one another. They talk very loud, very fast, and altogether."

If it was a garrulous and grasping Society it was also snug. Everyone knew everybody else. Even after its first English century had passed it was still a tolerant town, thanks in great measure to its Dutch heritage. And if by mid-century it was to be split into groups of conservatives or "solid men" on the one hand and "radicals," not all of whom were recruited from the "lower classes," on the other, class distinctions were less marked than in the New England corner. At least New York had never hung a witch or harried a Roger Williams from its borders! It had less poverty than Boston, although it had its share of the disenfranchised poor.

The city, headquarters of the British colonial troops and navy, made a pretty picture lying low-roofed at the tip end of the wooded island of Manhattan. The Fort, stretching like a half-moon on its fourteen-foot mound, with its one hundred and twenty guns bristling, was now all rebuilt and was the first object one spied from the sea. The Battery got its name from this English fort. But it was usually a peaceful fort, beneath which the fine ladies and gentlemen walked and lovers strolled. The guns were spiked. Beyond, to the east, were the docks and warehouses, and the river was dotted with white-sailed ferries plying between Whitehall Slip and Staten Island. Then came the other slips, Cruger, Rodman, Beekman, Peck and above them the shipyards where stout vessels were always building.

In the years just before the peaceful scene was disrupted by the Revolution, Broadway, even then the main street, was lined with the comfortable homes of such dignitaries as the captain of the Royal Navy, the resident collector, the speaker of the Assembly, Justice R. R. Livingston, and the van Cortlandts, who already had grown rich from their sugar refineries. On the street's other side was King's Tavern where the fancy elite gathered for their gay assemblies in the second-floor ballroom. Nearby were Trinity Church, St. Paul's, and the new King's College, as the British called Columbia University. Along the lower Hudson's banks, where the water was too shallow then for the docking of ships, above the college (on what is now Greenwich Street), lived the Lispenards, the Harrisons, the Mortiers, Lady Warren, the Jaunceys, and the Bayards, who had introduced sugar refining to the country.

Out Broadway, or the "Road to Bloomingdale" as it was more often called, lived the Apthorpes, Stuyvesants, de Lanceys, Dyckmans, all long-established families. Within New York itself were perhaps a dozen inns, but only one theatre, for New York then cared not at all for intellectual entertainment. Two or three newspapers were regularly published and these, with their coffee house gossip, supplied the city's cultural needs.

The symbols of New York were the warehouse and the dock. The ships that sailed down the Narrows were laden with peas, rye meal, Indian corn, apples, onions, boards, staves, horses, sheep, butter, cheese, pickled oysters, beef, pork, consigned, for the most part, to the West Indies. On their return they brought rum, sugar, molasses, mules, below decks, and often their decks were piled high with fresh fruit for the tables of New Yorkers. Those that cleared for Lisbon and Madeira, and they were many, carried wheat, flour, corn and lumber. They came back with hogsheads of fine wine, for the product of Madeira was a staple drink with New Yorkers then. Another lucrative commodity was "peltry of all kinds," bought then, as in Astor's more cruel time, "with rum, ammunition, blankets, and wampum," and especially rum! If New York was not as busy as Boston or Charleston, its anchorages were always crowded and its warehouses bulged with goods.

This commercially minded city was run by a local government not too far different from that which functions today. It was divided into seven wards. Its mayor and recorder were appointed by the British governor, but the Aldermen were chosen by the free citizens. There was a city hall, which housed a small library and a small fire department as well as offices. Outside were the cage and stocks and whipping post, for the public punishment of miscreants. There were several courts: a court of justices, of common pleas, a supreme court, a probate court, an admiralty court and finally a court of chancery from which appeals might be taken only to the Governor and Council of the Province.

These ruled twelve to fourteen counties, six manorial holdings in Westchester, the Philipse, Heathcote, Beeckman, and Schuyler preserves nearer home, seven townships controlled by the Livingstons, and the seven hundred square miles of van Rensselaer estates around Albany. With the exception of Morris of Morrisania every member of the Council, in the 1760's and 1770's, was engaged in commerce or industry of some kind, as, indeed, was nearly everyone, high or low in New York.

William Walton, the first of that once-powerful name to settle in the city, was the archetype of the merchant society. An extremely wealthy man, known as "the Boss," he sat on the Council with such others as de Lancey, Apthorpe, Watts, Morris. His mansion on Queen Street was so magnificent that reports of it, made in London as indicative of the prosperity of the colonies, were used in argument for the imposition of the Stamp Act. Within its grand rooms he entertained lavishly, lived in luxury and gave a rich flavor to the town. It may have been of him that Judge Smith, one of the city's earliest historians, was thinking, when he wrote:

"New York consists principally of merchants, shopkeepers, tradesmen, so sustains the reputation of honest, punctual and fair dealers. With respect to riches there is not so great an inequality as is common in Boston and some other places. Every man of industry and integrity has it in his power to live well. And many are the instances of persons who came here distressed by poverty, who now enjoy easy and plentiful fortunes."

These "easy and plentiful fortunes," in which members of the Roosevelt Family were to share, made it possible for many New Yorkers to enjoy life in a hearty way. They followed the London styles and fashions closely and met weekly at their many clubs, while their women enjoyed concerts and assemblies through the winter season. Fine furniture and ornaments filled the great houses where the tables groaned with great "quantities of flesh, fish and fowl, and all kinds of vegetables," which Negro servants served on fine plates.

But the people, at least *these* people, were not extravagant, Judge Smith took care to point out.

"Tinctured with a Dutch education," he wrote, "they manage their families with becoming parsimony, good providence, and singular neatness." He rejoiced because they did not gamble heavily, but he mourned because these virtues were negated by their distressing lack of interest in reading and, "indeed, all the arts for the improvement of the mind." The schools were "in the lowest order," and "our common speech is extremely corrupt."

There was, of course, a "rougher element" in the city. Those who, working on the docks or in the warehouses and the shops, dreamed, in their uncouth way, of someday making "easy and plentiful fortunes" for themselves: workmen, carters, shipwrights, mechanics, clerks, accountants, lawyers, newspaper men —common folk who were to listen to the Sons of Liberty and join the riots at The Fields—and make the Waltons and their Tory cronies tremble in their beds!

CHAPTER VI

The Roosevelt Family Melting Pot

THE CHILDREN of Nicholas Roosevelt I, the fur trader and shopkeeper, had all been born when this revolutionary century began and their way of life had been decided when he deserted distant Esopus for the busier streets of the town. His choice of an urban residence and occupation made inevitable their growing up in an atmosphere of commerce and trade. By all accounts Nicholas I had a keen sense of business values which he transmitted to his sons, and if he founded no great family fortune to be handed down generation after generation, as some of his contemporaries did, he at least left his descendants a heritage upon which to build and from which they became solid and substantial freemen of the city with which the name Roosevelt has been associated ever since.

His oldest son, Nicholas Roosevelt II, was born at Esopus in 1687, but he was reared in New York city. There he became an accomplished goldsmith, an able artisan to the proud wealthy families whose drawing room tables were weighted down with the finest ornaments money could buy. He lived a quiet life, escaping contemporary notoriety and future remembrance, content with his craftsmanship. He left politics and public affairs to his brothers and so his name seldom crept into the records of his time. When he was past middle age he became a freeman of the city. In 1753 the Common Council, desiring to honor His Excellency, Sir Danvers Osborn, Baronet, the new Governor of the Province, who was soon to commit suicide, with the freedom of New York, ordered a seal of the corporation struck off for the nobleman. Nicholas Roosevelt was commissioned to make a gold box for Sir Danvers to keep his memento in, and he was paid twenty pounds for his work.

In 1710 Nicholas Roosevelt II married. His wife's name usually is given as Sarah Fullman. She became the mother of his three children. The oldest, Catharina, was born in 1711. When she was twenty years old she married Steenwyck de Riemer, the son of Isaac de Riemer, who was Mayor of New York in 1700 and 1701. From this we may judge that the family moved in the best political circles of the day. Catharina's brother, Nicholas Roosevelt III, was born in 1715, and lived to a ripe old age, surviving two wives and the rigors of the Revolution, during part of which, at least, he served as a first lieutenant of a militia company. By his two wives, Catharina Comfort and Elizabeth Thurman respectively, he had a total of six children. One of them, also named Nicholas, settled at Stillwater, in Saratoga County, where he was a farmer. Another, who was called Jacob, eventually went to the Missouri frontier to live.

If Nicholas II stuck close to the shop and was happy with his trade his two brothers, Johannes and Jacobus, were to be caught up in the commercial and political whirl of the town. They were an active pair, sometimes partners in business and, on one occasion at least, co-partners with other favored citizens in a land deal that, to say the least, smacked of sharp political conniving. From Jacobus, the younger, sprang the so-called Hyde Park line of Roosevelts, and from Johannes came all the other Roosevelts of significance in the history of New York. Years later the descendants of the latter branch were to sniff audibly at the others as not being of the true faith. The grandsons of Johannes were scornfully to call the grandsons of Jacobus, "mavericks"—but in the early years of the Eighteenth Century the brothers walked hand in hand.

Johannes Roosevelt was born at Esopus in 1689, just one year before Nicholas I left his old friends, the Indians, to their traps and trails and set himself up in business in New York. There his brother Jacobus was born three years later. We do not know when Nicholas I or his wife Heyltje died, but it is likely that both lived until their children were grown and ready to strike out for themselves. That time came quickly enough, for Johannes was only twenty years old when he was definitely engaged in business.

The manufacture of linseed oil, that reeking essence from the ground seed of flax, had been introduced into New York in 1694 when one Isaac Lanser received the first license to make it at his mill. Now, eighteen years later, young Johannes Roosevelt and his brother-in-law Johannes van der Heul, built their own mill on Maiden Lane near the waterfront of Queen Street. This was adjacent to the Fly Market, precursor of the famous Fulton Market, which took its name from the Dutch "Smit's Vlei," or Smith's Valley, and which soon was to be the scene of one Heinrich Astor's shrewd operations as a butcher.

Young Roosevelt and his sister's husband must have had considerable influence with the General Assembly, for that powerful body gave them the exclusive rights in the entire Province of New York to manufacture "lintseed oyle." Their monopoly of the smelly business was to run for ten years, and their trade with the shipbuilders of the day was extensive, for the quick-drying linseed oil was widely used in the making of ships' paints.

But neither Johannes nor Jacobus Roosevelt was content with but one business. They had their hands in many local pies. When, for example, the sidewalk at the lower end of Wall Street needed fixing in 1720, Johannes and another partner, Philip van Cortlandt, won the contract for making the repairs. Johannes, it is interesting to note, had become an assistant Alderman three years before. He was to keep up this connection with the city government for many years, a political post that did no harm to the Roosevelts' welfare. Brother Jacobus, however, does not appear to have held a public post; perhaps, with Johannes on the board, it was not necessary.

Of the two brothers Johannes was the more versatile. Not only did he repair sidewalks and grind flaxseed, but he seems to have had some of his brother Nicholas's facility with his hands. When the new city charter of 1731 was adopted, he was entrusted with making a tin box for its safekeeping. This was several years before brother Nicholas designed the golden casket for Sir Danvers, and its manufacture was more in keeping with the pragmatic character of the family. Few creative or artistic spirits have appeared in the Roosevelt line, which has given the country several hard-headed men-of-affairs. The charter that reposed in Johannes Roosevelt's tin box was the third the city had adopted under British rule. John Montgomerie was Governor at the time and Richard Lurting, the thirty-sixth person to hold the office since 1665, was Mayor. Johannes was a political henchman of Mr. Lurting. Not only was he well paid for his essay as a tinsmith but he was made a fullfledged alderman at the same time.

From all this it appears that Johannes Roosevelt was doing well in his little world. When the new charter was adopted he had been married nearly twenty-three years to Heyltje Sjoerts, the sturdy Dutch daughter of Captain Olphert Sjoerts, who had deserted his own father's trade as a bricklayer and run away to sea. Johannes and Heyltje had nine children, the last of whom was born the same year he was made an alderman. Their oldest, Margareta, was already married at that time and to no less a person than William de Peyster, grandson of a wealthy burgomaster and Deputy Mayor of New Amsterdam in the old Dutch days, and himself the owner of docks and warehouses.

In the meantime Johannes's sister, Rachel Roosevelt, the youngest of the eight children of Nicholas I, had also been improving the family's position in society. Aunt Rachel was born in 1699 and, of course, was a native New Yorker. Although her father had never returned to Esopus to live after opening his shop in the city he had not broken all his ties with the up-river village of his furtrapping days. It is not strange, therefore, to find Rachel married in 1720 to Pieter Low, the son of Cornelius Low, who for many years had kept a store at Esopus. Pieter's ancestors had come from Holland in 1659 and the family had since then been identified with the village on the Hudson. Young Pieter, however, preferred New York, where he moved in the best Dutch circles. His children, as the saying goes, all married well.

Helena Roosevelt Low, the oldest, became the wife of Henry Kip, whose great-grandfather and great-uncle, Jacobus and Hendrick Kype, were wealthy landowners. Among their holdings was the large tract that now makes up the greater part of the once-fashionable village of Rhinebeck, New York. Old

Jacobus Kype, as the name was originally spelled, had married Marcia de Montagne, daughter of Dr. de Montagne, Governor Kieft's right-hand man, and he had built for her the famous Kip mansion overlooking the East River at what is now Thirty-Fifth Street. The region is still known as Kip's Bay. The other children of Pieter and Helena Low made alliances with van Duzens, Cloppers and Duryeas, all families of substance then and later.

All this while business ventures of one kind or another occupied the attention of the brothers Roosevelt. The aquisition of real estate was their greatest concern. Both were astute buyers. Before they died they owned together some of the most valuable property in New York. Jacobus Roosevelt seems to have been the first to see the inherent value of land and he began his purchases before 1720. Three years later he joined with Abraham van Wyck, Abraham Lefferts and Charles Sleigh, all prominent merchants in the town, and went before the authorities "praying a grant to them and their heirs and assigns forever of the lots of land . . . fronting Hudson's River to low water mark to the Green Trees near the English church." The land they coveted thus lay between the present Battery and Rector Street, a section of the city that had developed more slowly than the east side.

Soon Jacobus was looking for more land. In 1728 he was granted ten lots in Beekman's Swamp, a much more desirable location than its dismal name signified. This was the part of the city now occupied by Frankfort, Spruce, Gold and Cliff Streets and traversed by Ferry and Jacob Streets. At that time it was still swampy from the water filtering into it from the Collect or Fresh Water Pond, long since driven under ground, but then the largest body of water south of the Harlem River, covering the territory between White, Bayard, Elm, Canal and Pearl Streets of today. For many years the Swamp had been little more than a malodorous dump. But there was a good use for it. The city had at last rebelled against the existence of the smelly tanneries and slaughter houses that for years had clustered near the lower end of Wall Street. The lots which Jacobus bought in 1728 and 1733 for a total of about two thousand pounds he converted into sites for the new tanneries. Many years later, after the tanneries had gone, this region remained the wholesale leather district of the city. In the days before the Revolution, the muddy streets cut through by Jacobus Roosevelt were filled with vast mounds of tan. There, one ancient and nostalgic historian later recalled, gangs of neighborhood boys waged mimic warfare, using for weapons the horns of cattle picked up in the tanyards. Whether the dignified Jacobus Roosevelt, a pillar of the Dutch Reformed Church, allowed his sons to participate in these battles, has been forgotten long since.

Johannes Roosevelt, too, owned lots in the Swamp, and in 1749 the brothers asked the city for permission to build a street there. They reported that they had already spent "upwards of 200 pounds in order to have a convenient street or way from Queen Street" to the tanneries, and now they wanted to lay a thoroughfare fourteen feet wide through their property. The city willingly gave permission, but it was not until ten years later that the road which is now Ferry Street was conveyed to the city. Then it was turned over by Jacobus Roosevelt, John Chambers, Oliver Roosevelt, Jacobus Roosevelt, Jr., Cornelius Roosevelt, and William de Peyster. Since the last four were the sons and son-in-law of Johannes it is probable that he had died before the street was finished. More than a century later James Henry Roosevelt, the bachelor grandson of Jacobus I, passed his inherited share of the Swamp property to the Roosevelt Hospital, in New York City, which he founded, and in 1941 that institution still owned several of the original lots, now lowering under the shadow of the Brooklyn Bridge.

When Jacobus made his first Swamp purchases in 1728 the city specified that the money received should be put to the useful purpose of building a powder house for Fort George. At the same time he was told that he might "open the slip fronting the East River commonly called Hardenbroke's Slip." This undoubtedly was property owned at one time by his wife's family, for in 1713 he had married Catherina Hardenbroock, the descendant of a family of well-to-do merchants and landowners, allied through marriage to the grand Philipse family. They were to have several children, of whom Isaac Roosevelt, an outstanding patriot during the Revolution, was the most prominent.

By 1748 Johannes was generally known as John Roosevelt to his contemporaries and Jacobus was often referred to as James, so greatly had the Dutch language declined in New York. In that year John and James found themselves involved in the beginning of what, in a later age of politics and journalism, would be called a "land grab." The episode began innocently enough when the brothers, together with Cornelia Rutgers, a member of the affluent family of Albany brewers, Leonard Lispenard, a merchant who was to help found the Chamber of Commerce twenty years later, and Christopher Bancker, another merchant, quietly presented a petition to the Common Council. In this they stated that they were the joint owners of a parcel of land adjoining the East River which, they suggested, would be greatly improved if they might also own the beach, or water lot, which ran between it and the river. Undoubtedly they had in mind the building of a pier at which to dock the barges that brought hides to the tanners from the cattle farms of Long Island and Brooklyn. Since Johannes Roosevelt was a former alderman and Mr. Lispenard was then a member of the board, it is not surprising that their petition was favorably received.

The details of this deal did not attract attention until about five years later when the editor of *The Independent Reflector,* a gentleman well versed in the latest gossip, spoke his mind on what he said had become "a common Coffee-House topic." He boldly insinuated that there had been corruption in the Common Council's policy of disposing of the water lots and went on to expose what he called "the astonishing proposals" of Messrs. Roosevelt, Lispenard and Bancker, charging that they had had the effrontery to ask for the lots *gratis* for a term of twenty years, after which they proposed to pay but ninepence a foot in annual rent!

The editor's indignation rose when he figured that at the end of the twenty-year term the property so cheaply obtained would be worth at least six thousand pounds, or, in present money, approximately sixty thousand dollars, a fortune in those days. He demanded that the leases be rescinded and the lots resold at public auction, citing as a precedent that one Colonel Moore (who may have done some of the talking in the coffee houses!) had been forced to pay outright eighteen pence per foot for similar land. He added that none who had bought along the East River front had paid less than eighteen pence per foot, and some had paid as high as one shilling, ninepence!

But the Common Council had no intention of being browbeaten by any newspaper editor. It voted to grant the water lots at private sale, undoubtedly to the detriment of the city's purse and certainly in defiance of public opinion!

If the brothers Roosevelt were involved in what had certain aspects of a shady deal, Johannes, at least, was connected with one improvement of the city which certainly entitled him to respect.

In 1733 the Common Council proposed to rent some land "lying at the lower end of Broadway fronting to the Fort, to some inhabitants of the said Broadway in order to be enclosed to make a Bowling Green thereof with walks therein, for the beauty and ornament of the said street as well as for the recreation and delight of the inhabitants of the city. . . ." After a committee had surveyed and measured the land, leaving the street fifty feet wide on each side of the Green, it was decided to lease the property to such distinguished and sports-loving gentlemen as John Chambers, Peter Bayard and Peter Jay, father of the eminent jurist and statesman, John Jay. The lease was to run eleven years—and the annual rent was to be one pepper corn! The dried pepper berry or corn was often in those days stipulated in deeds as a nominal rent in a friendly transaction.

These gentlemen evidently did not take up the option, however, for the next year it was resolved by the Common Council that "the Bowling Green at the lower end of Broadway in the West ward of the city, as it is now in fence, be leased unto Frederick Philipse Esq., Mr. John Chambers, and Mr. John Roosevelt . . . for the term of ten years . . . for the yearly rent of one pepper Corne." The game of bowls, as the English game of skittles was then called, had been for many years a popular pastime among the fashionable young blades of the city. Whether Mr. Roosevelt and his partners rented the bowling

green out as a concession, or operated it gratis for the enjoyment of all-comers, does not appear in the record. The lease
was not renewed at the end of the ten years. Later the Green
was used as a parade ground and now, of course, it is a small
forgotten park and the name of a subway station.

During this time John Roosevelt had continued to run his
mills. Not only did he keep on grinding the odoriferous flax
seed, but he had also branched out into the manufacture of
chocolate and flour. Unfortunately his wooden mills burned
down in the winter of 1737, although the neighboring houses,
in the words of the contemporary New York *Journal,* being
"stately and according to the new Method of Building," escaped with a scorching. Presumably he rebuilt them after the
fire, for he was only forty-eight years old then and too young
to retire from a profitable business. But even if he did retire
he was kept busy at other affairs.

When, for instance, the Province of New York in 1741
adopted an act "for the better fortifying of this Colony and
other purposes," John Roosevelt was appointed one of the four
commissioners entrusted with carrying out its provisions. The
others were John Cruger, one of the most active merchants in
the Bristol trade, and then Mayor of New York, William
Roome, and Captain Henry Rowe of the British Navy. A fire
had recently swept Fort George, and in the words of an official
account of the affair, several buildings had "the misfortune
to be burnt down." To John Roosevelt fell the task of building
a new secretary's office in a more convenient location and of
safer construction. He was allotted £260 (or about $2600 to-
day) to put up the new building in the east garden of the
Fort. It was to be not less than forty-two feet long, twenty feet
wide, and one story of ten feet high. There was to be a chimney
in the middle, arched with iron and brick, "fit for two fire-
places."

As contractor John Roosevelt had to supply "all manner
of materials and workmanship, not only for building it, but
likewise to partition the same into two rooms and an entry,
and to make a writing desk and benches in each of them as
likewise a sufficient number of shelves with drawers and boxes

between them as well to put public papers in, as to remove them speedily with out loss in case of accident."

The specifications, which have been preserved, also called for four sashes with good glass and shutters, a proper light over the door, "if judged needful," a shingled roof, painted wood-work, two hearths "laid with one row of Bristol stones and the back part with bricks on their edges"—and he was ordered to "finish both the outside and the inside workmanlike to the turning of the key."

There was, however, one saving grace for a man with an eye to a profit. He could use the bricks "of the ruins of the old building" if he wished—and he probably did.

The Royal Provincial authorities must have been satisfied with his work—even to the turning of the key—for, three years later, he was again called into Royal service by the Assembly. In 1744 a bill was enacted which stated:

"The Colony has for some years past been at a vast expense to put it in good posture for defense, whilst his majesty was engaged in a war against the king of Spain only, but now he is engaged in another with the French King, whereby it is liable to attacks by land as well as by water, prudence and self preser-vation make it necessary to complete and augment the fortifica-tions thereof in such manner, as may of the one hand discourage an enemy to attack, and of the other excite our inhabitants cheerfully to exert their natural bravery in a vigorous defense, if such undertakings should be attempted."

For the next few months Commissioner Roosevelt and his fellow commissioners kept busy putting the city's defense in good order. John Roosevelt's activities ranged from erecting a flag pole with a top-piece to setting up a complete new bat-tery of eight guns on "the Red Hook of Nassau [Long] Island." He also spent certain funds for "maintaining prisoners of war," and he bought five hundred pounds worth of gunpowder. Thus he served colony and city well in payment for all the favors he had received.

James, too, took part in the public life of his time, although he was less conspicuous in public affairs than his brother John. He was a loyal member and senior elder of the new Dutch Church, whose cornerstone he laid in 1767, and although he was no longer a young man he was in tune with the changing manners of the Anglicised city. He had seen the old Dutch ways disappearing but, being no reactionary, had resigned himself to their passing. After all, as the father of several children, he knew the younger generation could not be held fast forever to ancient customs. And so, after giving the matter much thought, he joined with Philip Livingston, the wealthy and dignified Duke Street importer, in a campaign to modernize the church. Together they drew up a petition to the Consistory, or ruling body of the Church, which was signed by many members of the congregation and by "young men baptised and partly raised in our church," asking that an English-speaking minister be appointed.

One might think that by 1762 so simple a request would be readily granted. Instead it caused a great controversy. Seven meetings of the Great Consistory itself had to be called before the elders relented and approved an English-speaking minister for the ancient Church.

There were good reasons for Mr. Roosevelt's and Mr. Livingston's petition. Already Trinity Corporation, encouraged by many defections from the Dutch congregation, had voted to erect St. Paul's, and before the Dutch had got their English preacher, more than half the Dutch congregation could be seen on Sunday in Trinity's pews. James Roosevelt and Philip Livingston moved almost too late. But they saved their church from dissolution by their act, for with English spoken in the Dutch Church many members returned to its fold. Strangely enough it was the descendants of James who were to go over eventually to the Protestant Episcopal Church while those of John Roosevelt remained faithful for generations to the Dutch.

When James Roosevelt was about eighty years old he called for pen and paper and made out his will. It was a long document for, by the eve of the Revolution, James had become an extensive property holder and the possessor of several hundred pounds of New York money. He was far from being the richest man in town but if his last testament, a carefully arranged and meticulously worded document in the Dutch language, is an accurate indication of his resources, he could take his place proudly among the well-to-do citizens of the growing

commercial city. In his will he disposes of some four thousand
two hundred pounds, or about forty-two thousand dollars of
our money of today, in cash, as well as extensive real estate
holdings in New York City, across the Hudson in East New
Jersey, and at Bushwick, on Nassau Island, as Brooklyn was
then called.

The old gentleman did not intend his children and grandchildren to squabble over his money or lands. First, he set aside
two thousand eight hundred pounds as a trust fund for the education and maintenance of his eleven grandchildren, the children of Helena Roosevelt Barclay; specifying that its interest
should be used for this purpose until they became of age, after
which they were to share the generous heritage and share alike.
He then gave Isaac Roosevelt, his oldest living and favorite son
who already was a leading sugar maker in New York, six hundred fifty pounds. The rest of his cash he divided between other
grandchildren, giving five hundred fifty pounds to Nicholas
Roosevelt, one thousand six hundred pounds to James Crommelin, one hundred pounds to Sarah Roosevelt, Isaac's daughter, and five hundred pounds to Catherine van Ranst, another
grand-daughter.

James seems to have had a good understanding of his children and to have had some qualms about the generosity of
grand-daughter Catherine, to whom he left a house and some
land in New York and the Bushwick farm, for he warned her
to abide by the terms of the will, and to share her property
with other members of the family and let them use the houses,
or else be cut off with a shilling. He made Isaac the executor
of the will and presumably he chose a good one, for none of
the beneficiaries ever squabbled publicly about their share.

The will of John Roosevelt has not come to light, but he,
too, owned considerable property in addition to his lots in the
Beekman Swamp which he passed on to his several children,
and he probably had accumulated from his contracting business
a considerable fortune for those days. Both branches of the
Roosevelt Family thenceforth were well-to-do, although it is
not until generations later that any of them was ever listed
among the really rich citizens of their times.

CHAPTER VII

Roosevelt Cousins

THE BROTHERS John and James Roosevelt sired a total of twenty-two children. Not all, of course, survived the plagues and pests of New York City, which was intermittently swept by epidemics in the years during which they were born. It would be quite unprofitable to trace all the descendants of those who throve in Eighteenth Century New York down to the present time. But because a family cannot neglect its cousins, however much it may wish to do so upon occasion, it is interesting, and even important, to examine briefly the lives and doings of the Cousins Roosevelt at this time.

Of all the members of this third American-born generation of Roosevelts, the figure of Isaac the Patriot stands apart from the rest. Although the richest and most prominent of Eighteenth Century Roosevelts, he could hardly be called the Head of the Family, as one in each generation of the more genuinely dynastic Adams, Astor, Vanderbilt, or Du Pont families could be termed. Even at this time the Roosevelt Family was too diffuse, and its two branches too self-contained, to acknowledge any dynastic leader to whom they paid tribute or from whose bounty they accepted largess.

The marriage of Margareta Roosevelt, the daughter of Johannes, to William de Peyster was indicative of the society kept by the Roosevelts in the early 1700's. And other members of the family did nearly as well. Margareta had eight brothers and sisters. Nicholas III, born in 1710, went to sea and died at the age of twenty-five in the West Indies. Johannes, born in 1712, lived only a few years longer and died childless, as did his sister, Heyltje. Another brother, Jacobus, died in infancy. But Oliver, who was born in 1716, grew up and prospered. He married Elizabeth Lounsbury, a member of a family long settled in Westchester County. She gave him nine children in eighteen years. Maria Roosevelt, who was born in 1720, married Abraham Duryea, a merchant and a deacon of the Dutch Reformed Church at Flatland (Brooklyn). The next born was named Jacobus, for his uncle, and he added another generation in the direct descent to Theodore Roosevelt. Another sister died as a small child. But Cornelius, the last of the brood, grew up and became a man of some distinction.

Like most but not all the Roosevelt Family, Cornelius Roosevelt was an ardent patriot. Before the grim and bloody struggle with England he had served as a private in the Colonial troops and after the war began he was an ensign with Captain Roberts's company of the First Regiment of New York City. Before he was driven temporarily from his home on John Street in British-held New York, he had carried on the political tradition of the Roosevelts, established by his grandfather Nicholas I, by serving for four years in the aldermanic council. In 1751, when he was just twenty years old, he married Margaret Haering, a buxom Dutch lass, and in the next fourteen years they had seven children. Five grew up and prospered.

One, Cornelius C. Roosevelt, followed his father's footsteps and became a grocer. For many years he was the partner of John Duffie, the American-born son of an Edinburgh Scotsman, who married his sister, Maria Roosevelt. The firm of Roosevelt & Duffie was successful prior to the Revolution and, after the hostilities, reaped even greater profits in the salt trade. One of the young clerks who worked there, William Whitten Todd, was a nephew of John Jacob Astor. Young Todd married Maria Caroline Duffie, his boss's daughter and eventually became a partner of the firm. Their son, it is worth noting in passing, was the Rev. Cornelius Roosevelt Duffie, who became the first rector of the fashionable St. Thomas's Protestant Episcopal Church, in which all of New York "aristocrats" must be married and from which they must be buried.

Another son of Cornelius I was Elbert Roosevelt, who married Jane Curtenius, daughter of Colonel Peter Theobold Curtenius, Commissary General of the American troops during the Revolution. Elbert lived in a fine house at Pelham Bay overlooking Long Island Sound and thus escaped the ravages of the yellow fever epidemic which in 1789 spared neither rich nor poor. It counted among its victims Elbert's heroic old father-in-law who had sold his store, the Golden Anvil, to raise cash for the ragged Continentals during the worst days of the Revolution. Elbert had eight children: one, Washington Roosevelt, became minister of the Dutch Reformed Church at Bronxville. Cornelius I's youngest daughter, Aunt Elizabeth Roosevelt, had outlived her own generation when, a venerable spinster, she died in 1850.

Although Brother Jacobus I and his wife, Catherina Hardenbroock, had thirteen children, not all of them figured with any degree of prominence in their close New York world. John, the oldest, was born in that city in 1715, two years after his parents' marriage. His father may have had some idea of forming a dynasty, for he favored this oldest son, and even sent him to New Haven to attend Yale College.

The first Roosevelt of record to obtain a college education, John was graduated in 1735, nearly twenty years before the first class of King's College was held in the vestry of Trinity Church, supported partially by funds raised by a lottery conducted in 1753 by the Yale man's father. Young John Roosevelt served on the Board of Aldermen from 1748 to 1767. In 1775, when the crisis was fast approaching in the struggle with England, he became a captain in the Oswego Rangers, an independent company of footguards organized that year. He already had training as a private in the Orange County Militia. Captain John Roosevelt undoubtedly was a striking figure in his blue coat and white trousers and his brass-bound hat. His company sent him before the Provincial Congress in 1776 to offer its services as "Minute Men," and later he acted as a liaison officer between the Congress and the Continental troops. Captain Roosevelt married Annatje Luqueer of Bushwick, Long Island, a young lady whose French ancestor had come to America from Holland late in the Seventeenth Century. They had only one child, a daughter, who married Abraham van Ranst.

John's brother, Nicholas Roosevelt III, who was born in 1717, also became a storekeeper in New York where, in 1739, he married Annatje Brestede. Their only son, also named Nicholas, married Sarah van Ranst, a cousin.

If Margareta Roosevelt brought some degree of lustre to the Roosevelt Family by marrying William de Peyster, her cousin Helena did just as well. Helena was Jacobus Roosevelt's oldest daughter and the belle of the tribe. She spurned all the Dutch suitors who must have sought her hand. When she was only eighteen years old she met and fell in love with a serious-minded young Scot who had only recently come down from his native Albany to win a fortune in New York. Andrew Barclay was exactly her own age when they were married in 1737. His father was the Reverend Thomas Barclay, the first Church of England minister at Albany, and his mother, the former Dorothea Dranger, was the daughter of Admiral Andrew Dranger of the Danish Navy.

Soon after their June wedding young Barclay set himself up in business on Wall Street. Later his brother-in-law, Isaac Roosevelt, seven years his junior, became his partner in the sugar refining business, but Andrew's main attention was directed to his busy warehouse near the City Hall. There he dealt in rum and salt, chinaware, spices, Nicaragua wood, and lignum vitae, among other profitable commodities. Adolphus Roosevelt, his youngest brother-in-law, was one of his agents in the West Indies, where he lived for many years and eventually died. Andrew's trade was extensive and he became a wealthy man. New York, which has always honored its successful merchants, named Barclay Street after him.

Andrew's older brother, while claiming only a tenuous relationship with the Roosevelts, was an interesting personality in pre-Revolutionary New York. William Henry Barclay, also a native of Albany, was graduated from Yale College in 1734 and, attracted to the way of God, went to Fort Hunter, near his birthplace, as a catechist to the Mohawk Indians. He next attended Oxford where he took holy orders in 1738, after which he returned to the Mohawk Trail as a missionary. In

1746 he was inducted as rector of Trinity Church in New York, then one of the most influential ecclesiastical posts in the colonies. Oxford gave him an honorary degree and he busied himself translating the Book of Common Prayer into the Mohawk dialect on which he was still engaged when he died in 1764. His widow inherited his stanch Tory-Episcopal beliefs with the result that her property was seized after the Revolution. She herself did not follow the many other Tory New Yorkers to Nova Scotia but she sent three of her children there for safety's sake. So hated were the Tories in 1783 that she had to beg for an allowance from Sir Guy Carleton, the British Governor, to tide her over that cruel winter.

Unfortunately the Widow Barclay's brother-in-law, Andrew, could not help if he wished to, for he had died the year before the Revolution began and was safely buried in a vault in Trinity Churchyard. Whether he would have remained loyal to the Crown or sided with his partner and brother-in-law, Isaac the Patriot, is today an unanswerable question. Helena Barclay, Andrew's younger daughter, married Major Thomas Moncrieff of the British Army and two others made alliances with Tory families. One of them, Sarah Barclay, married Anthony Lispenard, of the Chamber of Commerce Lispenards, and thus became the great-grandmother of William Rhinelander Stewart, and another, Charlotte Amelia, became the wife of Dr. Richard Bayley, who was to become one of the first professors of medicine at Columbia College in New York.

Jacobus Roosevelt's youngest daughter, Sarah, who was born in 1730, married a widower named Charles Crommelin. She died before her father, and her only son, James Crommelin, fell heir to some of old Johannes's property at Peck Slip. Peter Roosevelt, who was two years younger than Sarah, was twice married, the old records reveal. By his first wife, Elizabeth Brinckerhoff, he had one son, Peter, Jr., who married but had no children. He died of scarlet fever a month after his second marriage to the widow of an Albany minister. Adolphus Roosevelt, born in 1735, took his bride, Elizabeth Dekker, to live with him in the West Indies, where he died, leaving two children. One, Catherine Roosevelt, married James Amory there, and the other, Sarah Roosevelt, married one Jan de Witt, a member of the prominent de Witt family of New York, who took her to England to live. Christopher Roosevelt, the last born of the children of Johannes I, married Mary Duryea of Albany, and they were the grandparents of James Henry Roosevelt, who was to make a fortune in real estate and give the Roosevelt Hospital to New York.

CHAPTER VIII

Isaac the Patriot and the Shot That Was Heard Around the World

MORE THAN ANY OTHER member of his generation Isaac Roosevelt moved in the main channel of the Revolutionary Age and approached that greatness so cherished by posterity. This son of Jacobus I, born just fifty years before the colonies revolted against British rule, was the first, and for four generations the last, of his breed to achieve a reputation extending beyond that smug world of shopkeepers, bankers, shipowners, and landlords in which the Roosevelt Family lived until Theodore Roosevelt broke the mold and shouted his way to the Presidency. Isaac Roosevelt supported the Revolution with his money and strength, was the second president of his city's first bank, helped write his State's first constitution, and stood with Alexander Hamilton for a strong Federal Union. He was typical of his class and time.

On the wall of his great-great-grandson's home in Hyde Park there hangs a portrait of this eminent man. He sits at a desk looking up from some papers that might be either notes on the proceedings of the Council of War—or a bill of lading for a shipment of rum. The eyes that look out at the room are set under cynically arched eyebrows and they are cool and shrewd. Above them is a high forehead surrounded by a powdered wig. Beneath, a long Roman nose casts a slight shadow over thin, determined lips. The whole effect is that of a keen, reserved individual quite likely to take seriously the world and his own presence in it. And yet there is an essential kindliness about this face and one feels that at the right moment Isaac Roosevelt would know how to smile.

Most of Isaac Roosevelt's life was spent under the shadow of a warehouse. Since he was one of Jacobus Roosevelt's younger sons, that well-to-do parent did not favor him above his other brothers. He was born on December 19, 1726, according to the notation in the family's old Dutch Bible, and shortly thereafter was baptized in the Reformed Dutch Church of New York. He probably was given as good an education as the rather indifferent common schools of that period afforded and then was set to learning the intricacies of book-keeping and letter-writing in his father's place of business. That at least was the educational custom in vogue in those days.

He grew up in his father's house on Queen Street (later Pearl) with his many brothers and sisters and, of course, knew all the other young communicants at the Dutch Church, with which his father was prominently identified. Since his father had never lost contact with the region up the Hudson, where grandfather Nicholas I had trapped and bartered for furs with the Indians, he was acquainted with many of the families who still lived in reasonable splendor between Esopus (which had been patriotically renamed Kingston) and Albany, where the patroons still ruled. When the summer sun beat too strongly on the streets of New York, the children were packed away to the healthier climate far from the tanner's swamp their father owned. At any rate Isaac was in Kingston in August 1752, and for a very definite purpose. On the twenty-fourth of that month, four months before his twenty-second birthday, he married Cornelia Hoffman, a wealthy and attractive girl of eighteen.

Cornelia Hoffman was the daughter of proud and military-minded Colonel Martinus Hoffman, who, as we have seen, owned vast tracts of land in Dutchess County, and of Tryntje Benson, whose Swedish grandfather had first come to Albany as a carpenter in 1648. The Hoffmans, descended from a Finnish soldier who claimed to have fought for the King of Sweden, had long been prominent and wealthy in both Dutchess

and Ulster Counties, and had already forgotten that their immigrant ancestor had been a common saddler by trade. Now
the Hoffmans ranked high among the gentry and lived leisurely
lives on rolling acres, attended by their Negro slaves.

Isaac had his own way to make and so did not stay long in
this rural community. Soon after his marriage he was counted
among the rising young business men of New York. He had
his own house on Wall Street and in its back yard he built,
at a date that is now forgotten, one of the first sugar refineries
in the city. The Bayards, who lived in a grand house on the
Hudson River front, had introduced sugar refining to New
York, and the mighty Livingston family also was engaged in
this business, probably before Isaac entered it. Nevertheless,
Isaac Roosevelt was one of the first large-scale refiners. Some
time later Isaac moved his sugar house to the swamp where it
stood on the site of the present Cliff Street. At his Wall Street
residence Isaac dealt in all kinds of loaf sugar—"double, mid-
dling and single refined"—and in "clarified, muscovado, and
other molasses"—and in rum. His business was such that it was
not long before he was recognized as one of the more important
citizens of New York.

Isaac's standing among the business men, or merchants, as
they were invariably called in those days, brought him into
contact with all the "best people" of the city, including the
Waltons. New York's commercial aristocracy has never boasted
a more formidable family than this. In their severe unbending
way the Waltons ruled the city. A proud, disdainful people,
they were little known to the mass of the population, but
their magnificent mansion on Queen Street was the envy of all.
There the British snobs gathered, for not even in London did
rarer wines grace the tables of the genuine aristocracy than in
William Walton's exclusive home.

Walter Barrett, author of the gossipy *The Old Merchants
of New York* and a delightful and garrulous predecessor of
Walter Winchell, boasted that William Walton was descended
from Robert Walton, who had been counsellor to the Earl of
Belmont when that gentleman was Governor of New York.
This is discounted by more recent genealogists, who say he was
the son of a fiery Staten Island farmer who was clapped into

jail in 1689 for having declared that, if he had 200 men, he would cross the harbor and retake the fort from that Dutch upstart, Leisler. He died shortly after his vain boast and left his son a small fortune. What is more important he left all his descendants an unperishable love for England and a hatred for all its foes. William Walton, the son of the boastful Thomas of Staten Island, used part of his patrimony to buy land on the East River where he established one of the busiest shipyards in the city. He had a passion for speed and his vessels were among the fastest built in America before the Revolution. Most of the ships he built were for his own use in trade with the West Indies and the Spanish colonies in Cuba, Florida and South America. During the frequent scraps between Britain and France his vessels became privateers and harried French commerce. His sons often commanded the Walton ships themselves and both father and the Walton boys became extremely wealthy. In fact, they had so much money that they underwrote the ventures of others, and they had their fingers in so many ledgers that William Walton became known as "Boss" Walton, which led Walter Barrett to remark: "the word 'Boss' had a meaning in Dutch, in 1754, not since as well understood. It was originally 'Baas,' and means 'master'—a name repugnant to democrats, although few object to recognize a 'Boss' "!

"Boss" Walton died in 1748, but his sons carried on. Jacob, the oldest, had married a Beekman in 1726, and had several children, but he died two years after his father. This left another William Walton at the head of the family and the powerful business house. William II was as aloof as his father, well aware of his own importance and dignity. It was he who built the famous Walton Mansion, the finest house in the city, situated on fashionable Queen Street in the section that later became Franklin Square. Its beautiful lawns and gardens extended to the East River. The house itself was of yellow brick, with a double pitch roof of tiles surrounded by a balustrade so that a Walton might walk there safely while watching his vessels in the harbor. Two fluted columns supported the portico that bore the "Walton arms." There was nothing Dutch, and everything English, about this mansion. There William Walton lived his splendid bachelor existence surrounded by his brother Jacob's children. During the Seven Years' War many a British naval officer was lavishly entertained at banquets in its huge dining room and the tales they took back to London were used as powerful arguments in support of taxing the colonies.

Isaac Roosevelt, whose own house was not far away on Wall Street, was a frequent guest at William Walton's house. He was a close friend of Abraham Walton, William's nephew, whose ownership of the Rutgers Brewery made him an independent fortune. Young Abraham married Grace Williams, a member of a family with some claims to provincial aristocracy. After 1766 he divided his time between New York and his vast country estate, "Pembroke," at Mosquito Cove (in 1836 changed to Glen Cove) near Hempstead, on Long Island. There most of their children were born. All were baptised in the Episcopal Church of St. George at Hempstead. Isaac was often a visitor at "Pembroke" and his children played with the Abraham Walton children in the rural and thoroughly British atmosphere of the garden estate. It was there that Isaac's son, James, first knew Maria Eliza Walton, whom he was to marry later, when the differences between the families, brought about by the Revolution, had been healed.

In the two decades between his marriage to Cornelia Hoffman and the firing of the shot heard 'round the world Isaac Roosevelt quietly devoted himself to commerce and the raising of an extensive family. Perhaps the most exciting event of his life came in 1772 when he moved his home and business from Wall Street to a more fashionable location on Queen Street. His older and unmarried brother, known as Jacobus, Jr., to differentiate him from others of that name, had originally lived there. But he had died and now Isaac took over the house which was, as his advertisement of that year proudly announced, "opposite to Mr. William Walton's." The sugar house was nearby. The alley leading to it crowded with empty hogsheads testified to the extent of its business. Everyone in the neighborhood used to come there to drink from the famous well of pure spring water which stood outside.

Like most of the New York merchants and members of the newly formed Chamber of Commerce, Isaac was a Whig in his politics. There was no English blood in his veins. Both his father and grandfather had been born in New York. He cannot have felt any close ties with England. All his natural sympathies lay with the cause of Independence. He was proud of his native city and he, at least, cannot have looked upon it as the sole province of the British king.

As a merchant the matter of taxation naturally vexed him and he felt strongly that the sooner the colonies broke away from England the better it would be for his business. A hope for better business was what originally made revolutionaries of most of Isaac's class. There were other reasons, it is true, and as the years passed passions other than economic were stirred, making conflict inevitable. But behind the oratory and pamphlets of the day there moved the inescapable economic force. It is quite unlikely that Isaac Roosevelt wanted a revolution, or felt that one was necessary, but once the drift towards "freedom" became a force he had no use for appeasement, no difficulty in determining where he stood.

Nothing in his background or his associations could make Isaac Roosevelt a member of a revolutionary mob. A landed gentleman by birth and marriage he had little in common with the landless and moneyless, the workers or pioneers, the artisans or small landowners, or the late comers to these shores. Had he been less a Dutchman he might have become a Tory. His friend Abraham Walton was a Tory of Tories. But those shrewd eyes of Isaac's that peered out beneath his arched brows looked clearly upon the New York scene and cut through the befogged issues of the day towards a goal he knew would not be easily won.

Isaac Roosevelt was not a radical. He did not belong to the Sons of Liberty and, so far as is known, never uttered the word "independence," then the most dangerous of words, in public. In the beginning of the long struggle he was a "moderate," inclined to follow the political views of such men as Isaac Low, Peter Jay and Philip Livingston, who were to be classed politically, but with doubtful reservations, as John Adams observed, with the Independence party. These gentlemen were all delegates to the first Continental Congress, an honor never accorded to Isaac Roosevelt. But in April, 1775, just one day before a dusty, travel-stained rider dashed into the city on his sweaty horse with the alarming news of Lexington, Isaac Roosevelt was elected by the city's freemen to the Provincial Congress. The story of the fight at Lexington set the city afire with excitement. The crisis was at hand. In that hour those whose minds were not made up were forced to a decision. Isaac Roosevelt, it was certain, could be counted on to stand his ground.

In the riotous city the "right-thinking" people agreed with the City Council that no longer could they hope to "maintain their antient Union with, and dependence upon Great Britain." No, all hope for reconciliation was now past. And what was equally important His Majesty's government in the Province had broken down. The drums beat up the temper of the people—gathered at The Fields—to seize the keys of the Customs House and to take the port by armed force. Men of Isaac Roosevelt's class and temper became the natural leaders and so they formed an Association which, as the timorous City Council grieved to say, was designed solely to "bring about firm Union with the rest of the Continent, and openly avow a Resolution, not only to resist the Acts of Parliament complained of as grievances, but to withhold Succours of all kinds from the Troops, and to repel every species of Force, wherever it may be exerted, for Inforcing the Taxing Claims of Parliament, at the Risque of their Lives and Fortunes."

Nobody, whether in the City Council or on the old and hesitant Committee of Sixty, felt equal to the task of running a government so suddenly broken down in the face of revolution. A Committee of One Hundred was named to administer the Province. Its roster was too conservative and the radicals, annoyed now at New York's hesitancy, rejected it coldly. In the ensuing excitement, with anarchy at hand and the mob growing ever more restless, a group of the "moderate men" met in New York. They issued an appeal to the people of the city to follow the recommendations of the Continental and Provincial Congresses, to oppose parliamentary oppression while waiting "a reconciliation between Great Britain and America," and to take the advice of the General Committee for "the preservation of peace and good order and the *safety of individuals and private property*."

To these tenets at first Isaac Roosevelt subscribed, as did his friend William Walton, and such merchants as John de Lancey, Curtenius, Brinckerhoff, and, indeed, almost all except the notorious revolutionaries and "radical" agitators. The motives of Walton and de Lancey, at least, were suspect. They wanted no independence, no break with England, but they feared the mob and what it might do to their warehouses and their fine homes on Queen Street. They would appease the radicals and hope for the best. But the current was too strong, and the Colony was swept into the Revolution in the end. They determinedly tried to stem the tide and under the leadership of Isaac Low, as chairman of the Committee of One Hundred, sought to restore order in the city. Isaac Roosevelt was a member of this Committee and of the Provincial Congress which tried to rule the Province in this unsettled May of 1775.

A change of temper soon came and most of the Loyalists were ousted from this body. Isaac, Low, James de Lancey and some others who still hoped to stave off conflict, managed to remain on it. But it was fast becoming to all intents and purposes a revolutionary body, although not yet committed to armed resistance. The Congress, so badly split, lasted only until July. In that month, realizing that war was inevitable, thanks mainly to the remorseless agitation of the Boston crowd, it delegated its assumed powers to a newly formed Committee of Safety—and New York was in the Revolution at last.

Many of Isaac Roosevelt's old friends and associates felt like John Alsop, who had served on many of the committees prior to the Declaration of Independence, but who, when that document was prepared, withdrew to his Connecticut home, saying:

"As long as a door was left open for reconciliation with Great Britain, upon just and honorable terms, I was willing to render my country all the service in my power . . . but as you have, I presume, closed the door . . . I must beg to resign."

Isaac Roosevelt, following the dictates of as an integral a conscience as that of John Alsop, did not care now if the door was closed. Who knows today his inner motives? The fact remains that he was committed to the Revolutionary cause.

To be patriotic was not an easy task. It meant severing his old ties, parting with close friends, abandoning his home and business the day the British Redcoats took New York. But he did all this. When the British filled the city—to the great delight of his friend Abraham Walton—he left, willing to face whatever the uncertain and dangerous future held. Abraham, too, had been an ardent Whig in 1775. Indeed, he had sat with Isaac at the Provincial Congress and had even signed the letter to London saying: "All the horrors of Civil War will never compel America to submit to taxation by Parliament." But he had not meant it! Isaac had. When the British took New York Abraham stayed as did many another merchant and member of the Chamber of Commerce, and, taking the oath of allegiance to the King, was pardoned for his former association with the American patriots.

Abraham's motto, like that of other Tories, was "business as usual." Having sworn allegiance, he felt safe, and since Long Island as well as New York City was under British control he spent the three first hot summers of the Revolution enjoying the sea breezes at "Pembroke." But one day in 1779 a French fleet hove into sight off Sandy Hook. A fellow Tory, who had been marauding on Long Island and robbing the homes of helpless patriot farmers feared this fleet would capture New York. Realizing that he would be in a peck of trouble without the protection of the Redcoats, the ruffian turned coat. Suddenly expressing a new-found "patriotism" he surrounded "Pembroke" with a mob of seedy followers, broke down the door, took poor Abraham's silver plate and money, and kidnaped the trembling Tory from his bed!

Isaac Roosevelt spent the years of British occupation at his wife's family home in Dutchess County. Although then a man of more than fifty years, he willingly bore arms in behalf of the cause for which he had risked so much, serving, although with no great military distinction, as a member of the 6th Regiment of Dutchess County Militia.

His real services to the country were of a different and more practical nature. Early in the war, before the British took New York, the price of powder had risen to forty pounds a hundredweight. The New York Committee of Safety, avid for arms, ordered Isaac Roosevelt to prepare an emission of paper money redeemable in three yearly installments beginning in 1779.

Once he even gave the lead window weights of his New York home to make bullets for the Continentals. Later, as the war progressed, he was elected a member of the Convention and took part in the debates that resulted in the first Constitution of the State of New York.

This notable document, to whose provisions Isaac Roosevelt heartily subscribed even if he may have had little to do with its actual writing, was proclaimed by John Jay from a barrel head in front of the courthouse at Kingston on April 22, 1777, and remained in effect for forty-four years. It was not the product of completely democratic-minded men, but it was a "working compromise" between the radical and conservative elements then united in the Revolutionary cause. In that its officials were elected by the people, it was a popular paper; but a property qualification was required for the electors and for members of the Senate, although not for those of the Assembly. A Governor and an appointed Council headed the government with the power to name many local military and civil officials. Another body, the "council of revisions," had limited veto power over legislation. Religious freedom was insured, but slavery was allowed—although in this last respect the document drew no color line. In short, it was exactly the constitution that one might expect from the property-conscious gentlemen who wrote it. The first Governor elected was George Clinton of New York, a former neighbor of Isaac Roosevelt, who defeated Peter Schuyler of the old and aristocratic family for the post.

Isaac Roosevelt was elected by the qualified, property-owning voters to the first State Senate and he served constantly on that body until after the declaration of peace in 1783. He was also, during some of that time, a member of the Governor Clinton's Council, and as such had many important duties to perform, including the licensing of privateers. During these years, of course, the legislature met at Kingston, Poughkeepsie and Albany and, since the British held the lower Hudson, the city and the western posts, its authority was confined to the Albany area and as far as Lake George, the Highlands and Lake Oneida. It instilled upon that region the political conservatism and deep respect for property that exists in up-state New York to this Republican day.

With the coming of peace the patriots were allowed to return to New York City even before the British had evacuated the port. Isaac was among the first to come back to his home, which thankfully had escaped the two disastrous fires that had ravaged New York during the long British occupation. His sugar house, too, still stood beside the famous pump in the Square. The British agreed to have all their troops out of the city by November 25, 1783, one of the greatest days in American history, marking as it did the final triumph of the American cause. On the autumn afternoon the victorious General, George Washington, marched down the Bowery at the head of his war-weary men while thousands cheered. Isaac Roosevelt was in the forefront of those who greeted the great General. He saw the American flag raised over the fort, despite the efforts of the British to prevent it by greasing the pole and removing the lanyards. His ears were delightfully deafened by the thirteen gun salute in the flag's honor that sounded before the British sailors had even got under way. That evening, in his white wig, his shrewd eyes shining under the arched brows, he sat at the dinner which Governor Clinton gave General Washington and his officers at Fraunces's Tavern.

Soon after that glorious November day Isaac Roosevelt picked up the threads of his business and resumed his place as a leading citizen of the city. When the French Minister arrived he headed the committee that tendered him a dinner in the old de Lancey mansion, by then turned into Cape's Tavern. General Washington and 120 guests also attended. Egbert Benson, Isaac's wife's cousin, helped him run the gala affair, and together they approved the bill for £156-10s for the food and wine. Nor did Isaac forego all his interest in politics in the ensuing years. In 1788, having reached his full years of dignity and put behind him an honorable and patriotic career, he was elected to the State Convention called to ratify the Constitution of the United States.

In 1784, but a few months after the evacuation of the city, the hard-headed businessmen who were engaged in the difficult task of readjustment, realized the need for a sound financial institution. The Bank of New York accordingly was chartered and on June 9, 1784, it opened its offices in the front parlor of

William Walton's home on Queen Street. One Alexander Mc-
Dougal was its first president, William Seton was cashier and
William Walton, already forgiven for his apathy towards the
Revolution, was on the board of directors. Two years later
Isaac Roosevelt was made president. He was to hold the post
five years.

During all these hectic Revolutionary years Isaac's family
had been growing up. His first two children, both boys, had
died in infancy. The next child, Catherine Roosevelt, was born
in 1756. She never married and died in 1807 when she was
nearly fifty years old. Sarah, her younger sister by two years,
lived only until her twentieth year when she died, in Dutchess
County, after a five days' illness, and was "interred there in the
family burying ground near her grandmother Hoffman."

Jacobus (James) Roosevelt, the third of this name in this
branch of the family, was born January 10, 1760, and so was only
fifteen years old when he left the city with his father at the beginning of the war. He was sent to the New Jersey College at
Princeton, and was graduated in 1780. Four years later he returned to New York with his father and became his partner in
the sugar business. The firm was known then as Isaac Roosevelt
& Son. In 1786 he married his childhood playmate, Maria Eliza
Walton, the first of his three wives, the niece of William Walton
and the daughter of the unhappy Abraham of "Pembroke."
Thenceforth Jacobus was to have an active commercial career.

Isaac Roosevelt's next child, Cornelia, lived only from a
Friday to a Monday, but Maria Roosevelt, born in 1763, grew
up to marry Richard Varrick, who had served as a colonel in
the Revolutionary Army and who was to serve, among other
political posts, as Mayor of New York from 1789 to 1801. He
was one of the city's leading lawyers and President of the Society
of the Cincinnati. They had no children.

Martin Roosevelt, Isaac's next child, was born in 1765, but
he died while attending Princeton College. Cornelia Roosevelt,
born in 1767, was nineteen when she met and married young
Dr. Benjamin Kissam, the son of a New York lawyer, who had
been graduated from King's College on the eve of the Revolution, and who had spent the war years studying at the University of Edinburgh, returning to New York in 1784. The next

year he began teaching in the Institute of Medicine at his alma mater, now proudly known as Columbia College. They had two daughters. Emma, the oldest, married Francis Livingston, and Helena C. married John Lefferts of Long Island.

Isaac's last born was Helena, born in 1768. In 1796 old Isaac sadly recorded in the Dutch Bible that she had "died of a lingering disorder, she bore with exemplary resignation and patience, was interred in the family vault."

In his latter years Isaac continued to occupy the mansion in Franklin Square near the sugar house. It was very handy to the Bank in the old yellow Walton House. Each morning Isaac would have an early breakfast and then could be seen trotting to the sugar house to give his son James his instructions for the day. This concluded he would run across the street to the bank, always arriving before the opening hour of ten o'clock.

The bank closed at 1 P.M., but Isaac and his clerk would be busy at their books and papers until the dinner hour, which was at three o'clock. But that was not all his busy day included. He was still interested in political affairs and often was closeted with his friend John Hancock, at No. 5 Cherry Street, near by or at the Congress Office on Broadway. Or he would be calling on Nicholas Low, who, unlike his brother Isaac Low, had been a vigorous Revolutionist. Nick Low now was in business on Water Street and a director of the Bank.

Or Isaac Roosevelt might be visiting another director, William Maxwell, whose snuff and tobacco store on Wall Street was a pleasant place for a business or political chat. Or he might be sitting with his close friend, Alexander Hamilton, the leader of the party "of wealth and talent," the Federalists, of which Isaac Roosevelt heartily approved. Mr. Hamilton practised law in his home on Wall Street and his theory of Federalism wherever he went. It was as a Federalist that Isaac Roosevelt attended the Constitutional Convention, for he was a believer in what he called "a firm National Government."

In 1791 the old gentleman of sixty-five began to feel that the time had come to take life a little easier. The sugar business could be safely left to his son James. In that year he retired from the Bank. Cornelia, his wife, had died in 1788, winning the following in President Washington's Diary:

"Received an invitation to attend the funeral of Mrs. Roosevelt (the wife of a Senator in this State), but declined complying with it, first, because the propriety of accepting an invitation of this sort appeared to be very questionable, and secondly, (though to do so in this instance might not be improper), because it might be difficult to discriminate in cases which might thereafter happen."

Six years later active Isaac Roosevelt himself died, and was duly mourned in the capital of the new nation, where he had been born and where he had passed his busy life.

CHAPTER IX

Hardware and Paddle Wheels

COUSIN JACOBUS ROOSEVELT, who was born in 1724, was a thorough-going Dutchman. He lacked the imagination and the flair of Isaac, whose contemporary he was. Politics held little if any interest for him; indeed, he mixed hardly at all in the public life of the city. He was content to tend his store and putter in the neat gardens that lay between his house on Green-wich Street and the river. His business was profitable, for he dealt in hardware and crockery, merchandise that was ever in demand, and he had a considerable trade with the shipyards that lined the East River, on either side of the small yard where Isaac used to repair the vessels that brought sugar, molasses, and rum to his store.

In the history of New York and of his own family this Jacobus played an inconspicuous role; in the case of the latter he is memorable primarily because he adds one more generation in the descent from the Little Fellow to Theodore Roosevelt. Had he been less phlegmatic, he might at least have sat on the Board of Aldermen. But this traditional Rooseveltian right he eschewed.

Even his marriage was hardly an event of social importance, for it failed to ally him with a family of wealth or prominence. His wife was Annetje Bogard (or Bogert) the daughter of one Jan Bogert and Hannah Peck, who had lived on Long Island most of their lives. If Annetje, whom he married about 1747, when he was twenty-three years old, brought him neither dowry nor social distinction, she did bring him happiness, and in the next several years they had eight children. All were born before the Revolution, in which Jacobus did his duty as a private in the State colonial troops. Annetje died sometime before 1774 and in that year he married Mrs. Helena Gibson Thompson, a widow, by whom he had one daughter, Ann.

Two of the eight children by his first marriage did not survive infancy. Anna, the oldest, was born in 1748 and, in 1771, married one Andries Heermanse; Johannes, the oldest boy, was born in 1751, and married a member of the old Schuyler family; Margareta, born in 1755, married Isaac van Vleck when she was seventeen years old; Helena, born in 1761, married John Ray; and Maria, the youngest daughter, born in 1763, married James Prevost. There were, of course, two other children—two sons who, each in his own way, added to the reputation of the name of Roosevelt.

The older of these boys was named Jacobus Roosevelt after his father but he was always known as James J. Roosevelt, the middle initial signifying that he was James the son of Jacobus. The appendage "junior" was seldom used in Dutch families. When the Revolution broke he was only seventeen years old, but he appears to have held some sort of reasonably responsible post with the Commissary Department of the New York State troops. After the return of peace he entered the hardware business in evacuated New York and, as early as 1797, had his own thriving place of business on Maiden Lane, and a substantial home across the street.

In 1793 Jacobus had married Maria van Schaack. He was then thirty-five years old. His bride, a charming girl of twenty, was of pure Dutch ancestry, the daughter of Cornelius van Schaack, of Kinderhook, N. Y., and a descendant of old Goosen Geritszen, one of the early settlers of Albany, where he had been commissary in the days of the patroons.

Like his father, James J. Roosevelt appears to have been a kindly, quiet and industrious man, whose life, as far as we can now tell, was wrapped up in the selling of hammers, nails and doorknobs in his store on Maiden Lane. He made a sizable fortune at this useful but prosaic business and raised a family of six children who played roles of varying importance in the commercial and social life of early Nineteenth Century New York. Cornelius van Schaack Roosevelt, his oldest son and heir to the hardware store, was to help found the Chemical National Bank and become the first Presidential grandfather in the Roosevelt Family. James I. Roosevelt, who might have stepped from a novel by Henry James, was to become the first glittering social light in the tribe. His marriage to the beautiful Cornelia van Ness in Paris was as brilliant an affair as "international society" had then known.

James J. Roosevelt's brother, the youngest of the eight children of Jacobus and Annetje, was given the old family name of Nicholas. Like its original bearer he was a restless and adventurous man. He was born in New York, but the war came when he was only nine years old and he was taken with his step-mother and his two younger sisters, Helena and Maria, to the comparative safety of the family haven at Esopus. His father was with his regiment. The British had taken New York and all the patriots had fled. His older brother and sisters were grown up and married and so he and the two younger girls were alone with their step-mother on the farm. There they were to remain until peace came again and they could return to their old home on Greenwich Street opposite their father's hardware store. Uncle Isaac was busy with his important political affairs and young Nick's other uncles, like his father, were with their troops.

Esopus—or Kingston—was a reasonably peaceful place, and there was plenty of work to keep the lad busy at farm-boy chores. But even at this early age Nick was an imaginative lad, with agile fingers and an active mind, and little of the Dutch stodginess that marked certain other members of his breed.

Nick's closest friend was an elderly farmer named Jacob Ousterhaudt, who had been tilling the Esopus soil for many years. Jacob liked his young neighbor and, when he learned that Nick had a mechanical bent, allowed him to use the workbench and tools in his big barn. He also gave the boy the use of an old punt that lay wide-seamed on the bank of a pond. Nick soon had this afloat and summer days would find him rowing and fishing on the small deep water. Nick hated to work and

wondered if there were not some way to propel the heavy flat-
bottomed punt that would be easier than pushing the oars.
One day, in the summer of 1782 he thought he had found the
answer to this problem that all boys in all generations have tried
to solve. Back of Jake's barn was an old set of carriage wheels
with their axle still intact. Why couldn't those wheels do the
work?

Young Nick moved them to the work bench and through the
bright summer days busied himself fitting wooden paddles to
the spokes. Next he cut in the sides of the punt and carefully
laid the paddle-wheels across the center of the boat. Handles
which he had placed in the center of the axle enabled him to
turn the wheels and paddles—and make the boat go. Old Jake
came down to the pond to watch his protégé and even ventured
out in the boat himself. But they soon found it was easier to
row or pole the punt than to turn the heavy wheels. Nick would
not give up the idea, however. Begging some old whalebone
from Jack Ousterhaudt he sought to make a spring contrivance
which would ease the work. With the whalebones and cedar
saplings he arranged a spring—all right—but somehow the result was a failure! Nick gave up the whole idea after that and,
boy fashion, went on to other adventures. Soon the joyful word
of the treaty of peace arrived—and the Roosevelts were hurrying back to town.

Although Nick's attempt to revolutionize the rowboat business had failed, he never forgot the youthful venture. Years
later his life was to be ruined by the memory. But now he was
busy at school where he developed a love for mathematics.
And when he had finished school his brother James, who already owned his own hardware store, wanted Nick to go to
work for him. But Nick was too energetic and restless to be
happy as a clerk. Instead he served his apprenticeship in a forge
and iron shop. By the time he was twenty-one he was as good
a mechanic as there was in town. If he had forgotten for the
time being his mechanical rowboat he must have remembered
it in that year, for in 1788 John Fitch of Philadelphia built a
steam engine that actually moved a boat. The piston of the
engine drove six paddles, Indian style, on each side of the craft!
News of this astounding contraption spread rapidly, especially

among the young mechanics of the day. Nick laughed when he heard about it and said that "wheels over the side," and not paddles, was the only right method. If he but had the money he would show what he meant.

Perhaps if he had had the courage he might have approached Uncle Isaac, then the president of the only bank in the city. Yet it is doubtful if that austere gentleman would have cared to put up cash for such a crazy idea.

Nick put all thought of boat wheels out of his mind, but crazy John Fitch went on experimenting until, four years later, he convinced a Congressional committee of the practicality of his steamboat and won a patent for his mad idea. In the meantime Nick saved his money, perhaps with the idea of some-day building a boat of his own. An opportunity, however, came along which seemed more immediately profitable for a young mechanic. In 1793 he invested all his hard-earned money in a syndicate organized to reopen the old and long-abandoned Schuyler copper mine in New Jersey.

Brigadier General Philip Schuyler was the prime mover of the New Jersey Copper Mines Association. Nicholas Roosevelt was the technical expert. The diggings, located at what is now Belleville, near Newark, on the Passaic, or as it was then called, Second River, were a deep shaft extending from the top of Schuyler Hill to three hundred sixty feet below the riverbed. The first thing that had to be done was to pump the workings dry. General Schuyler decided that it was more practical to build the engine right at the mine. Scraping together every cent he and his associates could lay their hands on, they bought a tract of land on the river bank and proceeded to erect a foundry and shop, patterned after the famous plant of Boulton & Watt at Birmingham, England. They named it "Soho." It was the first engine works in America.

The mine failed to pay dividends but the engine works was a success. Through Uncle Isaac and other members of the family, who knew every important shipping man in New York, Nick soon won contracts for rolling sheets of copper to cover the bottoms of vessels. Before long a dozen or more men, including two "graduates" of Boulton & Watt, were busy at "the works." Nick was a great admirer of Watt and thought his

steam engine the greatest invention of mankind. His burning
ambition, then and for many years, was to install one in a sizable vessel to turn "wheels over the side." But other men, with
more money than Nick ever had, were also interested in steam
navigation—men like Robert R. Livingston, the Chancellor of
New York. This powerful politician, who owned the biggest
iron foundry in the city, had been a close friend of Uncle Isaac
since before the Revolution.

Indeed, Mr. Livingston and Uncle Isaac Roosevelt went together one day in 1796 to watch John Fitch demonstrate his
small steamboat on the Collect Pond near New York's City
Hall. Nick had come over from New Jersey to see the demon-
stration, too, and stood silently respectful at his uncle's side.
Two years later Chancellor Livingston was to use his great
political influence to gain for himself exclusive rights to steam
navigation in the waters of New York. Nick, who never won
an exclusive right to anything, still dreamed of building his
own boat. But he was too busy, in the year of Fitch's demon-
stration, to do anything except run the Soho works. The plant
was humming with activity thanks to a contract Nick had
won—probably through Uncle Isaac's intervention—from the
United States Government, rolling out copper for the hulls of
three of the six 74-gun frigates for the new American Navy
authorized that year by Congress.

Unfortunately for Nicholas Roosevelt, General George Washington refused a third term and testy John Adams entered the
presidential mansion at Philadelphia in 1797. For political reasons Congress decided to suspend operations on the ships.
Nicholas, who had gone into debt to buy raw copper and to
hire men to roll it, now found bankruptcy staring him in the
face. But luck, of another kind, was with him. At this precise
moment Chancellor Livingston and his partner, Colonel John
L. Stevens, decided to build a steamboat. They had seen one
of Nick's engines pumping the water from the Schuyler mine
and gave him the contract to build the machinery for their
boat.

Work on the engine began early in January, 1798, at Soho.
Chancellor Livingston, an imperious and bull-headed aristocrat, sent his brother-in-law, Robert Fulton, an ingenious young

inventor, to act as consultant. Fulton insisted upon using a wheel with a vertical axle submerged at the stern of the ship. In vain Nick pleaded for "wheels over the side." Indeed, as early as September, 1798, he had written to Livingston making this suggestion. His letter on this subject was "the first record in America of the practical suggestion of the combination which eventually made steam navigation a commercial success." Roosevelt and Fulton were unable to agree, and so Nick decided to go ahead on his own. With typical Dutch obstinacy he hired John and William Sandford, two Belleville, New Jersey, shipwrights, to build him a river boat sixty feet in length. While the *Polacca,* as it was strangely named, was building, Nick made a one cylinder engine. On October 21, 1798, he fitted the boat with the machinery and wheels of his own design, one on each side just as he had done with Jake Ousterhaudt's punt. Steam was got up and on the still waters of the Passaic River the narrow sidewheeler was operated successfully at three miles an hour. But Chancellor Livingston sniffed. Young Bob Fulton went off to Paris. The Roosevelt-Livingston venture in steam navigation came to an abrupt end.

Hard pressed by the abandonment of the Livingston scheme and by the cancellation of his Congressional contracts, Nick nearly lost Soho. Luckily he met Benjamin Henry Latrobe, the eminent British-born architect, engineer and canal builder, who was then engaged in setting up the Schuylkill River water works in Philadelphia. Latrobe hired Roosevelt to build most of the pumping engines used in the water works and gave him other work to do. In 1808 Nick, now thirty-one years old and still a bachelor, met Lydia Latrobe, his benefactor's daughter. They fell in love and were married that year.

In the meantime Chancellor Livingston, who had gone to Paris as the American Minister, and Robert Fulton, fresh from his experiments on the Seine, returned to the country and decided to make use of Livingston's unpopular New York monopoly. They built the *Clermont,* named after the family seat of the imperious Livingstons—the first successful steamboat ever built. When Nicholas saw it he had a distinct shock. For the *Clermont* had "wheels over the side"—Nicholas Roosevelt's own invention, which had met only with Livingston's sneers and Fulton's scoffs when he had suggested it nearly nine years before!

Perhaps it was a guilty conscience on the great Chancellor's part; perhaps it was because he knew Roosevelt was the man who could do the job; but whatever the reason, the great Chancellor was to turn to Nicholas Roosevelt again before he was done. Looking inland, to the great rivers of the frontier, the Ohio and the Mississippi, Livingston realized that steam could conquer them. Accordingly in 1809 or 1810 he sent Nicholas Roosevelt on a voyage of exploration and of survey from Pittsburgh, about to become the "Birmingham of the new nation," to Natchez, in the South.

Like a grown-up Tom Sawyer, Nick made the journey on a flatboat. He spotted coal on the way and had several mines opened up. Then he returned to Pittsburgh, having by now given up Soho, and established a new foundry on the banks of the Monongahela. There the vessel was built, 116 feet in length, 20 feet by the beam, from white pine cut in the nearby forests. It had two cabins aft for ladies, a larger one forward for men. To turn the wheel at the stern (Livingston had reverted to his old scheme, and this time Roosevelt apparently raised no objection) Roosevelt built a 36-inch cylinder for the engine. The vessel cost at least three thousand eight hundred dollars. It was to run on regular schedule between New Orleans, for which it was named, and Natchez.

The *New Orleans* was launched in September, 1811. After a short, experimental trip up the Monongahela the craft was pronounced ready for the perilous voyage down the Ohio and the Mississippi to its home port. Nothing could stop Nicholas from going and nothing did stop Lydia—not even the horrified comments of her friends who felt she must be crazy when they learned that she expected to become a mother somewhere along the way. Besides the Roosevelts, there were aboard a captain, an engineer, a river pilot named Andrew Jack, six deckhands, two "female servants" for Mrs. Roosevelt, a waiter, a colored cook and a big black dog named Tiger. All Pittsburgh turned out to see them leave, cheering lustily as the *New Orleans* puffed upstream, circled and swung into the channel and then plowed around the bend into the Ohio and out of sight.

Two days later the vessel anchored in the stream off Cincinnati. Although nobody believed a steamer could ever go
upstream against the current, those who saw her steam into
Cincinnati were convinced the *New Orleans* would get down
all right. There the crew took on wood for her boilers and a
day or two later the boat was on its way again. On midnight
of October 1 they anchored quietly off the banks of Louisville.
The engineer pulled down the safety valve to let off steam.
Thousands of Kentuckians never forgot that midnight! They
leaped from their beds, rushed pell mell for the river, certain
that the comet of 1811 had dropped plumb into the stream!
It took Louisville days to recover from their fright. Then its
leading citizens tendered Mr. and Mrs. Roosevelt a public
dinner. Again it was said the boat could go down stream, but,
said the wise ones, it never could go up! Not to be outdone,
Nicholas invited the town notables to dinner aboard. Just as
they had seated themselves to the meal the boat began to tremble. Forks clattered and ladies screamed in a mad rush for the
deck. Louisville was already a mile down stream. The prankish
Mr. Roosevelt had proved the ship could go up as well as down.

Unfortunately there was not enough water at the Falls of
Ohio to insure a safe passage for the vessel and so for several
days the Roosevelts enjoyed the hospitality of Louisville while
they prayed for a rise in the stream. The skies were leaden; the
sun a red ball. Rivermen said it had something to do with the
comet. While they argued over the phenomena and waited for
a rise of water, Lydia had her baby. She was back on her feet
when at last soundings showed five inches clearance over the
Falls. Nick and the plucky Lydia clung to each other as the
boat plunged over, nearly capsizing as it went. But the *New
Orleans* cleared the scant bottom and went bravely down the
river, the shouts of all Louisville ringing in its crew's ears.

That night all aboard were practically thrown from their
beds. It was not until morning, when they met terrified rivermen and frightened Indians, that they realized what had seemed
like a terrific grounding of the boat had in reality been an
earthquake. They proceeded cautiously downstream. Once they
lost their bearings entirely and did not realize that the scraping

sounds came from tree tops of an island that had completely disappeared. Again the boat caught fire when one of the hands, left to watch a galley stove, fell asleep. They met many homeless, tragic victims of the earthquake, and scared the wits from scores of Chickasaw Indians who thought the strange ship had fallen from the skies. But at last—after a total of fourteen days of steaming—the *New Orleans* reached Natchez and anchored safely before the amazed thousands who lined the shore.

First to greet the Roosevelts was Edward Livingston, the younger brother of the Chancellor, former Mayor of New York and Congressman, and now New Orleans' leading lawyer. He had known Uncle Isaac well and greeted Nicholas as an old friend. Although Robert Livingston had withdrawn from the venture before the *New Orleans* sailed, Edward and his nephew John Livingston, Robert Fulton's brother-in-law, were quick to appreciate the commercial possibilities of river navigation by steam, and soon were involved in a mad legislative scramble in the various States for the right to navigate on the rivers. They neglected completely to secure patents to protect the man who had made the first steam voyage over an American inland waterway.

Nicholas Roosevelt, despite a patent obtained in 1814 and signed by President James Madison himself, never benefited from the pioneer voyage, or from the engine he had built. Patents were then handled by the Department of State, and, although Dr. William Thornton, the patent chief, later acknowledged to Lydia Latrobe Roosevelt's brother, J. B. H. Latrobe, the prior rights of Nicholas Roosevelt, poor Nick reaped no reward for his share in the development of steam navigation. Eventually Nicholas Roosevelt's claim became so involved with those of others that the matter was lost in a legal jumble none could ever hope to clear. In 1828 young Latrobe and Roosevelt's old partner, John Devereaux de Lacy, sought to have Nicholas's expiring patent confirmed and extended, but neither could raise one hundred dollars needed to press the claim!

Nicholas Roosevelt had tired long since of the whole business. Embittered at the whole Livingston tribe and at steam engines in general he had given up any idea of growing rich. With the faithful Lydia he retired to an old farm at Skaneateles, N. Y., and there, in 1854, he died, without having made a penny from the idea that had come to him so many years before, while paddling a leaky punt on old Jake Ousterhaudt's pond.

Book Three

THE RESPECTABLE AGE

Changing Times

NEW YORK HAS ever been a commercial city. In the days of the first Nicholas Roosevelt the Dutch set the pace. During the Nineteenth Century the pace quickened. Great fortunes were made, some honestly, more unscrupulously, as the Robber Barons reached out from their lairs across the rich country that was frontier America. No Roosevelt ever was a Corsair of Big Business, even in those expansive days, but on the whole, in the Nineteenth Century, the Roosevelt Family remained respectably immersed in business. Moses Y. Beach, that reverential chronicler of "the wealth and pedigree of the wealthy citizens of New York," remarked that "no family shines more honorably in the ancient Dutch annals of this province than the Roosevelts—venerated burgomasters of their day."

Mr. Beach's interest in his fellow men did not extend beyond their pocket-books. Was a man rich, Mr. Beach bowed. In the course of his investigations into New York wealth he bowed twice Rooseveltward: to Cornelius van Schaack Roosevelt I, and to James I. Roosevelt. The former, he estimated, was worth two hundred and fifty thousand dollars, and the latter was credited with one hundred and fifty thousand. These amounts did not place the Roosevelts among the richest of men but, if the estimates were true, they did allow the Roosevelts to walk securely on the same side of the street as the Astors, Vanderbilts, Drews, and their own relatives, the Howlands and Aspinwalls, whose fortunes, in those simple days, reached the incredible half-million mark.

None of the Roosevelts, it appears, was actually poor. Many members, especially on the Hyde Park side, married into wealthy families, and although the Roosevelts were credited in their obituaries with being of a charitable turn of mind, each generation inherited large sums from that which went before.

Roosevelt & Co., an investment and banking firm and a sort of family affair, played its not inconsiderable part in railroad history. Stores, warehouses, banks, blocks of real estate, and ships, all added to the solid, but hardly glittering, comforts of the tribe.

As the years passed the Roosevelts owned fine homes in comfortable mid-town New York or on more garish Fifth Avenue, the street of millionaires. Some became gentlemen-farmers along the Hudson and others lived in substantial ease on Long Island. One, at least, carried on the creative tradition started by Nicholas of the paddle wheels. Another dedicated his inherited wealth and considerable talents to political reform. A Paris branch, dedicated their lives to good living and sports. A member of another branch became a Bishop of the Church of Rome. There was an artist, of sorts. There was a lady bicyclist. And one Roosevelt, a proud and cranky collateral, lost his leg at Gettysburg and ended his days expounding military tactics at a European court.

Thus, in the Nineteenth Century, the Roosevelt Family continued to play its minor role in the economic drama of the turbulent times; while the two main branches of the line were hastening toward the time when, equal generations from the Little Fellow, they should each give a President to the United States.

CHAPTER X

The Missing Twins

THE ROOSEVELTS were an extensive family, with many ramifications, even in the early years of the Nineteenth Century, and it would be a dull and futile task to try to classify each member. Yet, apart from the two main branches, there were several who for various reasons deserve to be rescued from the obscurity into which they have fallen. There was, for instance, "Janet Roosevelt"; but she, alas, refuses to be rescued and must remain forever in the mysterious darkness where she was placed by our friend, Walter Barrett, that conscienceless chronicler of the lives and loves of the old merchants of New York.

It is quite probable that there never was a "Janet Roosevelt" any more than there apparently was a "Jansen Inderwick," and yet, prefacing his strange story with these precious words, "The following narrative is as true as gospel," the egregious Mr. Barrett sets down his scandalous tale replete with sources duly noted. Briefly it is this:

A Miss Janet Roosevelt, late in the eighteenth century, married a Mr. Jansen Inderwick, descendant of a Dutch family that had come to New Amsterdam in 1623 and at one time had owned "nearly one-tenth of all Manhattan Island."

"She was an extremely lovely person," says Mr. Barrett, "as her portrait, still in existence, shows that she must have been." But the marriage was a failure. "Eight years passed that they lived together, and she gave birth to *no* child."

This tragedy caused the wealthy and impotent Inderwick to

become morose and even cruel to his wife. In 1803 the beautiful, childless Janet packed up her extensive belongings and left her cold husband's town house on Courtlandt Street to take rooms, with her slave negress, at "a leading boarding house, in the lower part of Broadway." From that day on the unhappy husband never spoke a word to the lovely Janet, although she was always his charming guest whenever he gave a dinner party or a soirée at his home. He sent his carriage each day for her to ride in; whenever she needed money Jansen Inderwick saw that she received it. "Whether it was one hundred dollars or five hundred dollars, he sent the amount required back to her in Bank of New York notes." He was a director of that oldest of New York banks.

One day, as might be expected, a young and handsome gentleman, a Nova Scotian by birth but "a New York merchant of wealth and standing," whom Mr. Barrett calls "Richard Rupert" came to live in the boarding house. His suite was separated from Janet's by a large parlour. Despite this barrier the couple fell in love and before very long were having an "affair," of which the whole town soon knew, but of which the morose husband, brooding in his loveless Courtlandt Street mansion, took no notice. The affair, of course, reached a climax, and tongues wagged when Mrs. Inderwick left town for a New Jersey resort because of "ill health."

"It was reported that she had the typhus fever, and came very near dying," says Barrett with a smirk. "When she returned to her boarding house she was very much emaciated. Her husband sent every day to inquire after her health."

Following her return Janet Roosevelt-Inderwick took a curious interest in a young couple living nearby in Maiden Lane. They had come lately from the country with "a pair of twin children." She was extremely solicitous about one of the twins, a boy. The couple were William and Milly Seymour. One day Mrs. Inderwick quarrelled with the mother over Milly's fancied mistreatment of the boy and when, a few days later, she went again to the house prepared to apologize for her anger, the couple had vanished into thin air.

Mr. Inderwick died about this time and Janet returned to the Courtlandt Street home. Soon thereafter this advertisement, the veracious Mr. Barrett reports, appeared in *The Morning Chronicle,* in a January, 1806, issue:

"$1,000 reward will be paid for any information that can be given of a nurse named Milly Seymour, who in the year 1805 lived for several months in the upper part of a two-story brick house in Maiden Lane, two doors below Nassau Street, on the south side; or of a male child named Rupert, then a babe; or of her husband, William Seymour. Apply to Mrs. I., at No. 22, Courtlandt Street."

Apparently broken-hearted over her sin and the disappearance of her son, Mrs. Roosevelt-Inderwick herself died a few years later. Mr. Barrett says that a death notice appeared in the *Museum* of July 25, 1812. He says also that the request for information appeared in "all of the journals of 1809" and in the New York *Gazette* of 1810. He found it once more as late as 1856 in *The Herald,* with a lawyer's name appended. From this he surmised that if the son could be found, and if he could prove his claim, he would be heir to a vast fortune in New York real estate.

There would be no need of taking this fantastic tale seriously if the chronicler had not used the name Roosevelt. He was well aware of the standing of that family, for in early chapters he had written considerably (if sometimes inaccurately) about them, and he obviously held them in high esteem. It would seem from this that the name was deliberately used. But the Roosevelt genealogies list no Janet Roosevelt of this period—and the advertisements, even in altered form, *do not appear in any of the sources that he quotes!*

Thus the great Roosevelt mystery and scandal must be returned to its origin, the imaginative pages of *The Old Merchants of New York.*

CHAPTER XI

James the Democrat and Tammany Hall

ON WEDNESDAY, February 23, 1830, that fastidious poseur and ex-Mayor of New York, Philip Hone, wrote in his diary: "We were amused with a foolish piece of vanity by one of our townsmen now in Paris—a visiting card:

'James J. Roosevelt
'Membre du Conseil du New York et Attaché
'L'embassade des Etats Unis.
'Pres S.M.L.R. des F.'

"This," the caustic Hone added, "is one way of bringing a New York assistant alderman into notice and transforming a minister plenipotentiary into an ambassador."

Ex-Mayor Hone, whose social peregrinations brought him into frequent contact with members of the Roosevelt Family, did not like the contemporary Roosevelts. They were, he felt, pushing; and, besides, they were not politically acceptable. Only two years before he made the malicious entry in his diary, this same James J. Roosevelt had thrown himself into the campaign for the election of that dangerous demagogue, Andrew Jackson. He was a traitor to his class.

James J. Roosevelt was decidedly a man of parts. He was named James after his father and grandfather, but in family circles he was known as James J. J. or James I. Roosevelt, the "I" being used as a numeral, rather than as a letter, to distinguish him from others of this name in the Family. Like his brother Cornelius he was sent to Columbia College, but unlike the forerunner of the Oyster Bay branch, James Roosevelt was an apt student and was graduated with the Class of 1815. He did not immediately enter the family hardware business, as did his brother, who, as the oldest son, was to inherit the bulk of their father's fortune. Instead, he studied law, and, after being admitted to the bar, became the partner of Peter Jay.

He took an interest in politics from the beginning—but not in the affairs of the traditional Hamiltonian party which had attracted most members of the family up to this time. There was something of the rebel in him, as there had been in his great-uncle Isaac. He had no apparent personal reasons to espouse the cause of Jackson and Democracy, but he did. He even became a member of Tammany Hall, and at one time was among its more powerful leaders.

In the ten years that passed between his becoming a lawyer and the election of Jackson in 1828, James practiced law, dabbled in city politics, and engaged desultorily in the hardware business with his father and older brother. He was a gay young man, quite aware of his social standing, and a familiar figure at the balls and parties of the era. He liked to drive horses and gad about with the young blades and fashionable ladies of the town.

In 1830, having helped swing New York for "Old Hickory," whose rugged qualities he ardently admired, he gave up both his interest in the hardware business and his reasonably extensive law practice. He went to Paris where Louis Philippe, the Duke of Orleans, had just become king under the guise of a "revolutionary monarch," much to the disgust of the republicans. It was at this time that he passed around the calling card Ex-Mayor Hone thought so presumptuous. He had plenty of money to spend, he dressed in the height of fashion, and he naturally moved in the "best" circles of the international society of post-Revolutionary Paris. It was there that he fell in love.

The girl whose hand he sought was universally considered one of the most beautiful in America. The journalists of the day sang her praise and her many charms were glowingly described. As befitted one whom a Roosevelt courted she came of an excellent family. She had wit and charm and wealth as well as beauty, attributes that made her one of the most sought-after young ladies on either continent.

Cornelia van Ness was the daughter of Cornelius F. van Ness, who had been Governor of Vermont and United States Senator and who was to be Minister to Spain and a Justice of the New York Supreme Court. On May 30, 1831, she was married at the fashionable home of Mrs. Rives, in Paris—as charming a bride as Paris had seen in many a day. There, before a distinguished audience, she was given away by her father's friend, the great General Lafayette. After a European honeymoon, the happy couple returned to New York. Mr. Roosevelt resumed his law practice and his political affairs. Mrs. Roosevelt retired to a long life of child-bearing. Between 1832 and 1851 she was the mother of eleven children.

James Roosevelt was a member of the State Legislature in the sessions of 1835, 1839 and 1840. During these years the Whigs had, as usual, complained bitterly of the dishonesty of New York City elections, and had made many charges of the wholesale stuffing of ballot-boxes. In 1840, while Mr. Roosevelt was in Albany, they brought in a measure for the careful registration of voters in the metropolis. The bill passed the Senate easily enough, but when it came to the Assembly, it ran into the powerful opposition of the Democratic minority. Assemblyman Roosevelt, now somewhat of a behind-the-scenes power in Tammany, was the leader of this group.

Ex-Mayor Hone, whose love for Assemblyman Roosevelt was slight, as indeed it was for all Democrats, was his usual caustic self when he sat down to his diary in March of that year.

"James J. Roosevelt, the leader of the blackguards," he wrote, "in whose person, as its representative, our poor city is disgraced, takes the lead in opposition to the law and resorts to every species of vile, disgraceful conduct and language, in which he is supported by the whole pack!"

Roosevelt's tactics sound familiar. Echoing his fellow "Locofocos" of New York City, he charged that the bill was an upstate attack on the liberties of the city, and he declared that no such frauds occurred in Manhattan as in Albany and Hudson Counties. It was, of course, a spurious defense, for Tammany, even then, depended for its power to a great extent upon "repeaters" and the unnaturalized, alien vote.

In his history of Tammany Hall Gustavus Myers credits Mr. Roosevelt with being of considerable importance in that organization's inner circles. He was, in effect, liaison officer between the Hall and Wall Street, one who carried orders from the bankers to the politicians and dictated nominations and elections in a ruthless manner. Whatever the truth, he was a faithful Indian, even if he never was a "Sachem." He appears to have been no worse and probably some better than the others of the Tammany gang. His name was never involved in any notorious scandal. Mr. Hone gives us one more picture of him:

"We have in the House of Assembly a strong body of Whigs, the speaker, Taylor of Ontario, Wheaton of Albany, etc. There are many fine young men in our ranks. The other party is led by James J. Roosevelt of New York, the chief of a most unworthy delegation of a misrepresented city. *Roosevelt is a small man and very conceited* . . ."

If he used Tammany for his advantage, the Family nevertheless was to make amends, and through no less a person than James Roosevelt's nephew and Theodore Roosevelt's uncle, R. B. Roosevelt, who was in a few years to help unhorse the unsavory Tweed.

The Democracy to which James Roosevelt was faithful gave him his reward. He was elected to the House of Representatives in Washington from 1841 to 1843, during the administration of William Henry Harrison. The machine he had supported in Albany the previous year elected him with a substantial majority. He undoubtedly could have returned for a second term, but he rejected the nomination in 1844. Perhaps he was tired of New York politics and politicians, assistant Aldermen and others. At any rate he went abroad where he spent his time studying European law in the courts of England and France and in his ancestral Holland. Barrett tells us that he met James once in Rotterdam "and trotted him all about, during a great 'Kermis' (Fair) to ascertain whether the New York Dutch which he spoke was the same as spoken in Holland." As the Holland

Dutchmen could not understand Mr. Roosevelt, Barrett concluded that their dialect had deteriorated from that spoken by the Dutch two hundred years earlier "when the 'original Jacob' left Holland for New Amsterdam."

Upon his return to New York with his new learning James Roosevelt resumed his practice, but Democracy soon had further use for him. He was appointed to the New York Supreme Court in 1851, and for one term he was judge ex-officio of the State Court of Appeals. Judge Roosevelt resigned in 1859 to become United States District Attorney for the Southern District of New York. He retired the following year. The last fifteen years of his life he spent in New York and Paris. He died in his New York home April 5, 1875, at the ripe age of eighty years. His wife, the once so beautiful Cornelia, died the following year in Paris.

Of his eleven children only four lived to maturity. None distinguished himself in any line of endeavor, but one of them was the forerunner of an interesting line. Charles Yates Roosevelt was born in 1846, after his family's return from abroad. He married Cornelia Livingston Talbot, a distant relative, and the couple spent much of their time abroad. Their daughter, also named Cornelia, brought up in Switzerland and Italy, was not content to marry an American, but, after the fashion of the day, must find her husband among Europe's nobility. The man of her choice was Baron Clemens von Zedlitz of Berlin. He was an extremely wealthy man when they were married in 1889.

The von Zedlitzes had but one child, who was named Hilda. Her father, the Baron, died in 1901, and the widowed Baroness, née Roosevelt, brought the girl up in luxurious surroundings in Europe. When Mrs. Roosevelt, the mother of the Baroness, died in 1919, it was revealed that a will she had made in 1907 left the Baroness only one dollar, the rest of the reasonably large estate going to William O. Roosevelt, the Baroness's only brother. Since he had died before his mother the Baroness took the matter before the German courts. In 1921 she came to this country and had her cousin, W. Emlen Roosevelt, a banker, appointed temporary administrator of Mrs. Roosevelt's estate, valued at about one hundred fifty thousand dollars. In the meantime she was also having difficulty collecting about one million two hundred thousand dollars of the late Baron's estate, which had been seized in America by the Alien Property Custodian during the World War.

In the meantime Hilda was having her difficulties, also. She had been financially less fortunate in her marriage than her mother, for, although her husband, whom she wedded in 1913, had the imposing name of Gerhard von Koschenbahr Bruck, he was far from wealthy. He was an engineer in Berlin. Gerhard and Hilda Bruck had five daughters and five sons. When the Baroness sought the release of her late husband's funds she made the most of her daughter's plight in her plea to the court. Her poor daughter, she said, had been brought up "in the greatest luxury and ease, and in the manner which, in the opinion of her parents, *was worthy and fitting for a member of the German nobility and of the Roosevelt family. . . .*"

Most of the Baron's property was eventually released and it is presumed the von-Zedlitz-Bruck branch of the Roosevelt family was able to resume some semblance of a luxurious and easy way of life.

CHAPTER XII

A Million Dollar Will

ALTHOUGH THE OBITUARY notice of many a Roosevelt has recorded the charitable instincts of the deceased it remained for James Henry Roosevelt, the bachelor grandson of the first Jacobus, to perpetuate the family name by the endowment of an Institution.

The story of James Henry Roosevelt's life is both beautiful and tragic. His grandfather, Christopher Roosevelt, was the youngest son of Jacobus (the son of Nicholas I) who had married Maria Duryea, a descendant of a Huguenot family from Picardy. Their son, James C. Roosevelt, married a girl of Dutch descent named Catherine Byvank. As might be expected, this James C. Roosevelt was a merchant. He had inherited considerable of the property amassed by Jacobus I, and when he died he left a fair estate to his son James Henry.

James Henry Roosevelt was born in New York November 10, 1800. As a boy he was particularly bright and everyone expected he would have a brilliant career. He chose the law as his profession and went to Columbia, where he was graduated with honors in 1819. He then took up the study of law in earnest and was soon admitted to the bar. While in college he had met Miss Julia Maria Boardman, a charming young lady and a member of an old New York family, with whom he fell deeply in love. They intended to marry soon after he was established in his law office. But a bitter tragedy occurred which ruined their plans forever.

Almost exactly a month after he was admitted to practice he was stricken with paralysis. He was to be an invalid, able to walk only with the use of crutches, for the rest of his life. As was to be the case with a later Roosevelt, he refused to surrender to his infirmity. Although the law was shut to him, the doors of business closed, and society could hold but little pleasure for him, he decided to live as actively as the confinement of his home would allow. He was endowed with the Roosevelt business genius. He tended his estate with infinite care.

James Henry lived simply and unostentatiously, entertaining his close friends, keeping in touch with the world. He knew many people and never allowed himself to grow morose over his misfortune. Throughout the trying years his closest friend was the girl whom he had intended to marry. Neither ever did, and when he died, at the age of sixty-three, he left Miss Boardman an annuity of four thousand dollars and made her the executrix of his will.

Hitherto the name Roosevelt had been mainly confined to the society, financial, and occasionally the political columns of the New York press. But with the filing of James Roosevelt's will the name Roosevelt became front page news, for this little-known member of the family, whose infirmities had kept him long hidden from the public gaze, turned back the greater part of his fortune, which approximated one million dollars, to the use of the city from which it had been wrung.

Most of his property consisted of valuable real estate in Westchester County and in New York City and in valuable and available stocks and bonds. After deducting some personal bequests, including the annuity to Miss Boardman, he left the bulk in trust for the establishment of a hospital. The terms of the will are interesting. The hospital funds were left to "the several and successive presidents, ex officio for the time being of the respective managing boards of those certain five incorporations in the City of New York, known as the Society of the New York Hospital, the College of Physicians and Surgeons, the New York Eye Infirmary, the Demilt Dispensary, the New York Institution for the Blind and to the Honorable James I. Roosevelt, Edwin Clark, Esq., John M. Knox, Esq., and Adrian H. Muller, Esq., all of New York, for the establishment in the city of New York of a hospital for the reception and relief of sick and diseased persons, and for its permanent endowment."

Mr. Roosevelt bequeathed the use of his real estate—which included property that had been owned by Roosevelts since Jacobus and Johannes bought up the Beekman Swamp in the 1720's—to his nephew James C. Roosevelt Brown, of Rye, N. Y., and his heirs. But Brown died childless forty days after James Roosevelt's death on Nov. 30, 1863, and left the real estate to the same institution his uncle had endowed.

Roosevelt Hospital was opened in 1871 on the block bounded by Ninth and Tenth Avenues and Fifty-Eighth and Fifty-Ninth Streets. Today one of the largest semi-public hospitals in New York, it still draws sustenance from the early Swamp purchases of the brothers Roosevelt. Had no member of the family achieved fame, New Yorkers at least would know, and in many instances bless, the name borne by James Henry Roosevelt, the first outstanding philanthropist of the tribe.

CHAPTER XIII

Mother Seton and the Archbishop of Baltimore

THERE HAVE BEEN several Protestant clergymen in the Roosevelt Family. There was one Archbishop of the Roman Catholic Church.

James Roosevelt Bayley might have risen to a high place in the Protestant Episcopal Church if his Aunt Elizabeth Ann Bayley had not turned to the Church of Rome for spiritual solace and become Mother Seton, the founder of the Sisters of Charity, whose cause for canonization was begun at the Vatican in 1909. His great uncle was the first rector of New York's famed Trinity Church and there were other Episcopal ministers among his near relatives. And he himself went so far as to become briefly the rector of an Episcopal church in Harlem. But the influence of his almost sainted aunt and an innate mysticism of his own brought him into the Roman Church where he was deeply loved and highly honored for many years.

The future Archbishop was born at Rye, N. Y., on August 23, 1814. His father was Dr. Richard Bayley and he in turn was the son of *the* Dr. Richard Bayley, who had taught anatomy at Columbia College and waged an unremitting war against the "yellow jack" until he finally succumbed to "ship fever" contracted from attending Irish immigrants who caught it on the long, horrible voyages in the airless steerages in which they came to New York. His mother was the former Charlotte

Amelia Barclay, and she was the daughter of Andrew Barclay, the merchant, and Helen Roosevelt Barclay, the daughter of Jacobus and Catherina Hardenbroock Roosevelt.

Although the first Dr. Richard, a crusty Tory, had forfeited most of his property when he became chief staff surgeon to Sir Guy Carleton, the British Army commander of New York during the Revolution, the apostacy had been forgiven, the family fortune had been recouped and young James Roosevelt Bayley was sent away for his education to the fashionable Mount Pleasant School near Amherst, Massachusetts. There he decided upon following a Naval career and even went so far in this direction as to obtain a commission as a midshipman. But by the time he was ready for college he had changed his mind. Instead, he entered Trinity College at Hartford, Connecticut.

At Trinity he studied for the Episcopal priesthood. He was graduated when he was twenty-one years old and shortly thereafter was given charge of a parish in Harlem. Six years later, however, he resigned. His aunt had already become famous as Mother Seton and doubtless her influence had much to do with his decision. He had an idea of becoming a Jesuit monk when he left his Harlem parish and sailed for the Holy City. He was in Rome a year when he was baptised and received into the Roman Catholic Church. After his baptism he went to Paris to study at the theological seminary there. In March, 1844, he returned to New York and was ordained to the priesthood by Bishop Hughes. At once he was assigned to a professorship and to the vice presidency at the seminary at Fordham. His ecclesiastic career which was to take him much higher than many a Catholic-born priest has climbed, had begun.

After serving briefly as acting President at Fordham Father Bayley was given the busy parish at the Quarantine Station on Staten Island, to work spiritually among the immigrants whose condition in those days was hardly better than when his grandfather had administered to their physical ailments many years before. Next he was secretary to Bishop Hughes, who highly regarded his administrative abilities and who gave him leisure to collect the data for his valuable book *A Brief Sketch of the Early History of the Catholic Church on the Island of New York.*

In 1853, Rome decreed that the diocese of Newark be established, and Father Bayley was named as its first Bishop. He was consecrated at St. Patrick's Cathedral by the Papal Nuncio to Brazil who was in New York en route to Rome at the time. It was an elaborate ceremony, one of the most colorful held in the city up to that time, because the new Bishops of Burlington, Vermont, and of Brooklyn, New York, were consecrated at the same time.

The diocese of Newark consisted of some forty thousand Roman Catholics of Irish and German extraction and little else when Bishop Bayley crossed the North River to take up his duties. His executive capacities were taxed to the utmost, but within ten years he could boast a Benedictine and a Passionist monastery, a mother house of the Sisters of Charity, a college and seminary for potential priests, an academy for girls and a boarding school for boys, as well as churches and parochial schools.

James Roosevelt Bayley was Bishop of Newark for twenty-eight years and it was with great reluctance that in 1872 he left the diocese he had established to go to Baltimore to succeed Archbishop Spalding as the eighth archbishop of that important Catholic center. He was not to be archbishop long. During his first year he freed the cathedral from debt and consecrated it. Then illness overcame him. He asked for a coadjutor and James Gibbons, the Bishop of Richmond who was to become America's best-loved Cardinal, was sent to his aid. He went to Europe seeking health, but in the summer of 1877 he returned to Newark where he died in the simple house that he had occupied so long. At his own request he was buried at Emmitsburg, Maryland, beside Mother Seton, his beloved aunt.

Archbishop Bayley might have been a rich man. His grandfather, James Roosevelt, had named him among his heirs in his original will but when he became a Catholic he altered the will, cutting the priest entirely off. Walter Barrett is author of the legend that he did so in anger and left the money instead to found a Protestant seminary. The fact is that his grandfather labored under the delusion that a priest could not own property and, being meticulous in business affairs, wrote a codicil so that there would be no difficulty after his death. Much of the property that would have become Archbishop Bayley's passed to James Henry Roosevelt, who of course handed it along to Roosevelt Hospital at his death. Archbishop Bayley was urged by his friends to contest the will in court, but this he refused to do on the ground that it would be too worldly an act for one consecrated to the Church.

CHAPTER XIV

The Organ Maker

NOT MANY creative geniuses have graced the Roosevelt family. Perhaps the one member of this family who most nearly merited this description was Nicholas Roosevelt, the inventor and proponent of the side-wheeler. After his death in 1854 there was none to distinguish himself, outside of business and banking, until Hilborne Lewis Roosevelt came along.

Hilborne Roosevelt was the son of Silas Weir Roosevelt and the grandson of Cornelius van Schaack Roosevelt, Oyster Bay progenitor and the founder of the Chemical National Bank. His mother was the former Mary West. Although his father was essentially a business man, interested in the financial affairs of the brokerage firm of Roosevelt & Son, which was started by his brother, James Alfred Roosevelt, he was not without cultural interests. He was especially fond of good music. Hilborne was his second son, the others being Cornelius, who was to spend most of his life in Paris, James West, and Frank. None showed any great aptitude for business. They did not have to, for Silas Weir Roosevelt, through inheritance and his own initiative, was in comfortable circumstances.

Silas, in many respects, was an admirable father and close to his children, but even he was a little disappointed when Hilborne, whose musical interest was unquestioned, made up his mind to become a mechanic. Back in the days when Nicholas spurned the sales-counter of his brother's hardware store to become an apprentice in an iron works, the dividing line between the gentleman and the mechanic was not as strictly drawn as it had become when young Hilborne was growing up. He was born December 21, 1849, in New York. Some time in his early youth he had become fascinated with organs and had set his heart upon becoming an organ builder. Then, when his family, which by now took the Roosevelt social position very seriously, opposed his wishes, he was faced with a familiar dilemma. He solved it as many another youth has—as his own great-uncle Nicholas had done many years before—by spurning family pride and going to work. His first job was as an apprentice in the shop of Hall & Labagh, organ makers, in New York.

His uncles, with their fine offices in Wall Street, snorted, but this made no difference to the rather sensitive young man. He worked hard and learned all that he could be taught in Hall & Labagh's shops. Hard work did not curb his enthusiasm. When the time came he made several trips to Europe to study the finer points of organ making. He was particularly interested in the electric organ, realizing that the steadiness of electric control ought to produce an effect impossible with the old hand-pumped affairs which his sponsors manufactured. He was one of the very first to study the application of new electric devices to the manufacture of organs. Indeed, when he was only twenty years old, he took out the first patent for an electric organ ever issued in the United States.

Three years later he opened his own organ factory on Eighteenth Street in New York. Although primarily interested in the technical end, he seems to have had more of the Roosevelt genius for business than old Nicholas had. Within a few years he had moved to larger quarters and had established branch factories in Baltimore and Philadelphia. Undoubtedly by now the members of the family, who had shuddered to think that a Roosevelt would deign to be a factory-hand, had forgiven him. He was making money. Unlike the other inventor of the family his patents were secure.

It was at the Eighteenth Street factory that he built the first electric organ ever constructed in this country. He designed it for the Philadelphia Centennial Exhibition. There it attracted wide attention. Experts who heard it were amazed at its tonal qualities and said that it combined the best points of European "voicing" with effects never heard before on either continent. The officers of the Massachusetts Charitable Mechanic Association were so taken with this triumph of the mechanic's art that they bought it and had it installed in Boston's new Mechanics Hall, at that time one of the largest and most popular meeting halls and exhibition places in the East.

Hilborne Roosevelt built many organs during his brief career. Some of them were the largest then known in this country. Among them were those built for the Protestant Episcopal Cathedral, at Garden City, Long Island, for Trinity Church, and for the Grace Protestant Episcopal Church of New York.

But he did not confine himself to organ building. Electricity was a new science, and the telephone a coming business, in those days. Hilborne Lewis was attracted to the new device for communication and became interested in the Bell Telephone Company. For this he did a wide variety of work. Among the creative electricians of his day he was best known as the inventor of the automatic switch-hook, on which he received royalties for many years.

In 1883 he married Kate Shippen, the daughter of William Watson Shippen, of Hoboken, New Jersey. Three years later he died, at the tragically young age of thirty-seven years. For the next ten years his brother, Frank H. Roosevelt, continued the business. Then he sold the stock and patents of the Roosevelt firm to the Farrand & Votey Company of Detroit, Michigan, now out of business.

His was a brief, electric career. He had few interests except his work. The making of money meant less to him than good workmanship. He spent thousands of dollars developing the electric organ valve. H. C. Lahee and Alfred Dolge—historians of the American organ—agree that he was a significant figure in the development of the American organ and that all subsequent improvements stem from his defiance of his family's distaste for having a "mechanic" in their select fold.

CHAPTER XV

A Ship Builder and Sailors

THERE WERE, of course, many other scattered Roosevelts, by name or birth; most have been forgotten in the shuffle of time; but here and there one stands out slightly above the contemporary crowd and is worthy of mention in the family chronicle.

Briefly, then, let it be recorded that Solomon Roosevelt, Jr., the great-grandson of Nicholas, the goldsmith, played his small part in the nation's maritime history. He was born at Alburg, Vermont, in 1807, and evidently inherited his great-grandfather's love of craftsmanship, for at an early age he became a shipbuilder of considerable prominence. He spent his apprenticeship—this branch of the family, not being in Society, was undisturbed by any disagreeable contrast between a mechanic and a gentleman—with Webb, Allen & Eckford, shipbuilders. Then, after working for others, he moved to Keyport, New Jersey, where he founded his own shipyard. There, a few years later, he joined with Brown & Bell in taking the contract for the *Baltic* and *Pacific,* the first steamers to cross the Atlantic. Later, under the firm name of Roosevelt & Joyce he built several other steamers. In 1865, evidently tiring of the sea, he moved to Delaware County, Ohio, where he won a local reputation by erecting the first building in the town of Ashley.

All of the Rooseveltian love of the sea was not infiltrated into the blood from other sources. A grandson of Nicholas Roosevelt, the inventor, had a career in the United States Navy of some distinction. Nicholas Latrobe Roosevelt I was the son of Samuel Roosevelt and Mary Jane Horton Roosevelt. Samuel was a business man with extensive interests in the South prior to the Civil War and later in New York, where he held office in several financial institutions. A Northern sympathizer during that conflict he spent freely for the relief of prisoners of war. His son was educated at the University of New York, and then became a midshipman in the Navy.

After his graduation from Annapolis in 1869 Nicholas L. Roosevelt's active sea-going career began. He rapidly advanced from the rank of ensign to master, and then to lieutenant. He was attached to Admiral Roger's staff at the start of the third Korean expedition, that bloody foray of 1871 on which France and America revenged the death of French missionaries and American adventurers. During the attack by gunboats on the river forts he showed "great bravery" and was mentioned in dispatches. Later he served in Atlantic coastal stations, on vessels in European waters and the Pacific, and in Asiatic stations. He retired from the Navy in 1874—and entered the insurance business in New York!

Lieutenant Roosevelt had married a Miss Eleanor Dean of New York and in 1879, at their home in Morristown, New Jersey, they had a son who was to add naval lustre to the family history. He, too, was named Henry Latrobe Roosevelt. In 1896 the son entered the United States Naval Academy at Annapolis, Maryland, and during part of the Spanish-American fiasco served as a midshipman with the Marine Corps. That was to be his branch of the service until his retirement in 1920.

During his years in the service he saw wide active duty, being stationed at various times in Philadelphia, Panama, Cuba and Haiti. In 1916 and 1917 he was colonel of the gendarmerie at Haiti, after having served throughout the World War at the Marine base at Quantico, Virginia. After his resignation from active duty he was, for a time, engaged in the oil "game" in Oklahoma, but in 1923 he joined the Radio Corporation of America, a less messy business, and for five years was the European manager for the corporation. During these years he saw built the large radio stations that have since become familiar outlets of news at Ankara, Turkey, and Warsaw, Poland.

After his return to this country in 1933 to head the Radio Real Estate Corporation, Col. Roosevelt was recommended to his distant cousin, who had just become President, by Secretary of Navy Claude A. Swanson, who wanted him for his Assistant Secretary. He thus became the fourth bearer of the Roosevelt name to occupy this office.

In this post he was no idle figure-head. His own inclination, his Roosevelt drive, would not let that be. The poor health of his chief gave him opportunity and for a time he was the Acting Secretary. He made many tours of inspecion. Constantly, in public speeches and statements, he urged that the United States build up its navy to top strength. He expressed his credo thus:

"There is no such thing as second best in war. You either have to win or you will lose. Through having an adequate navy the chances of ever being engaged in a war are greatly diminished."

Other, greater Roosevelts had voiced similar statements while occupying the same post. But a war-weary America did not care for great navies then.

Henry Latrobe Roosevelt died in service on February 22, 1936, from a heart attack following influenza. Two sons, William Morrow Roosevelt and Henry Latrobe Roosevelt, and a daughter, Eleanor Katherine Roosevelt, survived to carry on the line descended from Nicholas, the inventor.

One other member of this branch deserves at least a passing glance. Samuel Montgomery Roosevelt, the brother of Henry Latrobe Roosevelt I, was a decided contrast to his salty brother. He had no interest in the active life. Instead he started out to be an artist, and as a young man he studied painting in Paris under Benjamin Constant, the popular Nineteenth Century artist who divided his interest between Oriental battle-scenes and portraits of Queen Victoria. Later Sam Roosevelt studied under other Parisians, but it does not seem to have done him much good. His only listed exhibitions were at the Art Students League and eventually he went "into business," where presumably he was a successful, if not happy, man.

CHAPTER XVI

The Sportsman Reformer

WHEN ALL STRIFE is ended and all wars are done and the historian sits down to contemplate the long history of the presidential administration of Franklin D. Roosevelt, it may be that his most important chapter will deal less with struggle and more with his policies of conservation and rehabilitation of the land. As one now looks back upon the work of Theodore Roosevelt his belligerency fades into nothing or, at most, into something comic, while his domestic endeavors to save the public property for the public's use re-establishes him as an important figure in the history of the United States. Undoubtedly the Long Island environment of Theodore's boyhood and the early years spent by Franklin in the fertile valley of the Hudson had much to do in conditioning both. Neither was exactly a "country boy" in the American tradition, but each grew up with soil and grass under his feet. In Theodore's youth, Long Island was still a highly rural region, a farming country that up to 1895 was the chief source of New York City's milk supply, a far different place from the country-club, golf-club, and Bob-Moses-park Long Island of the present day. Franklin Roosevelt's Dutchess County was even more rustic than Long Island— and it was his year-round home in his childhood days. Environment, then, had much to do with the interest of the two Presidents Roosevelt in "saving the land," but there was also, and perhaps it was of equal importance, a family precedent. There was Uncle Bob.

Robert Barnhill Roosevelt—some sense of delicacy made him forego family pride and call himself Robert Barnwell Roosevelt in after life—was the next-to-youngest of the five boys born to Cornelius van Schaack Roosevelt and his wife, the former Margaret Barnhill. In the nearly eighty years that followed his birth on August 7, 1829, in New York, he did many things and left his mark on several aspects of American middle class life. In several respects he was the outstanding member of the clan since Isaac Roosevelt's Revolutionary day. But the later, and naturally more publicised, achievements of his nephew Teddy and his cousin Franklin have combined to make him the forgotten man of the Roosevelt tribe. This is unfortunate, for within his limitations Uncle Bob stands shoulders high among the money-grabbing merchants, the Parisian sportsmen, the ineffectual doctors, the unknown artists, and all the others who bore the name Roosevelt in the middle years of the family's American existence.

Uncle Bob was completely aware of the fact that he was born a gentleman and a Roosevelt and expressed his interest in his ancestry by serving as President of the Sons of the American Revolution and a founder of the Holland Society. He could afford to do the things he wanted to do without having to worry at the same time over the vulgar problem of earning a living. In his generation there were several like him, and the next generation, that of Teddy, supplied several others who subscribed to the truly British-aristocrat theory that the young man of independent means should devote his life and dedicate his talents to the nasty business of politics in a democracy. Teddy, of course, was the outstanding example. Henry Cabot Lodge was another, to name but one of those genteel and erudite young men who must at one time or another have run across the name Machiavelli in the encyclopaedia or in the books they were induced to read at Harvard. Others of this ilk may be found by the interested student in the index of *The Education of Henry Adams,* or in the text of such an iconoclastic work as *The President Makers.*

The unfortunate fact regarding Uncle Bob's life, which was devoted to the thankless yet gentlemanly task of political reform both in the heart of the city and out where the wild duck flies, is that so few of his reforms reached into the immediate economic or social life of his contemporary America. But the truth remains: at their time and in their place and on the part of an upper-middle-class "gentleman" like Bob Roosevelt it required a modicum of personal courage to leave the purlieus of Wall Street and enlist in the unpopular ranks of politics. And so, if Uncle Bob's reforms did not "change the world," they were, at least, directed towards making that particular world in which Roosevelts had to live, willy nilly, a better spot for others as well as Roosevelts to occupy.

From young manhood Bob Roosevelt was interested in a number of things that were characteristic of the later years of his life. He liked to hunt; he sailed boats off the Long Island summer place his grandfather had built overlooking the ocean at Oyster Bay, Long Island; he enjoyed all the sports of boyhood: from hunting birds' eggs to riding horseback. Since his father could afford it, he was given an excellent early education, by private tutors and in "select" New York schools. He did not go to college. He spent long summers outdoors at Oyster Bay; during the winter, when he was confined to studying indoors, he showed what has been called a "precocious interest in politics and English composition."

There seems to be no doubt about his having been precocious. When he was twenty-one years old two major events happened. He was married and he was admitted to practice before the New York bar. Shortly after his marriage to Elizabeth Ellis of New York city, the daughter of the banker, John S. Ellis, and a member of a wealthy and socially prominent family, he moved into a brick and brownstone house on East Twentieth Street, next door to a similar small house occupied by the first Theodore Roosevelt, his youngest and favorite brother. He was to live there many years of his life. The house where brother Theodore lived, and where Teddy Roosevelt was born, is now preserved as a museum of the Oyster Bay Roosevelts— those whom Frank Sullivan once with delightful irreverence called the Out-of-Season Roosevelts. Known as Roosevelt House it contains many papers relevant to Bob Roosevelt, whose biography, strangely enough, still awaits writing. Among the relics preserved there is Bob Roosevelt's political "Black Book," which is not without interest for the politically minded historian.

In spite of his lack of an academic training Bob Roosevelt soon attracted attention to himself as a lawyer. Although he had the disadvantage of an "aristocratic" background he became definitely interested in politics. He was, as most Roosevelts were in those days before the Civil War, a member of the Democratic Party. Bob Roosevelt remained faithful to the party until his death. His brother Theodore flirted with Republicanism and was, so far as can be learned, the first apostate in the Family.

When the Civil War approached Bob Roosevelt identified himself with the Democratic supporters of the Union cause. He helped to found the Loyal National League and the Union League Club, two of the most powerful propaganda organizations established to further the Northern cause. While he, and his brother, also a Union League founder, were doing their bit for the Union by making speeches and supplying funds, the ladies of the Roosevelt tribe were active on several auxiliary committees. Two of Uncle Bob's sisters-in-law made a fine silk flag, embroidered with the words "For God and Right," which they proudly presented, with due ceremonies, to a troop of Negro soldiers recruited in New York. They were all very patriotic. But none was as actively patriotic, and at such a cost, as their cousin George.

George Washington Roosevelt of Chester, Pennsylvania, quit his job as a clerk in a store when he was seventeen years old to enlist in Company K of the Twenty-Sixth Regiment, Pennsylvania Volunteers. He was quickly promoted from private to corporal, to first sergeant. He soon saw enough service for the entire Family. In the grim and awful battle at Gettysburg he was so severely wounded that the army doctors had to amputate his left leg at the hip. He was breveted captain for his gallant services, and later he won the Congressional Medal for his meritorious conduct there and at the Battle of Bull Run. The great disappointment of his life was that after President Lincoln's second call for volunteers his physical condition prevented him from going again to the front with the company of soldiers that he had raised in Philadelphia. After the war he entered the consular service, and was consul at Aukland, New Zealand, St. Helena, Montanzas, Cuba, and Bordeau, France. Then he was made Consul General at Brussels, Belgium, where he became a friend of King Leopold, who never seemed to tire of his tales of Civil War strategy, on which he claimed to be an expert. He died there in 1907 at the age of sixty-seven.

While Cousin George was harrying the Rebels in the fierce campaign Bob Roosevelt and his brother Theodore were busy, in a gentlemanly way, in New York. Of the two, Theodore seems to have been the more active, for he helped to raise and equip regiments; he aided in the organization of the Sanitary Commission, which was founded to comfort the soldiers in the field and at home; he was a New York commissioner of the Allottment Commission; he assisted in founding the Protective War Claims Association, a society which collected dues owed to wounded war veterans; and, in his own house, he organized the Soldiers Employment Bureau, an important factor in post-war life.

When the war had ended Bob Roosevelt began to hit his stride as a political reformer. In 1864 he had become the secretary of the Citizens Association, an organization of well-to-do reformers interested in city affairs, and for many years thereafter represented the association in the courts and lobbied in its behalf before the legislature at Albany. One of his prosecutions resulted in ridding the city of incompetent health wardens and led to the setting up of a comparatively efficient Board of Health. He also had a leading part in the establishment of the paid New York Fire Department, that supplanted the old volunteer companies, whose alcoholic exploits and intense rivalry for too many years had added to the excitement if not the safety of New York life.

Sometime during this period Bob Roosevelt had become acquainted with Charles G. Halpine who, among other things, had been private secretary to P. T. Barnum and Stephen Douglas. At the present he was a member of the general committee of Tammany Hall and the recognized leader of the opposition to Mayor Fernando Wood's administration. He also edited *The Citizen,* the politely militant organ of the Citizens Association. Previously he had been editor of Boston's humorous weekly *The Carpet Bag* and he had written poems for the newspapers where, as Fitz-Greene Halleck observed, when they were published in book form, they should have remained forever. An Irish Protestant, he wrote under the name of "Miles O'Reilly," and his scorching letters sent from Southern army camps to vacillating Northern editors during the Civil War had done much good for the Union cause.

Bob Roosevelt, who already had several books to his credit (mainly about birds and nature), undertook the writing of editorials for Halpine's *Citizen*. His writings were a minor but still potent factor in the campaign against Boss Tweed, the corrupt leader of Tammany Hall. After the initial exposure of the "ring" by Editor Jennings of *The New York Times*, who presented documentary proof of Tammany's raids on the public till, Bob Roosevelt became a leader of the famous "Committee of Seventy," which was greatly responsible for Tweed's downfall. He addressed its first indignation meeting at Cooper Union and thereafter assumed leadership of the Independent Democrats who were opposed to the Tweed Ring's domination of the party in New York. He managed the 1872 reform campaign which resulted in the election of the eminently respectable William F. Havemeyer as Mayor. At this time Bob Roosevelt was also serving in Congress, where he found time to expose a corrupt political ring operating, Tammany-like, in the voteless District of Columbia.

But political reform was not Bob Roosevelt's only interest, nor was it, in the long run, his most important. Although much of his time was taken up by his legal practice he found the opportunity to get out into the woods and onto the streams that he dearly loved. The result of his native explorations were three books in a field then not greatly exploited. These were *The Game Fish of the Northern States of America and the British Provinces, Superior Fishing*, and *Game Birds of the Coasts and Lakes of the Northern States of America*. Favorably reviewed, they enjoyed a wide sale, and they had an important influence in creating the fad of the hunter-naturalist, a cult in which his nephew, Teddy, long excelled. He was, in the opinion of some natural scientists, a far sounder student than Teddy, who always prided himself on his standing as a scientist.

Even while enjoying Nature Bob Roosevelt was a reformer. He realized that it would not be long before all the game and fish would be destroyed by the greedy hunter if some measures were not found to check the national lust for slaughter. Thus he ardently promoted the work of state and national sportsmen's associations, An astute lobbyist endowed with a true Rooseveltian understanding of politicians, he induced the 1872 legislature to pass a law—later widely copied by other states—which set up the pioneer New York State Fishery Commission. For the next twenty years he was either a member or the chairman of this commission. He introduced new artificial methods of propagating fish and he fought for the protection of streams against pollution by the indiscriminate dumping of sewage and industrial waste.

In 1872 his father, Cornelius, died at Oyster Bay and the following year Bob Roosevelt received a large inheritance, made up mainly of stocks in railroad companies and large industrial firms. He retired then from the law and became a director of many corporations. Thereafter he was busy looking after his interests for many years. But in 1879 politics, or to put it more politely, public service, beckoned again and he began a three year term as a Commissioner of the great Roebling's engineering masterpiece, the Brooklyn Bridge. In 1882 he served in the ancient and traditional Rooseveltian post—a member of the Board of Aldermen, the first of his name to do so in many years. Most of his time was spent forcing through a pure food law for the city. Six years later, during the last portion of the first administration of Grover Cleveland, he was appointed Minister to the Netherlands, and when, later, the Boer War broke out, he was, as he recorded in his own sketch in *Who's Who in America* a "member of every committee to aid the Boers."

In 1887 the wife he had married when he was twenty-one and a bright young novitiate at the bar, died. The next year he married Mrs. Marion T. Fortescue, née O'Shea, a widow whose father hailed from Nenagh, Ireland. By his first wife he had four children, Margaret, John Ellis, Helen (who died young) and R. B. Roosevelt, Jr.

The love for reform and for politics was in his blood and

even in his later years he could not desert the battlefield. As the recognized leader of all Democratic reform groups he waged several unsuccessful fights against re-intrenched Tammany. His zeal for reform naturally robbed him of Tammany's support and his thoroughgoing support of the Democratic Party's major national policies prevented his endorsement by Republicans. Thus he was kept from realizing his one great ambition—to be Mayor of New York. He was treasurer of the Democratic National Committee at the time of President Cleveland's second election.

Uncle Bob Roosevelt lived to see his nephew become President of the United States. He never could understand Teddy's allegiance to Republicanism, which he knew was as corrupt as Tammany, but he took no little satisfaction from seeing his relative in the White House encourage the principles of conservation and political reform, to which he had devoted his life. When he died, at Sayville, L. I., in 1906, another relative, who was to further his beliefs under the banner of his beloved Democratic Party, was studying law at Columbia University— the young husband of Uncle Bob's grand niece.

Uncle Bob had bought a large estate near Lotus Lake in Sayville, L. I., in 1868, and there he had built a sumptuous home. Later, when his two sons grew up, they also erected dwellings next each other on the estate, complete with swimming pools and greenhouses and other gentlemanly necessities. A wire fence ran between the two sections. The brothers were not the best of friends and frequently quarrelled. Neither of the boys possessed their father's love of political battle. John Ellis Roosevelt, the older of the pair, became a Wall Street lawyer, and Bob, Jr., devoted himself to building up his inheritance; his fortune, at one time, was estimated as worth nearly two million dollars.

John Ellis Roosevelt was the central figure of a lawsuit which was widely reported in the New York press. It was, to say the least, distasteful to the Family. His first wife was Nannie Vance, the daughter of S. B. H. Vance, who was Acting Mayor of New York in 1874, completing the term of Uncle Bob's reform candidate, Mayor Havemeyer. They had two daughters. One married her second cousin, Philip J. Roosevelt, of Oyster Bay.

The other became the wife of Fairman Dick and was killed in 1926 at Westbury, Long Island, while riding to hounds with the Meadowbrook Hunt pack. Mrs. Roosevelt died at Sayville in 1913.

The following year John Ellis Roosevelt married again. His bride, the former wife of Lt. H. E. Briscoe, a United States Navy paymaster, was twenty-five years his junior and the younger sister of his brother's second wife. They had met at Sayville. As might be expected the marriage was a failure. It soon found its way into the courts. The second Mrs. Roosevelt sued for separation and alimony while he sought to have the marriage annulled. Because John Roosevelt was the cousin of Teddy, the newspapers had a minor holiday, especially when brother Bob came down from Washington, where he made his home, to tell of the unprintably abusive language he had heard brother John use to his bride—and Bob's sister-in-law. Although no divorce was granted, the couple was separated. When John Roosevelt died, in 1939, he left one-third of his estate to his estranged wife. The rest went to his daughter, Jean.

Bob Roosevelt, Jr., died in 1929 at his Sayville home, which he called "The Lilacs," leaving two daughters and a grandson. His only son, also named Robert Barnwell Roosevelt, was killed when he fell in front of a bus early one grey morning in New York.

CHAPTER XVII

Towards Oyster Bay

CORNELIUS VAN SCHAACK ROOSEVELT, the virtual founder of the Oyster Bay, or Theodore, branch of the family, was the last of the Roosevelt Dutchmen. The oldest of the six children of Jacobus and Maria Van Schaack Roosevelt, he was born in New York city on January 30, 1794, and from almost that very day he took the name of Roosevelt seriously. In his *Autobiography* his grandson Teddy recalls him vaguely and briefly as being "of almost purely Dutch blood."

"When he was young he still spoke some Dutch, and Dutch was last used in the services of the Dutch Reformed Church in New York while he was a boy."

In his rather heavy-handed way Teddy revived a family anecdote concerning Cornelius.

"In *his* boyhood Sunday was as dismal a day for small Calvinistic children of Dutch descent as if they had been of Puritan or Scotch Covenanting or French Huguenot descent— and I speak as one proud of his Holland, Huguenot, and Covenanting ancestors, and proud that the blood of that stark Puritan divine Jonathan Edwards flows in the veins of his children. One summer afternoon, after listening to an unusually long Dutch Reformed sermon for the second time that day, my grandfather, a small boy, running home before the congregation had dispersed, ran into a party of pigs, which then wandered free in New York's streets. He promptly mounted a big boar, which no less promptly bolted and carried him at full speed through the midst of the outraged congregation."

Never again, so far as is known, did Cornelius outrage anyone. His was a sedate and serious career. When he was a young man his father sent him to Columbia College, but he had no taste for the academic life and he was not graduated. He was, however, completely at home in the counting room. He became his father's partner, and when old Jacobus died he inherited a sizable share of the estate. This he tended well all his life and he died a rich man. The one thing that is most generally remembered about him is that he was one of the founders of the Chemical National Bank of New York.

On December 13, 1799, Cornelius married Margaret Barnhill of Philadelphia. Her forebears, as Teddy proudly recalled, had come to Pennsylvania with William Penn, "some in the same ship with him; they were of the usual type of the immigration of that particular place and time." Among them were Welsh and English Quakers, an Irishman who was not a Quaker, and "peace loving Germans, who were among the founders of Germantown, having been driven from their Rhineland homes when the armies of Louis the Fourteenth ravaged the Palatinate." There were Scotch-Irish immigrants in Margaret's ancestry also. Her father was Robert Barnhill, a merchant, and her mother was Elizabeth Potts, the granddaughter of a farmer who had been a member of the Provincial Assembly.

"My grandmother," Teddy recalled years later, "was a woman of singular sweetness and strength, the keystone in the arch of her relations with her husband and sons." She learned to speak Dutch, and even taught little Teddy nursery songs in that language. She was an educated woman, well read, gracious and able. She gave her husband six children. All were sons and five of them grew to maturity.

The oldest, Silas Weir Roosevelt, was born in 1823. He was followed by James Alfred Roosevelt, Cornelius van Schaack Roosevelt, Jr., Robert Barnhill Roosevelt, Theodore Roosevelt I, and William Wallace Roosevelt. Of these children Robert Barnhill Roosevelt was the only one who varied the pattern.

He was a sportsman, politician, reformer and writer. The others were businessmen, purely and simply.

Silas Weir Roosevelt's one claim to distinction is that he was the father of Hilborne Lewis Roosevelt, the organ builder. His wife was Mary West, and there were other sons. One, Cornelius, spent most of his life in Paris where he was known as a gentleman sport. He was a prominent member of the Racing Club and sponsored the Roosevelt Challenge Cup for the four kilometers footrace which, from the Gay Nineties until the outbreak of the World War, was run every year in October. He was married to a Frenchwoman in Paris and had three children. One, Hilda Roosevelt, became a singer, appearing in 1919 at the Opera Comique. The critics were kind. Edward returned to New York where he is now in business. André attained some fame as an aviator and explorer. His moving picture of Bali attracted some attention in 1937. Silas's other children were James West Roosevelt and Frank, who died unmarried in 1895.

James Alfred Roosevelt, the second son of Cornelius, was of the mold. He was born July 13, 1825, and when he was only twenty years old his father took him into his mercantile firm. Eventually he succeeded Cornelius as head of the firm. Cornelius spent most of his declining years at the Oyster Bay estate, which he built as a summer resort early in the Nineteenth Century. He died there in 1871, at the ripe age of seventy-seven years.

Seven years after his father's death, James Alfred established the brokerage firm of Roosevelt & Son and spent the rest of his life in or around Wall Street, where he had his finger in many financial pies. He was, of course, an officer of the Chemical National Bank. As president of the Broadway Improvement Association he was interested in New York real estate. Like many other fashionable men of his day he was on the board of managers of the Delaware & Hudson Canal Co., which later led his firm to become interested in railroads. He was a director of several insurance companies, a number of banks, and the Central & South American Telegraph Company.

James Alfred liked New York society, in which he and his wife, the former Elizabeth Norris Emlen of Philadelphia, were prominent. He belonged to the best clubs, Metropolitan,

Knickerbocker, Century, Riding, Coaching and Country, New
York Yacht, Seawanhaka-Corinthian, and the Hudson River
Ice Yacht Clubs. He was a typical, well-to-do New Yorker of the
proper family background, who did all the things that the right
people did. He had four children, just the fashionable amount.
Leila, the oldest of the three who survived, changed her name
to Cornelia, and when she was twenty years old married her
cousin, Montgomery Roosevelt Schuyler, the grandson of
Nicholas and Lydia Latrobe Roosevelt. Alfred married Katherine Lowell of the Boston Lowells and William Emlen married
Christine G. Keane of New York.

All of these people were pleasant, honest, and dull. They
contributed little to society, yet none of their acts ever bothered
society. Had greatness not come to the family they would have
long since been forgotten, their memory preserved only in old
copies of the *Social Register*. Their financial transactions were
hardly great enough to bring them footnotes in the histories of
the Robber Barons of the times in which they lived. They were
respectable, and so never broke into print in the sensational
newspapers. They went their way, like so many others of the
old families of reasonable wealth and social prestige. Their way
was narrow, and unwatched.

Robert B. Roosevelt was the liveliest and most interesting of
the lot but his older brother Theodore was the father of a
President. In his autobiography—which, singularly enough,
completely ignores Uncle Bob Roosevelt—Teddy wrote:

"My father, Theodore Roosevelt, was the best man I ever
knew."

In a heart-felt tribute, Teddy gives us a son's unforgettable
portrait of his father:

"He combined strength and courage with gentleness, tenderness and great unselfishness. He would not tolerate in us children selfishness or cruelty, idleness, cowardice or untruthful-
ness. As we grew older he made us understand that the same
standard of clean living was demanded for the boys as for the
girls; that what was wrong in a woman could not be right in a
man. With great love and patience, and the most understanding sympathy and consideration, he combined insistence on
discipline. He never physically punished me but once, but he

was the only man of whom I was ever really afraid. I do not mean that it was a wrong fear, for he was entirely just, and we children adored him."

This paragon of the paternal virtues was born in his father's New York home on Fourteenth Street near Union Square, on September 22, 1831. He was not spoiled by a college education. He followed the family tradition by going to work in his father's importing business and for many years he was known as one of the leading importers of glassware. When his brother, James Alfred, founded Roosevelt & Co., a banking and brokerage firm, the outgrowth of the general merchandising business established by Jacobus Roosevelt I and his son, Jacobus, in 1797, he became a partner. According to his son he was a tireless worker who spent long hours at his office desk. But he varied the dull mercantile regime by an interest in public affairs.

During the Civil War—he was in his thirties when Abraham Lincoln sent out his call for men—he helped raise and equip regiments of soldiers in New York. Although born and bred a Democrat, and married to a girl from Georgia, he became a passionate supporter of the new Republican Party. He was among the founders of the Union League Club of New York and served on the Allotment Commission, the Sanitary Commission, and other committees formed to further the cause of Union. He was patriotic, but not blustering, and generous with money as well as time and talk.

Not only was Theodore Roosevelt active during the Civil War but also during the "Dreadful Decades" that followed it, when the Democratic Tweed and the Republican Conkling typified the low estate to which politics might fall in either party. According to his son "he was interested in every social reform movement" of the time, and so, as was the case with his brother Robert, he worked with the Citizens' Committee in its fight against the Tweed Ring, and with the moderate Republicans who opposed the "Stalwart" machine of Conkling within the party. In New York he was regarded as an honest merchant with public spirit. He was not a professional politician, nor was he a professional reformer. He never held public office and never sat in the high, inner circles of his party. But his work was effective enough and his community standing sufficiently elevated so that, in 1877, President Rutherford B. Hayes, moving suddenly against Roscoe Conkling, nominated him as Collector of the Port of New York.

Senator Conkling, of course, was furious when this "tremendous patronage job, overseeing half the custom house business of the country," slipped from his hands. He could bring no charges against Roosevelt, for the man's probity was such that it could have withstood any investigation. Instead he invoked the "courtesy of the Senate," and for two years managed to block the appointment. Roosevelt died before his name could be forced through. Mr. Matthew Josephson in his book *The President Makers* remarks that this long-forgotten episode, which Teddy fails to mention in the *Autobiography,* can hardly have been unknown to the son and that it must have had some bearing on the younger Roosevelt's early opposition to the spoilsmen in politics.

Whether this event was deeply impressed on Teddy's mind or not his entire life was greatly influenced by memories of his father. He consciously patterned himself after the man of whom he wrote: "I never knew anyone who got greater joy out of living than did my father, or anyone who more wholeheartedly performed every duty; and no one whom I have ever met approached his combination of enjoyment of life and performance of duty."

"He and my mother," Teddy wrote, "were given to a hospitality that at that time was associated more commonly with southern than northern households; and especially in their later years when they had moved uptown, in the neighborhood of Central Park, they kept a charming, open house." This home was at 6 West 57th Street.

The senior Theodore was a "big, powerful man, with a leonine face." He wore a beard. Nothing pleased him more than to drive through the Park at great speed behind his four-in-hand, or the "spike team" of three horses of which he was very fond. He was a familiar sight on summer afternoons cantering with his wife and children home from the Oyster Bay station at "a rattling pace," his linen duster "sometimes bagging like a balloon." He liked to ride cross-country, too; both in the driver's seat and in the saddle he was known as an excellent horseman, daring and brave.

His crockery and banking business took a great deal of Theodore Roosevelt's time, and politics took some, but he never let either interfere with his philanthropies. One of his charitable hobbies was Charles Brace's Newsboys' Lodging-House. Another was the Society for the Prevention of Cruelty to Animals. Still another was "Miss Slattery's Night School for little Italians." He was an ardent believer in getting children off the city streets at night and in sending them out to Western farms where they might enjoy fresh air—and hard work. He led a Mission Class for poor young men. His church was the Presbyterian Church in Madison Square. He liked to walk to Church with his children. Then he reminded his sister-in-law of Great-heart in Bunyan.

Theodore Roosevelt, Sr., was not listed among the richest men in New York, but he was wealthy. He gave large sums to charities, served as Vice President of the State Charities Aid Association, and was a member and officer of the Board of United Charities and the State Board of Charities. He helped start the New York Orthopaedic Hospital for the treatment of spine and hip diseases and was one of the founders of the Metropolitan Museum of Art and the Museum of Natural History. He was, one might say, a Gentleman of the Old School, although he was only forty-seven when, worn out by all his many efforts, he died.

Martha Bullock Roosevelt, whom Theodore Sr., married in 1853, was, in her son's words, "a sweet, gracious, beautiful Southern woman, a delightful companion and beloved by everybody." Martha's first ancestor in this country was the Reverend Archibald Stobo who had come to the Carolinas from his grim experiences at the Isthmus of Panama at the very end of the Eighteenth Century. The first to bear the name Bullock was also a Scotch preacher who married the Reverend Stobo's daughter, Jean. The Bullocks had moved from South Carolina before the Revolution and had settled first in Savannah. Archibald Bullock, Martha's great grandfather, was the most important member of the family. He had been the first President of Georgia during the Revolution and had held other offices of local importance. The Bullocks were planters, and Martha's father owned an extensive estate in the Georgia uplands near Atlanta. He had a white, columned house in the town of Roswell where he kept many slaves. The Roswell home, on the line of Sherman's march to the sea, was looted by Union soldiers during the Civil War.

In the Roosevelt house at twenty-eight East Twentieth Street, which was crowded with black haircloth furniture, Theodore and Martha raised a family of two sons and two daughters. Another member of the household was Aunt Anna Bullock, Martha's maiden sister, who gave the children their lessons when they were small and told them stories in the "Uncle Remus" tradition. Uncle Bob Roosevelt published some of them in Harper's, but they were not successful.

Martha had two brothers. One, James Dunwoodie Bullock, familiarly known as "Uncle Jimmy," was a retired sea captain, who had been an admiral in the Confederate Navy and who had built the famous Confederate war vessel *Alabama*. Uncle Irvine Bullock, a midshipman on that ship, fired the last guns discharged in the fight with the *Kearsarge*. Martha and Theodore, despite their strong sectional differences of opinion, did not quarrel in their home over the war, and when it was ended the two doughty Southern heroes were guests there, although they had to travel under assumed names. They then went to England and lived in Liverpool where Uncle Jimmy became "a Tory of the most ultra-conservative school," hating Mr. Gladstone with a black fury.

These, then, were the Roosevelts who had descended from Johannes Roosevelt, the assistant alderman and petty contractor of the old city of New York: solid and stolid, unimaginative, comfortable, the old Dutch blood still running thickly in their veins. Very respectable and quite dull, they lived in the turbulent times that saw the nation rent, and when peace came again went on with their little affairs in the great market of New York. Bonds and stocks and railroad shares, old brick houses on Twenty-Second Street and Fourteenth Street near Union Square, and then out near Central Park. Offices on Wall Street. Roosevelt & Son. Country homes on quiet, cool Long Island, at Oyster Bay, where grandfather Cornelius had gone first, and where he died. Pampered children. Ease. Comfort. Standards, yes, of prim, upper middle class variety. Be good to the poor, go to church, be respectful to women, be moderate. Homely virtues. Puritanical, too. Like those of thousands of others of their Victorian day. Not a bad way to live, if you can afford it. Charity for your conscience's sake. New York and Europe and Long Island. No ostentation. The Roosevelt way of life.

Out of all this was to come greatness. Out of the more leisurely, more gracious, less stuffy way of life on the Hudson was to come greatness, also. Two branches of a tree with all too few colorful blossoms were about to grow brilliant fruit.

CHAPTER XVIII

Back to the Hudson

I

JAMES ROOSEVELT, Princeton 1780, the son of Isaac the Patriot, turned his back on New York City and the stony farm he owned at Harlem and sought the serenity of the Hudson River and the society of the last patroons. Had he been more avid for wealth and power than he was, or had he subscribed to the tight-fisted maxim of old John Jacob Astor and held firmly to his Manhattan acres he might have been the founder of a family fortune that to this day would enrich without labor the descendants of his line. At one time he owned the land that is now occupied by fully one hundred and twenty packed and rent-paying city blocks. But he could not wait for the city to creep past his fences. He lacked Astorian vision and sold his land for twenty-five thousand dollars—and started a new way of life.

His mother had been a Hoffman, and when he was born in 1760 her family had been settled up the Hudson for more than a century. His father's grand-father, too, had made his start at Esopus. It was not strange, therefore, that James Roosevelt should look nostalgically northward. But he did not make the move until late in life, after his children were grown and started on their own careers, and he had spent long years as a sugar refiner and banker in the post-Revolutionary city of his birth. That, in those years, he had substantially increased his heritage from Isaac, stands to reason. He, too, was associated with the Bank of New York, although he was never its president; and he had studied law, already a necessity for a business man, although he had never sought clients for his knowledge.

How great a fortune James possessed is not known. Doubtless it was not as extensive as that amassed by his cousin Cornelius, but it was enough to allow him every luxury he or his family desired, enough to educate his children well, enough to enable him to indulge in horse breeding, and to maintain a large home near Washington Square as well as an extensive estate at Poughkeepsie.

This only son of Isaac had his father's shrewd eyes, but he hid them behind steel spectacles, thus appearing more the merchant and less the statesman than Isaac when he sat for his portrait. The eyebrows were not as arched; the white hair was thin. His face was more benevolent than Alexander Hamilton's old friend; less sophisticated and less debonaire. Perhaps that was because he had an affinity for the soil, a trait never apparent in Banker Isaac. He liked farming and he loved horses. He did his best to make his extensive Harlem acreage pay, but the land was rocky, the drainage poor. When he acquired it much of the land—it lay between what is now One Hundred and Tenth and One Hundred and Twenty-Fifth Streets and Fifth Avenue and the East River—was timber covered. This he cut for lumber and fuel, a profitable venture. The rest he cultivated as best he could. The farm was not an agricultural success, but he raised some good horses there. On days when the roads were dry his fastest mares could carry him to his city home in about an hour.

Bred as he was in his father's mercantile-revolutionary tradition he, too, was a Federalist, and the college where he had studied was of course the breeding place of some of Alexander Hamilton's stanchest supporters, although its graduates included the Democrat, James Madison. But politics was not a passion with him. He sat with the New York Assembly during the uneventful term of 1796-97, and in 1809 he was a member of the city's Aldermanic Council. Beyond that he took no active part in the political action of his day, and he was the last of his branch of the family to indulge himself in public service until young Franklin Roosevelt, inspired by the success of his fifth cousin, Teddy, was elected to the State Senate in 1910.

Six years after his graduation from the college at Princeton he married Maria Eliza Walton, the daughter of Abraham the Tory, who had been his childhood playmate in the gardens of "Pembroke." Maria was his "affectionate and best of wives" from 1786 until her death in 1810, nearly a quarter of a century. Ten children, of whom eight survived infancy, were born to James and Maria.

Two years after Maria's death her husband married again. His second wife was Catherine Eliza Barclay, the only daughter of James Barclay. They were wed at the Protestant Episcopal Church of St. John the Baptist. The land for this church had been given by John Duffie, partner in the salt and grocery business of Cornelius Roosevelt I until 1805. He had married Cornelius's sister, Maria Roosevelt. Mr. Duffie was the son of an Edinburgh Scotsman. For many years he was a trustee of the Gold Street Baptist Church. His wife, however, was an Episcopalian. Indeed, their son, Rev. Cornelius Roosevelt Duffie, was the first rector of St. Thomas Protestant Episcopal Church. Mrs. Duffie persuaded her husband to give part of a large parcel of land he owned at Kip's Bay on the east side of Murray Hill for a Protestant Episcopal Church that was built at Lexington Avenue and Thirty-Fifth Street. This was named the Church of St. John the Baptist, and for years the irreverant insisted it had been named for its benefactor, John Duffie, the Baptist trustee.

Catherine Barclay's father had volunteered in New Jersey to fight for the king's cause during the Revolution, had been captured on Staten Island, and imprisoned with other active Tories at Trenton during the war. Catherine Eliza lived but four years, yet in that time she gave James two children. In 1821, when he was sixty-one years old, he took a third bride. She was Harriet Howland, a descendant of John Howland, John Carver's manservant on the *Mayflower,* and a member of the same family into which James Roosevelt's grandson was to marry. There were no children by this marriage.

During the early years of his active life James Roosevelt had his home at Number Eighteen South Street, then a residential thoroughfare, but now a water-front street crowded with docks and saloons. The old sugar refinery, whence had been ground the family fortune, had been moved from Isaac's old back yard near Hanover Square to Number Ten Thames Street. In 1823, however, James sold his South Street home and moved to the far more fashionable region of Greenwich Village. He took a house at Number Sixty-Four Bleecker Street, at the corner of Crosby Street, two blocks south from Washington Square. This was to be his New York home until his death, but he was to spend less and less time here as the years went by.

Having sold his Harlem farm—partly to John Jacob Astor— he bought a large tract of land at Poughkeepsie. On the hill top which dominated the green acres, flushed by the Hudson flood, he built a large, square and comfortable house. He called the estate Mount Hope. Here he lived during the long summer months, here he kept his horses, puttered with his greenery, lived fully his declining days. From 1819, the year of the purchase, he was there whenever the exigencies of his investments allowed. He was known as a kindly gentleman, well liked by his neighbors, some of whom had always lived in the region, others of whom, like himself, were New Yorkers attracted to the unspoiled countryside. On December 7, 1847, in his eighty-eighth year, the great-grandfather of Franklin Roosevelt died.

An indication of James Roosevelt's character may be found in the obituary that appeared in New York City and upstate newspapers a few days after he had succumbed to a stroke of paralysis:

"Having acquired a small fortune, he retired from commercial life many years ago to spend the remnant of his days in the luxury of sharing it with a large circle of friends, and the richer luxury of doing good in the cause of his Redeemer. Mr. Roosevelt was among the steady and liberal patrons of the various benevolent associations of his day."

The same account called him "a gentleman of the old school" —a phrase, interestingly enough, that was to be trotted out to describe both his son and grandson, when they, too, had died.

Philip Hone, realizing perhaps that this Roosevelt had not fallen victim to the scourge of Democracy, wrote in his diary:

"Died yesterday Mr. James Roosevelt in the 88th year of his

age; a highly respectable gentleman of the old school, son of Isaac Roosevelt, the first president of the first bank of New York [Mr. Hone was in error. Isaac Roosevelt was the second president] at a time when the president and directors of a bank were another sort of people from those of the present day. Proud and aristocratical, they were the only nobility we had; powerful in the controlling influence they possessed over the commercial operations of the city, men could not stand straight in their presence; and woe to them who bowed not down to the representatives of a few bags of gold and silver, the potential dispensers of bank favors."

"Commodore" Vanderbilt had wrung more than five hundred thousand dollars out of the shipping business by 1834 when he was forty years old. When Pierre Lorillard died, four years before James Roosevelt passed on, he left an estate worth one million dollars or more. Five years later old Astor was to surrender twenty million dollars worth of choice real estate when he departed this earth to test the truth of the adage of the rich man and the needle's eye. Journalists had been forced to coin the word millionaire in this era. Old Billy James, a penniless Irish immigrant and Albany cigar salesman had accumulated three million dollars when he died in 1837, ten years before James Roosevelt's death. His fortune smoothed the paths of literature and psychology for his famous grandsons, Henry, the novelist, and William, the psychologist.

No Roosevelt had climbed so high on the financial ladder. But there were acquisitive Roosevelts in the sprawling tribe. Most of them stemmed from Johannes, progenitor of the Republican Roosevelts of Oyster Bay, ancestor of Teddy, who scourged the malefactors of wealth and hated socialists all his well-fed life. In the first half of the Nineteenth Century, an era favorable to the founding of great fortunes, the cousins of Jacobus Roosevelt, progenitor of the Democratic Roosevelts of Hyde Park, turned from trade to live leisured, cultured, quiet lives on the Hudson's upper banks.

One who made the most of reasonable wealth and leisure was Isaac Roosevelt II, the oldest son of James and Maria Walton Roosevelt. He was born April 21, 1790, in his father's South Street house. Although named for his patriotic grandfather, he despised politics; although the son and grandson of bankers, he hated business. Among the Roosevelts he was a strange figure, almost a queer duck. His father, of course, sent him off to the college at Princeton, where he was graduated in 1808 just after his eighteenth birthday. He then came back to New York and entered the College of Physicians and Surgeons at Columbia University. Just why he did so is a mystery to this day, for he patently was cut out to be neither a physician nor a surgeon. Four years later he was admitted to the practice of medicine, but he never opened a doctor's office although, with his social connections, he undoubtedly might have become one of the most fashionable physicians in the city. Instead, he continued to study under Dr. David Hosack, the noted New York physicist and botanist, whose famous gardens were where Rockefeller Center is today. In 1820, he gave up all connection with the profession.

Isaac's retirement and his father's completion of the house at Mount Hope coincided. Young Doctor Isaac went there to live. He had inherited his father's love for country living. Also he was shy and studious. As long as he could confine his medical studies to books, especially on the history of the subject, he was happy—but he could not bear the sight and sound of human pain. One cannot escape feeling that he was a singularly ineffectual young man in whom there appeared many signs of a line that was beginning to go to seed. Physically he was far from robust. Compared to his father and grandfather, whom he strongly resembled, his face lacked strength of character. The nose is longer and thinner, the eyes lack sparkle and the mouth is weak. But whatever his lacks he did one thing to redeem his apparent ineffectualness. He married an Aspinwall.

That simple act fused old and sturdy Yankee blood with the once vibrant Dutch blood of the Roosevelt strain.

Mary Rebecca Aspinwall's immigrant ancestor was Peter Aspinwall, an Englishman, who had settled in Dorchester, Massachusetts, in 1645, and then had become a founder of the town of Brookline. There he married for his second wife Remember Palfrey, daughter of Peter Palfrey, whose grandsons were to be the well known New England historians and theologians. Their son of this union, Joseph Aspinwall, had followed the sea all his life, owned his own ships, and been a scourge to the French. In the late Seventeenth Century he had moved to New York, where he married a girl named Hannah Dean, before finally settling down for his old age at Dedham, Massachusetts, a testy old sea dog who would have driven the Spaniards out of South America if he had had his way. He sent his son, John Aspinwall, to sea, and lived to see him one of the most prosperous of New York merchants and traders, a leader of mercantile society, and a dignified vestryman of Trinity Church.

This John Aspinwall married, in 1766, Rebecca Smith, who was descended from the Reverend Thomas Shepard, that "humbling, mourning, heart-breaking" New England divine whose sermons in defense of ecclesiastical authority are among the grimmest in New England history. Another member of the Aspinwall family was Dr. William Aspinwall, director of an army hospital at Jamaica Plain, Massachusetts, during the Revolution, and a pioneer in inoculation against smallpox. He, evidently, did not tremble at the sight of human pain.

This John Aspinwall was the founder of the New York Aspinwalls, who, with the Howlands from New Bedford, formed two of the wealthiest merchant families in the city in the early Nineteenth Century. He had a large estate at Flushing—Philip Hone once was his guest and his mouth watered remembering the vegetables raised in the Aspinwall gardens— and he owned shipyards and warehouses along the East River in New York. His vessels knew every port of the world. When he died he was assured that the Aspinwall fortune would continue, for his young son, also named John Aspinwall, had been trained in a hard mercantile school. The third John Aspinwall increased his heritage, expanded the family fleet, and became even wealthier than his crusty old father. In 1803 he married Susan Howland, a descendant in the fifth generation of John Howland and of Captain Ephraim Bill, a salty old fellow who at his yards in Saybrook, Connecticut, built the fourteen-gun ships-of-war *Oliver Cromwell* and *Defense* for the Colonial Navy, thus giving the British many nasty moments during the Revolutionary War.

Mary Rebecca, the daughter of John and Susan Howland

Aspinwall, who married Dr. Isaac Roosevelt in New York, in 1827, was two years younger than her brother, William Henry Aspinwall, the last great New York merchant of that name. He, too, was the product of a stiff commercial education of the kind recently described in the short stories of *Young Ames*. After the most rudimentary common school education he was apprenticed in the counting house of his uncles, Gardner C. and Samuel Howland, proprietors of the firm of G. C. & S. Howland of New York, whose father had made a fortune in the New Bedford whaling trade, and whose sister, Harriet, had been James Roosevelt's third and last wife.

When William Henry was twenty-five he was made a partner in the Howland brothers' firm, then at the height of its vast business with Mexico, England, and the Mediterranean countries, and was given a quarter interest, which netted him the not inconsiderable annual income of fifteen thousand dollars. Five years later the brothers Howland turned over the business, which was capitalized at two hundred thousand dollars, to William Henry Aspinwall and his cousin, William Edgar Howland, and it became known as Howland & Aspinwall. Although the young men took charge during the panic year of 1837 they withstood the depression and from then until 1850 ran with an iron hand the largest general trading, importing, and exporting business operating from the port of New York.

During these years Howland & Aspinwall sent its ships steadily to England and to the Mediterranean; in the Pacific the firm was without a rival; and there were few to challenge its supremacy in the West and East Indies shipping routes. The famous clipper ship *Rainbow*, a vessel of seven hundred and fifty tons and the first of its type to come off the ways in New York, was only one of the many to carry the H. & A. house flag in those busy, wind-jammer days. In 1846 the *Rainbow* startled the waterfront by making the round trip to Canton, China, in the time formerly taken to reach that eastern port. Remembering this, one finds it easy to realize how the salt got into the bloodstream of President Franklin D. Roosevelt. Later another salty jet was to come from the Delano family, whose members knew and owned and sailed ships as fast and as fine as the *Rainbow*.

Franklin Delano Roosevelt's great-uncle, William Henry

Aspinwall, had a streak of adventure in his soul. He was no stolid, ledger minded trader; instead he was a man of singular vision. The gold fever that swept the country in 1849 did not find him immune. He astounded his conservative associates by resigning his active leadership of Howland & Aspinwall to throw his lot with the Pacific Railroad & Panama Steamship Company. For years he had been a power in South and Central America, and his friendship with the President of Venezuela had long enabled him to maintain a virtual trade monopoly with that country. Now, after obtaining a charter for the new one million dollar corporation, Panama Railroad, Inc., he experienced no difficulty in persuading the government of New Granada, as the future Republic of Colombia was then known, to permit him to build a railroad across the Isthmus of Panama.

Associated with him in this daring and expensive venture were Lloyd Aspinwall, his brother, Samuel W. Comstock, Henry Chauncey, and John L. Stevens, all men of affairs in or near Wall Street. They sent the famous engineers, George M. Tooten and John C. Trautwine, into the jungle and within five years forty-nine miles of steel rails stretched to the port of at Aspinwall, the terminal on the western coast named in William Henry's honor.

Meanwhile Aspinwall, Chauncey, Richard Alsop, the Howland brothers, and Edwin Bartlett had, in 1847, formed a partnership, established the Pacific Mail Steam Ship Company, and taken over an existing charter for bi-weekly ship schedules from Panama to Oregon. This, too, had been a daring venture and thoroughly speculative in nature for the West Coast was hardly opened up and almost all the business consisted of delivery of mail to the settlers of Oregon. However, the discovery of gold, which at once brought about a vast increase in the traffic of passengers, freight, and bullion, soon gave the line, and its rival, United States Mail Steam Ship Company, more business than both could handle. Within two years the line's four hundred thousand dollar capitalization was increased to two million dollars, and when the railroad across the Isthmus was completed, Aspinwall and his associates had control of a through water-rail route from New York to San Francisco that was the envy of their greatest rival, Commodore Vanderbilt. Within ten years of the gold strike the railroad alone had netted six million dollars and for another decade, or until the last spike was driven into the rails of the Union Pacific Railroad, in 1869, the Aspinwall interests had a monopoly of the western carrying trade.

Before that year W. H. resigned, content to be called "one of the richest men in New York." He maintained directorships in numerous shipping concerns, banks, insurance companies, railroads, was a leader of the Chamber of Commerce, and active in society, where he was known, at least journalistically, as a patron of the drama and the fine arts. Occasionally the public was admitted to his picture gallery. He was a trustee of the Lenox Library. His home at Thirty-Three University Place was a "center of hospitality," and his summer home at Tarrytown was a "show place." During the Civil War he did his patriotic duty by accompanying John Forbes of Boston on a mission to persuade the British from building iron rams for the Rebels. Philip Hone, who was related by marriage to the Howlands, visited him in 1846:

"I dined today with Mr. and Mrs. William Aspinwall, in their new house, University Place, one of the palaces which have been lately erected in this part of the city. A more beautiful and commodious mansion, or in better taste in every particular, I have never seen. This gentleman is one of the merchant princes of New York; long may he enjoy his prosperity. He deserves it. He is an upright and honorable merchant, a liberal and public spirited citizen, and a hospitable and right-minded gentleman."

William's brother-in-law, Dr. Isaac Roosevelt, seems to have been singularly unaffected either by the Aspinwall opulence or the stirring times in which the merchant prince played so imposing a part. Undoubtedly he was a frequent guest at University place, and at Tarrytown, and it is also quite likely that he entrusted W. H. with his and Rebecca's investments. He himself spent most of his time tending his live stock and his gardens and reading about the history of the profession he had so strangely abandoned. He liked the quieter aspects of country life, but he was not unsocial. About 1832 he left his father's house at Mount Hope, and moved across the line into the township of Hyde Park, on the west side of the post road. There he had brought a large estate and there he now built his own house. He called it Rosedale.

Dr. Isaac spent the last thirty years of his life at Rosedale. There his two sons, James Roosevelt and John Aspinwall Roosevelt, grew up, learning, like their father, to love the rural, but not the rustic, atmosphere of Dutchess County, where both were to make their homes. James was born in 1828; John not until 1840. Upon their father's death James inherited Mount Hope while Rosedale went to the younger son.

Of Dr. Isaac, his brother-in-law, Dr. Guy Carleton Bayley, wrote:

"Though well educated in his profession, and fond of its literature, its practice was distasteful . . . and being removed from the necessity of practise he never engaged in it, choosing rural enjoyments and agricultural pursuits. He was of delicate constitution, with refined tastes, a gentleman of the old school."

Ineffectual though he was, Dr. Isaac left his branch of the Roosevelt Family deeply rooted in the shores of the Hudson when he died in 1863. Rebecca Aspinwall Roosevelt lived on at Rosedale or in New York until her death in the city in 1886. Their sons became well known in business and especially in society—that gay society of town and country, of paddock and ballroom, of New York and Europe, that made life pleasurable, for those who could afford it, between the Civil War and what John Hay, Teddy's cynical and bearded friend, called that "splendid little war" of 1896.

II

James Roosevelt, the son of Dr. Isaac and the father of President Franklin D. Roosevelt, was a gentleman of some importance in his own little world and in his time. He was a dashing figure among the sports-loving descendants of the Hudson River patroons; ranked high in the exclusive social circles dominated by Mrs. Caroline Astor, the leader of the Four Hundred; he was a charming guest in his friends' houses in England, Germany, and France; and he was an able lawyer and business man

whose talents aided materially in the post-Civil War development of an important link in the railroad system of America.

A distant kinsman of James, Joseph Alsop, the Washington
newspaperman, has called him a "period piece," and his most
familiar portrait bears out this description. He loved horses
and dogs and so he posed for his picture in a high-buttoned
coat and flowered cravat, quite the fashion in the 1880's among
sportsmen. Seated at a small table, he is holding a riding crop
in his large, strong hands. A ring decorates the little finger of
his left hand; another bands the ring-finger of the right. The
arched eyebrows inherited from old Isaac the Patriot, lend a
familiar, half-humorous and half-cynical expression to his face.
Mutton chop whiskers adorn each cheek. And a heavy watch-
chain falls below the carefully unbuttoned portion of the three-
button coat. Henry James, the novelist, knew this type well,
especially away from its native Hudson habitat.

The Roosevelt fortune, handed down through three generations from Old Isaac's sugar house, and amplified, no doubt, by
the wealth of the Aspinwalls, had been carefully nurtured. If
Dr. Isaac was no great shakes of a man, he at least had not
squandered his heritage, and he saw to it that his sons had every
advantage of gentlemen. In the 1840's, when James was growing up, it was not considered a social necessity in New York
State for a son to attend Harvard. The up-river gentry were
quite content to send their sons to Union College at Sche-
nectady, home of Sigma Phi, the first college fraternity. It
boasted an excellent faculty in those days. Young James was
graduated from Union in 1847, and after the fashion of the
day immediately set out on the Grand Tour.

An ardent youth and a born Democrat, he was in Europe in
stirring times. Like others of his class he joined up for awhile
with Garibaldi's legions, with which he played at fighting for
that tenuous thing called Freedom. When he returned home,
unscathed, he entered the Harvard Law School, from which he
received his degree in 1852. With this decided asset he was well
equipped for the business of handling his estate. And despite
his great interest in living, he never neglected business during
his entire life.

The year after his graduation from Harvard he married Miss

Rebecca Brien Howland. His plump and pretty bride could trace her ancestry back to John Howland, of the *Mayflower*. Rebecca was, of course, a member of *the* Howland family of New York, so long associated with the Aspinwalls in their great shipping ventures. The Howlands were already related to the Roosevelts, for Dr. Isaac had married Rebecca Aspinwall, and her mother was Susan Howland. Rebecca was a pious young lady, but used to wealth and privilege. One of her brothers was a sportsman, who married a French woman, and Mme. Howland's Paris salon is described in Marcel Proust's *Remembrance of Things Past* as a special haunt of members of the Jockey Club.

James had inherited the Mount Hope house on the Poughkeepsie hilltop across the post road from Hyde Park. He loved the life of this region, hunting, riding horses, superintending the care of his trees and lawns and gardens. He liked the people who surrounded him: men of affairs, like himself, but who had plenty of leisure and knew how to use it; and capable farmers who knew how to turn the soil to best advantage and who knew a good piece of horseflesh when they saw it. Mount Hope burned down in 1866, and since the state had already bought the land to the southward for the site of a hospital for the insane, he decided to sell his inheritance to the state and build a new home elsewhere. Later he served as superintendent of the hospital erected on the land he had once owned.

The place which James selected for the new home of his wife and only son, James Roosevelt Roosevelt (who was born a year after his marriage) was an old estate known as Springwood. He did not like that name and called it Hyde Park, the name by which it has been known ever since. Its history dated back at least to 1699 when it was one of several Hudson River "water lots" divided up under the terms of the so-called Nine Partners' Patent. For fully a century it had been tilled by tenant farmers placed there by owners alien to Dutchess County. In 1826 one Ephraim Holbrook, who lived on the next "water lot" to the north, bought Springwood and built a rectangular, two-story, frame house there. About twenty years later James Boorman, president of the Hudson River Railroad, took over Holbrook's place and bought Springwood as a gift for his daughter and son-in-law, Mr. and Mrs. Josiah W. Wheeler. Mr. Wheeler added north and south wings to the old house, and it was this that James Roosevelt purchased in 1867.

The estate, incidentally, has never been known as Krum Elbow, despite Franklin Roosevelt's insistence that it had been. Krum Elbow was the name of a nearby turn in the Hudson River. It was a contraction of an apt old Dutch term, meaning Crooked Elbow.

When James Roosevelt bought the estate it comprised one hundred and ten acres of rolling, wooded land with a magnificent view of the broad sweep of the Hudson. Within a few years he purchased three adjacent tracts until his acreage totalled six hundred acres. The house stood above and behind slopes of hemlock. To the north he built stables for his trotting horses and it was there that he bred Gloster, the first horse to trot a mile in less than 2.20. After that record-breaking performance he sold Gloster to Senator Leland Stanford. The horse never broke another record. He was killed in a train wreck on the way west. His tail, about all that was saved, now hangs in President Roosevelt's bedroom on the second floor of the White House.

James Roosevelt followed his investments in railroading and became the vice president and legal advisor of the Delaware & Hudson railroad, which was a favorite investment of the better families of the day. He also, at one time, was President of the Louisville railroad and the so-called New Albany. His railroad interests after the Civil War (in which he seems to have taken no active part; perhaps because he was an ingrained Democrat) led him into Southern Securities. He became president of that outfit, and helped in the post-war housecleaning of the "carpet-baggers," which resulted in the organization of the Southern Railway System and the Louisville & Nashville road. It has been estimated that he accumulated a fortune of three hundred thousand dollars from his railroad ventures.

Although this was no huge amount—some of the Oyster Bay Roosevelts would have sniffed at it—it was enough to allow him to live the spacious kind of life he most enjoyed—the life of last century's Hudson River gentry; the life of those who moved leisurely over the green, clipped lawns of Algonac, Staatsburg,

Steen Valletje, Mount Hope, Tivoli, Rosedale; the life of those who played at being the Last Patroons.

Almost every year he went abroad, for he had friends in Paris and in London, and he was a welcome visitor at more than one English country house. He knew the life of the German spas, the hunts at Pau, the grouse in Scotland. And back in New York City he was a popular figure in Society. He was a patron of the Patriarch's Ball in the days when the ineffable Ward McAllister was telling *the* Mrs. Astor who was nice, and who wasn't.

He knew the garish Astor mansion at Three Hundred and Fifty Fifth Avenue well. There, with Caroline the Magnificent beaming haughtily over the assembled guests, he mingled with such worthy rich as Mrs. Jonathan Edwards, the C. O'D. Iselins, the August Belmonts, the James F. Ruggleses, the Robert Goelets, Miss Hamilton J. Jay, the Schuyler Hamiltons, Jr., General and Mrs. Lloyd Aspinwall and the De Lancey Kanes. There too he might meet his own relatives, the Theodore Roosevelts and the Elliott Roosevelts, and who knows how many relatives near and far? When autumn painted the Hudson's landscape he would be seen enjoying Caroline's hospitality, with the other Dutchess County élite, at Mrs. Astor's between-season retreat, Ferncliff.

All this time his son was growing up. The fastidious James disdained the appellation "Jr." and so he called the only child of his first marriage James Roosevelt Roosevelt. To all the young blades of the day the son was known as "Rosey." He was a bright and personable lad who was graduated with honors from Columbia University in 1877, when he was twenty-three years old, the year after his mother died. He was not to have much use in the future for his undoubted scholastic talents for in that very year his engagement was announced. Thereafter there was little for him to worry about, at least financially, for the girl of his choice was Helen Astor.

As the daughter of William H. Astor (the grandson of old John Jacob Astor) and of Caroline Webster Schermerhorn Astor (*the* Mrs. Astor) Helen was, without question, the catch of the season. Not only was she socially impeccable, but she brought to the marriage a four hundred thousand dollar trust fund, probably a greater sum than any Hudson River Roosevelt had ever known. Rosey gave, in turn, a modest fortune, and an ancient name—doubled. They were married at Grace Church, New York, November 18, 1878 with the Right Reverend Horatio Potter, society's favorite Protestant Episcopal Bishop of New York, officiating with the aid of two other ministers. The newly-weds then moved into Three Hundred and Seventy-Two Fifth Avenue, the mansion the late William Backhouse Astor had built for himself shortly before his death.*

Like his father, Rosey Roosevelt was a Democrat and he remained faithful to his party even after his marriage to an Astor. His mother-in-law, the magnificent Caroline, it has been said, felt towards Democrats about the way her Episcopalianism made her feel towards Baptists or atheists. Perhaps this devout Republican forgave Rosey because he believed in sound money and so could not be hopelessly lost. His Democracy, however, brought him a pleasant reward. He was a generous contributor to the campaign chest of Grover Cleveland, his money helping the ex-sheriff of Erie County to win the election of 1884. Accordingly he was made the first secretary of the legation at Vienna, whither he took Helen. As an Astor she naturally was the leader of American society there, and was invited upon occasion to be the guest of a Hapsburg. Mr. Cleveland unfortunately was defeated in 1888 and the Astor-Roosevelts had to postpone their diplomatic career until 1892.

In that year James Roosevelt Roosevelt gave ten thousand dollars to the Cleveland campaign fund and his prize was the post of the first secretary of the American Embassy in London. This meant that Henry White, who had held the post for ten years, had to make way for a Roosevelt who had "bought" his way in. From the Republican side there arose a great clamor,

* Another Roosevelt-Astor relationship is interesting, for it brings Assistant Secretary of State Sumner Welles into the Roosevelt Family. His father, Benjamin S. Welles, married Katherine Schermerhorn, the sister of Caroline Webster Schermerhorn Astor, who was the mother of Helen Astor Roosevelt (Mrs. James Roosevelt Roosevelt). Katherine was the daughter of Abraham and Helen White Schermerhorn, the latter being the granddaughter of Augustus and Catherine Barclay van Cortlandt, the great-granddaughter of Andrew and Helena Roosevelt Barclay and the great-great-granddaughter of Jacobus and Catherine Hardenbrook Roosevelt, the parents of Isaac the Patriot and the great-great-grandparents of Franklin Delano Roosevelt.

which grew louder when it was announced that another Astor
son-in-law, James J. Van Alen, who had given fifty thousand to
the Cleveland chest, had been appointed Ambassador to Italy.
President Cleveland was condemned for entering the "world of
pure fashion" in making his diplomatic appointments. Van Alen
eventually resigned. Roosevelt went to London. Mrs. Caroline
Astor was greatly pleased, for she could have an even more en-
joyable London season with the American Embassy backing her
up. She sailed to meet her daughter and family—they had two
children, James Roosevelt Roosevelt, Jr., and Helen Rebecca
Roosevelt—but when she arrived her daughter was dead at the
country estate the Roosevelts had taken at Heathfield, Ascott.

Helen Astor Roosevelt left to her children an estate of one
million five hundred thousand dollars, but Secretary Roosevelt,
"hard-pressed by the social standards of the Court of St.
James's," asked an allowance of thirty thousand dollars from
the trust fund for the maintenance of his son, then aged fourteen, and his daughter, then aged twelve. The New York judge
who heard the petition did not think the children needed that
much money and said: "It is difficult to conceive of any circumstances that would justify it. Such a sum is certainly out of
the question in the circumstances. . . . The incomes (from the
trust funds) should not be dissipated merely to accustom these
children to luxury. When they are of age they can do what
they will with their own. In the meantime they should be
taught the value of money and should be habituated to prudence and moderation rather than to extravagance in the grati-
fication of every luxurious desire." The judge decided that
seven thousand five hundred dollars apiece was enough for the
children.

After his term as Secretary was over James Roosevelt Roosevelt returned to New York. He later became a guardian of the
Astor Estate, along with Douglas Robinson, William A.
Dobbyn and Nicholas Biddle, and had to spend at least some
of his time at the Estate's office at Twenty-Three West Twenty-
Sixth Street. But most of it he passed at his home in Hyde
Park. He sent his son to Harvard. In his senior year the youngster, who sowed his wild oats with a profligacy, fell in love with
a girl named Sadie Meisinger, but whom the newspapers called

"Dutch Sadie." He met her first at the Haymarket, the lush cafe on New York's Sixth Avenue that was haunted by *fin de siécle* Harvard students on the loose. Both sides of his family were deeply shocked and hurt when he married her. The newspapers made much of the affair and said he went to Florida to live under an assumed name because of it. He separated from his wife and years later quietly returned to New York, where he now lives, greatly interested in the affairs of the Salvation Army. Young "Rosey's" sister, Helen, made a happier marriage, her husband being the late cat-belling Assemblyman Theodore Douglas Robinson, the son of Douglas and Corinne Roosevelt Robinson and a nephew of Teddy.

In the later years of his life James Roosevelt became intensely interested in religion. Not only did he contribute to many religious charities but he became a trustee of the Protestant Episcopal Cathedral of St. John the Divine. He gave a quarter of a million dollars to the Saint Francis Hospital at Poughkeepsie. One of his closest friends in his declining years was the late Cardinal Patrick Hayes of the Roman Catholic Diocese of New York, with whom he often visited.

In 1914, when the *Kronprinzessen Cecilie* sailed from New York with its ten million dollar cargo of gold, only to put back into Bar Harbor in the darkness of night when war was declared, Mr. Roosevelt was aboard. Also on the ship was Miss Elizabeth R. Riley. The couple had known each other for many years and their friendship had now developed into love. Thwarted by war in their desire for a European wedding they slipped from the steamer and went quietly to the Roosevelt house at Campobello Island, which Mr. Roosevelt's father had built for his summer home in 1890. There they were quietly married. Their friends knew nothing about it until the *Social Register* appeared in November. They were then living in seclusion at Mr. Roosevelt's Hyde Park estate of four hundred acres, a quarter of a mile south of Springwood where Franklin was born.

James Roosevelt Roosevelt died at Hyde Park on May 7, 1927. He left his estate to his widow for her life use. She is still living there. When she dies it will go to Mrs. Helen Roosevelt Robinson, if she survives, and upon her death to President

Roosevelt. He also left four hundred and fifty thousand dollars to his widow. His daughter received an adjoining estate and her four children were left twenty-five thousand dollars each. James Roosevelt, who always regarded Franklin Roosevelt more as a son than a much younger brother, left him one hundred thousand dollars in securities and all his fishing paraphernalia in England, Scotland and the United States. He also left fifteen thousand dollars to aid in completing the Cathedral of St. John the Divine.

III

Two years after James Roosevelt Roosevelt had married Helen Astor, his father, now a widower of fifty-two, who had given up his stables because trotting races were no longer fashionable and who otherwise had withdrawn from the whirl of society, married Sara Delano, his neighbor on the Hudson shore.

This marriage brought an even closer alliance between the House of Roosevelt and the House of Astor than that which already existed through the marriage of "Rosey" and Helen. In 1884 Helen Astor's aunt, Laura Astor, the daughter of William Backhouse Astor, the unimaginative son of the old fur trapper and Landlord of New York, had been married to Franklin Hughes Delano of Fairhaven, Massachusetts. Young Mr. Delano was a descendant of Philippe de la Noye, the French Huguenot who had come to Plymouth in 1621 when Robert Cushman made his only visit to the Colony he had struggled so desperately to found.

Laura Astor brought to the marriage a trust fund of two hundred thousand dollars, which enabled young Delano to withdraw from the shipping firm of which he was a partner and live the life of a gentleman. Now and then he delved in a real estate deal with his father-in-law, and he indulged in an occasional shipping venture. But most of the time he divided between Steen Valletje, a part of Rokeby, the Astor's up-river estate, which W. B. Astor had given Laura, and their town-house in Colonnade Row in La Fayette Place, a gift of old John Jacob himself. The fortunate couple, who were very happy together, were nevertheless childless and the name of

Franklin Delano might have vanished forever had not his niece, Sara Delano, given it to her only son. When William Backhouse Astor died, in 1875, he left Laura Delano one million one hundred thousand dollars in cash and property and made Franklin Delano, with whom he had got along exceedingly well, executor of the estate. Sometime before that he had given Laura a fine house on Madison Avenue at Thirty-Fourth Street. Franklin Hughes Delano died in France in 1893.

The Delanos, however, did not have to depend upon any Astor largess, for they were wealthy in their own right. But wealth was not the criterion of the family. Sara Delano was Franklin Delano's niece and the daughter of the second Warren Delano who divided his time between Fairhaven, Massachusetts, New York City, and his summer estate, Algonac, at Balmville, near Newburgh, New York, across the Hudson River from Hyde Park. It is through him that President Franklin Delano Roosevelt can trace his ancestry, in a direct line, to Isaac Allerton, the Pilgrim's business agent who was banished first from Plymouth and then from Massachusetts and who became one of the first wealthy English traders on Manhattan Island. Through him also President Roosevelt can trace his ancestry directly back to Robert Cushman, who did not settle at Plymouth but who helped found the Plantation; to Mary Allerton, who arrived with her father on the *Mayflower;* to Thomas Cushman, the son of Robert, who was for many years the ruling elder of the Plymouth Church and to Francis Cooke, also a *Mayflower* passenger.

Sara Delano's mother was Catherine Robbins Lyman of Northampton, Massachusetts, and this meant that she, too, was of ancient Yankee lineage. Neither the Robbins nor the Lyman family dated back to the *Mayflower,* but Lymans had fought in King Phillip's War, in Queen Anne's War, and in the Revolution. The early members of the family were hardy farmers and stockraisers who had prospered in the fertile Connecticut Valley. Two grandsons of Richard Robbins, who settled in 1639 on the banks of the Charles River, that runs between Boston and Cambridge, had fought at the Battle of Lexington as members of Captain Parker's immortal company of "Minute Men"; other members of the family had been noted New England divines, related through marriage to Ann Hutchinson; and the family could boast a Speaker of the Massachusetts House and a Lieutenant Governor of that proud Commonwealth.

The Delanos, ancestrally, need bow to no one. In 1854, when Sara was born at her father's Newburgh estate, the Yankee blood had not run thin. Action was the family word as much as ancestry. All the Delanos had been seafaring men; they had commanded New Bedford whalers; they had sailed around the Horn in search of the China trade. Sara's father was no different from the rest, as hard-headed and driving as his uncle Amasa Delano, who had helped blaze the clipper-ship trail to the Orient. In her earliest years Sara lived for awhile in the sea port of Boston, where she had the whooping cough, which was doctored by no less a physician than Dr. Oliver Wendell Holmes, the Autocrat of the Breakfast Table and father of the famed dissenting Justice. Ralph Waldo Emerson, the sage of Concord, was a family friend. Later the family moved to New York.

As a young man Sara Delano's father had commanded his own clipper ships, plying between New England ports and China and the West African coast. It was in Hong Kong that he met one of the largest tea merchants established in the Orient. This gentleman took a fancy to young Delano and offered him a partnership in the firm that was known as Russell & Co. Its American headquarters were in the then sail-crowded port of Boston. Later Warren Delano became the president of the company, a post which made it necessary for him to spend many years in the Far East, where he learned Oriental ways.

By the time of his marriage to Catherine Lyman, Warren Delano had amassed a sizable fortune and had decided to retire to his Hudson acres and live on the income of his soundly invested wealth. It was then that he purchased Algonac for he needed a large place. He had five daughters and two sons.

But it was not written that Warren Delano should retire. In 1857 a financial panic swept the country. Many of his friends lost all their wealth and never recovered; but he was of too hardy a stock to let a mere Wall Street panic put an end to his dreams of leisure. With true Yankee fortitude he packed his bags, kissed his wife and seven children good-bye, and took the next clipper to Hong Kong. Before he went he tried to sell Algonac—but, in that grim and moneyless year, Hudson River estates were a drug on the market.

It took Warren Delano five years in the Orient to recoup the losses that he had suffered overnight in 1857. Then, once more a wealthy man, he sent for his family to come out to the East to join him. Catherine Delano gathered the brood and boarded the clipper, *Surprise,* for the long journey eastward. All her life Sara Delano was to remember that voyage, that long, slow, wind-tossed voyage down the South American coast, around the dreaded Cape Horn, and across the Pacific Ocean. Four months were consumed in the passage of the *Surprise,* but the Delano children enjoyed the life on the ship, with its little farm of cows and chickens, brought along to supply fresh food, and the husky sailors who sang on any provocation. Sara learned the chantey, "Down the river hauled a Yankee clipper and it's blow, my bully boys, blow," and all her life she could sing it as the Yankee sailors sang it making landfall at Java Head.

In Hong Kong the Delano family lived for a year. There was born Sara's brother, Frederic Adrian Delano, who was later to become a man of prominence in New York and Washington. But at last Warren Delano was ready to return home. This was a longer journey than the last, for the family journeyed first to Germany and then to France, taking two years in the passage. In Paris they took a house on Avenue l'Imperatrice, and from its balcony Sara used to see the Empress Eugènie, ride by in her fine carriage with her courtiers and her royal consort, Napoleon III.

Then and later Sara loved to dress in the height of fashion. In one of her diaries—the Delanos, perhaps because they were friends of Emerson, were inveterate journal-keepers!—she tells how she "peacocked up and down in a new Paris bonnet and coat" in front of the Delano home on Lafayette Place. After returning from Europe the family divided its time between Colonnade Row and Algonac, which is now owned by Mrs. Roosevelt's brother. Sara was now growing into a beautiful, cultured and charming young lady, one of the fascinating "Delano girls."

The sisters were beautiful and charming. All had lovely features and dark brown eyes. Laura, the oldest, died when she was eighteen. Dora married William H. Forbes, a trader in China tea, and lived for many years in Paris, where her husband had his headquarters. During Dora's long life she was to cross the Pacific ten times and the Atlantic more than fifty. Her merchant husband died in 1893 and thereafter she divided her time between Newburgh and Paris. During the first World War she helped found The Lighthouse, a charitable organization which assisted countless *poilus* who were blinded during the war. Dora stayed in Paris throughout the long conflict, and when the second war was about to envelop all Europe she was in that city for her annual visit. Only the importunities of her nephew, President Roosevelt, caused her to return at the last. She arrived in this country in November, after the war had begun, and the following June, within a month of her ninety-third birthday, died peacefully at Algonac.

Sister Annie, who married William Hitch, lived for many years at Algonac and was a leader in Newburgh charitable affairs. She gave a large tract of land for a public recreation park in that city. Sister Katherine, who also made the voyage around Cape Horn, married Price Collier. The brothers of the family became business men with the exception of Frederick. He distinguished himself as chairman of the Regional Plan of New York and its Environs, as president of the American Civic Association, as a vice-governor of the Federal Reserve Board before Franklin Roosevelt became President, and as chairman of the National Resources Planning Board.

It was difficult, when they were young, to tell which was the most beautiful of the Delano girls. The accolade might well have gone to the brown-haired, brown-eyed Sara, who grew into as delightful a young lady as any who graced the drawing rooms of Lafayette Place, or Tivoli, or Newport, or even Fifth Avenue. Undoubtedly many beaux sought her company but she spurned whatever offers of marriage came her way until she was twenty-six years old.

Then, one day in the early spring of 1880, Mr. and Mrs. Theodore Roosevelt, Sr., gave a dinner party at their comfortable home on Twenty-Sixth Street. The lovely Sara was placed next to another member of the Roosevelt family, James of Hyde Park. The tall, middle-aged gentleman had a hearty, infectious laugh, and a fund of fascinating stories. When something amused him, his mutton-chop whiskers danced gayly, and after dinner, Sara noticed, he smoked his cheroot with a fine flourish. She was enchanted with him and he fell in love with her.

James Roosevelt, who had a son as old as the girl he met at the dinner party, made a gallant suitor. He was in constant attendance upon her all that summer and made frequent trips across the Hudson to woo her at Algonac. Sitting together on the shaded lawn she talked of her childhood travels, they mentioned all the people they knew, and discovered that they were sixth cousins, among their joint ancestors having been Ezekiel Cheever, who taught Cotton Mather his Latin and who was the first master of the ancient Boston Latin School. Despite the difference of twenty-six years in their ages they had much in common, and not the least was their love for the shores of the Hudson, the old homes that they both cherished.

On October 7, 1880, they drove by carriage from New York, taking the front seat and putting the coachman in back, and were married in the drawing room at Algonac before members of clans Delano and Roosevelt, who tactfully hid whatever amazement they may have felt over this December-May romance. And then Sara Delano crossed the Hudson to become mistress of Hyde Park.

For twenty felicitous years James and his young wife Sara made Hyde Park their home. Together they traveled widely in this country and in Europe, they passed one winter in Washington, another in Spain. They went to Mexico together. But they also spent long, happy days, as Sara once recalled, "just sitting before the fire at Hyde Park—like Darby and Joan."

Happiest of all the days at Hyde Park was the 30th of January, 1882. On that day James Roosevelt set down these historic words in his wife's diary:

"Monday, January 30, 1882. At quarter to nine my Sally had a splendid large baby boy. He weighs ten pounds without his clothes."

His Sally, years later, revealed that it came close to being a

tragic day, for she and her son inhaled "too much chloroform."
But they both quickly recovered and within a few days Sara
was doting over her "plump, pink, and nice baby," whom they
named Franklin Delano Roosevelt, after Sally's uncle.

Sara was ideally happy during the next eighteen years and
then the inevitable happened. Her husband was now seventy-
two years old and she was forty-six. Franklin was away at Harvard when James Roosevelt became ill. With his wife he left
Hyde Park and came to New York where they took rooms at
the old Hotel Renaissance in order to be near the family physician. Franklin was called from Cambridge and both mother
and son were at James's bedside when he died. A few hours later
Sara Delano Roosevelt wrote in her diary:

"All is over. At 2.02 he merely slept away. As I write these
words I wonder how I lived after he left me."

Before her marriage the greatest influence in her life had
been her father, who had devoted his life to support and protect his children. Having invested his money wisely in Pennsylvania coal mines and real estate—he had been a railroad
director, as James Roosevelt also was—she now had all the
money she needed to satisfy every material want. Her husband
also left her a not inconsiderable estate. During her marriage
Sara had received from James Roosevelt the same kind of consideration that her father had always given her. Although she
had traveled widely and knew more of the world than many
women, hers had been a cloistered existence, and always she
had leaned on her men for support.

Most women of her age and circumstances would have sought
another sanctuary in this tragic time. Her own brothers, or her
stepson James Roosevelt Roosevelt, might well have taken the
place of her earlier protectors, and to them she might have
clung, asking from them constant tribute to her helplessness
and her grief, for she was approaching middle age and was a
distinctly mid-Victorian lady. Instead, she took into her own
hands the management of Hyde Park, with its farms and ten-
ants and the big, empty house. From that time on she managed
her own affairs. Her interests expanded. She began to grow.

The greatest of her interests, of course, was her son Franklin.
Her future life, so different from that which had gone before,

was dedicated to his welfare, from the day they sat together in
the suddenly silent house at Hyde Park after the funeral in St.
James' Church in the nearby village until her own death early
in September, 1941, at the age of eighty-six. But through those
many years she never forgot her husband. She insisted that she
be called Mrs. James Roosevelt and not Mrs. Sara Delano
Roosevelt; and she placed a window in St. James Church, "giving thanks to God for the beloved memory of James Roosevelt."

Many honors and distinctions were to come to her in the
ensuing years, those historic years that saw her son grow up and
move from one public office to another until he became President of the United States. One she shared with but seven other
women in history for, along with the mothers of George Washington, James Madison, James K. Polk, Ulysses S. Grant, James
A. Garfield, and William McKinley, she had the rare distinction of seeing her son elected to that post. She was the only
woman to have that honor three times.

At the beginning of her son's political career Mrs. James
Roosevelt was not inclined to take his ambitions seriously. She
expected that he would be content to pursue the same gentlemanly life that had appealed to her husband or that at the
most, he might, eventually, become a "diplomat," such as James
Roosevelt Roosevelt had been in the Cleveland era. When
Franklin won his first election, much to her surprise, the gracious grande-dame went to Albany and superintended the large
reception for his constituents which her son held at the opening of the session. She must have been greatly startled, a few
weeks later, when his name began to appear in the headlines
as a new scourge of Tammany Hall.

But as the years passed and it became apparent that Franklin
was more interested in politics than in anything else, she willingly reshaped her life to suit his. Mother Roosevelt never
could become quite reconciled to some of the queer, even radical and long-haired, individuals whom Franklin brought home
to Hyde Park. They were not her kind. But Mrs. Roosevelt,
who was the mistress always of her own home, was able to hide
her distaste. As the years passed she actually came to like the
frequent disturbances of the ancient tranquillity of Hyde Park.

Franklin's illness in 1921 revived all her maternal and protective instincts. She sought to shield him against jarring disturbances. Eleanor Roosevelt saw the error of Mother Roosevelt's way and with infinite tact was able to take charge. If there
was animosity then, it later disappeared. The two women—one
the matriarch, the other the modern woman of affairs—were
friends. Each admired the other, although each disapproved of
some of the things the other did. Mrs. Roosevelt could not understand why Eleanor wanted to run a furniture factory, or
study shorthand, or teach school. Eleanor, perhaps, resented her
mother-in-law's well-intentioned desire to manage things. But,
as far as is known, the friction never developed beyond that
stage.

When Franklin Roosevelt became President it was only natural that the sweeping spotlight should rest on Mrs. James
Roosevelt. She rose to the occasion. She was proud of her son,
but not so proud that, if she thought it necessary, she could not
take him down a peg. Like Teddy Roosevelt, Franklin was not
always sure of his facts, but was stubborn in maintaining his
errors. He once told reporters that he was going to call the
estate at Hyde Park by what he insisted was its old Dutch name,
Krum Elbow. Better informed on the ancient history of
Dutchess County, Mrs. Roosevelt also told the reporters that
the name of the place was Hyde Park, that it had never been
Krum Elbow, and she intimated that as far as she was concerned it never would be.

"Franklin doesn't know everything," she added, with a firm
nod of her head.

With the passing years the two, mother and son, looked more
and more like each other. Most noticeable was the likeness in
their firm, determined mouths and chins. Their smiles, too,
were alike, although Mother Roosevelt, not being a politician,
did not smile as readily. Looking at Mrs. Roosevelt, proud, determined, aristocratic in her bearing, one knew that Franklin's
stubbornness was not all Dutch. It was part Yankee.

Age crept with graciousness upon Sara Delano Roosevelt. To
the end she kept up her interest in many things. She served on
committees, she lent her name to causes; but she never joined
a cause that might in any way embarrass her son. Wherever she

went, to Europe, to the World's Fair of New York in 1939 or 1940, she was a commanding person. But not demanding. It seemed, as one watched her ingrained dignity, that she had been born to be a President's mother. In another age she could have been a queen. Even those to whom the name of Roosevelt—of Franklin Roosevelt—made the blood boil bowed, as it were, before her. A tall, white haired lady, who seemed like some one out of the past, kindly but not sentimental, cultured, patient, and charming, she went quietly through the two administrations of her son, accepting the homage paid to her in his name, not in her own. She never tried to hide her pride in her son; nor he, his love for his mother. For sixty years the closeness between mother and son had been remarkable. When it ended in September 1941 with her quiet death in the old house at Hyde Park to which she had gone as a bride, millions of Americans who had never known her felt as if something especially strong and fine had gone from the American scene.

Book Four

PRESIDENTS

Greatness At Last

GREATNESS CAME to the Roosevelt family in the seventh generation.

Tracing the line of descent from Claes Martenszen van Rosenvelt to the twenty-sixth and the thirty-second Presidents of the United States, Theodore Roosevelt and Franklin Delano Roosevelt, one finds that both were born an equal number of generations from what Teddy once called their "very common ancestor."

This direct descent from the scrubby Manhattan farm of the Little Fellow to the magnificence of the White House can best be understood by a glance at the following simple chart:

CLAES MARTENSZEN VAN ROSENVELT

Nicholas Roosevelt

(1658)

Johannes (1689)	Jacobus (1692)
Jacobus (1724)	Isaac (1726)
Jacobus (1759)	James (1760)
Cornelius (1794)	Isaac (1790)
Theodore I (1831)	James (1828)
Theodore II (1858)	Franklin (1882)

It was James Roosevelt, the father of Franklin, who was responsible for the difference of twenty-four years in the ages of the two Presidents. Teddy Roosevelt was born when his father

was but twenty-seven years old. Franklin was the child of James
Roosevelt's second marriage, and he was not born until his
father had passed his fifty-fourth birthday.

Exactly two centuries had passed between the birthdays of
Nicholas Roosevelt, the fur trapper and shopkeeper, and Theodore, the President, and it now is a little more than a decade
less than three centuries since the name Roosevelt first crept
into the records of American history.

Comparisons between the two great Roosevelts who, within
our own time, have commanded the attention of the world is
inevitable. But comparisons are no less odious now than they
have always been and even with the inescapable record before
us, it is futile to say that one was the greater man. They were
much alike in many ways; but by ancestry as well as by temper-
ament they were vastly different. And so were their times.

We must remember that the problems which Theodore faced
were not those which Franklin Roosevelt had to solve. Perhaps
if Theodore Roosevelt had been able to carry through his ideas
and ideals to a conclusion, or if he had been sprung from a different environment, or if he had seen the world more clearly
and compromised less, then the world that Franklin Roosevelt
faced so squarely in 1932 would have been far different.

But "ifs" are not history and both Theodore and Franklin
and their separate worlds are facts.

When Teddy was born, the Civil War had not begun to rend
the nation; it was nearly two decades past when Franklin was
playing with his first toys in his crib at Hyde Park. Teddy became a national hero in the cruelly comic war with Spain
when Franklin was a schoolboy. When the World War broke
Franklin was Assistant Secretary of the Navy and Theodore,
already an old man, was trying desperately to find one last
heroic place for himself in a changed world. He was gone from
the scene when Franklin replaced the New Freedom (sprung
in part from Teddy's own attacks) with the New Deal. He was
gone when Franklin, taking a clue from Teddy's great political
mistake, remained silent about the third term and was kept in
the White House by a people who did not dare to turn the
country back to the old rulers, the spiritual heirs of Teddy,
who lacked his fire and drive.

The lives of the cousins have stretched over the most momentous years of our history since old Isaac Roosevelt broke with his Tory friends and became a Patriot. Although of the same generation of descent, they are of different generations of thought, action, and history. Although of the same family they are nevertheless of different families, with different strains of blood running through them. Franklin is, mostly, Dutch and Yankee; Teddy was Dutch, and, to a lesser degree, Southern. Which strain—paternal or maternal—was greater in each it is easy to see. In Theodore the Dutch stubbornness and ruggedness came to the fore. In Franklin, the dry Yankee strain mingled with the Dutch and became volatile. The Allertons, the Aspinwalls, the Delanos (who were Yankee despite their French origin) seem to have enriched Franklin more than the Bullochs and Stobos and Barnhills enriched Teddy.

But does all this conjecture really matter? Both branches flowered in greatness, and both transcended their ancestry. Both have proved that heredity *plus* environment is what counts; and that deeds count more than either.

CHAPTER XIX

Theodore Roosevelt

I

IT IS A MYTH of long standing that Theodore Roosevelt, who was to become the twenty-sixth President of the United States, stepped suddenly and without reason from the guarded circles of an upper class family, that had never been touched by so common a thing as politics, into the hurly-burly business of rulership, burning with a passion for reform, and became the Great Crusader of his age. For many years he was considered the supreme example of the young man of wealth, culture and leisure who bravely dedicated himself, in the manner of an English gentleman, to those mundane affairs which members of his "class" had long held beneath contempt.

This was far from being the truth. Theodore Roosevelt was born with politics in his blood. His father played at the game; his Uncle Bob worked at the business. It would have been unusual if some member of the family had not, in his time, entered the lists. The family was ready, through years of careful nurture, to produce a "great man," and the time had come, in the national development, for exactly the kind of greatness that was stored in the frail, asthmatic body of the son of Theodore I and Martha Bulloch Roosevelt.

Theodore II was born at twenty-eight East Twentieth Street, New York, on October 27, 1858. The small brick house still stands there, known as "Roosevelt House," a museum to his memory. He was the second of four children. Anna, his sister, was three years older; Elliott was two years younger, and Corinne was two years younger still. Elliott, who was to be the father of Anna Eleanor Roosevelt, the wife of Franklin Roosevelt, was the huskiest of the group, and its natural leader. Teedie, as young Theodore was called, was far from healthy as a child, suffering from asthma and weak eyes. He was naturally pampered by his father and mother, his grandmother Bulloch, who lived with the Roosevelts, and by his Aunt Anna Bulloch, who also stayed in the house. Aunt Anna was the children's tutor, although for a while a French governess was employed. In the New York house they had all the playthings they desired; in the country, where they spent the summers—usually on Long Island although sometimes at Dobbs Ferry on the Hudson—they had all kinds of pets, cats, dogs, rabbits, a coon, and a pony named General Grant. Their father invoked a benevolent discipline, but, as remembered by Teddy in later years, nothing harsh ever entered the lives of these children.

Because of his asthma Teddy was more pampered than the rest. When he was ten years old the severity of this affliction caused his parents to take him to the Catskills for the summer. He made his first trip to Europe when he was eleven, and, when he was fourteeen, accompanied his father on another long journey that included a voyage up the Nile in a sailing vessel. He did not enjoy his travels nearly as much as he did the long summers in the country with his brother and sisters— a bespectacled barefoot boy with prominent teeth and an infectious grin.

When he was about sixteen his father decided that he should go to Harvard. For the next two years private tutors came to the house to prepare him and for a time he attended the nearby private school of a Professor McMullen. He never went to a public school or a private boarding academy, nor was he ever away from his family until he left for Cambridge in the autumn of 1876. There was no family tradition for choosing Harvard, although the sons of most of the "best" families went there in the 'seventies and 'eighties. Hitherto such Roosevelts as had received a higher education had taken it at Princeton or Columbia. The first Harvard Roosevelt was James Roosevelt of

Hyde Park, the father of Franklin, who studied law there in the 1850's.

Before he went off to college Teedie had become, as he said, an embryo zoölogist. He even learned, as his cousin Franklin was later to learn, the messy science of taxidermy; he collected butterflies, birds and small beasts; he kept notebooks on his investigations; and he even sent information about his zoölogical discoveries to obscure semi-scientific publications. He learned Latin because he had to understand the strange names of flowers, birds and beasts. He read books of adventure—the stories of Captain Mayne Reid were his favorites—and he learned, mainly because of his travels, to speak German and French. But he was not by any means a "grind" when he left home for the Cambridge adventure.

Summers spent outdoors and the careful nurturing of his health by his indulgent family had filled out the spindling lad by this time. With his father's encouragement he had learned to box, a sport he enjoyed despite his weak eyes. He had been wearing spectacles since he was thirteen, and was to wear them all his life. After 1908 he was totally blind in one eye. But he did not allow this affliction to rob him of any pleasures in life and he seldom complained about it.

In the meantime Teedie's brother Elliott had been having his own struggle for good health. Always apparently far stronger than his older brother, he had been sent to fashionable St. Paul's School, at Concord, New Hampshire, to prepare for Harvard. But there he had a physical breakdown and was removed after attending for only a year. Accompanied by a physician friend of the family, he was sent to Texas, where he lived with the officers at Fort McKavit, a frontier post. In this healthy if hardly cultural environment he hunted wild turkeys and other game and even accompanied his older friends on their sorties, scouting for hostile Indians. One can imagine the envy with which young Teddy must have received his letters in the less adventurous environs of Oyster Bay! After several months in Texas, now apparently in robust health, Elliott returned to New York, with two accomplishments, an imperishable love for hunting and the ability to ride unruly horses. He did not pursue his education further.

At Harvard Theodore was far from popular. True, having come from the "best circles" in New York Society and being the son of a reasonably rich New York merchant, banker and philanthropist, he was acceptable to the "best circles" of student society. But even there he was not well liked by his fellow students. Most of his teachers disliked him immensely; he had the habit of making them feel he knew more than they did. Having stepped so suddenly from a pampered existence—there is no question that he was a spoiled child—he had developed an inferiority complex that he now tried to hide through being bumptious. A thin, bespectacled youngster, he sought to obscure his youthfulness behind a ridiculous pair of red side-whiskers. He over dressed like a dude. His toothy grin accentuated his obnoxious, know-it-all manner, which was particularly offensive in the class room.

Theodore was not a brilliant student, but neither was he dumb. His social standing made him acceptable to the "right" clubs, and he was admitted to them all, including Porcellian. His native intelligence, and the sobering effect of his father's death—which occurred in February of his sophomore year— kept him from "flunking." In the end he "made" Phi Beta Kappa and, in his senior year, stood with the first tenth of his class.

After his father's death, by which he inherited about two hundred thousand dollars, Theodore became more fashionable than ever and showed more fully that touch of exhibitionism which was to mark him all his later life. But he was not wild, like that far richer young man, William Randolph Hearst, who came to Harvard two years after Teddy had left and whose adventures in vulgarity did not end with his college days. He had, even then, a serious side. This led him into the study of history as well as zoölogy, and for four years caused him to teach a class each Sunday at Cambridge's select Christ Protestant Episcopal Church, although he was not confirmed in the Episcopal faith. Perhaps this was his way of paying tribute to the memory of "the best man I ever knew," his father, who for many years had devoted much time to his own Presbyterian Bible class.

There was a fertility in Teddy's mind. There was also a fear of being bored. He might very well have lived an idle life devoted solely to the pursuit of pleasure, with the same alcoholic result that was to afflict his older brother Elliott, for he could afford to be idle. But this prevalent aptitude of his class did not appeal to him. Neither did it appeal to certain other young men he knew at Harvard,—men like Owen Wister, who one day would be a famous author and Teddy's biographer, and especially the older Henry Cabot Lodge, who was later to be Senator from Massachusetts and who was to make Teddy president. At this time he was already approaching his career through history. Before he left Harvard he had begun to write his history, *The Naval War of 1812,* and he dreamed of a life devoted to historico-literary pursuits. No Roosevelt, except perhaps his Uncle Bob, had ever shown these traits so markedly before.

Yet before he became the ambitious young scholar who delighted to associate with men like Henry James and Edward Everett Hale, because they were doing delightful things, he fell in love. He passes over the episode in his *Autobiography* yet there is no more beautiful chapter in his life. Alice Hathaway Lee was a lovely and lively girl. She was a true Brahmin of Boston and Brookline, the daughter of George Cabot Lee, one of State Street's leading bankers. Her father was a descendant of George Cabot, Alexander Hamilton's close friend. He was a confirmed Mugwump, as those who held themselves superior to their party in character and intelligence were called in the 80's, and deeply interested in the same polite measures of political, if not financial, reform that had taken up so much of Teddy's father's time and strength. He was a partner of Major Henry Lee Higginson, founder of the Boston Symphony Orchestra and cultural leader of Boston. His political beliefs were those of the greater Mugwumps of the day—of Carl Schurz, Edwin L. Godkin, editor of the *New York Post,* and George William Curtis, that Emersonian young man in whom, as Van Wyck Brooks once said, "Transcendentalism had gone to seed" but who was admirable as a "driver out of money changers." Their ideals and their way of life fitted admirably to Teddy's dream of that "far distant salon, wherein we are to gather society men who take part in politics, literature and art, and politicians, authors and artists whose bringing up and personal habits do not disqualify them from society."

Although Teddy glowed in the company of George Cabot Lee and the other progenitors of *The Late George Apley,* Marquand's satirical novel of Brahmin Boston, he did not go to Brookline primarily to listen to their elder wisdom. He was in love with Mr. Lee's tall, brown-haired daughter. He courted her ardently, so ardently that he was the butt of his more uncouth classmates' jokes, and he pursued her to the detriment of his studies. The lovely girl, who was noted for her straightness of carriage and her up-tilted Cabot nose, was vastly amused at first by the impetuous New Yorker with the foreign-sounding name of Roosevelt, who still collected bugs and frogs and knew their Latin names. But she could not resist him long. He was so deadly serious, so hopelessly in love with her. Their engagement was announced about the time of his graduation in June, 1880, and they were married the next October.

II

After leaving Harvard young Teddy was at loose ends. He did not, of course, have to work for a living. Harvard, he felt then, had not done much for him. It had not made him a scientist, as he had half-hoped it would, nor had it taught him to be a writer. His history of the War of 1812 was gathering dust—although it was later to be finished. His friend Cabot Lodge, as the young politician was always known to his intimates, had not yet begun his long drive to make the young man president. He could, of course, follow his brother Elliott's example, and go hunting big game in the jungles of India and Ceylon. But there seemed to be something futile to this. At about this time, in a letter to his sister Anna, who had become Mrs. William S. Cowles, he was complaining bitterly about the dull life led by certain of his classmates—"fellows of excellent family and faultless breeding, with a fine old country-place, four-in-hands, tandems, a yacht, and so on; but, oh, the decorous hopelessness of their lives!"

In order to escape this boredom and salve his troubled Presbyterian conscience, the young bridegroom decided to accept his Uncle Bob's offer of a clerkship in his law firm. Most of the time, however, was not spent poring over legal books. Instead, he again took up his study of the Naval War. When Autumn came he desultorily entered the Columbia University law school. In the meantime, he had taken the first step of his career as a politician—although he was unaware of this fact at the time—by joining the Twenty-First District Republican Association, better known as the "Jake Hess Club" after a city henchman of Tom Platt, the "Easy Boss" of up-state Republican politics. The meetings were held in Morton Hall, a barnlike room over a saloon, on the corner of Fifth Avenue and Fifty-Ninth Street, a site now occupied by the Savoy Plaza Hotel. Teddy's action caused much amusement among the "men of cultivated taste and easy life" who were his and his father's friends. He had chosen the Republican party because "in 1880, a young man of my bringing up and beginnings could join only the Republican Party"—although it would seem that Uncle Bob and his Reform Democrats might have welcomed a young man of his stripe in theirs.

The law appealed not at all to the young, blond, bespectacled and overdressed Teddy, and after a year at Columbia he put it aside for good and all. He then went abroad with his bride of a year and had a splendid time in England, on their belated honeymoon. During his trip he corresponded with Henry Cabot Lodge, then already a member of the Massachusetts House of Representatives, who spent his days alternating between his scholar's library and the smoky South Boston counterparts of the "Jake Hess Club." Upon Teddy's return his mind was made up. He would "enter politics" seriously. The cynical hostility of Society to public life angered him and made him feel that its members did not belong to the "governing class," as they thought they did, but that the governing class was made up of those "saloon-keepers, horse-car conductors, and the like" with whom he would have to associate if he followed his plan.

Courageously Teddy approached the rough and ready politician, Jake Hess, who must have been startled to see the young gentleman enter the clubroom over the saloon, and ask to be given an active part in the district's politics. Hess, who was absolute boss of the Twenty-First District, and who personally

supervised all nominations and elections, was more annoyed
than pleased, but Joe Murray, a district captain who had been
"raised as a barefooted boy on First Avenue" and had deserted
Tammany for the Republicans, took a liking for the "silk stocking dude." When Murray was ready to scalp his chief and win
for himself the coveted leadership, he decided to make young
Teddy his foil. Accordingly he forced through Teddy's nomination as Assemblyman. This won, and with the election approaching, the astute Murray let Teddy campaign on Fifth Avenue while carefully concealing him from Sixth Avenue, where
he felt a better result could be achieved for "the dude" if he
were not seen. The result was that Teddy carried his district by
1,911 votes—thanks to the obedience of the machine, and, in the
upper brackets, to the aid of such respectable residents of the
Twenty-First district as Elihu Root and Joseph H. Choate,
corporation lawyer and famous leader of the New York bar.

When Teddy and Alice Lee went to Albany he was not, of
course, the first Roosevelt to occupy a seat in the legislature.
But James Roosevelt, the Tammany brave who had helped
sabotage the Whigs' election reforms of 1840, had long since
been forgotten, and there were few to remember that Isaac
Roosevelt, the Patriot, had been one of the first Senators of the
State. Even if these facts had been recalled they would hardly
have made his fellow-legislators less hostile to him. He came as
representative of the richest district in the city of New York;
he was, himself, a rich young man; he was, therefore, doubly
suspect. But he was placed on the important Committee of
Cities by the Democratic house, which hardly suspected so
naive a youngster could do any real harm.

Teddy soon realized that what he had suspected when he first
entered the Jake Hess Club—that Republicans were no more
honest than Democrats—was true upstate as well as in the city of
Tammany Hall. The "Black Horse Cavalry," so-named because
of its unbridled raids on the public till, accepted bribes and
extorted in return for passing or thwarting legislation. Much
to naive Teddy's horror, it was composed of members of the
Republican Party. Teddy estimated that "probably a third"
of the legislators were crooks and those who were not were
unable to make their honesty effective. Sensibly he did not

plunge immediately into "reform." When he did, his first effort was in vain. One day he managed to push through a resolution calling for an investigation of various scandals involving elevated railway financing in New York and charging the all-powerful Jay Gould with the corruption of a State Supreme Court Judge. The *New York Times,* perhaps remembering the work of the elder Roosevelts during its own fight against the Tweed ring, commended him in these words:

"There is a splendid career open for a young man of position, character and independence like Mr. Roosevelt who can denounce the legalized robbery of Gould and his allies without descending to the turgid abuse of the demagogue, and without . . . the cowardly caution of the politician."

If little but a few commendatory editorials came of his initial attack on "bossism," the gesture was not entirely wasted. Attention had been drawn to the young Assemblyman. Mr. Godwin approvingly recommended him to other young society men who might by chance read *The Evening Post* or *The Nation,* and several eminent Mugwumps dined him at Delmonico's. In his own little world he was looked on as a heroic young man, even if some of his more experienced friends, including Mr. Lodge, were beginning to wonder if he would know how to control himself at a crucial moment.

During this first session Alice had stayed with him at his Albany hotel. Now they returned to New York, where they took a house on West Forty-Fifth Street with Teddy's mother, the widowed Mrs. Martha Bulloch Roosevelt. That autumn Teddy was re-elected for a second term and returned to Albany, ready to throw himself even more ardently into the business of politics. Except for the fact that he won the minority vote of his party as Speaker of the House—an empty honor in the Democratic body—his second term was quite uneventful. When it had ended he went to the Dakotas to hunt buffalo and while there invested fourteen thousand dollars of the two hundred thousand dollars inheritance from his father in a cattle ranch at Chimney Butte, near the hamlet of Little Missouri in the Bad Lands of the Dakotas. He then was elected for a third term. When he returned to Albany this time he left Alice in the West

Forty-Fifth Street home. Albany was no place for an expectant mother.

Meanwhile Teddy's brother, Elliott, had come back from his Eastern hunting trip to attend the wedding of their younger sister, Corinne, to Douglas Robinson. At about this time he met Anna Hall, one of the reigning beauties of New York society, a member of a socially prominent family and descendant of Chancellor Livingston. They were married in December, 1883. Elliott had none of his brother's drive or interest in politics and little of his bride's intense preoccupation with society, but more of the latter than the former. As the young son of Theodore, Sr., he had inherited enough wealth to live comfortably without exerting himself. With his wife he was to carry on some of his father's philanthropies, particularly those related to the welfare of newsboys and crippled children, but on the whole his was an aimless existence in contrast with that of his brother. Teddy, the family now believed, was already destined to be a Great Man.

While Teddy was in Albany, leading an abortive investigation of vice conditions in New York and trying to force through the passage of a law to stop the manufacture of cigars in New York's squalid tenements (not because he was interested in the welfare of the exploited cigar-maker but as a measure of "public health"—for the smoker!) his first child was born. A girl, they named her Alice for her mother.

Very elated, Teddy returned to the State Capitol, but soon he was called suddenly home and Corinne and her husband were summoned from Baltimore, where they were visiting friends. They were greeted at the door by the distraught Elliott, who mumbled something about there being a curse on the house they were about to enter. Both Alice and Mrs. Roosevelt were dangerously ill. In fact, they were dying. Early on the morning after Teddy's dash from Albany his mother passed away. That afternoon Alice, his wife, whom he had loved so dearly, followed her. Two days later Teddy sat grimly at the double funeral service that was held in the Fifth Avenue Presbyterian Church. Back in the house on Forty-Fifth Street, a small baby gurgled in her nurse's arms. Twenty years later, when her father had at last become the Great Man, she was to be known as Princess Alice and her marriage to Nicholas Longworth, the rich young Congressman from Ohio, was to be blazoned on the front pages of the world's press.

Fortunately for Teddy he could find some measure of forgetfulness in his work and after pausing to write a beautiful tribute to his dead wife, which he had printed for their friends, he returned to the legislative halls and the hotel rooms of Albany. Strangely enough when he came to write his *Autobiography* at Sagamore Hill in 1913, he had erased all memory of his beautiful first wife from his mind. Or perhaps, even then, after all the struggles and all the triumphs, the memory was too sacred to bring before the public gaze.

There was, indeed, much to occupy his mind these days. The Presidential campaign of 1884 was in the offing. In the meantime, however, he had suffered a cruel set back to his political ambitions and a cruel blow to his ineffable pride. When he had begun his third term the Republicans had gained a majority in both Houses. Since he had been named Speaker in the previous year when the honor was as empty as an old tin can, he thought, now that the Speakership meant something, it should come his way again. But the hard-headed politicians deemed otherwise. Despite much running around, cornering of members, and open pleading on Teddy's part, they gave the post to a trustworthy "regular." Teddy, smarting under the lash of party discipline, blamed his "independent" actions and his open hostility to "bossism," for his defeat, as he was to blame other set backs later on in the career that was now so definitely begun.

Teddy had his first major experience with the hard and bitter reality of practical politics at the Republican national convention of 1884. Accompanied by his friend, the scholarly, gentlemanly, yet thoroughly unscrupulous Henry Cabot Lodge, then a Representative, the young delegate from New York went to Chicago filled to the bursting point with a zeal for reform. In Teddy's eyes no person within the Republican ranks was more distasteful, more revolting than the "Plumed Knight," the "Man from Maine"—James G. Blaine. Every instinct for decency within Teddy rose against supporting a candidate against whom the finger of suspected corruption was so darkly pointed, and who undoubtedly had sold his influence in Congress to save him from financial ruin. He worked with Lodge, the avowed mouthpiece of the Boston Independents, for the nomination of the colorless but honest Senator George F. Edmunds of Vermont, but he promised Lodge that he would support Blaine, of whom he had spoken openly in terms of disgust, if their own candidate should lose. There was, of course, no real hope that Edmunds would become the compromise choice. The cards were stacked for Blaine from the beginning by the "regulars" who preferred him, his soiled plume and all, to President Chester A. Arthur or Vermont's favorite son. To shouts of "Blaine! Blaine! James G. Blaine!," Maine's adopted son "swept" the convention.

Teddy was in a quandary. "By all his lights," as Matthew Josephson has said in *The President Makers*, "Roosevelt, too, should have 'switched to Cleveland'," as most of the men "of the broadest culture and highest character," to use Teddy's own phrase, in the Party were preparing to do. That he was wracked by doubts there is no question. Should he, in the words of Carl Schurz, "obey a noble impulse," and bolt? Or should he remain within the ranks on the specious Lodgian excuse that by so doing "I can be of some use. By going out I destroy all the influence and power for good I possess?"

In this moment of indecision the soul-tortured young man fled to the solitude of his ranch at Chimney Butte. There, prodded by his older friend Lodge, who had broken with his Reform friends—that gentle but gallant Independent, Moorfield Storey, did not speak to Lodge for forty years!—Teddy reached his decision: he would follow the party line. Personal ambition had triumphed at the cost of his honest, inward beliefs. It was a bitter Teddy who came back East to campaign in Massachusetts —unsuccessfully—for his friend and adviser, and even to take the stump for Blaine, of whom he had said: "I hope to God he will be defeated."

God must have listened to the young man's prayer. Grover Cleveland became president and for the next four years Teddy, posing as "an humble party man"—although that was something he never could be long—cast about for a new starting point for his interrupted career.

III

Even a young man with the income from two hundred thousand safely invested dollars and a fourteen thousand dollar cattle ranch that presumably would some day pay dividends cannot happily remain idle long, especially a restless individual like Teddy Roosevelt.

After the disastrous election he went again to his Billings County, North Dakota, ranch, where he put on his chaps and sombrero, rode madly and lived a healthy life "roughing it." Forgotten, for the time, was politics. Forgotten, too, was the dream of the "far distant salon" of society men, politicians and writers, all happily engaged in decent work. He remained in the West, thoroughly enjoying himself, from April until October, 1885. Then he came East again. He might have had the Republican nomination as Congressman but he rejected the offer and laid his plans for bigger game. He would be what his Uncle Bob had never succeeded in becoming—Mayor of New York! The young politician who had lost the love of the Mugwumps, who could not conceivably win any support from the Democrats, captured the futile Republican nomination and pitted himself, in a ridiculous and disastrous campaign, against that magnificent eccentric, Henry George, the father of the Single Tax, and Abram S. Hewitt, the successful contender.

Soon after the last returns were in Teddy fled from unkind New York. This time he accompanied his sister, Mrs. Anna Cowles, to England. The journey had a deeper purpose than mere rest. Teddy was planning to be married again. After they had arrived in London, Edith Carow, whom he had known almost all his life, and with whom perhaps he had been in love even before he knew Alice Lee, joined them and they were married in St. George's Church, Hanover Square, on December 2, 1886. When the officials at the Registry Office asked him his father's occupation Teddy set down the single word: "Gentleman." They had a delightful time in Florence, Italy, and then they returned to England, where Teddy mingled with the "very nicest people." He went fox hunting, which was great sport. He had access to the Reform Club, where he met Lord Bryce, ambassadorial author of *The American Commonwealth,* and others—the very type of political gentlemen he found so rarely in America—the "real thing" that he and Cabot Lodge hoped they might be.

Shortly after his return from Europe with his bride, Teddy built a large house at Oyster Bay, Long Island, which was to be his family seat until his death. He kept busy writing, but all the time he was, as President Cleveland once remarked, "looking to a public career, studying political conditions with a care that I had never known any man to show." Just when or where he would find the spot from which to spring was not clear. The campaign of 1888, which saw that "little grey man," Benjamin Harrison, defeat Grover Cleveland, did not afford any magnificent opportunity. He spoke against Cleveland, it is true, but the services of the defeated mayoralty candidate were not so valuable as to get him an imposing award. Indeed, Henry Cabot Lodge had to exert considerable pressure to induce President Harrison to offer Teddy the relatively obscure post of Civil Service Commissioner at three thousand five hundred dollars a year.

Teddy occupied this berth for six years. During this time he seized every opportunity to make himself heard. He had, even then, a loud voice, and he stirred up this hitherto moribund office. That pious merchant prince, John Wanamaker, who was accepting the reward for his campaign contributions in the office of Postmaster General, suffered frequently from Teddy's lashing tongue. Senators and Congressmen fought his often successful efforts to dislodge their more onerous appointees from the public payroll. President Harrison treated him with a "cold and hesitating disapproval." More than once Henry Cabot Lodge had to step hastily into the picture and place a restraining arm on his friend's shoulder. After all, there were elections coming up in the future. After these admonitions Teddy would quiet down, although it irked him to have to pull his punches for the sake of party harmony.

When Cleveland was returned to office after his Harrisonian holiday he retained Teddy in the Civil Service post and, strangely enough, Teddy got along better with the Democratic President, whom he had known in Albany, than he had with Harrison, although he tangled frequently with other Democrats. He managed to enforce the merit and examination system better than most Commissioners could have done. He rid the government of some dishonest men. And from time to time the newspapers, who had such a bad habit of forgetting him, sang his praises.

In 1894, as a result of the Lexow Committee's exposure of the corrupt status of the street-cleaning and police departments of New York city, the Reform elements were able to force through the election of William L. Strong as Mayor. At their suggestion he offered Teddy, who was already tired of his Civil Service job, the post of Street Commissioner. This he wisely rejected, but when the offer was followed with the promise, arranged by Lodge, that if he would accept a post on the police board he would be given its presidency, Teddy realized that the break he had been awaiting was at hand. He accepted.

Meanwhile Teddy had become very much of a family man. His adored daughter Alice was now ten years old and as much a member of the growing family as if she had been Edith Carow Roosevelt's own child. Much of her early childhood had been spent in New York, in Oyster Bay, and in Washington, with frequent visits to her Lee relatives in Boston. Already she had two half-brothers, Theodore, Jr., a toothy youngster like his father, and Kermit, and a half-sister, Ethel. All these children Teddy loved dearly and he strove, in every way, to earn from them the love he had borne for their grandfather. Edith, who shared many of his memories with him, was like his own mother, an ideal mother and a gracious hostess. At home, where he had to make no decisions involving his conscience, as he did almost daily in the political battlefields, Teddy was an ideally happy man.

The post of president of the board of Police Commissioners was exactly what Teddy needed to revive his interest in politics and to restore his faith in his own future. He was, at the time he took office, only thirty-six years old—but six of these years had been spent in a minor political post in Washington, and three, long forgotten by the populace, in Albany. It had hardly been the brilliant career he had dreamed of carving for himself when he had braved the jeers of his fellow society men and joined up with Jake Hess and Joe Murray; hardly the brilliant career he must have hoped for when he basked in the light of Lord Bryce at the Reform Club in London. But now, wait and see!

Ten years ago, when he had first gone to Albany, he had tried without success to expose the conditions of vice and police corruption which the Lexow Committee had at last brought to light. He now rolled up his sleeves and with his inordinate gusto went to work cleaning the Augean stables. At the start it looked as if he might accomplish great things. Richard "Chief" Croker, the Tammany boss, went darkly to Ireland "for a vacation," and Teddy persuaded his fellow Commissioners to oust Tom Byrnes from his graft-ridden office of Chief Inspector of Police. Then came his famous order to enforce the Sunday closing law of the saloons. This was followed by scores of raids and hundreds of arrests.

All this made marvelous newspaper copy and such socially-conscious reporters as Lincoln Steffens and Jacob Riis did their best to heroize Teddy. They succeeded. His friends, as in the past, warned him to go slowly, that the law was unpopular, that he was heading for trouble. He kept on enforcing the law. He scoured the city by night, a dark cloak hiding his dinner jacket, and reporters covering his trail. The press cuttings grew, the cartoons increased, and Teddy was, as he modestly admitted, a hero.

But Henry Cabot Lodge, ever the realist, pointed out that being a hero among the Reformers might prove an embarrassment. Lodge was right, as he usually was. The politicians, ever aware of the trend of popular opinion, soon began to realize that Teddy and his reforms were heartily disliked by the masses. He had closed their only recreational centers, the saloons, and now they had to sneak down dark alleys for a drink on Sunday, or stay at home and listen to the yelling of their children in their crowded slums.

Then came the passage of the unhappy Raines Law, presumably a liquor-control act, but which turned out to be a great boon to organized vice. This doubled the work of the police—and its widely publicised Commissioner's unpopularity. He again won the enmity of Tom Platt, the Republican boss, and soon found himself, as he said, "living in a welter of political

intrigue of the meanest kind." He knew that the alliance between Republicanism and Tammany was too strong for him to
combat much longer. Nevertheless he determined at last to
fight the Republican machine. When he wrote Lodge to this
effect the little terrier from Nahant, then in Europe, cabled him
frantically to refrain. Even Teddy's wife could see that he was
making a political mistake if he went after Platt's scalp, and told
him so. Cabot kept after him, hinting slyly that if only he remained "regular" the presidency of the United States might
some day be his. Once again he drew in his horns.

"I do not say you are to be President tomorrow," Lodge
wrote him. "I do not say it will be—but I am sure it may and
can be."

Lincoln Steffens, then a young reporter who later was to be
among that group of liberal writers whom Teddy disdainfully
called "muck-rakers," knew at this time that every act of
Teddy's was done with this goal in mind. If his two years as
Police Commissioner had accomplished little in the way of
lasting reform in New York, they had accomplished one thing.
Teddy, as a result of his nocturnal raids and his mass arrests,
had made himself a nationally known figure. He now moved to
the national scene and threw his support to Thomas B. Reed,
Speaker of the House and one of the most intelligent and
incorruptible men in the Republican Party. But Mark Hanna,
Senator from Ohio and undisputed boss of the Republican
Party, whose "coarse ways are pretty hard to stand," had picked
William McKinley to be President. And so Teddy bowed before the inevitable, and went forth into battle on McKinley's
side.

Teddy had to crawl on his knees to Boss Platt before he
could get that man's necessary endorsement for the only post
open to him in the McKinley administration, that of Assistant
Secretary of the Navy. Henry Cabot Lodge, now a United States
Senator, and other powerful friends had to beg McKinley, who
did not trust Teddy's temper, before the President would send
his name to the Senate. The appointment was confirmed April
8, 1897. But it was worth all the effort. Teddy was heartily sick
of New York and longed for the pleasant life of Washington,

where he could bask in the pleasant company of his literary-political friends whom he so greatly admired.

In spite of his years in office Teddy had not given up writing. Biographies and political studies had poured from his pen —his *Life* of Thomas Hart Benton, whom he admired because of his early interest in "Manifest Destiny," as American imperialistic expansion was romantically called,—*The Winning of the West,* in which he extolled the imperialistic qualities of the hardy pioneers and other lesser works. All of them exhibited his growing interest in his own peculiarly virile Americanism. It was an anti-democratic, imperialistic Americanism full of red blood and the conquest of land.

Now in Washington, already stirring with predictions of war —the war that Cleveland had warned McKinley against—Teddy could discuss these momentous matters with his friends: Don Cameron, the Senator from Pennsylvania; Henry Adams, the historian; the bearded and cynical Secretary of State, John Hay; and all the rest of that precious group immortalized in the pages of *The Education of Henry Adams.* There were teas and dinners and musicales; good talk, good music, good food. In Washington one was not bothered by the masses as in New York. One could be aloof from humanity and work for the greater glory of America—and Teddy. One could help get on with this war.

Teddy had read and written much about war, but he had never known it except in the pages of books. He thought it was a bully thing. Within a year of his return to Washington, under Secretary of the Navy John D. Long of Massachusetts, whom he called a "perfect dear," he told the Naval War College:

"No triumph of peace is quite so great as the supreme triumphs of war. The diplomat is the servant, not the master, of the soldier."

At this time the talk in "influential circles close to the imperial McKinley regime embraced not only national affairs but, more than ever . . . international relations, the course of empire and trade, the acquisition and completion of the Isthmian canal, naval bases, expansion on the ocean to the south and west, all the various moves in the game of world power politics, and America's part in them."

These things Teddy understood and believed in. He wanted excitement, it is true, and personal glory, but he also desired to see America grow big and strong. But he was afraid McKinley, whom he likened to a chocolate eclair, was "bent on peace," and he sighed because he could not "poison" Secretary Long's mind "so as to make him more truculent in international affairs." At every chance he agitated, and young William Randolph Hearst took up the cry, and Mr. Pulitzer of the *World* joined him in a bloody battle for circulation. Then Mr. Hearst printed a letter in which the Spanish Ambassador said unkind things about President McKinley. And the *Maine* blew up. And Teddy had his "bully" war.

In fairness to Teddy, whose military exploits in the next few months were foolish enough, it must be recalled that he was never merely carried away by his own enthusiasm. He wanted war, but he believed in preparedness first. He sounded the late Nineteenth Century *leitmotif* of the imperialists: "We must have a great navy." He was an old friend and admirer of Admiral Mahan, the great expert on the role of sea power in international affairs. A year before the war came, Teddy, as Assistant Secretary of the Navy, had laid plans for the seizure of Hawaii, for the sending of munitions and supplies to the all-important Pacific Fleet, and for an attack upon the Philippines. He knew always the exact position of every ship. He even had made plans to "prevent the Japs from chipping in." He was ready, a year before the war, to "take Manila."

With the coming of the war Teddy craved action. The office of Assistant Secretary of the Navy would be, he felt, too cramped. He wanted to be in the thick of things, to see the "splendid little war" at first hand.

The first thing he did was to telegraph Brooks Brothers in New York for a lieutenant-colonel's uniform "without yellow on the collar and with leggings." Then he resigned from the Navy Department. Beginning with a nucleous of his friends of his ranching days he organized the Rough Riders. He went with them to Cuba. Perhaps the kindest thing we may do is to forget, now, the ridiculous Teddy, in his gay uniform, storming this hill or that, and "winning the war." The best evidence now available, thoroughly explored by Mr. Walter Millis in his delightful, ironic and carefully annotated *The Martial Spirit* does not leave Teddy the great military hero he appeared to be in, let us say, the contemporary despatches of Richard Harding Davis.

"I do not want to be vain," he wrote to Henry Cabot Lodge, "but I do not think any one else could have handled this regiment quite as I have handled it."

There were few to disagree with him when he came triumphantly back from the wars. Indeed, he had handled the regiment, and himself, in such an open way that he had hardly stepped off the transport at Montauk Point when the Republican nomination for Governor of New York was handed to him, as it were, on a flag-draped platter. He was Colonel Teddy, the great national hero. He could have for the asking almost anything he desired—except the Congressional Medal of Honor. He wanted that, then, above everything. He was still wanting it when he died.

The gubernatorial convention was held that year at Saratoga. Before going there Teddy had made his peace with the "bosses," who had always thought him arrogant and who now realized no man could possibly defeat him. Chauncey M. Depew, a power in Republican circles and then president of the Vanderbilts' New York Central Railroad, placed the Colonel's name in nomination. After that all he had to do was go around in uniform with a few Rough Riders, also in uniform, to lend color to the procession. Augustus Van Wyck, the Democratic opponent, having no Rough Riders to guard him, did not stand a chance.

When Teddy entered the executive mansion at Albany in 1898 he had agreed, in writing, to recognize Boss Tom Platt's supremacy in party affairs and, after much heart-wringing during which he once broke down and "cried like a baby," he had publicly broken with the Independent, or Goo-Goo, party in New York. He had entered another stage of compromise; another step in his career.

His term as governor was hardly distinguished. It was, of course, turbulent at times, for Teddy could never be peaceful, or docile, for long. He accomplished no great, lasting reforms. But he did manage to tangle momentarily with corruption. He had been his party's choice primarily because the Republicans had needed his brass bands and cowboys to drown out the cries that had arisen over a scandal in the administration of up-state canals during the previous administration. Now another indication of corruption within the Republican ranks arose. Boss Platt insisted upon the reappointment of his man, Lou Payn, as Superintendent of Insurance. Teddy refused to make the appointment on the ground that Payn had borrowed money from banks that were dominated by the insurance companies. Platt in the end let him turn down the nomination, but the man whom Teddy did appoint was also from Platt's camp, albeit his record was clear. The episode is remembered today mainly because it was at this time that Teddy said:

"I have always been fond of the West African proverb: Walk softly and carry a big stick."

Teddy, of course, hoped to step from Albany to the White House. Cabot Lodge, his alter ego, had other ideas. (Henry Adams was convinced Lodge wanted to "cut his throat.") At any rate Lodge told him that he should seek the vice presidency with McKinley. Had Teddy's governorship been more brilliant he might have withstood the pressure; but as it was he was not even sure he could capture the renomination. And so, going against his higher hopes, but in the realization that any other move would be suicidal, he agreed. His popularity, he knew, was still ascendant throughout the country, even if it had dulled somewhat at home. McKinley was overwhelmingly renominated, and, with wise old Tom Platt, and sly Matt Quay, boss of the Pennsylvania Republican machine, and the juicy Boise Penrose, Senator from that State, winking at each other behind the scene, Teddy was handed the anonymity of the vice presidency. He was, they thought, safely shelved at last.

But Mark Hanna, cautious and far-seeing, stood out against him until the end. He bitterly remarked of the man he called the "mad cowboy":

"Don't any of you realize there's only one life between this madman and the White House?"

None did, and none cared, and Teddy was back in Washington again.

IV

After the strenuous campaign, during which Teddy toured, the country, baring his prominent teeth and waving his sombrero while Mr. McKinley, safe in the dignity of office, stayed close to his front porch, triumphant Republicanism settled down for what it believed would be a long period of unending power and prosperity.

Teddy presided over the Senate in his new office of Vice President just five days when that august body adjourned until the following November, leaving seven long months in which to plan for the future—for the Presidency he hoped to wrest for himself four years later. The restless Teddy had no intention of being swallowed in the obscurity of the Vice Presidency. He did not have to wait his chance long. Two months before he was scheduled again to mount the Senate rostrum President McKinley fell mortally wounded. On September 6, 1901 while attending the Pan-American Exposition at Buffalo, New York, he was killed by a bullet from the gun of Leon Czolgosz, that strange little anarchist whose mind had become unbalanced by reading too many Emma Goldman articles.

Theodore Roosevelt became the twenty-sixth President of the United States at exactly 4:10 P.M. on September 14, 1901 and consternation spread rapidly from its focal center on Wall Street where the heart and brain of Republicanism was centered. It is true that any broker or banker, willing to look at the record and plunge beneath the verbalisms of Teddy's past career, can hardly have found anything to have alarmed him deeply. The new President's entire background—his family, his breeding, his education, and his years in public office—showed conclusively that his "radicalism" was slight. He hated Socialism in any form; indeed, he had openly opposed many a "reform" measure since his first days in Albany on the very ground it was "socialistic." He did not hate wealth, as so many believed; he merely felt that those who flagrantly abused the power of great wealth would hasten the day when the masses, led by demagogic politicians, would seize power and the result would be chaos. Mr. Josephson, in one brief sentence, has defined the cause of the fear of Teddy when he said ". . . this political soldier, this playboy of reform politics, had never worked seriously at any trade; he *had never had important business men as his clients nor acquired the respect for money that McKinley instinctively showed."*

Mark Hanna, the man behind McKinley and the undisputed ruler of the Republican Party, stepped quickly into the picture. He warned Teddy to go slow, go slow! And once again Teddy agreed. By his own compromise he became, for the time being at least, the creature of Hanna. Teddy's own relatives, his sister Anna, his brother-in-law Douglas Robinson, beseeched him to do nothing reckless. Elihu Root begged with him to be good. He promised and pledged himself to carry on the policies of McKinley, that "very supple and highly paid agent of capitalism," as Henry Adams called him. He kept McKinley's arch-conservative Cabinet; even kept McKinley's private secretary for his own. He appointed Robert Bacon, a Morgan partner, as Assistant Secretary of State. He went for advice to Senator Aldrich, the nabob of Newport, Rhode Island, and the very epitome of Republicanism. What else could he do? Was he not the youngest president in the history of the republic, and a Republican thrown into office by accident. But never think that Teddy did not know what he *intended* to do. He warned his brother-in-law, Douglas Robinson, New York real estate man and Wall Street broker:

"I intend to be most conservative, but in the interests of the corporations themselves and above all in the interests of the country, I intend to pursue cautiously, but steadily, the course to which I have been publicly committed . . . and which I am certain is the right course."

And that is what, it now appears, he proceeded to do.

The difference between Teddy and his advisors lay in his belief that it was his duty, in the words of Herbert Croly, founder of *The New Republic,* to give a democratic meaning and purpose to the Hamiltonian tradition and method of which the Republican Party was the heir.

In order to do this he played, partly, the boss's game, especially in the matter of patronage, but in return for his complacency he made his own demands. For example, he agreed not to disturb the protective tariff system, of which Aldrich was the arch defender, or the monetary system, but he demanded his head on all things outside the realm of economics and finance. Yet, on the matter of the eight hour day, then a burning issue, he kept silent, nor did he attempt to dislocate any of the economic set-ups of his day. By his own admission Teddy had no deep understanding of, or interest in, economics: give him a "moral crusade," however, and let him have his way in foreign policy, and he was content.

He chose, for his crusade, those "heejous monsthers," as Finley Peter Dunne made his famous character, Mr. Dooley, call the trusts. And so, without consulting the Elder Statesman, he "cracked down" on J. P. Morgan's Northern Securities Company and after two years of acrimonious debate and court action won at least a paper victory when a dissolution order was issued by the Supreme Court. Of course, the order was not as effective as it sounded, but it had the effect of making Teddy even more of a hero to the middle class, which had learned to fear the trusts as much as it feared Labor.

In most of his public utterances against the Trusts Teddy attacked them as a moral, not as an economic problem. He spoke of evil, and of wickedness, and pitted his campaign on the belief that he was preventing the misuse of property and preventing wrongdoing lest worse evil and wickedness follow. He attacked "great wealth" never; always it was the "malefactors of great wealth"—and there was a vast difference.

He spoke his mind in Boston in 1902 when he said that he was not against property, in asking that the question of trusts be taken up, but that he was acting in the most conservative sense "in property's interest" because "when you can make it evident that all men, big and small alike, have to obey the law, you are putting the safeguard of law around all men."

In the autumn of 1902 Teddy was faced with the greatest crisis of his career, the settling of the great anthracite coal strike that had begun the preceding spring. This he handled with consummate skill and added immensely to his popularity. Although he laid plans to declare a national emergency and take over the running of the mines he did not have to do so. He forced J. P. Morgan and the obdurate operators to meet with the strikers and present their case to a board of arbitration. In the end peace was restored, with the miners getting a nine-hour day instead of eight and only half the wage increase they had asked. Union recognition was denied, a bitter blow to the miners and the real reason for the strike. Teddy never "loved the laboring man"—indeed he feared him—and in this instance had in reality done little for him. But in the middle class mind he had brought capital and labor together, forced a compromise, and "saved the country from anarchy."

If Big Business hated and feared Teddy it had a strange way of showing it. When the election of 1904 neared, who should pour their gold into the Republican coffers but the great financiers, magnates, capitalists, and "robber barons" like Frick, Harriman, Stillman, Gould, H. H. Rogers, the despicable Archbold of Standard Oil, and even J. P. Morgan himself. Teddy, of course, averted his noble head. It was always his belief that as long as wealth, however concentrated, did no wrong, he would see that no harm befell it. Let the corporations obey the law, that was all. And so he made much noise. He would get angry. He would shout and pound. And in their Wall Street offices the lawyers would find ways to prove their clients were not disobeying the law. All was well.

Some substantial reforms did emerge from the hubbub of Teddy Roosevelt's administration. There was, for example, the Hepburn act, which greatly enlarged the powers of the Interstate Commerce Commission, and the Pure Food and Drug Act, and far from least, there was his conservation program. Teddy, history shows, was the first President to make a decent and an effective campaign for the preservation of our natural resources and our national beauty spots.

During his first two years in office Roosevelt had clashed with Hanna, in several noteworthy political skirmishes, some of which Roosevelt won. Now, in February, 1904, Hanna died, and the situation changed, for he was the last of the active bosses to whom Teddy had to turn. Matt Quay was dead, aging Boss Platt was retired, others had disappeared. But even with Hanna's passing Teddy was not to have a free hand. It was Teddy himself who had plead with the rich men for funds for his campaign; it was he who would have to pay. He was swept into office almost by a landslide. In bringing this about he had stirred the emotions of the common people, as well as the coffers of the rich.

The most sensational achievement of Teddy's first term, his *unelected* term, had been the taking of the Panama Canal Zone, as abysmal a piece of imperialism as any in our history.

When the U. S. S. *Oregon* made its historic dash around Cape Horn during the Spanish American War, the need for a Central American canal became apparent. Even before the war, in 1894, Teddy had expressed the hope that "Republicans would annex Hawaii and build an oceanic canal." The war showed it as a defense necessity. When Teddy took office he was in favor of the route across Nicaragua. He inherited from McKinley a treaty in the process of negotiation with Great Britain, one clause of which was that the canal, if built, should not be fortified. Teddy could not see it that way at all. He changed the treaty so that military control was vested in the United States although neutrality was guaranteed to all ships of commerce.

Already a French effort to cut through Panama, at a spot not far from that on which Archibald Stobo had wrestled with the godless Scots—had cost millions and accomplished little. But William Nelson Cromwell, a New York corporation lawyer, for reasons of his and his clients' own, favored Panama over Nicaragua. His influence in Republican circles and his money prevailed, the French rights in Panama, and the partly dug canal, were made available for forty million dollars, but still Congress favored Nicaragua. God then intervened, in the form of the eruption of Mont Pelée at Martinique and the threatened eruptions on Mount Monotombo at Nicaragua. Congress capitulated, Cromwell went ahead with his schemes. Teddy stood by.

The Hay-Herran treaty, providing a cash payment and an annual rental to Colombia, was jammed through in gangster-like manœuvres, but Colombia, avid for part of forty million dollars, held up the deal. Teddy called the Colombians "dagoes," "jack rabbits" and "inefficient bandits." He was now determined that the United States should get the Panama route at any cost; and while he knew, and said, that this country could not "foment secession" he admitted, in a private letter, that he would be "delighted if Panama were an independent state." Cromwell took the hint. The Republic of Panama was formed—in a room at the Hotel Waldorf-Astoria in New York!—and soon thereafter four warships, two on each side of the Isthmus, fortunately happened to be headed that way. There followed some more clever manœuvring, which resulted in the establishment of the new republic, the landing of American troops to "protect American lives," and the recognition of the new republic by Teddy as President of the United States.

In 1911 in California Teddy boasted in a speech, "I am interested in the Panama Canal because I started it. I took the canal zone and let Congress debate, and while the debate goes on so the Canal does also." This was a vain and ungentlemanly boast for a President! When Woodrow Wilson took office one of his early acts was to draft a treaty offering apologies and indemnity to the Colombians.

Teddy, of course, had had no official part in the revolution that made the Republic possible, but he had been a silent partner, knowing full well what was going on. Perhaps one of his great acts was the building of the Canal, but it reeked of jingo imperialism of the worst order. Teddy's friends in Washington throughout his lifetime blocked efforts to pay indemnity. It was not done until Warren G. Harding's regime, when the discovery of oil in Colombia made it necessary, in order to protect American oil interest there! When Teddy's fifth cousin became President, and set forth his "good neighbor" policy, he went even further, renounced our guarantee of Panamanian independence and made other concessions in an effort to pacify Central American animosity towards the Colossus of the North.

Teddy, in 1904, was fearful that he could not be re-elected. He was so fearful that he publicly and unequivocally promised to seek no third term if he were. He went bear-hunting, and mountain-lion-hunting, and otherwise used the agents of publicity to keep the public interested in his vital personality. In 1904 and 1905 he was at the crest of his popularity, independent, powerful, and a living threat to his own party. He continued his drive to put Big Business in its place through corporation control. During his second term he engineered legislation for railroad control; he chastised Standard Oil until Judge K. M. Landis levied his famous, but futile, twenty-nine million dollar fine; and he concluded the peace between Russia and Japan. His greatest piece of showmanship, in keeping with his imperialistic beliefs, was his sending the fleet on its good-will trip around the world, thus, perhaps, staving off war with Japan, and his settlement of the Alaska boundary dispute with Great Britain.

Always interested in foreign affairs,—for in that field one could be a statesman!—he stepped into the matter of the partition of Morocco, at the request of the Kaiser. Although he believed he had prevented partition, the later revelation of the treaties between France, England and Spain, showed that he had not accomplished what he had expected. Big Business, of course, blamed his anti-trust policies for the panic of 1907, which broke when he was hunting bears. When he returned, the market was in a fearful state that was only partially alleviated when the Treasury placed in the national banks twenty-five million dollars in government bonds. In the midst of the panic U. S. Steel, the creature of Gary and Frick, pounced upon Tennessee Coal & Iron Co., a two hundred million dollar property, and took it for a paltry fourteen million dollars—because Roosevelt felt it not in the public interest to "interpose any objection"!

His second term was stormy. He fought with everyone, including his old friend and president-maker, Henry Cabot Lodge. Power and glory, it seemed to friend and enemy, went to his head. Even those who believed in the sincerity of his reforms could not miss seeing signs of his messianic complex. He scrapped with Congress, the Court, the Army. And not without reason. He intended, when his term was done, to step aside for four years and then come back to carry on. He made Taft his "political legatee"—and Taft was nominated on the first ballot. Taft's opponent was the softening Bryan, now fat and bald, his silver tongue grown harsh. But Taft did not sweep the country—many states returned to the Democratic column—and Roosevelt went off, convinced that four years later he could stage a comeback such as the country had never seen.

He went to Africa and hunted elephants, successfully. He lectured at Oxford, in Germany, France and Norway. In Rome he had what he called "an elegant row" with the Pope, who made "a proposition that a Tammany Boodle Alderman would have been ashamed" of by offering him an audience—if he would ignore certain Methodists then in the Holy City who had offended the Vatican. He represented the United States at the funeral of King Edward VII of England. He had been at Christiana receiving the Nobel Peace Prize for settling the Russo-Jap war when the King died, and there he had proposed a League of Peace between the great powers "not only to keep the peace among others, but to prevent, by force if necessary, its being broken by others." His proposal fell on deaf ears.

When Teddy and Mrs. Roosevelt returned to America he was tumultuously received by huge crowds all the way from the Battery to Oyster Bay. He felt that the hysterical quality of the reception boded no good for his political future. He was right.

Robert M. La Follette, then leading his confused but hopeful Progressives, so he thought, towards the New Nationalism, invited Teddy into his party. He entered, took it over and became its nominee. But Woodrow Wilson, with his New Freedom, was on hand, and it was he who became President in 1912, a fateful year in world history and in Teddy's career.

Although he did not believe it, when Teddy bolted the Republican Party he jolted himself from public life.

In 1913 he was the central figure in a libel suit he brought against an editor who had foolishly called him a drunkard. He won a six-cent verdict, vindication, and reams of publicity. Then he went to Brazil and explored the famed River of Doubt. This brought more publicity. He was defendant in another libel suit, brought by Boss Barnes, a New York up-state political leader. Many political secrets came to light and there was more publicity. Ex-President Roosevelt could not keep out of the limelight if he had wanted to, but that he did not!

Teddy, who always had posed as a he-man, a virile, and masterful American, the hunter and cowboy and explorer and scientist, who had never missed a chance to impress these robust qualities upon the public, admired the German people because they, too, were a "stern, virile, and masterful people." At the beginning of the World War he was "accused" of being pro-German, primarily because, as an old "military expert," he justified the invasion of Belgium as a military necessity. But he changed with the winds of war. The sinking of the Lusi-

tania sickened him and he called it murder on the high seas.
The ship had hardly settled on the bottom before he was crying
for war. He wanted to get out his old Rough Rider costume
and charge the Kaiser's troops. He had never liked Wilson.
Now his hatred knew no bounds. When the President, in his
wisdom, proposed indemnifying Colombia for the seizure of
Panama—Teddy's greatest glory—he was furious. He stormed
for preparedness, he vilified every peaceful move of Wilson.
And when, at last, we entered the war, he demanded a commission. President Wilson refused.

In July, 1918, Quentin Roosevelt was shot down behind the
German lines.

"Only those are fit to live who do not fear to die," the
broken-hearted but still belligerent father began his moving
tribute to his hero son.

After that, the old exuberance seemed to have oozed from the
old crusader.

Six months before his son's death he had been treated for
abscesses of the ear. Although he had lost his hearing on one
side and was not well he stormed the countryside, demanding
the unconditional surrender of Germany, and war to the end.
For *The Outlook* he wrote vigorous editorials, even as his own
health failed.

When the Armistice came he was in Roosevelt Hospital in
New York suffering from an attack of inflammatory rheuma-
tism. But he came home to Sagamore Hill for Christmas. He
lived until January 6, 1919, when an arterial embolism ended
his life. He was buried in the simple grave on a hillside at his
beloved Oyster Bay, beneath the trees he climbed with his
children years before.

V

The influence of women in the life of Teddy Roosevelt was
great. His gracious mother; his gay first wife, Alice Lee; his
second wife and life-long helpmeet, Edith Carow; these of
course exerted immeasurable influence upon his career. But
Teddy was always close to his two sisters, Anna and Corinne.

Anna, the older of the two, was as near to her brother as any
person, male or female, to whom he turned for advice during

his political life. Her public activity was slight, but "Darling Bye," as Teddy called her in his frequent and revealing letters, which she published some years ago, was a powerful factor in life behind the scenes in the White House. He wrote to her with an amazing candor, seeking her advice at every crucial moment from 1870 until his death.

Whether he was worrying over his future as Police Commissioner, or debating the problems of a combative Assistant Secretary of the Navy, or preparing to bolt like a Bull Moose from Republicanism, he always found time to write at length to "Darling Bye," explaining his half-formed views, seeking her judgments and advice. It is impossible to estimate, with any pretense to accuracy, the power she exerted on her brother, his friends and associates, indeed upon the country of which he was the leader.

Educated at Fontainebleau, France, and in New York, Anna's early life was spent in furthering the interest of her father's charities, the Orthopaedic Hospital and the Children's Aid Society. In those days the whole Roosevelt Family was more closely knit than it has since become, and so when her cousin James Roosevelt Roosevelt's wife died while he was secretary of the American Embassy at London she crossed the ocean to act as his official hostess. There she pleased the most fastidious of the international circle with her charming manners and there she met Lieut. Commander William Stirling Cowles of the United States Navy. This son of a New York broker, who rose to the rank of Rear Admiral before his retirement in 1908, was then Naval attaché in London. They were married at the Embassy in 1895 and soon returned to New York, where they took a house at Six Hundred Eighty-Nine Madison Avenue.

But it was in Washington that Mrs. Cowles shone. The Cowleses went there about the time of the Spanish-American war, taking a house at Seventeen Hundred Thirty-Three N Street, which became the center of Capitol society through Teddy's presidency. As a brother-in-law of Teddy, the Naval officer had no difficulty in advancement, in spite of the fact that he had run the *Despatch* ashore on the Assateague Shoals, sixty miles off Cape Charles, in 1891, while on the way to take the President and the Secretary of the Navy to Annapolis, or that

his battleship *Missouri* had once collided with the *Illinois,* or
that he was commanding the *Missouri* when a powder explosion
killed thirty-three sailors. When Teddy was President he made
him his Naval Aide. As such Rear Admiral Cowles accompanied Prince Henry of Prussia on his tour of America and
represented the United States at the Coronation of King Edward VII.

Mrs. Cowles left Washington after her brother's second term
and lived for many years at her ancestral home "Oldgate,"
Farmington, Connecticut, which, until her death in 1932, was
a shrine frequently visited by the old Roosevelt crowd. She
assiduously refrained from talking for publication, devoted her
life to keeping her brother's memory green, and served the
cause of history well by editing the frank and often naive letters
he had written her over the tumultuous years.

Although Teddy never opened his heart to his sister Corinne
as freely as he did to Mrs. Cowles, she was an integral part of
his life. She adored him and believed he was the greatest man
who ever lived. She loved to tell stories about him, especially
of his childhood, and a great deal of the Roosevelt myth has
come from her remembrances of Rooseveltian things past.
When she was twenty-one she was married to Douglas Robinson, a New York banker and real estate dealer, whose conservative beliefs were to receive many a rude shock from his
brother-in-law.

Corinne devoted much of her time to charitable affairs and
to the care of her brother Elliott, whose heavy drinking was
the dark problem of the Family until his death. She wrote
poetry, lectured, and took some interest in politics. She served
on the Republican National Committee and in other political
capacities. Family ties, in the end, meant more to Corinne
Robinson than the bonds of party. She set an example in 1932
that was not to be followed by other Roosevelts when she refused to become a Republican elector-at-large:

"You must understand," she said, "my own beloved niece is
the wife of the Democratic candidate. She is the daughter of
the brother who was nearer to me in age than Theodore. For
her I have the deepest affection and respect. So, much as I would

like to pay the highest tribute to President Hoover, I cannot do so in this campaign."

Thus the woman who had bitterly attacked President Wilson, who had worked for the greater glory of Republicanism during a great part of her life, turned from the lists because, above all else, she was a Roosevelt.

Douglas and Corinne Robinson had three children. The oldest, Theodore Douglas Robinson, was once a member of the New York Assembly. There he distinguished himself by sponsoring a bill for the licensing of cats. His sister, Corinne Robinson, married Joseph W. Alsop, a Connecticut tobacco merchant who was at one time Public Utilities Commissioner of the Nutmeg State. Thus she became the mother of Joseph W. Alsop, Jr., the Washington columnist. Their other son was Monroe D. Robinson.

VI

Throughout the greater part of Theodore Roosevelt's career as a politician there was always at his side the gracious figure of his second wife, the mother of five of his six children. As such she takes her place in the history of America, a genteel, somewhat Victorian, Abigail Adams whose major duty for more than thirty years was to care for her tempestuous husband.

If the Roosevelts had become a proud family by 1888—as they had—Edith Kermit Carow, when she became a member of it was of equal social and patriotic standing. Indeed, she could trace her family history in this country back almost as far as Teddy could and did trace his. Her great-grandfather was Colonel Daniel Tyler, a Revolutionary officer and fellow townsman of Israel Putnam, the hero of the Battle of Bunker Hill. Her father was Charles Carow and she was born at Norwich, Connecticut, on August 5, 1861, in the tumult attending the opening of the Civil War.

Edith Carow had known the Roosevelts from childhood and had always admired Teddy, an admiration that never lessened while she was his wife. And yet she never let her admiration sway her better judgment. When Teddy was presumably being shelved by the bosses in the anonymity of the vice presidency she easily saw through their tactics. She did not want him to seek that office, believing that his public record, including particularly his popular actions in Cuba during the Santiago campaign in 1898, entitled him to first place on the ticket. But Teddy was committed beyond his wife's desire and all turned out for the best in the end.

Edith Carow Roosevelt was a perfect mistress of the White House in those days when women were not supposed to transcend their traditional role as hostess and mother. Her soft voice, her quiet dignity, and above all her self-possession fitted her admirably for her position as the First Lady of the Land. Of course, any place where Teddy happened to be would be lively, but Edith, too, was able to add to the elan of White House life. She was an excellent conversationalist, an adept musician. She loved to be surrounded by her children—Teddy, Jr., Kermit, Ethel, Archibald, and Quentin—and to listen to their breathless tales of adventure, and their childish problems. Alice, her stepdaughter, was her constant companion.

After the mourning for the martyred McKinley had properly ended she cleared the White House of its ungracious mahogany and horsehair furniture and transformed it into a more nearly livable place. She was an excellent housekeeper and kept her eye on housewifely affairs, always seeing to it that Teddy's table was amply provided with the things he and his cronies liked best. When political duties left her free she spent her time sewing, for Edith was an accomplished needle-worker. She was happiest when making clothes for the babies of her friends.

Her one habit that approached ostentation was her liking to drive in her carriage from the White House to the Capitol. She was the leader of the "Social Cabinet," which consisted of the wives of Cabinet officers, and as such undoubtedly wielded some political power. She loved balls and State affairs, and the debut she arranged for her step-daughter Alice was as magnificent an event as the White House has ever seen.

When the exigencies of democratic politics retired Teddy to private life she retired with him to live, at Oyster Bay, the reserved existence befitting an ex-President's wife. She took no part in public affairs until many years after her husband's death in 1919. Indeed she had no reason to do so, for during most of that period the Republican Party was in power, and she was always at heart a Republican. In 1932 she made a public statement in behalf of Herbert Hoover and even flew from Roosevelt Field to Washington to attend the notification ceremonies. Asked if she would vote for Franklin D. Roosevelt she replied stiffly:

"Franklin Delano Roosevelt is a distant cousin of my husband. I am a Republican and voting for Herbert Hoover."

The political break between the two branches had come to a head in 1920 when Franklin was seeking the Vice Presidency with James M. Cox of Ohio. At that time her son, young Teddy, Jr., had said publicly that Franklin "does not have the brand of our family" and had called him a "maverick," a statement politically true, as of that year, but genetically hardly accurate!

Later, in 1933, the aging Mrs. Roosevelt, living comfortably at Oyster Bay on a generous income inherited from her husband and a five thousand dollar annual pension from the Government, expressed the feelings of her leisured and moneyed class when she said:

"We expected Franklin Roosevelt to take us out of the mud when he went into office, but he has led us into the mire!"

When her son, Teddy, then known as Colonel Roosevelt, was Governor-General of the Philippines the old lady visited Manila, taking the long route by way of China. Later she went to Guatemala and San Salvador. One of her great desires was to visit the River of Doubt in Brazil, which Teddy had explored after leaving the Presidency in the unhappy hands of Mr. Taft in 1908. Relatives, however, dissuaded her.

And now she still lives in the house at Sagamore Hill that Teddy built for her. Once she wrote to the widow of a soldier, "We must take it standing. Afterward we can live with our memories." She has many—crowded memories of life in Washington—of Japan and the Emperor who once opened the Akasaka Palace so that she might see the gardens—of a visit to Greece in 1934—the inaugural ball at which she wore a one thousand dollar gown of Alice blue—the visit of the Prince of Wales to her Long Island home in 1924—the death of her beloved son Quentin, who was shot down in France in the Great War—these and many, many more. With the death in 1941 of

Mrs. James Roosevelt, Franklin Roosevelt's mother, she became the matriarch of the Roosevelt Family.

Once she said, "Nothing could please me more than if, when I die, they put this inscription on my tombstone: 'Everything she did was for the happiness of others.'" And, it might be added, especially for the happiness of her own brood.

VII

Teddy Roosevelt, Jr., was born with a dual disadvantage. He was the oldest son of a President and he bore that popular hero's name. To have overcome either handicap would have been asking a great deal. Only one President's son ever reached the White House, John Quincy Adams, the son of John Adams, the second President.

Teddy, Jr., has never quite lived up to the expectations of his early admirers who professed to see in him "a chip of the old block." Although he sought public office several times he was elected only once; and although he held appointive posts he was never able to use them as a stepping stone to greatness as his father had done.

He was born Sept. 13, 1887 at Sagamore Hill, the home his father had built shortly before he went to Washington as Civil Service Commissioner. Like his father he was a sickly child with weak eyes, and he was given the same treatment that Teddy had received from his father—outdoor life and exercise. It worked. After attending public school at Oyster Bay and in Washington he was sent to Groton School, that training ground of the socially elect, where he was fitted for Harvard. He was a bright youngster and finished his Harvard course in three years.

After working for a short time on the Mesaba Range properties of United States Steel, under an old Rough Rider friend of Teddy's, he came East. He held a job briefly in a Connecticut carpet mill, then became a salesman and worked his way up to the managership of the company's West Coast office. Before he left for San Francisco he married his childhood sweetheart, Miss Eleanor Butler Alexander, a New York girl of excellent social standing.

Thus far he followed the family tradition, showing no signs of rebellion nor any interest in politics. When he returned to New York in 1912 it was to sell bonds for a Wall Street brokerage house. Two years later he was New York manager for a firm of Philadelphia investment bankers. If it had not been for the World War it is quite probable that the rest of his life would have been spent in or around the financial district. But when the Plattsburg Training Camp was founded he and his two brothers, Quentin and Archibald, went there to learn to be soldiers.

Quentin was to die in France and become a sort of national symbol of the brave young hero, for he died fighting in the air in a fierce combat over foreign soil. Young Teddy survived, but his heroism, if less romantic, was as great as that displayed by his younger brother. He arrived in France in June, 1917, as Major, and emerged from the war a Colonel, but only after having been gassed and wounded at Soissons and having returned to lead his troops in the Argonne and on into Germany. For this he was decorated by the United States, France, Belgium and Montenegro.

While Teddy was at the head of his troops, his wife, Eleanor, had left their two babies at Oyster Bay, donned her own uniform and followed her husband to France as a volunteer worker for the Young Men's Christian Association. It was she who organized the famous "leave area" at Aix-les-Bains.

Lieutenant Colonel Roosevelt was in Germany with his regiment when word came of his father's death. He came hurrying home. Before he left, however, he had laid plans with Colonel Bennet Clark (later Senator Clark, Democrat, of Missouri) and others for an organization of ex-service men from which the American Legion was to emerge within a year. At about this time Teddy began to have visions of taking up his father's gaudy mantle and entering the lists. His first public appearance was before the New York County Republican Committee where he brought down the house by baring his Rooseveltian teeth in a typically Rooseveltian smile and shouting to the crowd:

"It's bully to be home again!"

Young Teddy might have used the American Legion as a political springboard but he refrained when the word became widespread that he would seek its leadership. The political implications were clear and he was placed in a difficult position. After all, the World War was not in the same category as Secretary Hay's "splendid little war," nor was the Argonne another San Juan Hill. Teddy refused the command of the Legion, crying to the noisy first convention at St. Louis:

"They say I'm a politician and that I am starting this organization as a grandstand play!"

He returned to New York to begin his political career on a less pretentious footing. The Nassau County Republicans, stronghold of J. P. Morgan and his crowd, sent him to the Assembly. There he played the Roosevelt game of bolting, in a minor way, by insisting upon the retention of the Socialist Assemblymen whom the red-baiting Republican machine was seeking to oust from their duly elected offices. He also sided with some of the reform measures of the day, including the bill for shorter hours for women.

When that great and good poker player, Warren G. Harding, became President he made T. R. Jr., Assistant Secretary of the Navy. It was during his service in this post that the valuable oil reserve leases in California and Teapot Dome were transferred from the Navy Department to Albert B. Fall's Department of the Interior, whence they found their way into the hands of private oil interests. In the investigation that followed and rocked the national conscience Teddy and his chief, Secretary Edwin Denby, were cleared of any wrongdoing, but the jolt was a severe one to young Teddy's political ambitions.

Nevertheless he did not give up. He sought the Governorship of New York in 1924. An Irish-American politician from the Fulton fish market of New York's East side had no difficulty in defeating him. Al Smith won by one hundred and five thousand votes in a year which saw Calvin Coolidge carry New York by eight hundred thousand votes! Teddy trailed the entire Republican State ticket. After that bitter blow he again emulated his father by taking a long hunting trip in Asia.

In 1929, just on the eve of the depression, President Hoover appointed Teddy Governor of Puerto Rico. In the second year there he balanced the budget, something that had not been done for sixteen years, and in 1932 the Treasury showed a surplus. He won the respect of the natives by learning their language. President Hoover next sent him to the Philippines as Governor-General, in 1932, but his tenure there was short-lived for his "maverick cousin" soon became President and he resigned.

Since then he was for a time chairman of the board of the American Express Company and a member of the firm of Doubleday, Doran & Co., publishers. He has flitted around Republican politics, being president of the National Republican Club in 1934, in which year he lost the Republican nomination for Governor to Robert Moses, the park builder. He was "receptive" again in 1936, but made no active bid for it, spending his time and energy in the futile effort to replace his cousin by a man named Alfred Landon from Kansas. The New Deal has had no more bitter critic than young Teddy.

Young Teddy, as he is still called, maintained his interest in military affairs and was a Colonel in the United States Army Reserve until the emergency of 1941, when he went back into active service and was stationed at Fort Devens, Massachusetts. Shortly after the United States entered the war against the Axis, he was promoted to Brigadier General and placed in command of the 26th Infantry of the First Division.

Politics, business, travel, and hunting were interests inherited from his father. But like Teddy and Uncle Bob, the first of the literary Roosevelts, he had a flair for writing. His first book, written with the aid of his brother Kermit, was a war story called *Average Americans*. Most of the others have been travel books. His most recent and most serious one, published in 1937, was *Colonial Policies of the United States*.

Young Teddy and Eleanor cared little for Society as such. They abandoned their New York town house after the war and since have lived at Oyster Bay. There they raised four children, Theodore Roosevelt III, Grace Roosevelt, who married William McMillan, Cornelius and Quentin.

Kermit, President Roosevelt's second son, was born at Oyster Bay on October 10, 1889, in the administration of President Benjamin Harrison. He, too, went to Groton and Harvard, but his childhood was more spectacular than that of his brothers. When T. R., Sr., went off in 1912 to hunt big game in Africa and cogitate on ways and means of retrieving the Presidency from Mr. Taft, young Kermit accompanied him; and later, when Teddy explored the dark Brazilian River of Doubt, the young man, who already had had some engineering experience in South America, went along, too.

Like his father, Kermit was an advocate of the "strenuous life" and he had, also, a good streak of belligerency in his make-up. He did not wait for America to enter the war to become a soldier. Instead, he joined up with General Sir Frederick Maude and saw active service almost at once in Mesopotamia and Palestine as a captain of the Motor Machine Guns. When America entered the conflict he was transferred to the First Division as a commander of a battery of the famous French 75s.

The war ended, he became an executive of the Kerr Steamship Line and also devoted some time to writing. *War in the Garden of Eden* recorded his Palestine ventures. He also helped immortalize his beloved brother Quentin with a biography. Later he resigned from the Kerr Line and founded the Roosevelt Steamship Company to operate vessels leased from the United States Shipping Board, which later was merged with the International Merchantile Marine Company. He stayed on as a vice president until 1938, when he quit business, and went abroad. No enemy of the New Deal, he has often been a guest of his cousin Franklin at the White House.

Kermit was in London when England and Germany again went to war. He quickly re-enlisted in the British forces and received a major's commission with the Middlesex Regiment. Later he raised a regiment of volunteers for the aid of Finland, but Russia had crushed that country before he could see service. He returned to his regiment and, in 1940, had a brief tour of duty in Egypt before resigning and returning to the United States.

He married Miss Belle Willard, a Virginian, in 1914, and has three children, Kermit Roosevelt, Jr., Belle Roosevelt, and Joseph W. Roosevelt.

Of all of Teddy's six children the most volatile, of course, is Alice, the child of his first marriage. Least volatile is Archibald, whose career followed the familiar pattern of Groton,

Harvard, the war, and Wall Street. He is now a broker, and the father of two children, whose mother, the former Grace Lockwood, he married in 1919.

Ethel married Dr. Richard Derby at Oyster Bay in 1913. They still live there, and are the parents of one son, Richard, Jr., and three daughters, Edith, Sarah and Judith.

All of Theodore's children married young, after the racial dictates of their father, and all followed his famous advice and raised at least reasonably large families. To date the record shows no divorces among them.

CHAPTER XX

The Princess and Little Nell

IN THE THREE-HUNDRED-YEAR HISTORY of the Roosevelt family in America two women, both Roosevelts to the core, have attracted almost as much attention as that accorded to the men. Their private lives and their public accomplishments alike have filled countless columns of the public press. One, the daughter of President Theodore Roosevelt, became a national heroine in the days of her youth. The other, a niece of Theodore and the wife of President Franklin Delano Roosevelt, became a national force in the days of her maturity.

The story of Alice Roosevelt Longworth and Anna Eleanor Roosevelt is one of contrasts. Alice grew up under the spotlight. As a young lady she was suave, smart, witty, sophisticated, the toast of Newport and Washington, a glamour girl of the years before the first World War. The spotlight did not shine on Eleanor until after her first grandchild was born. As a girl she was a homely, lonely, queerly dressed orphan, whose father had made a tragic failure of his life and whose mother had died when Eleanor was very young.

Although they were only a year apart in age and were first cousins Alice and Eleanor lived in different worlds. Alice was the daughter of Republicanism, of prosperity, of wealth and social position. Eleanor was the step-daughter of Democracy, of the depression, and of a social conscience. Alice burgeoned in the age of individualism. Eleanor came of age, very late, when individualism was no longer a national virtue. When

Alice was a girl they called her The Princess and all her life she strove to live up to the undemocratic title. Eleanor never had a title. They called her Little Nell when she was a child.

I

By virtue of her birth and ancestry Alice Roosevelt was destined to be an American princess. Although her mother, the tall and brown-haired Alice Lee, died when Alice was only two days old, the aristocratic influence of her family was to be a strong one in the little girl's life. Not as strong, of course, as that of Teddy, for Alice's father dominated everything and everybody with whom he came in touch, but the blueness of her Boston blood has never run pale in her veins.

Alice did not long remain motherless. For she did not regard the second Mrs. Roosevelt as a step-mother. Edith Carow always treated little Alice as though she were her own child. Indeed, upon more than one occasion when she had grown up, Alice spoke of her step-mother's "fairness, charm and intelligence, which she has to a greater degree than anyone else I know." Alice was never a lonely child. From birth she was healthy and imaginative. Her early years were divided between the comfortable homes of her Boston relatives on Beacon Hill in Brookline, the Roosevelt's New York house, and the ancestral acres of Oyster Bay.

From her father Alice inherited a stubbornness of will that was typically Rooseveltian. From him also she received an active mind. In her own words she could spend hours of time pretending that she was "a fiery horse, preferably cream colored, like Cinderella's horses, able at a bound to cover vast regions of the earth and also able at will to turn into something quite different, such as a princess with very long hair, or an extremely martial prince."

Teddy, of course, adored her, as he did all his children, and although she probably was his favorite, he successfully managed to refrain from showing it. He brought her up as an individualist. By her own admission she was a "spoiled child." Governesses and tutors took care of the fundamentals of her education, teaching her mathematics and the languages of her own and other nations. When the family was living in Albany, during Teddy's governorship, she stubbornly refused to go to school. Teddy, who was to insist that his other children go to the public schools, did not make her conform to the rule. Perhaps he felt that he was quite capable of educating his own daughter. His methods were simple, Rooseveltian. He fed her a strong diet of Kipling's imperialistic poetry and the ancient British ballads. Many years later, she could still recite offhand from the *Saga of Olaf the King,* that martial song from the *Tales of a Wayside Inn:*

> I am the God Thor,
> I am the War God,
> I am the Thunderer!
> Here in my Northland,
> My fastness and fortress,
> Reign I forever!

She read, or had read to her, more of poetry than anything else, but philosophy and history and literature were also on her list. Her step-mother watered the diet somewhat with Maria Edgeworth's didactic tales of English and Irish rural life and the romances of Sir Walter Scott. But reading did not occupy all her time. Never was she, or her step-brothers and sister, happier than when skating or sledding on the hills of the Oyster Bay estate with father, who had the priceless virtue of being contemporaneous with his children.

Alice was only six years old when she lived in Washington for the first time, while her father was Civil Service Commissioner in the Harrison administration. She used to play then on the Capitol lawn, which she was sure belonged personally to Henry Cabot Lodge! Again, when her father was President McKinley's Assistant Secretary of the Navy, she lived in the capital, but she was equally at home in Back Bay, Newport, and fashionable New York.

As the daughter of the Vice President, Alice attracted no overdue attention, but suddenly she was the President's daughter.

Not for many years had any President so challenged the imagination of the people as Theodore Roosevelt. Ever since he had been Police Commissioner of New York in the 1890's, Teddy had been the newspaper reporters' delight. They were not long in discovering that if Teddy were a national hero there was also in the White House a young girl who could be made a national heroine. In those simple days when there was no Hollywood and Ethel Barrymore was young, they took Alice to their hearts.

Smiling seventeen-year-old Alice was quite capable of bearing up under the floods of adulation that swept around her from the moment of her famous coming-out ball at the White House in January, 1902. That was a gala and historic affair. It marked the end of the period of mourning for the martyred McKinley. It marked also the start of seven years of tireless effort on the part of the press to marry off its princess to a variety of suitors ranging from a lieutenant of artillery to the Emperor of China.

The summer, after the coming-out party, Princess Alice—she was so continually referred to by that title that several small countries in remote parts of the world actually believed it was her official designation!—was a gay addition to the summer colony at Newport, where castles are "cottages" and one has to have a pedigree to play tennis at the Casino. As the guest of such socially correct families as the Ogden Millses and I. Townsend Burdens she was quite in the swim of things at Bailey's Beach.

Alice, however, was disappointed at having to spend the summer at Newport. She should have been in London, attending the Coronation of King Edward VII. She had been invited and Teddy had been anxious for her to go. Indeed, her status as an entirely unofficial young woman, who happened to be the daughter of the President of the United States, had already been decided by the bigwigs at court. They had reached the momentous conclusion that she could sit in the space reserved for ambassadors' wives. But unfortunately 1902 was the one hundred and twenty-fourth anniversary of the birth of the Irish patriot Robert Emmet and Irish-Americans were making the occasion an excuse for many bitter attacks on England. Several societies protested against Alice's attendance—unless she take with her a condemnation of England's treatment of Ireland, signed by millions of American mothers, and give it to the King as soon as he was crowned. Teddy was all for letting Alice go, anyway, but when he saw the tenor of the hundreds of letters received by Mark Hanna in his capacity as chairman of the Republican National Committee, he sacrificed his daughter's happiness to save his own political scalp.

It was during the summer at Newport that Alice first broke into the newspapers of her own accord. The previous winter, of course, she had received much publicity when she broke a bottle of champagne over the bow of Kaiser Wilhelm's new yacht, the *Meteor,* as it slid down the ways at Shooter's Island, New York. The Emperor sent her a bracelet with his miniature set in diamonds, and Prince Henry of Prussia, representing the Kaiser at the launching, also gave her a gift. Later a despatch boat in the German Navy was named *Alice Roosevelt.* But all this was of an official nature. The Newport adventure was not.

With her friend, Ellen Drexel Paul, of the Philadelphia aristocracy, Alice rode in an automobile from Newport to Boston, covering the seventy-four miles in six hours, with only a stop at Fall River for an ice cream soda. They made the amazing speed of twenty-four miles an hour on open roads, but had to slow down to eight miles in the towns, The daredevil escapade, as it was regarded in that horse-drawn age, shocked America, and Teddy. He told Alice to stick to horses. But the next year Alice bought a car, a bright red affair with red upholstery, two cylinders and a wheel base of six feet, eight inches. This, in the words of one reporter, caused more talk in Washington than the new tariff bill. She did not drive it long, however, and went back to the safer tandem team and four-in-hand, much to Washington's relief.

For the next several years the success of the Newport season depended on Princess Alice. No ball, no tennis tournament, no yacht race was considered complete if Alice was not there. The gay young set tried to keep up with her. If she appeared at the Casino carrying a cane, then one of her rivals had to show up, the next day, with a live parrot tethered to the hood of her automobile! That was in the era when Harry Lehr startled America by playing tennis in his two-piece bathing suit; when Natica Rives went out in public with her hair down her back. But when Alice dove to the bottom of Newport bay in a submarine torpedo-boat she reached the height of feminine daring.

As a result of the publicity which followed her every move, America became definitely Alice-minded. Babies were christened Alice in her honor. Ball games couldn't start until she was in her box. Roses, colors, and hats bore her name. And if she went to a racetrack, owners of winning horses presented her with the victor's shoes! In Washington Society it was seriously debated whether her invitations were to be regarded as commands and whether women, as well as men, should rise when she came into dinner late, as she most often did. By the end of her father's first term as President there were many who had wearied of her name. In Paris a conservative newspaper estimated, with its editorial tongue in its cheek, that in the previous fifteen months Alice had attended 408 dinners, 300 parties, 350 balls, 680 afternoon teas, 1,706 calls, and 32,000 handshakings, and suggested that she take the next year off! But America, taking the affair seriously, began worrying that dear Alice didn't get enough rest. Teddy, exponent of the "vigorous life," told the public not to be alarmed. Alice, he said, "does not stay in the house and fold her hands and do nothing. She can walk as far as I can, and often she walks several miles at the pace I set for her. She can ride, drive, ski, shoot—although she does not care much for the shooting. I don't mind that. It is not necessary for her health. She gets plenty of outdoor exercise. That is necessary."

During this period the great topic of journalistic speculation was Alice's choice of a husband. This had begun at her coming out party, when a great rivalry arose between a Major of the Marine Crops and a Lieutenant of the Artillery, each of whom sought the honor of leading her out for the German. (The Artillery won the engagement!) The newspapers carried rumors of her engagement to Prince Gustav Adolf of Sweden; Paul Loubet, the son of the President of France; Marconi, the inventor of the wireless; Prince George of Greece; Grand Duke Michael, brother of the Czar; and Prince Adelbert of Prussia. Sandwiched between royalty were Yale and Harvard football stars, bright young men in the diplomatic corps and at the foreign embassies in Washington, and any number of Rough Riders who presumably had been willing to give up their lives for Teddy at San Juan Hill. In 1905 the Sultan of Sulu actually did send her a proposal!

Alice's closest friend during the Princess period was Countess Marguerite Cassini, "daughter" of the Russian Ambassador at Washington. Their common interest was a love for pedigreed dogs and blooded horses. They were frequently together and soon the gossips noticed that the two girls were often in the company of two popular young members of Washington society: Nicholas Longworth, then Ohio's *jeune* Congressman, and his brother-in-law, Viscount de Chambrun of the French Embassy. The quartet, almost always together at balls or dinners, were soon the recognized leaders of the younger set.

While the nation whistled and hummed such an ineffable tune as "Alice, Where Art Thou?" (for no good reason, as one wit put it, because everybody always knew where she was every minute!) the inspiration of the melody sat in the gallery of the House of Representatives paying particular attention to the debates in which Nick Longworth spoke.

Young Mr. Longworth was a worthy suitor for Princess Alice. He was handsome, he was rich and he belonged to a good family. His father, Nicholas Longworth, Sr., was one of Ohio's most respectable citizens whose considerable wealth had been wrested, by others, from coal mines. He was also a Federal court judge. Nicholas, Jr., had had every advantage. After Harvard he had gone to law school and then had returned to Cincinnati to move freely among the social, financial, and political nabobs of that city. Old George Cox, the Republican boss of the slum-infested First Ohio District, liked the young man, took him in hand, and shoved him through the two houses of the State legislature until he reached Washington as a Congressman.

Although there were frequent denials of an engagement, Nicholas was often observed entering the White House with his violin under his arm. Alice, who had hated her childish piano lessons and who preferred a banjo, nevertheless could play the piano well enough to accompany the Ohio virtuoso. Shortly after his inauguration in 1905 Teddy sent William Howard Taft, his rotund Secretary of War, to the Philippines to make a study of that island's affairs. Included in the party that accompanied him was Mr. Longworth, a young politician from Kansas named Charley Curtis (he was to be vice president with President Hoover), and Princess Alice. Her status was quite unofficial. With the band dinning "Alice, Where Art Thou?" wherever they went, and the newspapers keeping the public informed, the party crossed the continent, visited Hawaii (where Alice learned the hula-hula), and on to Manila.

On the ship Alice the irrepressible was the life of the party. One day she pushed Nick, in his smart flannels, into an improvised swimming pool. Mr. Secretary Taft, careful of his dignity, often gave Alice what she called "curtain lectures" and every so often he would call her aside and sternly say, "Alice, I think I ought to know if you are engaged to Nick." Her reply was coy: "More or less, Mr. Secretary; more or less."

The official junket ended at Manila, but Alice went on to the Orient where she was received in a regal manner by the Emperor of Japan, and the Dowager Empress of China who, so the newspapers said, offered the Emperor in marriage to the American princess!

Alice's engagement to Nicholas was announced formally after her return. The King of England joined the rest of the world in sending his congratulations and Teddy dashed off a reply, perhaps more revealing of himself than of his future son-in-law.

"Longworth is a good fellow," he wrote, "one of the younger men who have really done well in Congress; he was from my own college, Harvard, and there belonged to my club, the Porcellian, which is antique as antiquity goes in America, for it was founded in Colonial days; he was on the varsity crew and was, and is, the best violinist that ever came from Harvard."

As goldsmiths, silversmiths and tapestry makers all over the world went to work making gifts for nations and rulers of nations to send to the American princess, the wedding was set for February 17, 1906, at the White House. This was to be the first wedding in the executive mansion since President Cleveland married Frances Folsom in 1886 and the tenth to take place in that historic house. The East Room was crowded with members of the Cabinet, the Supreme Court (but not in their black robes), the House, the Senate, and representatives of every nation who had embassies at Washington. Priceless gifts were piled on tables elsewhere in the White House—gifts from the Empress of China, the Kings of Italy and Spain, from obscure kings of forgotten Balkan countries, from the great financial barons of New York. There was a twenty-five thousand dollar necklace of aquamarines and diamonds, a genuine Gobelin tapestry, and, tied up in the kitchen, a bull dog in an Alice blue blanket. Outside a great throng milled behind police lines to get a glimpse of the bride.

After the Right Reverend Henry Yates Satterlee, Bishop of Washington, had pronounced them man and wife, Nicholas and Alice boarded the Elysian, their private railroad car hired for the occasion, and departed for Florida on the first lap of their honeymoon. This was spent in Cuba, where the legislature had just finished a long debate as to whether that nation should present Alice, as a wedding gift, San Juan Hill, where her father had made his famous charge. The legislature decided against the hill and sent her twenty-five thousand dollars worth of jewelry, instead.

The following June the couple went abroad. In Paris the President of France tendered them a lavish dinner at which the King of Cambodia's dancers performed, and the next two months were hectic with dinners, balls, and receptions given by the cream of diplomatic and royal society. The King of England, whose coronation the Irish had deprived her of seeing, received her, and the Kaiser dined her aboard the yacht which she had christened.

Back in Washington Alice made an effort to settle down as Nicholas Longworth's wife. But she was too volatile to lose her identity in marriage. In 1910, while Teddy, so he thought, was resting on his laurels and Mr. Taft was President, and the country was following young Louis D. Brandeis's exposures of corruption in the Forestry Service, Alice once again seized the headlines. She smoked a cigarette in public! At once the women of the nation, or at least those who belonged to women's clubs, started to scream. "Unladylike" was one of the mildest epithets hurled at the ex-Princess's head. Editorials were written, speeches were made, apologies demanded, and any club president, no matter how obscure, merely had to issue a statement to get her name in the papers.

The controversy raged for months. It reached its climax in a near riot in Pittsburgh when a member of the Daughters of the American Revolution said: "We women of Pittsburgh needn't get up our feathers because Mrs. Longworth smokes. Let us not forget our maternal ancestors smoked corncob pipes."

Perhaps because of her active life as a girl, when other young ladies looked with frightened eyes upon any form of outdoor exercise, and because she dared to smoke when cigarettes were taboo among nice women, Alice deserves her chapter in the long history of the emancipation of American womanhood.

Alice was to spend thirty years in Washington as the wife of the handsome and popular Republican Representative from Ohio. The three decades were to her liking for during that time she was a considerable power in the capital. Although socially the position of a Congressman is not great, either in Washington or back home, she continued to be a leader in those circles which take birth and breeding, wealth and position seriously. As the daughter of a former President, as a Lee-Cabot and a Roosevelt, her position was such that she could live up to her old, grand title. And although it was not incumbent upon her, as the wife of a Congressman, she could afford to entertain lavishly. Through inheritance of extensive coal and oil properties in the Southwest, Nicholas was a man of means; Alice, although not wealthy in her own right, had an assured income of at least five thousand dollars a year from her grandfather Cabot of Boston.

Politics was what interested her the most. She was a close friend of Ruth Hanna McCormick, the daughter and former secretary of old Mark Hanna. Unlike Ruth, who had served her apprenticeship in her father's office, Alice did not take an active part in Republican affairs; she preferred to work behind the scenes. Those who disliked her, and they were legion, said she was a Lady Lobbyist who used her tea parties and soirees to influence legislation. It is difficult to say how much power she actually wielded. Her one great fight was with the Battalion of Death, the clique led by Senator Lodge and Senator Jim Reed, the Missouri Democrat, to kill American entrance into the League of Nations. Like her father, she hated Woodrow Wilson venomously, and when the great debate over Wilson's fourteen-pointed dream was going on in the Senate, Alice was a daily gallery visitor. She fed and comforted the embattled Battalion, providing them late suppers and early breakfasts. She goaded the men to bitter warfare against the League and all its work. No little of the credit for America's staying out of the League must go to Princess Alice, which may or may not, according to one's own politics, make her a great woman.

She preferred always to be an onlooker. More than once she said, as she turned down suggestions that she take a place on one or another committee, that she preferred to work as an individual for the success of the Republican party. She seldom made speeches. She never held posts, One woman perhaps best described her political attitude when she said, rather unkindly:

"Alice is a good Republican by inheritance and conviction and she wants, and expects, the Republican Party to do its duty by her and hers."

On election night, in 1908, when her old friend Mr. Taft received the news of his election to the Presidency, Alice and Nick (one always seemed to think of them in that order!) were his guests at his home in Cincinnati. But four years later, when Teddy took his memorable bolt from the Republican Convention and during his ill-fated Bull-Moose campaign, she stuck to her father's cause. On each occasion Nicholas supported Taft. This caused no family friction: each knew that the other was doing what loyalty expected. That year Longworth suffered his only defeat between his first Congressional election in 1902 and his death in 1931.

Alice, noted for her caustic wit which, like that of many other brilliant conversationalists seldom bore translation into print, was also known for many years as the most delightful hostess in Washington. Her parties were never stiff. She refused to abide by the conventions, to pay official calls, or do the other tiresome things expected of a Washington official's wife. She didn't have to. She could, and did, dress as she pleased. Usually she was, to put it frankly, sloppy, and invariably, night or day, was encumbered by a huge handbag. But when she deigned to dress and put on regal airs, the bravest women quailed before her imperious walk. She could play the haughty princess whenever the spirit moved her.

Once when she and Mrs. McCormick arrived on a tour at a hotel in the Yellowstone Park they found the place crowded with distracted tourists who were at their wits' end because the maids and waitresses were on strike. Alice summoned the manager, dug into her handbag, and produced enough money to pay the overworked girls five dollars a day during their stay. The newspapers, which reported this act, forgot to say what happened to the girls after the princess left.

Alice was thirty-nine years old when her daughter was born on February 14, 1923, at the Lying-In Hospital in Chicago. Quite naturally this event rescued Alice from the journalistic oblivion into which she had fallen. But she disappointed the papers when she refused to allow the child to be photographed. Alice was determined not to let her daughter grow up in the spotlight that had dazzled her own eyes. She seems to have succeeded for in the morgue of one great New York newspaper no clipping bearing her name has been filed since 1931.

It might have been expected that Alice would name the child Theodora. She had no intention of loading her infant with the name of a president. Had the child been a boy it would have been called Paul, for next to Theodore Roosevelt, Alice's favorite historical personage was Paul, the tentmaker who fought with wild beasts at Ephesus. Since the baby was a girl she was named Paulina.

"That," said the mother, "is so she can have a personality of her own."

Although the next few years found Alice absorbed in the upbringing of the baby, and the perambulator (English style) was the most popular vehicle parked in front of the Longworth's Massachusetts Avenue home in Washington, Alice could not remain in the background forever. An erudite newspaper woman once described her as a combination of "Aspasia, Queen Elizabeth, Mme. Récamier, Diana of the Crossways, Mrs. Hauksbee, and Tennyson's Princess." That, of course, was laying it on a bit thick. She never was as lively as some of the ladies mentioned.

What really set Alice apart was her refusal to be hampered

by the *minor* conventions. As a sub-deb she had shocked the
dowagers by sitting on a piano, swinging her legs while talking
with M. Jusserand, the Ambassador; and in her early travels she
had startled more than one person by carrying with her a cool,
green snake named Emily Spinach ("Emily in honor of a very
thin aunt, and Spinach because it was green.") Fundamentally
she never really went much beyond that and there was one
celebrated occasion when she demanded, with a hauteur worthy
of her blue Cabot blood, that the conventions be observed.

Herbert Hoover was President and Charles Curtis, who had
known Alice since the Manila junket that ended in her engagement to Nick, was Vice President. Within a few months the
whole world was to descend into the great depression. But in
the warm spring of 1929 Alice put on an act that amused the
whole country. For years, as one newspaper put it, Alice had
made her own social laws, and to challenge her freedom was to
be barred from her "brilliant salon." But now she demanded
that the social laws be observed! Charley Curtis was not married and so he "appointed" his sister, Mrs. Dolly Gann, as his
"official hostess." In this role her place was at the right of every
host at dinners not attended by Mrs. Hoover. Such was the
burning Washington issue of 1929! Alice determinedly and
defiantly said no! To her suddenly socially rigid mind that
right belonged not to the *sister* of the Vice President—but to
the *wife* of the Speaker of the House! And the wife, of course,
was Alice.

Poor, harried President Hoover, who so soon was to have
greater matters on his mind, sent the problem to the Department of State, which promptly passed the buck to the diplomatic corps. As *The New York Times* put it, "The corps, not
being disposed to offend the Vice President of the United
States, gave the Perpetual Right to his hostess-sister."

Dolly Gann won in protocol, but Alice won in practice. Mrs.
Eugene Meyer, wife of the banker-politician who later became
publisher of *The Washington Post,* gave a dinner party at her
swank home on Crescent Place. She informed Alice that Dolly
would precede her at dinner. Alice, deeply offended, sent her
regrets. The joker was that the Vice President and Mrs. Gann,
having heard that the Speaker and his wife would not attend,

failed at the last minute to appear. The great social battle of Washington was declared a draw. But the victory was Alice's. She had spoiled Mrs. Meyer's party and kept Dolly Gann at home.

The nation guffawed loudly over the affair in those easy-going days, but it did not laugh long. The market crashed and Alice Roosevelt Longworth's fifth cousin once removed became the man of the hour. When he moved at last into the White House Alice was his guest upon one or two occasions. But soon she waxed caustic about the New Deal and all its works. She was induced to write a newspaper column as a sort of counter-irritant to Eleanor's *My Day*. A bitterness marked her words and they soon found few readers. She was still patiently ex-pecting the Republican Party to do its duty by her and hers. She faded from public notice. She became a ghost, or better still, a princess dethroned and forgotten. During the bitter campaigns to unseat her distant cousin—and her first cousin, his wife—she occasionally came to the fore, but few heard her voice. And after Franklin Roosevelt's third term began, Alice, remembering her old hatred for the "entangling alliances" of the League of Nations, took her stand with the isolationists. She still lived in Washington. Paulina was growing up, a young lady of eighteen. Maybe she will someday take up the torch.

II

The autumn of 1884 was an exciting one in the Roosevelt family. Young Teddy, then an Assemblyman at Albany, was doing his best to bring about the election of the "Man from Maine." It was a busy time for the embryo politician who had turned from Reform to cast his lot with Republican Party regu-larity. Up the Hudson at Hyde Park, James Roosevelt was living his quiet, rural existence, playing with his two-year-old son, Franklin, and following the campaign of his old friend Grover Cleveland in the newspapers. His older son, James Roosevelt Roosevelt, was awaiting the election less patiently, for he had contributed heavily to Cleveland's war chest and, along with *the* Mrs. Astor, his mother-in-law, was wondering what his re-ward would be. In New York Teddy's brother, Elliott Roosevelt, was hardly moved at all by the bitter campaign. He was younger than Teddy, a charming, delightful, somewhat spoiled young man, already showing that liking for drink which was to become a major problem for himself and his family. To Elliott, still grieving over the death of his mother, whose favorite he had been, the impending birth of his first child was more important than anything else in the world.

On the 11th day of October, 1884, the baby, a little girl, was born. Elliott was delighted and thought his daughter, whom he named Anna Eleanor after her mother, was "a miracle from Heaven," but Anna Livingston Hall Roosevelt was frankly disappointed. She herself was a beauty; indeed, for several generations, all the Halls and Livingstons had been proud of the good looking women in their families. Little Anna Eleanor was definitely not beautiful. Elliott, who adored her from birth despite her plainness, was amused by her solemn attitude as she grew older and he called her his Little Nell, after the tearful child in Dickens' *The Old Curiosity Shop*. Her mother had a less literary nickname: she called the child Granny, because, as she told her guests, Eleanor was such a "funny child, so old-fashioned." Elliott used to let her dance for his guests, but her mother made her self-conscious in their presence with her general attitude of disapproval.

Young Mrs. Roosevelt liked the activity of society, but Elliott, who had been content to live the very kind of life of "decorous hopelessness" that Teddy had complained against in his senior year at Harvard, was somewhat bored. He had little to do, no job or business, nothing with which to occupy himself except the work for crippled newsboys that his father had begun. When Little Nell was about four he broke his leg while riding in a Long Island horse show. After the slow process of healing was over he began to drink more than was good for him. This growing habit cast a shadow over the household. Even Little Nell was aware that something was happening which was making many other people unhappy, although she did not know the real reason.

In 1890 Elliott, Jr., was born and soon thereafter the Roosevelts decided to go abroad, hoping that treatments in European sanitariums might help Elliott regain his health and rebuild his selfcontrol. It was to be a far from gay journey for Little Nell.

After traveling on the Continent with his family Elliott entered a sanitarium and Mrs. Roosevelt settled down in a small cottage in Neuilly, near Paris, with little Elliott. Because there was no room for her, and because her mother was again pregnant, Little Nell was placed in a convent. There she was extremely unhappy. The children spoke a strange language and they were all being taught a religion that was strange and confusing to her Protestant mind. Six years old, horribly lonely, craving affection, she did the best she could to get away. Her desire was gratified one day when she told a nun that she had swallowed a penny. The nun knew she was lying. Her mother was sent for and she was taken away in disgrace. At the cottage her father, who had come for the birth of his second son, Gracie Hall Roosevelt, understood and was kind to her.

Little Nell's father had not been "cured" and so now he went back to his sanitarium and the mother and her three small children returned to New York. The unfortunate Elliott was to stay under doctors' care many months until his brother, Teddy, found time to journey to France and bring him home to this country. In the interim at the Halls' New York home Little Nell was lonely without her gay father, who loved to sing and read to her. Her mother did not understand how alone the little girl was.

Oh, there was plenty to do: she learned to read and write and memorize Bible verses and to sew pretty things, as all little girls of her class did in those Victorian times. Sometimes she overheard her mother and aunts talking about her father's "weakness," but although she did not understand what they meant, their words added to her childish woes. She spent a summer at Oak Terrace, the Livingston estate at Tivoli, New York, twenty-six miles up the Hudson from Hyde Park, and when she was seven her family took a house in East Sixty-First Street, New York, not far from where Aunty Bye was playing host to motherless Alice Roosevelt, Uncle Teddy's daughter. Little Nell was afraid of the self-confident, laughing Alice, but she worshipped her in her shy, solemn way, and was envious of her carefree poise.

That winter a fashionable teacher came each day to the East

Sixty-First Street house to give the three Roosevelt children their lessons. Although she was very busy with her social engagements, her teas, and dinners, and dances, Little Nell's mother set aside part of each day to be with them. But Eleanor never grew close to her beautiful mother. When her father finally came back to America he went into exile at Abington, Virginia, where the climate was better and he could busy himself with the affairs of a land-development company in the hope that by keeping busy he could forget the craving for alcohol. Little Nell longed for him. Her first thought was of him when, early in December, her mother was suddenly stricken with diphtheria. Before Elliott could reach her side, Anna Hall Roosevelt died.

This first experience with death had little affect on the eight-year-old Eleanor but she was heart-broken to see her father so crushed by the tragedy. He had worshipped his beautiful wife. It had been her mother's dying request that Little Nell's grandmother, Mrs. Valentine G. Hall, act as guardian for her children. An imperious woman, decidedly aware of her own status in society, Mrs. Hall scorned Elliott's protestations that he was capable of caring for his own children and insisted that they come to live with her in the sombre town house on Thirty-Seventh Street. Eleanor spent several grim winters there. Nor were the summers at Oak Terrace much happier. The Hall menage was dominated by Mrs. Hall. There were also her two daughters, Edith Livingston and Maude, her two sons, Valentine, Jr., and Edward, and a full complement of French and German maids, as well as a governess for the three grandchildren.

The young aunts and uncles were kind to the children and older members of the family did their best to bring them up properly. Eleanor's great-aunt, Mrs. James King Gracie (whence Hall Roosevelt's unmasculine first name), took her to visit the poor crippled children at the Orthopaedic Hospital, which Eleanor's grandfather, Theodore Roosevelt, Sr., had helped to found; Aunts Edith and Maude, who devoted an hour or so each week to singing hymns to the unfortunate derelicts in the Bowery Mission, took her with them; and at Christmas Uncle Valentine let her help with the trimming of the tree which he

set up at another "mission" for the impoverished wretches of
New York's most hideous slum, Hell's Kitchen. All the aunts
and uncles of the fashionable circle of which the Roosevelts
were a part in the 80's and 90's felt it their Christian duty to be
"good to the poor" in such ways as this, and the young people
were early initiated into social service, even if the causes of
poverty were taboo as subjects of discussion in their households.

The first winter with Grandmother Hall was tragic. Young
Elliott died of scarlet fever and little Hall nearly died. Eleanor
was sent to live with a cousin, Mrs. Henry Parish, Jr., a young
society matron, during this trying time. When summer came
she went back to Oak Hall. There, in August, she received
word that her father—her gay, happy father, who had loved his
Little Nell with such tender understanding, who had written
her such lovely letters from the South, who had planned with
her the home they would someday occupy together—had died in
New York. The child was stunned. She did not believe what she
had been told. Indeed, months passed before it dawned upon
her that her father would never sing to her again, or ask her to
dance for him. . . .

After his death Grandmother Hall took even more seriously
the upbringing of the sensitive, imaginative, and desperately
shy child. There was to be no new-fangled nonsense about it.
She dressed Eleanor plainly and sensibly—sensibly, that is, from
her Victorian point of view—with plenty of flannel petticoats,
long black stockings, high-laced shoes, and short skirts when
all her playmates—and they were few—had dresses that came
half-way down their legs. She made her take cold baths in the
morning, forbade her candy (which Eleanor stole, anyway) and
disapproved of the girl's love for reading. Eleanor learned ballroom dancing, the ballet, and even toe dancing, because proper
children had to know those arts if they were to be introduced
to Society later on.

At Tivoli, where her grandmother lived in the feudal manner
of a descendant of the old patroons, her only playmate of her
own age was a girl who lived five miles away. She had many
duties of a Victorian nature to perform, among them teaching
the Protestant Episcopal Catechism to the coachman's daughter.

But life was not always grim. Her aunts and uncles, themselves rebellious against the Puritanical background of their lives, took her riding and camping on the estate, and visited her in the little house in the woods which her grandmother had built for her to play in. There she taught herself to cook; there she dreamed and remembered her father; there she read every book she could get, from her Grandfather Hall's tomes on theology, his favorite reading, to the latest novel, whether she understood it or not. She had a bicycle, too, and other toys. She was lonely, repressed, but she was not altogether neglected or unhappy in the summer months.

Mrs. Hall, in her imperious way, disapproved of the Roosevelts. They were too rambunctious, too happy-go-lucky to suit her staid tastes. And so Eleanor was not allowed to see them as much as she had when her father was alive. When she did visit Oyster Bay she was painfully aware of her own awkwardness, her strange dress, and her timidity. She forgot her own gauche figure only when her Uncle Teddy read poetry to the children in his resounding voice. At other times the athletic cousins of that household scared her. In New York she was allowed to go to parties only at Christmas time. Seldom did she see or talk to a boy, and she had no idea how to get along with them. But at one Christmas party given by Aunt Corinne Robinson her distant cousin, Franklin, whom she had seen at Hyde Park once or twice before, was kind to her. He asked her to dance, the only boy at the party who did not shy away from the strange little girl in the unfashionable short skirts and black stockings.

When she was fifteen, Grandmother Hall became worried at her grandchild's gawkiness and a family conference was held. Aunty Bye suggested that Eleanor be placed in a school in England which was run by a Mlle. Souvestre, who had been Mrs. Cowles's teacher in Fontainebleau, France, many years before. And so, accompanied by another aunt, Mrs. Stanley Mortimer (her mother's older sister) but with no new or fashionable clothes in her trunks to make her happy, she was taken to Allenswood, as the school near London was called. Mlle. Souvestre, an understanding mistress, did her best to transform Eleanor, but the stay at Allenswood was not entirely a happy venture. For one thing, Eleanor had no spending money, because Grandfather Hall had died without making a will, thus leaving Mrs. Hall only her dower rights. Mrs. Hall's sons and daughters, gay and extravagant, had run haphazardly through their own inheritances, and the old lady had developed an unreasonably parsimonious nature as a result. Later, although she was not then aware of it, Eleanor was to inherit her share of the Hall wealth, but now she was poor as a church mouse in a school of wealthy English and American girls. To have to wear second-hand dresses, remade from the clothes of her aunts, at as fashionable and international a place as Allenswood was an experience that must have galled her girlish soul! Nevertheless she got over much of her nervousness—she learned to stop biting her fingernails—and when she came back to America for the summer, although still shy and uneasy in the presence of boys and girls her own age, she did not feel quite as out of place.

After another year in England and on the Continent, which she visited with schoolmates chaperoned by Mlle. Souvestre, Eleanor went to Oak Hall for the summer season. A change had come over that place. Her uncles, who lived there, had taken to drinking heavily; sometimes Eleanor would have to drive down to Tivoli and rescue Uncle Valentine from the local saloon and lead him home to Oak Hall. Proud Mrs. Hall was ashamed of the situation and kept all but close friends of the family who knew of Uncle Val's weakness, away from the estate. Now seventeen years old Eleanor more than ever wanted to escape from this unhealthy atmosphere, but when she told Grandmother Hall that she would like to go to college that worthy matriarch raised her aristocratic eyebrows and chillingly informed her that such was "not done" by young ladies! Eleanor bowed to the ruling and after taking her young brother, Hall Roosevelt, up to Groton School in Massachusetts, she went to New York for her first "season in society."

Although Grandmother Hall did not give her a "formal debut" Eleanor was invited to the Assembly and all the "proper" parties and dances. She began to make friends. Every now and then, at a social affair for young people, she met her cousin, Franklin, who had come on from Harvard for the occasion, and they became close friends. Nobody then expected the handsome, tall young student to fall in love with the tall, shy girl. When she went to a dance one of Mrs. Hall's maids went along to accompany her safely home. Eleanor did not care so much for formal dinners and parties as for the informal, but utterly respectable, studio parties to which she sometimes was invited. There, among artists and writers, she had fun. The highlight of the season was a visit, with other cousins, to Hyde Park. Mrs. James Roosevelt, a much younger woman than Grandmother Hall, although of a somewhat similar social background, was nice to her. Franklin was pleasant, too.

Grandmother Hall closed her Thirty-Seventh Street house when Eleanor was nineteen and the girl went to live with cousins, Mr. and Mrs. Henry Parish, Jr., in a pleasant but rigidly run house on fashionable East Sixty-Seventh Street. There she could entertain her friends at formal teas, and she was welcome at Mrs. Parish's rather stiff luncheons and dinners, all planned long in advance and run on schedule. Cousin Henry, now that she had come into money of her own, taught her how to cast up her checkbook and keep her bills paid, something she had never done before. She joined the newly organized Junior League and spent several hours a week at the Rivington Street Settlement House teaching fancy dancing and simple calisthenics to the girls from the sidewalks of the East Side of New York. Once Cousin Franklin came to take her home and she did not understand what one of the little girls meant when the child asked the dancing teacher if that handsome young man was her "fellow"! She helped the Consumers' League investigate conditions in New York factories, and otherwise did the right things that were expected of young ladies of her class. None of them were things that she particularly wanted to do, but she did them, because she was well brought up, the proper child of American Victorianism, cloistered, protected, innocent of life.

In her own autobiography, *This Is My Story*, Eleanor wrote many years later that she had at this time "painfully high ideals and a tremendous sense of duty . . . entirely unrelieved by any sense of humor or any appreciation of the weakness of human nature." She had not learned the truth about her father until long after his death and then her troubles with her alcoholic uncle had been a load difficult to bear. So things were either black or white, right or wrong. But her adventures in social work and the comparative freedom of life away from the ever-watchful eye of Grandmother Hall had broadened her. She was ready and eager for more of life.

III

Eleanor and Franklin Roosevelt saw a great deal of each other during the summer of 1903. That autumn, before he went back to Harvard, Franklin, who was twenty-one years old, asked his eighteen-year-old cousin to marry him after his graduation in June. Eleanor did not give him her answer at once, but went for advice to Grandmother Hall and Cousin Susie (Mrs. Parish, Jr., with whom she was still making her home). They thought she should wait awhile. Mrs. James Roosevelt, Franklin's mother, was sure that both were too young to know their own minds. Indeed, Mrs. Roosevelt was considerably disturbed over Franklin's devotion to his young cousin. No formal announcement of an engagement was made at that time. Eleanor resented the delay, but she made the best of it. Franklin invited her to Cambridge for proms and football games and, of course, saw her during the holidays. They were certain everything would come out for the best, whatever their families might think of it.

Mrs. Roosevelt was hopeful that her son Franklin, if properly distracted, would forget what she was sure was only a passing fancy for his cousin. While Eleanor went to Washington, as a guest of her Aunty Bye, she took Franklin and his roommate, Lathrop Brown, on a West Indian cruise. Although resentful at this interference Eleanor could do nothing about it. She resigned herself to the inevitable and enjoyed Washington. Aunty Bye's house was much more lively than Cousin Sue's New York home had been. Mrs. Cowles was delightfully informal and as a result Eleanor met some stimulating young people; she heard talk of politics and world affairs, topics that had never been discussed in the stuffier New York circle that she had known. Her own Uncle Teddy was President; Aunty Bye's husband was an important figure in Naval and political centers. And so she became alive in this new and vivid world. When

Franklin returned from his cruise to complete his senior year at Harvard they were still in love.

In June, 1904, Eleanor went to Harvard with Mrs. James Roosevelt and a host of other proud members of the Roosevelt family to see her handsome cousin graduated. Then she went to visit Aunt Corinne Robinson at the latter's summer place at Islesboro, off Dark Harbor, Maine. Franklin came for a weekend and then, with a maid as chaperone, the dashing swain took his cousin-fiancée by train to his mother's summer cottage on Campobello Island, New Brunswick, Canada. They had a happy vacation there together, walking and talking, and sailing on the Bay of Fundy, these two children who had so much in common: their lonely childhoods, their travels on the Continent, their love for serious books on history and literature, their inherent dislike for the surface pleasures of society. Franklin thought he might enter the United States Naval Academy or that he might go to the Harvard Law School. But he decided that he would do neither. He would study law at Columbia University in New York, where he could be nearer Eleanor. By autumn Mrs. James Roosevelt was convinced that the young couple were extremely serious. Their engagement was properly announced.

Time flew quickly. Franklin had his studies to attend to and Eleanor had her trousseau to select. There were many parties. In March they went to Washington to see Uncle Teddy inaugurated as twenty-sixth President of the United States. Then they hurried back to New York, for Uncle Teddy had said that he would be in that city to make a couple of speeches on the seventeenth of the month and he would be delighted to give his niece away in marriage to his own fifth cousin.

On St. Patrick's day Teddy arrived, primed for his speech to the Friendly Sons of St. Patrick after the annual parade on Fifth Avenue. The wedding took place in the twin brownstone houses of Mrs. Parish and her mother, Mrs. E. Livingston Ludlow, at Numbers Six and Eight East Seventy-Sixth Street, just off Fifth Avenue. On the Avenue the parade was in full panoply as the guests arrived in their carriages. The strains of *The Wearin' o' the Green* all but drowned out the ceremony as Uncle Teddy gave the bride away.

Eleanor wore a white satin dress covered with Grandmother

Hall's rose-point lace, which also formed the veil. Mother Roosevelt had given her a dog-collar of pearls, and Franklin, a chatelaine watch and pin, with her initials in diamonds on the watch. The pin which Mrs. Roosevelt still wears, was shaped in the form of three feathers from the Roosevelt crest. The Reverend Endicott Peabody, Headmaster of Groton School, officiated. After the ceremony everyone—the Vanderbilts and Astors, Hoyts, Chapins, Schiefflins, Delanos and Roosevelts, who had filled the double parlors of the joint houses for the occasion—crowded around the President, who was still chuckling over the way the paraders had drowned out the soft strains of *Oh, Promise Me* and forgot about the bride and groom.

The newlyweds, postponing an extended honeymoon until Franklin's summer vacation period, spent a few days at Hyde Park and then settled down in a small apartment in the West Forties. Franklin went back to his classes at Columbia and Eleanor tried her best to keep house. She was no better at it than most brides, and no worse; but as soon as Mother Roosevelt left her New York home for Hyde Park in the spring they joyfully moved in there, and Eleanor let the housekeeper assume the responsibility of running the home. After school closed she and Franklin took their belated honeymoon abroad, visiting London, Paris, Venice, Germany, and the Swiss Alps. At Paris they were the guest of Franklin's aunt, Mrs. Dora Delano Forbes; they visited Scotland, where Franklin's half-brother, James Roosevelt Roosevelt, loved to fish and hunt and knew the owners of many large estates. The whole summer was a gay adventure. On the way back Eleanor, always a poor sailor, was seasick, and more so because, as she knew, she was soon to have a child.

One domestic worry did not confront Eleanor upon her arrival in New York. She did not have to hunt out a place in which to live. In her characteristic way, Mother Roosevelt had arranged everything. She had rented a house for the young couple at One Hundred and Twenty-Five East Thirty-Sixth Street, not far from her own home, and she had furnished it and decorated it before her son and his bride had a chance to say a thing about it. She had even hired the servants. Instead of

being resentful, Eleanor was glad to be relieved of this responsibility, for she was quite ignorant of housekeeping. Although
Franklin had money of his own from his father, Mrs. Roosevelt,
whose fortune was far greater, was extremely generous to her
son. Both accepted her largess gratefully.

Eleanor's first child, Anna Eleanor Roosevelt, was born May
3, 1906, and for the next ten years, as she later said, she was
always "just getting over a baby or about to have one." In the
winter of 1907 she had to undergo a serious operation, from
which she nearly died, but on December 23 she had James, her
second child. Both Anna and James were somewhat sickly
infants, and the Roosevelt home saw a succession of trained
nurses. The house was crowded, especially at holiday time, for
Hall Roosevelt, Eleanor's brother, now made his home there.
Mother Roosevelt decided something must be done and so she
bought two plots of land at Numbers Forty-Nine and Fifty-One
East Sixty-Fifth Street and built twin houses there, one for herself, another for her son and his family. While the houses were
being built Franklin and Eleanor took a cottage by the ocean
at Seabright, New Jersey, where the young mother and two
children grew strong in the sun. Eleanor nearly wrecked the
little automobile Franklin had bought and she who one day
was to travel thousands of miles annually in her own car, was so
distressed that she refused to touch a steering wheel for many
years!

When they moved into their new home that winter Franklin
went to work in his law office. Eleanor, expecting a new baby,
stayed at home much of the time. One day, shortly after moving in, Franklin found her in tears. She suddenly hated not
having a house of her own choosing, she cried, one she had not
planned, one that did not suit her own ideas! Her husband,
who had never seen her in this mood, did not understand her
outburst; as she later said, he thought she was "quite mad,
told me so gently, and said I would feel different in a little
while and left me alone until I should become calmer." And
so Eleanor sublimated herself to the desires of her strong willed
mother-in-law and her husband—and made the best of the situation. After all, there was little she could do about it. Their
third child, "the biggest and most beautiful of all the babies,"

was born in March. He died of influenza the following November. This tragedy made her morbid, for she thought if she had watched the child's nurse more closely, or if the baby had been breast fed, he might have lived. This unhealthy state of introversion continued for some months, despite all the assurances to the contrary which Franklin made to her. The next summer she went to Campobello, sending the children to Hyde Park. Franklin was at Hyde Park, making his first campaign for the New York Senate. But he came to New York to be with her when her next child was born, on September 23, 1910, in the East Sixty-Fifth Street house. They named him Elliott, after her beloved father.

IV

Much to the surprise of everyone who was interested, Franklin Roosevelt was elected to the Senate. Almost at once a new life opened for Eleanor. She who had spent a lifetime under the domination of other people—Grandmother Hall, Mother Roosevelt, and her numerous uncles, cousins, and aunts—was to become mistress of her own home for the first time. True, it was not really her own home, but one which the Roosevelts rented in Albany, an old house, furnished, not far from the Capitol. There she installed an English nurse, a German maid, and a Slovak wet-nurse for little Elliott. The day she arrived the house was in a turmoil because Franklin was holding a reception for about one thousand constituents! But as soon as that was over, and the house thrown into order, Mother Roosevelt left for Hyde Park.

Occasionally Eleanor visited the legislative galleries to watch her tall, blue-eyed, fair-haired husband. Every afternoon she had tea with the children, read to them, and played with them. She gave luncheons for Franklin's political associates, and opened the house to his fellow "insurgents" making for them a comfortable place to meet and map the anti-Tammany Hall strategy that was to make young Senator Roosevelt something of a hero. She saw that they had sandwiches and beer, and threw herself wholeheartedly into supporting her husband's political career. Many years later Franklin said that it was during her

first year at Albany that Eleanor's "political sagacity and cooperation" had their beginning.

There was always Hyde Park for the children. They stayed
there while Eleanor, Franklin and Hall Roosevelt, just graduated from Harvard, went on a visit to New Mexico, and there
they played, under the benevolent and watchful eye of their
grandmother, while Franklin and Eleanor attended the Democratic National Convention at Baltimore in 1912, at which
Franklin worked in the dreadful heat and racket for the nomination of his political idol, Woodrow Wilson.

But the Convention was too much for Eleanor. She fled to
cool Campobello, taking the children, to stay for the first time
at another house she could now call her own. A friend of the
Roosevelts, knowing how Franklin liked the island, had suggested in her will that Mother Roosevelt buy her cottage there
for Franklin at a "nominal sum." This Mother Roosevelt had
done, taking it with all its furnishings, silver, china, and glass.
It really was more than a cottage—three stories high, six bed-
rooms, spacious living room, servant-quarters, many porches,
a tennis court, rolling lawns, a boathouse, a stony beach!
Eleanor was enjoying the place when Franklin, returned to
New York after the Convention, was taken ill with typhoid. She
rushed to his side, was stricken herself with the fever, but
nursed him back to health. During that illness Franklin was
reëlected to the State Senate through the clever manipulations
of Louis McHenry Howe.

This year the children stayed in New York, with Mother
Roosevelt helping to keep an eye on them. Eleanor was with
them, too, except from Monday to Thursday, when she stayed
with Franklin at an Albany hotel. In the spring of 1913 President Woodrow Wilson appointed Franklin Roosevelt Assistant
Secretary of the Navy, Uncle Teddy's old post, and another
change came into Eleanor's life. With her head crammed with
advice to a young secretary's wife, given by Aunty Bye out of
that lady's long knowledge of Washington political life, Eleanor,
now twenty-nine years old, went proudly and bravely off to the
capital with her husband. They settled at Mrs. Cowles's old
house on N Street, which had not rattled with the sound of
political small talk since Uncle Teddy had been President.

Life was full, exciting, and busy. There was, of course, the inevitable round of official calls, entertainments, and "at homes," those grim necessities of official life. But there was fun, too. The Roosevelts were not wealthy, by any reckoning, even when they added their inherited joint incomes to Franklin's salary. They could not entertain lavishly, nor give large dinner parties. Instead, they held informal gatherings on Sunday evenings for Franklin's political friends, and Eleanor presided over the chafing dish, a wedding present, in which she concocted scrambled eggs. This same dish was to become a White House favorite years later, when she transported to that austere mansion the same informality that marked these early Sunday parties. When Franklin went on tours of inspection of Navy Yards, which was his end of Navy Department business before the war, Eleanor often accompanied him. She had developed some of the charm that was to mark her later life, an attribute Franklin had aplenty then as later, and they made many friends throughout the country.

In August, 1914, that grim summer which saw war spread over Europe, Eleanor was at Campobello, having another baby, Franklin D. Roosevelt, Jr. That year her ambitious husband was busy trying to further his political career, but Eleanor was too busy with the new baby to pay much attention to his unsuccessful attempt to win the Democratic nomination as junior Senator from New York. When he went on a junket to the San Francisco Fair the following Spring she went along. It was her first trip across the United States. That winter and for several months thereafter, Washington was a busy, rumor-ridden town, what with all the talk about the war in Europe and the possibility of American entrance into the conflict. But life, on the whole, went on as usual. At least it did for Eleanor. She was not yet done "having babies." On March 16, 1916, however, her last was born. He was named John Aspinwall Roosevelt.

When Eleanor's first child was born, Mother Roosevelt, Grandmother Hall, and even Aunt Susie had warned Eleanor that she must give up her social welfare work—in which she had been interested purely as a duty expected of her ever since her return from Mlle. Souvestre's English school. They feared, if she did not, that she might bring back from the "dreadful slums" some "awful disease" which the dear children might catch. Obedient, as always, she had done so, and in the ensuing twelve years she had been inactive outside of her own home. She had not yet learned to follow the creed for living given her by Aunty Bye the first time she had gone to Washington:

"No matter what you do, some people will criticise you, and if you are entirely sure that you would not be ashamed to explain your action to someone whom you loved and who loved you, and you are satisfied in your own mind that you are right, then you need never worry about criticism nor need you ever explain what you do."

It had been easier to follow the line of least resistance, to let herself be dominated by Mother Roosevelt and Grandmother Hall. The war was to change that.

Suddenly it became her duty to be busy, to do things, to work hard inside and outside her home. In those days they called it "doing your bit." Eleanor's bit was much more than the word signifies. Franklin, of course, was up to his neck in work for the Navy Department. Eleanor, too, was soon one of the busiest women in Washington. She worked for the Naval censor, going over letters from sailors stationed in the capital; she slaved in the canteen of the Red Cross in the Washington railroad yard, passing out food to troop trains on their way to camps; she helped at the Naval Hospital. One day she discovered that St. Elizabeth's Hospital, in the rush of war time activity, was overcrowded and ineptly managed. She got the ear of her old friend from the days of the scrambled-egg parties, Secretary of War Franklin K. Lane, and induced him to order an investigation. As a result, St. Elizabeth's became a model hospital for the insane and the shell-shocked under the able administration of Dr. William White.

In the humid summer of 1918, Hyde Park's cool lawns and the sea breezes of Campobello were forgotten (or wistfully remembered!) as she worked twelve hours a day at the canteen, a hot iron-roofed shack. That summer her husband went to Europe on an official mission and was stricken with pneumonia on his return. Eleanor nursed him back to health in New York —and then, back in Washington, she, her husband, her five children, all came down with influenza during the epidemic that swept the East. With her three servants also sick, she cooked for them all, and for the neighbors, and even helped with a Red Cross unit caring for victims among government clerks in the crowded wartime capitol.

Eleanor had changed. New vistas had opened for her, new ideas of service, and she threw herself wholeheartedly into the hard work. Women who knew her then were unstinting in their praise.

When, after the 1918 armistice, Franklin again went abroad on an official errand, she accompanied him. In London she had a severe attack of pleurisy. Franklin had to go to Paris with the Wilson peace mission, but Eleanor soon was on her feet again and met him in Paris in time to return to America with President Wilson's party.

Grandmother Hall, full of years and virtue, the grand Victorian dame to the end, died in 1919. Franklin was still with the Navy Department but neither he nor she was as busy as during the war. The next year Eleanor rushed to New York to take charge when her Aunt Puss (Mrs. Edith Livingston Hall Morgan, the wife of Forbes Morgan) and two of her three children were burned to death in a fire that swept the converted stable in which they lived on Ninth Street. Except for the death of her father and her son this was the greatest personal tragedy that so far had touched her life.

In the autumn of 1920 Franklin was busy running for Vice President on the Democratic ticket with James M. Cox, the Ohio publisher. Mrs. Roosevelt placed young James in Groton that year and then joined his father on the campaign trip that took them over many miles and into almost every state in the union. Mrs. Roosevelt gave her first newspaper interview while on that trip. But her help and Franklin's speeches were of no avail on election day when a couple of Republicans named Harding and Coolidge became the people's choice. The Roosevelts settled down in New York. The children were sent away to school. Franklin went hunting in Louisiana with Mrs. Roosevelt's brother Hall, who had lived with them until his own marriage to Margaret Richardson, and who was to be very close to them both until his death in 1941. Then Franklin started to practise law. Because their own house had been rented during the Washington years they lived at Mrs. James Roosevelt's adjacent home.

Away from the excitement of war-time Washington and with her children all in school, Eleanor found time hanging heavy on her hands. Of course, there were visits to Hyde Park at holiday time and many social engagements of one kind or another. But there really was not much to do. Eleanor studied shorthand and typewriting, and cooking, an art in which she had never been too adept. And she joined the New York State League of Women Voters for which she prepared a monthly report on national legislation. Mother Roosevelt, always interested in charitable causes, induced her to join the boards of several organizations, but, as Eleanor soon learned, all she was expected to do was to lend her name while paid employes did the work. She found that dissatisfying.

In the summer of 1921 the Roosevelts went to Campobello as usual. Franklin came up, tired from his work in the law office and for the insurance company with which he was associated. It was at this time that he was stricken with infantile paralysis. At once all of Eleanor Roosevelt's strength of mind and body and will were directed toward bringing about his recovery. There was more to contend with than her desperately ill husband. There was his mother, whose only child he was and who had cared for him with a possessive tenderness since his birth. To Mother Roosevelt he was still her baby. To Eleanor he was a wonderful man with a magnificent future before him who must, at all costs, get well. The struggle between two strong-willed women—for Eleanor no longer was the little girl completely under the sway of her elders—was titanic.

With firm determination Eleanor set herself against the defeatist attitude of Mother Roosevelt, whose instincts of protection and possession told her that her son would never get strong, would never again enter the political lists which she abhorred. Aiding Eleanor was the gnome-like Louis McHenry Howe, who long ago had joined his future with that of Franklin Roosevelt, giving up his own career to foster that of the man whom he had known from his first day in the State Senate. Together they battled for his recovery—and they won.

Eleanor Roosevelt knew that her husband's salvation lay in

getting him back into the whirl and excitement and hard work of the political action that heretofore had been his whole life. For this reason she deliberately began to take an interest in politics. Within a year of his stroke she had become chairman of the finance committee of the Women's Division of the Democratic State Committee. How that must have amused Franklin and Aunt Susie, both of whom, years before, had struggled to teach her how to keep her accounts! With the same abandon that had kept her in the hot canteen in Washington twelve hours a day Eleanor threw herself into the work. If her job was to lick stamps she licked stamps. If her assignment was to tour the State on a speaking tour with Mrs. Henry Morgenthau, Jr., her Dutchess county neighbor, she visited every place on the schedule. She became an ardent, active Democrat. To the Junior Leaguers she wrote that the Democratic party, in her mind, "seems to have been more concerned with the welfare and interests at large and less with the growth of big business interests." If such heresy fell on deaf ears, it did not matter. She was forming her creed.

V

When 1928, an election year, rolled around Mrs. Roosevelt was politically more active than her husband, who had spent the last seven years restoring his health. Except that he could not use his legs he was now physically well. But he had not returned to politics. Indeed, he had pretty well made up his mind that he would not for some time to come. But through such organizations as the League of Women Voters, the Consumers' League, and the Women's Trade Union League, Eleanor had kept up the family's association with politics and she stood high in the ranks of women workers for the Democratic Party. She had campaigned for the 1926 election of the German-born liberal, Robert F. Wagner, against aristocratic Senator James Wadsworth—whom, in several of her speeches, she accused of having the "Marie Antoinette type of mind— 'Let them eat cake!' "

During the seven years between the time Franklin was stricken and the 1928 Democratic National Convention, which was to see him once again in the forefront of party affairs, other matters than politics had interested Eleanor. Near his mother's home at Hyde Park, Franklin had bought a small farm. A creek, still bearing its old Dutch name of Val Kill, ran through this property, and Eleanor had long wanted to have a cottage beside it. In 1926, at her husband's suggestion, the cottage was put up, primarily as a place to which Eleanor could bring her growing circle of women friends for quieter, more intimate week-ends than was possible at Mrs. James Roosevelt's Hyde Park estate. Later Franklin built a swimming pool on the lawn in front of this house, and still later he designed and erected a small white house for himself—which, much to his disgust, the newspapers called his "dream house" —on the hill overlooking Eleanor's retreat.

The year her cottage was built, Mrs. Roosevelt, with her close friends, Nancy Cook, Marion Dickerman, and Caroline O'Day, who was to become representative-at-large from New York in 1934, also built a furniture shop on this property. Its purpose was to provide employment for the unemployed farm men of the region. They hired an expert to train the men in making reproductions of fine old furniture. Later a pewter forge and weaving looms were established. Mrs. Roosevelt continued to supervise the plants, on a non-profit basis, until she went to the White House. Then the factories were turned over to the people who had worked in them and were continued elsewhere in the neighborhood.

The desire to do things was growing on Eleanor, in whom the Roosevelt vitality and urge for expression had been kept suppressed for so many years. In 1927 John, her youngest child, went off to boarding school leaving her with more free time than ever. She was, therefore, receptive to a suggestion now hesitatingly made by Miss Dickerman. This estimable lady, a school teacher from Oswego, New York, whom Eleanor had known and liked for many years, was offered a chance to buy the Todhunter School for Girls on East Eightieth Street, New York, a fashionable school run by an Englishwoman who now wished to retire. Mrs. Roosevelt, Miss Dickerman, and Miss Cook, each purchased a one-third interest in the school.

Eleanor, much to the disgust of Mrs. James Roosevelt, who

couldn't understand her daughter-in-law's restlessness, became vice principal and, although completely untrained for the task, teacher of English and civics. In these days, of course, the name Roosevelt was not yet anathema among people who could afford to send their children from their Central Park and Park Avenue homes to a private school. The new Todhunter, which had a reasonably progressive curriculum, prospered. Mrs. Roosevelt taught her classes there faithfully until her husband became President, and retained her interest in the school until she resigned in 1938. The following year Todhunter was merged with another school and the proceeds of the sale were turned over to Mrs. Roosevelt's two partners. From this venture, as from the Val Kill industries, she received no profit, except her salary while a teacher.

Thus, when the campaign of 1928 opened and she was assigned to take charge of the women's work to wrest the Democratic nomination for Al Smith, Eleanor Roosevelt's life was a full one. Through bitter experience she was personally a "dry," but she worked tirelessly with the late Mrs. Belle Moscowitz, Al Smith's famous advisor on social matters, for the nomination of the nation's outstanding "wet." She gave luncheons, teas, dinners, and worked day and night in the office of campaign headquarters. That June, at the National Democratic Convention in Houston, Texas, Franklin Roosevelt made his famous speech in which he gave to Al Smith the title of "The Happy Warrior"—and the Governor of New York was nominated to run against Herbert Hoover, whom Franklin and Eleanor, in their Washington days, had known and liked and whom they had tried to persuade to become a Democrat. Franklin went off, then, to Warm Springs, Ga., where the swimming was doing him worlds of good. Eleanor, staying in New York, continued her hard work for the Party.

As the campaign progressed Al Smith realized that he could not possibly defeat Mr. Hoover unless he could carry New York State—and he knew he could not carry New York unless the Democrats could win the governorship. Mr. Roosevelt's felicitous nominating address at Houston had made him a popular figure; besides he did not have the political disadvantage of being a Roman Catholic. Vainly Al Smith begged Mr.

Roosevelt to seek the nomination, but Franklin had no intentions of letting anything interfere with his recovery: he flatly refused. But Al Smith did not give up hope, although his own situation was growing daily more desperate as the New York State Democratic Convention approached. Roosevelt continued to remain adamant. Eleanor, of course, attended the state meeting at Rochester, but Franklin stayed at Warm Springs.

There, in his stubbornness, he would not answer the telephone, although many an old and close friend tried to reach him and implore him to accept the nomination. On the day when the most frantic efforts were being made to persuade him, he went on a picnic with other patients at the Warm Springs Foundation. At last, in desperation, Al Smith sought out Mrs. Roosevelt and begged her to telephone Franklin. She told Mr. Smith that she did not believe he would accept, that he needed more time at Warm Springs. But still, she said, he should make his own decision, and so, reluctantly, she agreed to telephone. When Franklin was told she was on the wire he dragged himself to the second floor of a neighboring house to talk to her. But the connection was bad on the party line, and he could not hear. When Mr. Roosevelt got back to the Foundation, he telephoned Eleanor at the Rochester headquarters to see what she had wanted. She told him that Al Smith, hovering anxiously at her elbow, wanted to speak to him. At first Franklin hesitated and then agreed to talk. Without a word Mrs. Roosevelt handed Smith the receiver and then, glancing at her watch, rushed off for her train. She had a class at Todhunter in the morning.

On her way to the school Eleanor saw in the morning newspapers that her husband had accepted the nomination.

"I don't want Franklin to be Governor," she cried with tears in her eyes, when the first reporter sought her out. "It will spoil our lives. He doesn't want to be Governor. What shall we do?"

Franklin, whether he wanted to or not (and that is a question still debated by political experts!), became Governor, although Al Smith lost the state to Herbert Hoover.

VI

The years at Albany were probably the least interesting in Anna Eleanor Roosevelt's life. She took her duties as governor's wife seriously. Her new position barred her from active politics so she confined her activities to annual summer tours of State institutions with Governor Roosevelt. These were hardly exhilarating but gave her a chance to see many interesting things, in hospitals, asylums, jails. She kept open house each Wednesday in the sombre and barnlike Executive Mansion. She gave teas and luncheons, and retained her interest in several organizations. Also she kept up her teaching in New York. But on the whole it was neither thrilling nor interesting, being a Governor's wife.

Nor did Eleanor become excited when Franklin Roosevelt, in that grim year of 1932, asked the democracy to make him its candidate. Although she could not lend her name openly to the work, she "advised" her old political associates and helped organize democracy's women behind her husband. When he was nominated she proudly climbed into the airplane and accompanied him to Chicago where he shattered precedent by accepting the party's gift during the Convention.

Mrs. Roosevelt, tall and straight, invariably dressed in styles befitting her forty-eight years, with a charm of manner that transcended her plain features, made an ideal candidate's wife. To the women of America she was not well known. Few even knew that she was a grandmother. But she was. Anna, her oldest child, was married to Curtis Dall, a New York broker, and they had two children, Anna Eleanor ("Sistie") and Curtis ("Buzzy"), tow-headed youngsters whose photogenic qualities were soon to be known by everybody. James, who had married Elizabeth Cushing, daughter of the world-famous Boston brain surgeon, was the father of a daughter, Sara, born March 13, 1932; and Elliott's wife, Elizabeth Donner Roosevelt, the daughter of a business associate of that arch-Republican financier and distiller, Andrew W. Mellon, was to present her with another grandson, William Donner Roosevelt, shortly after the November election.

At that time a phrase frequently on her husband's lips was,

"Eleanor and I think this, or that—." It became a respectful byword at campaign headquarters, where Mrs. Roosevelt was in frequent consultation with James J. Farley, the campaign manager, Louis Howe, and the other political advisors of her husband. Franklin and Eleanor were known, then, as a great "political team," and many a behind-the-scene quarrel was left to her to be smoothed out. When election night came she gathered her entire family, and Mrs. James Roosevelt, at campaign headquarters in New York city, to join in the celebration of her husband's landslide victory.

After the election she was busier than ever. She was preparing one evening to catch a train to an Ithaca, New York, conference of farm women when a pain-wracked and insane man, Guiseppe Zangara, tried to kill her husband as he returned from a yachting trip at Miami, Florida, and killed Mayor Cermak of Chicago, who was riding beside the President-elect in his car. Although shocked by the news the first thing she did was to rush next door to comfort her mother-in-law. When both were reassured about Mr. Roosevelt, she took the midnight train to Ithaca, saying:

"One must have a philosophy about such things. One realizes it is always possible for such things to happen to men in public life and then one thinks no more about it. I cannot imagine living in fear of a possible death."

Even if she had wanted that kind of life, the times were unpropitious for any display of ostentation when Anna Eleanor Roosevelt became the First Lady of the Land. The country was in the midst of the worst depression it had ever known. This was no time for fancy balls, gay parties, lavish dinners. It was a time for desperately hard work, faith in the future, and old-fashioned simplicity in the present. But this did not mean that one had to be gloomy. Mrs. Roosevelt expressed her hopeful philosophy when she said at that time:

"There never was a time when life was more worth living. I believe that if we are not afraid there is a chance to make this a wonderful new world. We must not be content with what has been told us in the past, because now nearly everything is being weighed in the balance."

Few women ever set out to do more things on more different

fronts than Mrs. Roosevelt did as she began her search for her wonderful new world.

First, she took pains to fit the White House into the kind of place that would suit the type of administration her husband was about to inaugurate. Years before, when Eleanor was not yet a bride, her aunt, Mrs. Theodore Roosevelt, coming into the White House still heavy with the aura of McKinley plush, had shifted things about to please her volatile Teddy and her active, banister-sliding children. Now Eleanor rid the mansion of Hooverian stuffiness, and she and her husband filled it with things like ship's clocks and bells, naval prints, cartoons, furniture from Val Kill, and other objects personally and pointedly Rooseveltian. She spent nine thousand dollars of Government money for new china, although some caustic people called it an extravagant thing to do in 1933.

Later, at the cost of one hundred sixty-five thousand dollars Eleanor had the Government modernize the kitchens, although she kept the historical old fireplace where they cooked meals in the days of Jefferson, and she rescued from oblivion the marble trough from which Andy Jackson's cow had drunk in those early Democratic days. Many other improvements were made because Mrs. Roosevelt, to the delight of women's page editors everywhere, said: "I think the White House should set an example of a standard of decent living for those who have to work in somebody else's house."

"Sistie" and "Buzzie," of course, enlivened the place in those days for they lived there days at a time. Anna was staying there, too, not yet divorced from her husband, Curtis Dall. The place was busy and gayer than it had been for years. It was to remain that way—a place of "delightful domesticity" and equally delightful informality. Mr. Roosevelt, of course, was confined to the White House more than any predecessor, and Mrs. Roosevelt made it, as much as possible, a comfortable home.

Although, when she moved to Washington, Mrs. Roosevelt had to give up many of her old interests, she quickly found others to take their place. Val Kill was turned over to other people and moved from the estate. She no longer taught school. But there were compensations—many of them. Too many, said some critics—who would have kept her out of the limelight and restricted her doings to tea parties. But she ignored the critics. She was no longer Grandmother Hall's ward. She had made a life and was determined to live it. And she did, with gusto.

Mrs. Roosevelt accepted contracts to speak for the radio on time sponsored by manufacturers of soap and other commercial products. For a while she edited a magazine called *Babies, Just Babies,* an ill-starred venture of the barefooted, raw-carrot-eating publisher, Bernarr Macfadden. She wrote books and magazine articles. And she was forever, as they say in New England, on the go. She went and saw and did so many things that the jokesmiths were kept busy overtime thinking up gags about the eternal peregrinations of the Lady of the White House who was never home.

In 1935 Eleanor signed a contract to write a daily column for the United Feature Syndicate, which she has done six days a week without interruption ever since. Sometimes it was as inoccuous as the post-presidential animadversions of the late Calvin Coolidge; sometimes it contained inside political information; occasionally she used it as a sounding board for new ideas broached by herself or her husband. The first column appeared in forty newspapers. When she signed a new five-year contract in 1940, one hundred and thirty-five papers published it every afternoon. When, in 1941, the pro-Roosevelt *New York Post* offered to take it over from *The World-Telegram,* long a bitter critic of every Rooseveltian policy, the latter, knowing its popularity, refused to relinquish it. (Alice Longworth's column, started shortly after Mrs. Roosevelt's began, died painlessly within a few months. Alice's vaunted wit, somehow, never seemed so witty when transferred to paper. She had the aid of a ghost. No one but Mrs. Roosevelt has ever written *My Day.*)

Mrs. Roosevelt, who now drove her own Chevrolet car, usually accompanied only by her secretary, Malvina Thompson, traveled uncounted thousands of miles. She wanted to see America and Americans at first hand. In order to do this she went deep down into mines; she visited factories; like an inquiring reporter she showed up unannounced in the strangest places. Many people accused her of meddling in affairs that were none of her business. But she ignored all the gibes and went her way.

Conscious of labor's new dignity under the New Deal she refused to pass picket lines. Later, as a working newspaper columnist, she joined the American Newspaper Guild, the first successful newspaperwriters' union in the history of the American press, and took an active interest in its inner affairs. She moved steadily Leftward in the early years of the New Deal. Because she had her own column, and because she was the first First Lady to establish a weekly press conference for the women reporters in Washington, the public always knew her views.

Sometimes Mrs. Roosevelt expressed herself on dangerously controversial subjects. Her greatest interest was in the youth of America and, perhaps because she allowed her own children to manage their lives in their own way, she was often criticised for lending her support to the so-called Youth movement. Her adversaries, and they were many, suggested that she learn better to manage her own domestic affairs before trying to tell American youth how to manage its business! Perhaps her greatest political mistake was her loyalty to the American Youth Congress even after that organization had been "exposed" as one of many organizations under allegedly Communist leadership. When severely condemned for giving so radical an organization her support, and even inviting its "Red" members to the White House, she "got up her Dutch" in typical Rooseveltian style. She refused to resign, and by her actions added fuel to the anti-Roosevelt fire so faithfully tended by those who hated the New Deal and all its aims. Her loyalty may have been admirable, but tactically it was mistaken. Eventually she turned on the Congress, read it a motherly lecture, and became the object of Communist derision until the breaking of Stalin-Hitler pact brought the Reds back into the New Deal camp.

It would be impossible, in this chapter, to chronicle all the events of her crowded life from the time she first went to the White House, through the years of the depression, until the beginning of her husband's third term as President and the dangerous days when the second World War drew closer to American shores. Few women at any time have been more publicised. Her annual visits to the New York shops to buy her clothes—which some women feel are excellently chosen to display her personality and which others feel are the antithesis of fashionable taste—her closeness to her children, her rushing to their bedside when ill, her presence at their second marriages—her long absences from the White House—her writing of books and columns—all these things millions of women admire and thousands of other women hate.

But these years from 1929 to 1941 were years of growth for Eleanor Roosevelt and the hustle and bustle of her life was, in reality, merely her own Rooseveltian way of making manifest what *The Nation* once called her "intelligent and dogged defense of democratic principles." A year or so ago Miss Ruby Black wrote Eleanor Roosevelt's biography. Miss Black, one of Washington's most experienced newspaper women, had known Mrs. Roosevelt for many years. Towards the end of her biography she gives, in a brief paragraph, an unforgettable profile:

"Her hard won courage gives courage to others—to the bewildered, the simple, and the voiceless. Thousands upon thousands are not afraid because she has learned not to fear. Her enduring faith in the people sustains the faith of others in democracy, in a time when democracy is seriously and widely questioned. Her laboriously gained knowledge inspires others —many others—to learn about their country and its people, their government and its aims, successes and failures. Her humanization of politics and government spreads its influence, slowly but effectively. Her intelligent and informed struggle for peace where there is no peace keeps others working patiently. Her deep distaste for 'Lady Bountiful' kind of charity sets an example to help people help themselves. Her belated boldness in making a life of her own leads other women to realize that they, too, are persons. . . ."

In some sections, and among a certain type of women, these words will fall as superfluous praise of a woman who "gads about" too much to learn, of a woman who would do better to step from the spotlight, close her notebook, and take up her knitting by the fireside. Eleanor Roosevelt has not had, or needed, the support of these women. She has had the love of millions of other women, poor, hard working, striving, dreaming, women, in factories, on farms, in small homes. To them, struggling in a world wracked first by depression and then by war, she has taken on a largeness of spirit that few other women have attained in this generation.

The child of American Victorianism, the Little Nell of the 1880's, the pig-tailed, black-stockinged girl who stood in awe of Alice, her cousin, has lived a life most women would envy. She has taken her full share from life. Her fifty-seven years have not all been happy, but as wife and mother and then as Eleanor Roosevelt, she must have long since felt that on the whole they have given her greater riches than she ever dreamed of in her little house under the trees at Tivoli, or in the sombre town house of Grandmother Hall.

VII

More than once, in her later years, Eleanor Roosevelt has wondered if she did not make many grave mistakes in the up-bringing of her children and in her early close relationships with them. When she was a young mother she built her life around the needs, real or fancied, of Anna, James, Elliott, Franklin, or John; sometimes she worried herself sick fearing she was not doing everything for them that she should; at other times she was sure she was "spoiling" them with her attentions. But as mother and children both grew older she became, in the eyes of many, the ideal mother, unwilling to criticise and determined that they should lead their own lives, in their own way, and with as little parental interference as possible.

The children were given all the advantages that were in the power of their parents; they were sent to the best schools and colleges and when their education was complete they were al-lowed to follow their own dictates in the choice of careers. In college they did their best to live as much out of the spotlight as possible, an exceedingly difficult task which was made no easier for them by their father's many political enemies, who delighted in exaggerating each diversion from the normal routine. This, of course, was true with Teddy's children, also; the old newspaper files are filled with scattered stories in which each childish escapade, such as an arrest for speeding, is sensa-tionalized far beyond the probable facts. That this could be otherwise is unlikely in a democracy—the sins of the children of public servants become the faults of the father—if the purposes of politics can thereby be served.

James, the oldest, inherited his father's fine physique and both his father's and mother's charm of manner. The Roosevelt love of politics was in his blood from the start. Undoubtedly at one time he aspired to take his father's place in the White House, a second John Quincy Adams, and there is good reason to believe that his father, too, may have cherished this dream. It is doubtful if this will happen, but prophecy of any kind is futile in this assailed democracy of today.

Jimmy was born December 23, 1907, in New York City. He received his first training at the Cathedral School for Boys in Washington and then was sent to Dr. Endicott Peabody's famed finishing school for young gentlemen at Groton, Massachusetts. After that, came Harvard. At Cambridge he was an extremely popular although serious-minded young man, a member of several of the "best" clubs, and president of the Philips Brooks House Association (for serious diversion). He broke an ankle trying to play football. He rowed on the crew. And, like Teddy and his father, he fell in love while still a student. While riding one day on a Cambridge bridle path he met Miss Betsey Cushing, the daughter of Doctor Harvey Cushing, one of America's most distinguished brain surgeons. Jimmy was only a sophomore then. He courted Betsey throughout the rest of his time at Harvard and in the spring of 1930, two days before his class was graduated—he received no diploma because of a deficiency in language requirements—they were married at St. Paul's Church, Brookline. They went to Europe for their honeymoon and then came back to Cambridge, where they settled down in a little white cottage, the gift of Doctor Cushing.

Jimmy had his first taste of politics at Harvard. In 1928 he and two friends bought a car for thirty dollars in which they toured Massachusetts in the interest of Al Smith's presidential campaign. By the time of his graduation Jimmy had made up his mind that politics should be his life interest. But he believed in a pragmatic maxim often expressed by his father; that any man who enters public life should be able, at any moment, to fall back on his own fortune or business and not be

dependent upon public office for a livelihood. He therefore
entered the Boston University law school to learn a profession.
At the same time he joined the insurance firm of Victor de
Gerard in Boston, determined, as he told friends, to make a
competence for himself and his family as soon as possible so
that he could devote the rest of his life to politics. He soon for-
sook the law, however, because he saw that he could make more
money quickly in the insurance business. Many Roosevelts
have been in this business. The Oyster Bay branch boasts several directors of insurance companies. In 1921 Franklin D.
Roosevelt was eastern manager of the Fidelity and Deposit
Company of Maryland, at a salary of twenty-five thousand dollars a year, and underwrote nearly five hundred million dollars
in risks.

The struggle between his father and Al Smith for the 1932
nomination game Jimmy his chance in politics. In spite of his
youth Massachusetts political circles admitted him to their
inner circles because of his name and the certainty that his
father would be nominated. Soon he joined hands with James
Michael Curley, then Mayor of Boston and later Governor of
Massachusetts, in a vigorous effort to deliver the Commonwealth's thirty-six delegates to his father. The regular Democratic machine, however strung along with the loser, Al Smith.
Jimmy acted as his father's secretary during the campaign that
followed his nomination and, after the election, Mr. Roosevelt,
who obviously owed nothing to the machine in Massachusetts,
let "my little boy, Jimmy"—as he described his six-foot-four
son to campaign audiences—handle the Federal patronage in
the Bay State. Thus, at the age of twenty-five Jimmy became a
figure of national significance.

The next three years Jimmy worked industriously at his insurance business and for a time prior to the death of Prohibition headed a grain yeast company at the comfortable salary of
twenty-five thousand dollars a year. Jimmy's political activity
at this time was confined to the Young Democratic Clubs of
America, of which he was secretary. In 1936 he toured the country in behalf of his father's re-election. He took a commission in
the Marine Reserves in that year, and then, in November, he
accompanied his father to the Pan-American Good-Will Con-

ference at Buenos Aires. Upon his return from the pleasant and exciting trip he became an executive assistant at the White House at six thousand dollars a year. He could afford this meagre salary for he was receiving two hundred and fifty thousand dollars a year or more from his insurance firm of Roosevelt & Sargent in Boston. Whispered criticism of Jimmy's phenomenal success in the insurance business annoyed President Roosevelt and Jimmy was sent back to Hyde Park for a time to manage "the farm."

His father soon relented, however, gave Jimmy a better job as a full White House secretary at ten thousand dollars a year and put him in charge of coordinating the various Federal agencies. There was much criticism of this among the anti-New Dealers, but even David Lawrence, next to Mark Sullivan and George Sokolski perhaps the most bitter of columnar critics of the New Deal, publicly admitted that Jimmy was a capable and competent young man and well equipped to handle this important assignment. The white light of publicity, which beats nowhere more mercilessly than on the White House, now shone in full force upon Jimmy's baldish head. Just before the 1938 Senatorial primaries he visited Florida where he said that "we hope" Senator George Pepper, an ardent New Dealer, would be re-elected. Loud were the cries about White House interference in State affairs, but Mr. Pepper won that nomination by a huge majority, and Jimmy was hailed as the wonder-boy of politics. He tried a similar stunt in Iowa, where Senator Gillette, a very cool Democrat, was seeking re-election, but it did not work. The attempt to "purge" Mr. Gillette boomeranged, and gave the New Deal a severe, though temporary, headache. And then, in the summer of 1938, Jimmy received a major setback to his political hopes.

For some time there had been whispers about Jimmy's insurance activities, most of them, it is true, emanating from other agents' offices and all of them elaborated upon for political purposes. Now Alva Johnson, a former newspaper reporter, wrote an "exposé" of the large insurance accounts which Jimmy and his Boston partners had taken "from under the noses" of many better-known and presumably better-equipped firms. The charge was made in a sensational article, which appeared in the bitterly anti-New Deal *Saturday Evening Post,* that Jimmy had got the accounts only because the prospective clients thought it would be good policy to give the business to the President's son. It had became a byword in insurance circles, Mr. Johnson said, that when some agent thought he had an account sewed up he would be told, "Jimmy's got it!"

At the time the article appeared Jimmy was a patient in the Mayo Brothers' clinic at Rochester, Minnesota, where he was being treated for a serious gastric ulcer. He was very angry at the article which strongly inferred that he had used the Roosevelt name and political connections to get business which he could not otherwise have obtained. But Jimmy was already trained in the hard school of politics and early in his life he had learned that a public man cannot afford to answer personal attacks. He did not rise to the bait until some time later when he wrote a reasoned and reasonable answer which he published in *Collier's* magazine, the *Post's* greatest rival for the nickel magazine trade.

Sometime thereafter Jimmy resigned from the board of directors of Roosevelt and Sargent. His mother took his place on the board, not, as some said, to keep the name Roosevelt in the firm, but to protect the interests of her son, who was still majority stockholder, and to warn the other directors against selling insurance to corporations, such as shipping and radio concerns, which might have or seek governmental connections.

Jimmy's marriage was a failure, in spite of the birth of two daughters. One, born in 1931, he named Sara Delano Roosevelt, after his grandmother. The other, born in 1936, he named Kate. He and his wife decided upon a divorce before her father's death in 1939. Jimmy had fallen in love with Romelle Theresa Schneider, his nurse at the Rochester clinic, who had gone with him to a ranch near Hollister, California, to help him recuperate. Jimmy and Betsey were divorced in 1940. This event saddened Mrs. Roosevelt, but she made no effort to interfere, even as she had withdrawn when Elliott, a few years earlier, had secured the first divorce in her family. She felt it better for them to separate if they were unhappy together, if love were gone, reasoning that when marriage "ceases to be good for the family, with no basis for gracious living, then it should be ended." She remained a close friend of Betsey Cushing Roosevelt even after the divorce.

A year afterward Jimmy married Miss Schneider, the daughter of the late Jerome Schneider, of Independence, Wisconsin. Although she was a Roman Catholic James Roosevelt did not espouse her religion. The ceremony was a civil one, performed at the home of George Converse and his wife, the former Anita Stewart of the movies, at Beverly Hills. Mrs. Roosevelt flew from New York to attend the wedding and gave the bride an old gold pin to wear. It once had belonged to Mrs. Sara Delano Roosevelt.

Before his marriage Jimmy had withdrawn from politics. He resigned as his father's secretary and apparently abandoned forever the dream he once cherished of returning to Massachusetts, becoming Governor of the Commonwealth, and heading from that vantage point towards high Federal office, even to the White House. He had entered the motion picture industry, first as an aide to Sam Goldwyn, later as a producer and distributor in his own right. But at the height of his Hollywood career, and shortly before his second marriage, he was called to active duty as a Captain in the United States Marine Corps. Immediately after his marriage he left on an extended tour of the Orient and embattled Europe as a military observer.

His brother, Elliott, the most individualistic member of the tribe, also sought to carve for himself an independent career. After attending Groton for awhile he was placed in the Hun School at Princeton, New Jersey, from which he was graduated in 1930. His first great interest in life was aviation. Soon after he left school, instead of entering Harvard, he went to work for the Hearst newspapers as aviation editor. He became an experienced flier and in 1934 the Aeronautical Chamber of Commerce looked upon him as sufficiently expert in this line to make him its vice president by unanimous vote. Later he became interested in the radio business. He managed stations for the Hearst chain, was president of the Transcontinental Broadcasting System and ran a chain of stations in Texas. An articulate youngster, with a flair for phraseology, he liked best his role of commentator. As such he strove for independence and occasionally said things which were embarrassing to Democrats and Republicans alike, and to his own family. Once it was believed he, too, had political ambitions in Texas, where he had gone to live after his second marriage, but he said, "I'm not going into politics. Three politicians in the family are enough."

"Three?" he was asked. "There's your father and Jimmy. Who else?"

"Mother's pretty good at it," Elliott replied.

At Hun School Elliott had been adept at polo and swimming and he played around with the "society crowd." In this way he met his first wife, Eleanor Donner, the daughter of William H. Donner, builder of the National Tinplate Works and the Union Steel Company and a close associate of that arch-Republican, Andrew Mellon. They were married in an elaborate ceremony at Bryn Mawr, attended by social and political bigwigs. Governor Roosevelt came over from Albany and the newspapers gave columns to the event, playing up the relationship of the Roosevelts, through the Delano family, to the Astors, as befitting the merger of the Roosevelts with one of Philadelphia's richest clans.

Although there was one child, William Donner Roosevelt, this marriage lasted little more than a year. Mrs. Roosevelt tried to patch things up between the young couple. She failed. A few days after a Reno court had dissolved the marriage Elliott was married to Miss Ruth Googins, of Texas, whom he had met at a rodeo. They went to live on a ranch near Fort Worth. President Roosevelt did not meet his new daughter-in-law until the next summer when Elliott brought her, and their baby daughter, Ruth Chandler Roosevelt, who was born May 9, 1934, to Hyde Park. A second child, Elliott, Jr. ("Tony") was born later.

Elliott was president of the Texas State Network when his father signed the draft law and his mother declared publicly that her four sons should be among the first to go if married men were drafted. Elliott did not wait to be conscripted. He volunteered, and was accepted as a captain in the Army Air Corps Specialist Reserve at a salary of two hundred dollars a month. Instead of being hailed for his act he became the butt of some of the cruelest jokes of the bitter 1940 campaign. Someone wrote a song entitled "I Wanna Be a Captain, Too."

Elliott, stung by the unjust criticism, denied seeking a special rank or assignment in volunteering and then offered his resignation. His superior officer refused to accept it and stated that Elliott had special qualifications for the procurement division of the Air Corps. Most critics, if they had ever known, had forgotten that Elliott was an experienced aviator, a former aviation editor, and a former vice president of the Aeronautical Chamber of Commerce!

During the World War the Roosevelt family was well represented in the armed forces, even if Mrs. Valentine Hall had imperiously suggested that Eleanor's brother Hall buy a substitute, when he was called to duty in the Air Corps, just as gentlemen of the North did during the "War Between the States"! All of Teddy's boys saw overseas service at the front. A dozen or more close collaterals were in uniform. Alice Longworth was in France. Eleanor was working herself sick in Washington. The crisis that confronted the Nation in 1940 and 1941 found a similar situation as regards the Roosevelt Family. As had been the case during the Revolution, when most of the brothers and cousins of Isaac the Patriot joined the regulars or the militia, so now the four sons of the President obtained working commissions. James, Elliott, Franklin, Jr., and John, found their places with the Marines, the Army and the Navy.

Franklin, the next to youngest son of Franklin and Eleanor, was born August 17, 1914. He was sent to the Buckly School in New York when a small boy and later to Groton. From there he went to Harvard, with the class of 1937. Sometime in his freshman year he met Ethel duPont, a descendant of that romantic powder-maker, Pierre Samuel duPont de Nemours, who had come to this country from France in 1800 and established one of the most powerful and richest dynasties in American history, the duPonts of Delaware. That year young Franklin attended a wrestling match in Philadelphia with Miss duPont and gallantly smashed the camera of a newspaper photographer, on the theory that he was protecting the young lady from vulgar publicity. Later he was among the thousand guests who attended Ethel's debut at her father's Wilmington home. Thereafter they were often seen together, this daughter of wealth and privilege and this son of the New Deal President.

They were at the boat races at Annapolis, in which Franklin participated, and at other functions of high society. When Ethel returned from a European tour in 1935 Franklin chartered a plane to meet her boat down the bay.

In November, 1936, Mr. and Mrs. Eugene duPont, from their Owl's Nest mansion in Wilmington, announced their daughter's engagement. All America (or at least a great part) was thrilled by this romance, for the fact that the parents of the couple were as far apart politically and economically as any two important families in America could be made the situation one greatly to the liking of democracy.

Shortly thereafter young Franklin was laid low with a serious streptococcus infection. He was taken to exclusive Philips House at the Massachusetts General Hospital. Ethel duPont and Eleanor Roosevelt took turns sitting at the youngster's bedside. He was dangerously ill. When he had recovered he sat resting in the sun at the duPont home in Florida. A short while later Ethel was a guest at the White House where she was stricken with appendicitis and raced to a hospital. But both recovered, and on the last day of June, 1937, they were married at Little Christ Church at Christiana Hundred, set amid the rolling Delaware estates of the duPont domain. On the left of the satin-covered aisle sat the bride's parents and other relatives, 100 per cent Republican; at the right were the bridegroom's parents, President and Mrs. Roosevelt, and relatives, 100 per cent Democrats. Forty telegraph wires in a nearby garage clicked the news to a waiting world.

Franklin took his bride to Charlottesville, Virginia, where they lived until his graduation from the law school of the University of Virginia in 1940. That autumn the twenty-six-year-old lawyer registered for the draft, listing himself as "unemployed." A few months later, on his own initiative, he became a clerk for the huge law-mill of Wright, Gordon, Zachary & Perry at Sixty-Three Wall Street. In spite of his marriage into the stronghold of Republicanism he had worked for the re-election of his father for a third term as President and sometime during that period he had written and published the lyrics of a popular song, "The Rest of My Life." At Harvard he had been for four years a member of the Reserve

Officers Training Corps, and, in the summer of his marriage, as an ensign in the Naval Reserve, he had gone on a training cruise on the battleship *Wyoming*. In 1940 he had another tour of training duty on the destroyer *Lawrence*. In the following spring he was ordered to active duty, the third of the President's sons to don a uniform in the armed forces of which his father was commander-in-chief. He was "somewhere at sea," on active duty, when his son was born, exactly three weeks after the Japanese attack on Pearl Harbor on December 7, 1941.

The baby of the family, John Aspinwall Roosevelt, was born on March 16, 1916, and was brought up according to the Roosevelt formula. After Groton came Harvard, and after Harvard came marriage. All of the Roosevelt children married young. John was just twenty-two when he and Anne Lindsay Clark, the daughter of Mr. and Mrs. Haven Clark of Boston and Nahant, were wed. John had grown up with Anne at Campobello during their summer vacations. She was just a year younger than he. They were married in June, 1938, at Nahant, that cold little island on Massachusetts Bay, which in the past had sheltered Longfellow, Motley, Prescott, Agassiz and other great New Englanders, and over which Teddy's mentor, Henry Cabot Lodge, had long played czar from his spacious mansion overlooking the sea. Four generations of Roosevelts, beginning with Mrs. Sara Delano Roosevelt, attended the wedding in the old Union Church. Once again the President, the nation's leading Democrat, smilingly invaded a Republican stronghold to see a son married.

John, of course, was named for his Aspinwall ancestors, those great merchants of an older day in New York, and so it was perhaps not surprising that he should forego both law and politics in favor of a commercial career. He went to work for the Filene department store in Boston and to live with Ann in a small apartment. Early in June, 1939, their first child was born dead. A year and three days later another child was born. They named it Haven Clark Roosevelt. Early in 1941 John obtained a commission as an ensign in Naval Reserves. That June he was called to active duty and assigned to the Navy Supply Corps School at the Harvard Business School, the last of the four Roosevelt boys to find his place in his country's defense.

The oldest of the five Roosevelt children and the only girl was Anna, who was born in New York on May 3, 1906. A delicate child, she inherited much of the Hall beauty that had escaped her mother. When her father was State Senator she was placed in a private school in New York, and when the family first moved to Washington she was a pupil at the Misses Eastman's school there. A tall girl like her parents, Anna loved the excitement of living in a political household, thrilled when she was allowed to sit at the luncheon table with her father and his fascinating guests. As she grew older she became a gay and vital young lady, who loved parties and excitement. It was during her father's severe illness that she and her mother came to know each other well, an understanding that was typical of Mrs. Roosevelt's relationship with all her children, who still come to her for advice. In 1926 Anna met and married Curtis Dall, a young and personable New York stock broker. Their first child, Anna Eleanor ("Sistie") was born March 25, 1927, and their second, Curtis Roosevelt Dall ("Buzzie") came along on April 19, 1930.

When her father moved into the White House Anna and her children were frequent guests, and Sistie and Buzzie helped transform the staid mansion into such a lively place as it had not been since Teddy's children were sliding down its banisters nearly two score years before. Anna and her husband began to drift apart after the start of the New Deal. Tall, blonde Anna was seen frequently in the restaurants and night clubs of Washington. Often she was accompanied by one or another of the newspapermen who covered the White House. There was much whispering in the gossip-ridden capital and eventually Anna and Mr. Dall were divorced. Anna retained the custody of her children. Soon after the divorce she married John Boettiger, a newspaper reporter for *The Chicago Tribune*, and went with him to Seattle, where he became manager of a Hearst-owned newspaper.

Anna Roosevelt Boettiger inherited a great deal of her mother's amazing energy. Completely happy with her second husband, whom Sistie and Buzzie adore, she helps him with his newspaper, writes and edits its woman's page, and takes part in the social activities of the Northwestern outpost. Mrs. Roosevelt frequently visits her; she flew there to be present when Anna's third child, John Roosevelt Boettiger, was born on March 29, 1939.

CHAPTER XXI

Franklin Delano Roosevelt

I

IN THE LONG SHELF of the biographies of the American Presidents one searches in vain for the story of a childhood more serene and secure than that enjoyed by Franklin Delano Roosevelt. Perhaps the secret of his unending battle for the social welfare of all Americans may be found in the comfort of his own sheltered youth. He was happy; he was healthy; he had whatever he wanted, not in excess but in sufficient quantity to gratify his childish desires; he lived according to a routine designed not only for his own benefit but for those around him as well; his physical wants were satisfied, his cultural wants were not neglected; he was allowed to let his imagination soar and at the right time become reality; he was nurtured but not pampered; and he was taught, at any early age, that the joy of freedom is not individual but collective.

The fact that Franklin did not run up against the sharp edge of life until he had reached maturity may have deepened his appreciation of his youthful security and made him the more understanding of those to whom the peace of mind and body, which had been his lot, was denied through circumstances over which they had no more control than he had over his own childhood at Hyde Park. The aims and purposes of his New Deal, one may well surmise, have been to extend the spirit of those peaceful acres—those acres never threatened by the sheriff nor darkened by fear—to the entire land.

In James Roosevelt young Franklin had an ideal father, one who seems in a quiet way to have justified his wife's description of him: "straight and honorable, just and kind, an upstanding American." Although he was past fifty when Franklin was born he became the close companion of his tall, blond and blue-eyed son. The boy never had for this impressive man with the arched brows the kind of respect that is half awe and half fear. His love for the father approached worship, for the man had a deep understanding of his son's problems: he never laughed at the boy, but often with him. They spent long hours together poring over their stamp collection in the library at Hyde Park or riding along the old trails of the father's many unfenced acres.

Hyde Park was both a gentleman's estate and a working farm which paid its own way and was not dependent upon the Roosevelt pocketbook for survival. Although he did not have to rise in the cold dawn to milk the cows in the true Presidential tradition, his was distinctly a rural boyhood, which may well account for his later sympathetic efforts, as Governor of New York and as President, to solve the "farm problem." He was, after all, the fourth generation of his branch of the family to have roots in the farming country around Poughkeepsie, and his great-grandfather had tilled stony Manhattan acres long before he left them for the richer lands of the Hudson Valley.

Franklin was an only child living in the country in a large and comfortable house, far from neighbors. Friends of the Roosevelts, at Hyde Park for a week-end, often felt that he was a lonely child. If he was, he gave few indications that his loneliness did him any permanent harm. He taught himself to enjoy his solitude. He liked to read, especially about the sea. He undoubtedly also heard tales from his own mother and other members of her salty family. But he did not become a bookworm. There was too much happening out-of-doors to occupy his mind.

A mile or so distant was the large estate of James Roosevelt's close friend, Colonel Archibald Rogers, the Standard Oil magnate, whose son Edmund was Franklin's own age. Edmund was to grow to be a president, too—of the Fulton Trust Company of New York—but in those days he and Franklin knew nothing of banks or politics and were close friends. Once they built a "ship" in the branches of a tree where, in their fertile imaginations, they duplicated the hardy adventures of Grandfather Delano rounding the Horn. Later they made a raft from logs which they cut. It sank in the creek under their own weight, but it was fun!

Franklin learned to handle a gun when he was eleven and his father, a true sportsman, taught him never to kill needlessly. He had a boyish instinct for collecting and shot one specimen of every bird in the neighborhood. Some he stuffed himself, but most of them were prepared for his "museum" by more expert hands. When he was a small boy he had a pony; later he had his own riding horse, a three-quarter Texas fellow of which he was inordinately proud. He was a true shot, a good rider, and an expert swimmer and skater before he was fourteen years old. He could handle an iceboat or a sailboat at an early age.

Without any exact pedagogical knowledge, but with true instinct, Franklin's father and mother achieved a balance in his physical and educational development. His father took care of the former because the man and boy were close to each other and derived true satisfaction from being together on the trails or in the fields and woods and waters. His mother was his first teacher; later tutors came to the house to hear his lessons. He arose at seven in the morning, breakfasted at eight, and studied from nine until noon. Between then and lunch, at one o'clock, he played out-of-doors. The long afternoons were his own, to sit by the big living room fire drawing or reading, or to roam the snowy woods seeking a winter wren for his collection, or to ride with his father.

The boy's reading was undirected, but the house was filled with substantial books. He especially liked history and, before he went away to school when he was fourteen, he had practically memorized Admiral Mahan's *History of Sea Power*. For this boy, the multi-colored autumns, the white winters, and the lush Hudson springs were a continuing delight—except that he had to take piano and drawing lessons. He learned to play the piano fairly well; he was a natural artist, but uninterested. In order to earn spending money he did chores around the farm, but he had no regular allowance. There was little need for cash at Hyde Park, his toys and books were bought for him, but when he wanted something special there were many ways to earn the needed money.

Franklin's mother tried to keep him a baby as long as she could. She later admitted that she loved to dress him in the fashionable styles for little boys of that day, which probably means that he was forced to wear those outlandish costumes of velvet and lace inspired by Reginald Birch's drawings for Mrs. Burnett's *Little Lord Fauntleroy*. But he was, as a boy, as indifferent to clothes as he has been since. He rebelled, boy-like, at having his yellow curls combed.

In spite of her adoration of her child, Sara Delano Roosevelt seems to have been as sensible as any mother of her day. Both she and James Roosevelt agreed the boy should not be "spoiled" and together they tried hard to teach him self-reliance and responsibility. When, for example, Uncle Warren Delano gave him Marksman, a beautiful Irish setter that would delight any boy's heart, he was not allowed to accept the gift until he had promised to care for the dog alone. He did, faithfully, every day. His love for dogs was to last him always. Now his constant companion in his White House bedroom and office is Falla, an engagingly self-important Scottish terrier.

Hyde Park was not the limit of Franklin Roosevelt's youthful existence. His parents first took him to Europe when he was only three years old. His father was an almost yearly visitor to the German spas and "cures" and so, nearly every year while his father was alive, Franklin was taken to the Continent or England, or both. During these journeys he had French and German governesses from whom he learned to speak those languages, and for good measure he was taught Spanish in his early 'teens.

In his eleventh year, while staying in London, Franklin was invited to visit friends who lived in the country and who owned a fine collection of birds. Unable to accompany him at the last moment his mother permitted him to travel by train alone. The mother later recalled that he was a shy boy, but he could overcome this shyness when it might interfere with something he really wanted to do. In his mother's recollections he was also a tractable boy who responded better to reasoning than threats.

Probably because he spent so much time with adults the boy developed an instinctive understanding of their problems. Money matters—hardly a problem in the comfortable circumstances of Hyde Park—were never discussed in his presence: as they seldom were, before the children, in any good Victorian middle-class home. But once he tried desperately to get his parents to bring back to Hyde Park with them a nurse whom they had hired in Europe for the summer. Since it was known that he did not like the young woman his father was at a loss to understand the sudden solicitude. Franklin confessed his reason was that Papa had gone to such trouble and expense to hire her in the first place!

At Hyde Park, or while traveling, certain mild rules of deportment and punctuality were established. They were rigidly observed, but his parents were never strict merely for strictness' sake. James Roosevelt believed in "keeping Franklin's mind on nice things, at a high level; yet he did it in such a way that Franklin never realized he was following any bent but his own." Thus, without realizing it, he became an adept geographer and stamp collector, two hobbies his father did much to encourage.

When he was still in his early 'teens Franklin's father and mother went for the summer to Bad Nauheim, Germany, to "take the cure" at the springs, as was the fashionable custom of the time. They allowed him to go off on a bicycle tour of the Black Forest with his tutor, supplying him with enough money for the trip, although the sum hardly allowed extravagances. This was the first time he had been permitted to handle his own money. Instead of spending with youthful recklessness, the youngster who one day was to spend more billions of dollars than any President in history, returned with a surplus in his pocket. He proudly told his mother that he had been arrested four times by the *polizei* for violating minor regulations but had talked himself out of his predicament each time in his "best company German!"

When he was fourteen years old his mother and father arrived at the decision that the time had come to send him, as his mother later said, "out into the world whose boundaries

were not limited by the barriers the very intensity of our devotion had imposed." They sent him to Groton School where
he was placed in a form made up of boys who had already been
in the school for two years. Instead of being frightened and lost
he immediately forgot his timidity, became sociable and gregari-
ous, and took to the pleasant school routine without hesitation.

Although he went out for baseball and football, he never
made the first teams, but he did establish a new school record
for the high kick. He was elected manager of the baseball nine,
a rather ignominious job, as every schoolboy knows. He was
a good student, especially in English and history, but he was
no prodigy. His greatest delight was the debating team which,
in the next few years, discussed such important topics as capital
punishment and independence of the Philippines. His side
argued for independence—and lost the debate.

Once he contracted scarlet fever. His mother rushed to
Groton, and, rather than be quarantined, made her daily visits
to the infirmary by climbing a rickety ladder and talking to her
son through the window. He also had the mumps and the
measles, from which the isolation of Hyde Park had previously
spared him. The attack of measles came just at a time when,
undoubtedly inspired by Uncle Teddy's Rough Riders as much
as by any patriotic fervor, he and some other boys were planning to run away and enlist in the Navy for the War with
Spain. Of course he indulged in several of those minor schoolboy pranks which perennially enliven the days—and nights—
of schoolmasters and become the exaggerated stories of "old
grads"—but none seem to have become embedded in the tradi-
tions of the school. In his final year he sang in the school choir.
Perhaps there, and on the debating team, he laid the foundation of the magnificent voice which was to make famous his
fireside chats of later years. Certainly his accent and intonations,
as clear as those of any man in public life, were learned at
Groton School.

Groton meant a vacation from European tours. In 1890,
when Franklin was eight, James Roosevelt had bought land and
built a cottage on the salt-sprayed island of Campobello which
lies in the Canadian province of New Brunswick, two miles off
the easternmost tip of the Maine Coast in Passamaquoddy Bay.

Here in the tumultuous, tide-swirled waters, Franklin learned to sail. When he was fifteen his father gave him a twenty-one-foot center-board type knockabout, rigged with mainsail, jib and spinnaker, with a small cabin forward for lockers and two bunks. Almost from the time that he laid his hand on its tiller, he was a good seaman, justifying his heritage from the Delanos and Aspinwalls and Isaac Allerton.

He soon knew the entire tide-beset currents of the waters from Campobello to Owl's Head, and as a young man he could sail, as they say, blindfolded through such difficult Down East cruising grounds as the Eastern and Western Ways of Mount Desert or the Eggemoggin Reach, and he knew his course through summer fog to the fashionable anchorages of Dark Harbor and Northeast Harbor, where his relatives and his Groton friends spent the summer months.

There is no better training in discipline than learning to handle a boat in Maine waters. But sailing was not all that Franklin learned. At Northeast Harbor he went to the dances of the conservative rich. One summer, at least, his partner was Eleanor Roosevelt, home from her school in England. He learned to play golf there, too, and later he "built" a golf course on some Campobello cow pastures where he taught others the game and became the island "champion."

Although he was not a brilliant student, Franklin managed to pass his Harvard entrance examinations with honors. He was eighteen years old when he entered Harvard as a freshman with the class of 1904. At this time he was a tall, well-proportioned youngster, a little thin, perhaps. He parted his yellow hair in the middle, after the collegiate fashion of the day, but unlike his cousin Teddy he did not attempt to startle the Harvard Yard with loud clothes. Indeed, he attracted very little attention at Harvard, and that was mainly because his rather unusual surname was then splattered all over the front pages of the newspapers.

He lived in the exclusive region known as the Gold Coast, where all the sons of well-to-do and fashionable New Yorkers had their "diggings." His room-mate was Lathrop Brown, a rather handsome lad, also from New York, whose father was the partner in the real estate business of Douglas Robinson, Uncle

Teddy's brother-in-law. Young Brown was a more brilliant student than Franklin, but his great interest in Greek was later to be subjugated to his father's business. Before the war, he was a political dilettante who managed to get sent to Congress in 1912, but who gave up all interest in politics after he and one other New York delegate bolted the 1924 Democratic Convention rather than support the candidacy of Al Smith. At Harvard the two boys lived in rooms chosen, arranged and decorated by Franklin's mother.

Franklin entered Harvard in October, 1900. Early in December his father was taken ill at Hyde Park and went to the Hotel Renaissance in New York to be near Dr. Ely, his family physician, who found that he was suffering from endocarditis. Franklin was summoned from Harvard and his half-brother, James Roosevelt Roosevelt, was also called. The four, the two sons, the wife, and the family doctor, were with James Roosevelt when, on December 8th, he died. After the funeral and the burial in St. James's Churchyard at Hyde Park, Mrs. Roosevelt went back to Cambridge with Franklin. There she took a house. She wanted to be near Franklin, but more than that, she could not bear to stay alone in the memory-filled house to which she had gone as James Roosevelt's bride.

Franklin had not particularly wanted to go to Harvard. If he had been allowed his choice in the matter he would have entered the United States Naval Academy at Annapolis. But his father had dissuaded him from this course. He did not distinguish himself as a scholar. At Groton the highest academic honor that had come his way was the All-School Latin Prize; at Harvard he maintained a fair standing in his studies, but not enough to win him a Phi Beta Kappa key. (He later was made an honorary member of this Scholastic society.) His distant cousin Teddy, now Vice President of the United States, had not been a notable scholar, either, in the days when he had sported his dude clothes and stickpins made of mounted five dollar gold pieces. In this respect only were the cousins alike. Franklin was quieter, he had no red whiskers, and, according to accounts, he was more democratic.

Indeed he was considered not only democratic but a radical by many of his wealthy classmates. For one thing he headed a committee to aid the Boers in their struggle with England. It was all right for Uncle Bob Roosevelt to boast openly, in his account in *Who's Who In America,* that he belonged to "every association formed to help the Boers," for he was treasurer of the Democratic Party and not a Harvard man. At Harvard, England was right. At least on the Gold Coast!

Six feet and one inch tall, reasonably well proportioned and athletically inclined, Franklin played on the freshman football team and pulled a freshman oar, but his athletic prowess was not of the kind to impress Varsity coaches. He never tipped the scale at more than one hundred and fifty pounds while at Harvard, and after his freshman year he gave up participation in sports. He had found another outlet for his energy, one which was to absorb his interest until his graduation. It was the student daily newspaper, *The Harvard Crimson.*

Franklin Roosevelt won his place on the staff of this journal through an ordeal by fire. The bitter, silver-streaked presidential campaign of nineteen hundred was nearing its close when he went to Cambridge and sought election to the newspaper's staff. President Charles W. Eliot, the austere head of the University, had consistently refrained from endorsing either candidate, McKinley or Bryan, and the young reporter thought, rightly, that it would make an excellent story if he could get Dr. Eliot to make his choice in a *Crimson* interview.

Unaware of the rule that forbade *Crimson* candidates to interview a Harvard president, Franklin went to the Eliot home with innocent heart. So eloquently did he make his plea that Dr. Eliot, after sternly rebuking him for his unprecedented breach of decorum, told him that the *Crimson* might announce that the President of Harvard favored the imperialist McKinley over the unsound Bryan. The choice was a blow to young Roosevelt, who would have voted for Bryan had he been of age, but it made a great scoop for the paper and assured Franklin's election to the staff. The *Crimson* printed the story under black headlines; press associations picked it up and sent it flashing to first pages all over the country.

After this auspicious beginning Franklin Roosevelt was successively sub-editor, managing editor, and president of the newspaper. But he became no great crusading editor, nor did he ever markedly transcend the bounds of Cantabridgian propriety, although, in addition to a campaign against "listless hockey practise" and the poor record of the football team, he did conduct a campaign to force the Overseers of Harvard to install fire escapes on dormitories.

His summers were spent mostly at Hyde Park or Campobello. His boyhood playmate, Edmund Rogers, was learning to be a banker at Yale, but on holidays he brought his New Haven friends home with him. They mingled with Franklin's chums in the two houses at Hyde Park, at gay parties, dances and picnics. One summer Franklin and his mother took a North Cape cruise. He lived, on the whole, the typical life of a typical Harvard boy of his social standing, working as hard as he had to but no harder. At the end of his third year he had done well enough with his studies to win his degree and enter the Law School. However, he preferred to continue his academic course, primarily because of his interest in the *Crimson*.

It has been asserted frequently that Franklin was not popular with his fellows at Harvard. Whether or not this is true he was elected to such select groups as the Hasty Pudding Club, the Yacht Club, the Fly Club, and the more seriously inclined Political Club. He celebrated his twenty-first birthday with a gay bachelor dinner at the Fly, but he never "made" his cousin Teddy's beloved and ancient Porcellian, snootiest of all Harvard undergraduate societies. He often went over to New York, for week-ends or holidays, especially in his senior and junior years while he was courting his cousin, Eleanor; and he was a far from unpopular figure in the younger social circles of that city where his relatives and friends were many. In his senior year he wrote several editorials demanding an "honest" Class Day election, insisting that they be conducted democratically and freed from the log rolling tactics usually indulged by the clubs and societies. He defeated six candidates for the post of permanent Class Day secretary.

His final year at Harvard was interrupted by the cruise he took to the West Indies with his mother and room-mate, Lathrop Brown. Ostensibly the trip was a reward for his good work at college but in reality it was intended to take his mind off his cousin Eleanor. It did not, as we have seen, for they were married in New York on the next Saint Patrick's Day.

After his graduation from Harvard Franklin entered the law school at Columbia University. He was not graduated, but he passed his bar examinations easily enough.

These were the formative years of his life. Thus far nothing had happened to indicate that Franklin Roosevelt was on the road toward greatness. His life had been different in no way from that of thousands of other young men in the colleges and universities of his day. He had been given everything he wanted, and accepted it gratefully. He had reasonable wealth, social position, a good name. His mother had a substantial income, a beautiful home, a country place on the shore where he could pass happy summers. He had fallen in love. The death of his father had not been painful or unexpected. These twenty-two years had been full and happy, and the future held no obvious darkness. He was tough enough to sail a boat on the Bay of Fundy, bright enough to head a daily student newspaper, and he was independent enough to favor the Boers over the British and Bryan over McKinley while living on Harvard's Gold Coast. But he had, thus far, done nothing to indicate that he would become anything but what he had been, a Hyde Park Roosevelt . . . a happy, average, well-bred young man.

II

Much has been written about the domination of Franklin Roosevelt's life by his adoring mother. He was only eighteen when his father died, and scarcely more than four of those years had been spent away from home. His mother, widowed at the age of forty-six, naturally felt drawn towards her boy and, since her own life had been secure and restricted, it must have been her instinctive desire to protect him as much as she possibly could against the world. He needed her protection much less than she imagined. The paternal insistence upon self-reliance had not been in vain. There was, however, another reason for her close watch. In his will James Roosevelt had written:

"I do hereby appoint my wife sole guardian of my son Franklin D. Roosevelt and *I wish him to be under the influence of his mother.*" [Italics the author's.]

That Franklin Roosevelt's mother, who had deeply loved and obeyed the author of those words, took them as a solemn obligation, there can be no doubt.

James Roosevelt, after several minor bequests, left his estate in three equal parts to his wife and two sons. Mrs. Roosevelt's share, which included all her husband's "furniture, pictures, linen, wines, carriages, horses, harness, stock, farm and garden tools and implements of all kinds in . . . my country place at Hyde Park," was to be divided among Franklin Roosevelt and James Roosevelt Roosevelt, or their heirs, upon her death. In 1900, when James Roosevelt died, there was in existence no inheritance tax demanding an exact appraisal of an estate, and so it is impossible to determine the size of his estate. However, it has been estimated that Franklin Roosevelt probably received about one hundred thousand dollars, which would yield him, under ordinary circumstances, an annual income of about five thousand dollars.

Hyde Park, the estate on the old Wheeler Place, including the house, was bequeathed to Mrs. Roosevelt, along with the Roosevelt family plate and silver, for her "use and enjoyment" during her life. Thus Hyde Park did not belong to President Roosevelt until her death in 1941. This situation undoubtedly was the source of the many unfriendly intimations that President Roosevelt, all his life, was dependent upon his mother for a place to live. He made Hyde Park his home because, in truth, it was, and when he lived there the expenses of operation were his. The rarely beautiful relationship that existed between this mother and this son made any other arrangement unnecessary.

When Franklin Roosevelt married his cousin Eleanor in 1905 he had an income of about five thousand dollars a year. His mother had inherited about one million dollars from her father, Warren Delano II, who had invested most of his China-made money in Pennsylvania coal mines and other similar industrial property. Eleanor Roosevelt also had inherited from her father, Elliott Roosevelt, and from her grandfather Hall, enough money so that she, too, was assured of about five thousand dollars a year. The young Roosevelt couple were not financially dependent upon his mother when he was married and he has been independent of her since. Her generosity towards him was great, however. It was she who rented and furnished their first home in New York while he was studying law at Columbia, and the welcome Mrs. Roosevelt always extended to Franklin and his family at Hyde Park or Campobello more than once helped lighten his financial load, especially when the children were small. His annual income was hardly enough to have enabled him to buy and build an estate like Hyde Park, the existence of which enabled him and his family to live on a somewhat higher scale than most people of their means.

When they were married their joint income of about ten thousand dollars was certainly enough to keep the wolf a long way from the door. But Franklin Roosevelt did not earn a cent in salary until, at the age of twenty-five, he became a law clerk with Carter, Ledyard & Milburn, attorneys for the Astor Estate, the American Express Co., and the Atlantic Mutual Insurance Co., among other wealthy clients. Some years later, when he set up a law practice with Langdon P. Marvin and Henry S. Hooker, his income undoubtedly increased. He received one thousand five hundred dollars a year as State Senator. When he became Assistant Secretary of the Navy his salary was five thousand dollars. After the war, and the vice presidential fiasco of 1920, he had no "business to fall back upon." But his friend, Van Laer Black, publisher of *The Baltimore Sun,* found a job for him as vice president and Eastern manager of the Fidelity and Deposit Company of Maryland at twenty-five thousand dollars a year. In the following eight years Mr. Roosevelt devoted himself to this business and his law practice with Basil O'Connor in New York, except when he was bed-ridden with paralysis between 1921 and 1923.

In January, 1927, he received a one hundred thousand dollar bequest from his half-brother, James Roosevelt Roosevelt. As Governor of New York he earned twenty-five thousand dollars a year. Before the depression he probably had an annual income, earned and unearned, of about thirty-seven thousand dollars. Mrs. Roosevelt's inheritance, through careful management, by then brought about seven thousand five hundred dollars more. She earned no money until she became connected with Todhunter School at a salary of two thousand dollars a year. The peak of her income from all sources prior to 1932 was never more than ten thousand dollars, making the total family income never more than forty-seven thousand dollars in a single year.

With five children to put through school and college and with all the entertaining that they had to do in Albany and in Washington, the Roosevelts could hardly be called wealthy. Of course, they were far from poverty-stricken, but they could not afford to be extravagant. They had to let their charm, their social position and their innate graciousness do for them what others could accomplish only through lavish expenditures, if then. It is reliably reported that during his last year as Governor of New York Franklin D. Roosevelt wore a suit of his father's until James Roosevelt hid it!

This charm, the greatest of Rooseveltian assets, one is inclined to believe, is the fruit of heredity and environment. It stems both from the Dutch and the Yankee blood of Franklin Roosevelt's heritage, was shaped in the woods and fields and library of Hyde Park, and moulded into lastingness there by a wise father and a kind mother, who had no dreams of greatness for their child, who certainly never thought he would be president, and who trained him only to be self-reliant and grateful for the security it was in their power to give.

III

Thus far in his life Franklin Roosevelt's career had followed much the same direction as that of his cousin Teddy's. Both had spent a great deal of time abroad. Teddy's health had kept him from attending a fashionable preparatory school but he had, of course, gone to Harvard, and afterwards had studied law, first with his Uncle Bob, the Democratic Party's treasurer, and then for a year at Columbia University. Their family background and social connections had been similar. But Teddy gave up all thoughts of a legal career almost as soon as he first entertained them. Franklin, on the other hand, went through the Columbia law school and, although he never bothered to take his LL.B. degree from that institution, he passed his bar examinations easily and went to work at once in the law firm of Carter, Ledyard & Milburn, probably through the influence of his half-brother, James Roosevelt Roosevelt, an executor of the Astor Estate, whose counsel that firm was.

He was a good lawyer, but not a brilliant one, undoubtedly because the law, per se, did not really appeal to him, any more than it had ever appealed to his father. He had, then, no literary ambitions to occupy his mind, as Teddy had with his unfinished treatise on the Naval War of 1812. He did his work well, first in municipal court cases and later in admiralty law, which must have been more interesting to him. At this period, little Anna and James had arrived and he had to keep his nose fairly close to the grindstone, but he was restless and dissatisfied with the prospect of what must have appeared to him as a colorless if comfortable future. He loved to break away from the law office and the life of New York city for week-ends at Hyde Park which, even then, he planned some day to make his permanent home. Naturally, because of his father, he was well known in Poughkeepsie, the nearest city to Hyde Park. He was made a director of the First National Bank of Poughkeepsie, and he joined the Hyde Park township's volunteer fire department.

Just when he first thought of politics as a career, or a supplement to his professional life, or how greatly he was influenced in this direction by the career of his cousin Teddy, he alone knows. Theodore Roosevelt, of course, was his wife's uncle, and his own distant cousin. Theodore's brother had been his godfather. If Franklin, as he undoubtedly did, thought that Teddy and Teddy's father were apostates for being Republicans (the first of such breed in the Roosevelt Family), nevertheless he was fond and proud of the older Roosevelt who had become President of the United States. When he first became President he told an interviewer that the characters in history he most admired were Benjamin Franklin, Thomas Jefferson, Benjamin Thompson (Count Rumford, a Tory genius of Revolutionary days),—and Theodore Roosevelt. But being a Democrat he could not turn to Teddy for material aid.

In fact, politics were thrust upon him. Teddy, indeed, was away hunting tigers and wondering about his wisdom in leaving the presidency in Mr. Taft's hands, when Franklin Roosevelt entered the political lists. Teddy had become an Assemblyman through the machinations of the petty politics of the "Jake Hess Club" when Joe Murray of First Avenue had sought to wrest the leadership of the Silk Stocking district of New York from the man who gave the club its name. The situation in the 26th Senatorial District (Dutchess, Columbia and Putnam Counties) in 1910 was not entirely analogous, but fundamentally it was similar in that the nomination for Senator was handed to him with the same wink that had accompanied Joe Murray's proffer of the Assemblyship to Teddy. In neither instance did the wise ones on the inside really expect their candidates to win. And in both instances the candidate was expected to foot most of the bills.

The idea of running young Franklin Roosevelt for Senator probably originated in the mind of John K. Sague, the Democratic mayor of Poughkeepsie, who had been disappointed but not surprised when Lewis Stuyvesant Chanler indignantly spurned the offer.

Lewis Stuyvesant Chanler was one of the turbulent Chanler boys of fabulous memory. One of his brothers was Sheriff Bob Chanler, the artist, and another was John Armstrong Chanler, who was sane in Virginia but insane (legally) in New York and who added to the American idiom by cabling to Sheriff Bob, "Who's loony now?" when that magnificent eccentric was being hounded in Paris by his wife, the glamorous operatic diva, Lina Cavalieri. The Chanlers were the children of Margaret Astor Ward, the great-grand-daughter of old John Jacob Astor, and beneficiaries of his tremendous fortune. Lewis Stuyvesant Chanler was a Democrat who had run for Lieutenant Governor in 1906 with William Randolph Hearst. The publisher was cut by Tammany, but Chanler, who had spent his youth in Ireland fighting with Parnell for freedom, was elected with the Republican, Charles Evans Hughes. Another brother, William Astor Chanler, had been a Congressman. Together they planned to make Lewis President. In 1908, he won the Democratic gubernatorial nomination. However he was defeated by

Governor Hughes. Naturally after he had lost the White House he was not interested in a State Senatorship, especially from a district which had elected but one Democratic State Senator since 1856, and that one as far back as 1884!

To take a nomination that even so distinguished a politician as Chanler spurned was taking the short end of a bad bet, but Franklin, either in innocence or because he remembered that Uncle Teddy had done the same thing, was glad to accept. He knew that he must pay his own campaign bills and he knew, as Teddy had found out in 1880, that he would be laughed at by his friends, and considered a nincompoop by his legal associates. But, in a way, he could afford to run for the Senate. Had not Isaac Roosevelt, his own great-great-grandfather been a member of the first Senate ever to sit under the constitution he had himself helped to write? Hadn't Judge James Roosevelt of Tammany Hall wrangled for Democracy in the Hall of Assembly in Albany back in the 1840's? Hadn't Robert B. Roosevelt stuck to Democracy, battled the Tweed Ring, sat in Congress, and handled Democracy's finances in the days of Grover Cleveland? And, of course, there was Teddy himself. There was precedent aplenty. Perhaps Franklin thought it was time to bring all the Roosevelts back to the Party they had adhered to at least from Jackson's day to the Civil War.

With practically no backing from the Party Franklin Roosevelt, much to the amused amazement of his immediate family, went after the vote. He hired an automobile and rattled through the countryside, preaching, as it were, from a text torn from Teddy's book: "Down with the Bosses!" Three generations of Roosevelts had lived in the region. The name was known. The farmers liked the young man who, even then, had the facility of talking their language without talking down to them, and since in the past candidates had ignored the rural regions, they were mighty glad to have him come out to see them, even if his car did scare some horses. With a heavy preponderance of votes in the country districts he carried the three counties by 1140 votes. The farmers, Franklin, and the politicians were all surprised. Especially the politicians! Very soon they were going to be more surprised.

The year 1910 was a significant year in the political history

of New York State. The Republicans, who had ruled the capital for a generation, were badly beaten and Democracy controlled both Houses of the Legislature as well as the executive.
When Franklin Roosevelt went to Albany in January, 1911, to
attend his first session he owed nothing to Tammany or the
up-state machine. If it had not been for a peculiar situation
which existed, he might still owe them nothing, for it is quite
possible that he would have disappeared from the public scene.
But the situation was there and he took advantage of it with a
courage and acumen remarkable in a political tyro. Within a
few weeks of the opening of the session the new Roosevelt in
politics had attracted national attention, and W. A. ("Baron")
Warn, the political correspondent of *The New York Times*,
attracted by his independent attitude, had written a glowing
account of the young senator for that newspaper's magazine,
prophesying that the name Roosevelt would reach new heights
of glory at the hands of the young gentleman from Hyde Park.

Although its members were then unaware of it, the New
York Senate was meeting that year for the last time to elect a
United States Senator. Soon the right was given directly to the
people, in great measure because of the ensuing events. The
minority Republicans were pledged to the re-election of the
Vanderbilt lawyer, Chauncey M. Depew, who had so eloquently
nominated Teddy for Governor at the close of the Spanish-
American war. Tammany Hall, through its leader, the shrewd
Charles F. Murphy, proposed to send William ("Blue-Eyed
Billy") Sheehan to take his place in Washington. Young
Roosevelt, of course, could not and would not support Depew,
nor would he, as an independent up-State Democrat with no
obligations to Boss Murphy, line up for Sheehan. There were
also other Democrats who also were not under the Tammany
Tiger's paw. These Franklin Roosevelt gathered together, and,
with Mrs. Roosevelt throwing open their rented house for a
meeting place and serving them sandwiches and beer, they laid
their insurgent plot. They seemed a forlorn group fighting for
a lost cause, especially when the Tammanyites resorted to the
caucus to put over Sheehan, in spite of the fact that there was
a state-wide protest over his selection.

In addition to Franklin Roosevelt there were eighteen in-

surgents, enough, if they stuck together and boycotted the caucus, to hold a balance of power on the joint ballot of the two
Houses necessary for election. For sixty ballots, through three
months, the battle raged. Roosevelt held the insurgents tightly,
nothing Boss Murphy could do made any difference. They put
forward a candidate of their own, a little known but eminently
respectable New York city lawyer, Edward M. Shepard. In the
end both he and Sheehan were killed off in the contest and, on
the sixty-fourth ballot, Judge James A. O'Gorman, a Tammany
compromise, was elected. Mr. Depew retired to his law office
and after dinner speeches. Franklin Roosevelt, having tasted
victory, was in politics for the rest of his life.

This epic battle had three outstanding results. It brought
about the direct election of United States Senators at the next
session, an act Roosevelt supported. It caused the gnome-like,
chain-smoking Louis McHenry Howe, a newspaperman, to believe that this young Dutchess County gentleman might some
day be President, even if Grover Cleveland, James Roosevelt's
friend, had, upon the occasion of a White House visit many
years ago, fervently prayed that little Franklin would be spared
that awful fate. It also marked the beginning of the friendship
between Franklin Roosevelt and Alfred E. Smith.

When it became time for Franklin Roosevelt to campaign
for re-election he was seriously ill, confined to his bed in New
York with typhoid fever. Louis Howe, then Albany correspondent for the old New York *Herald,* was given a leave of absence
from his newspaper to manage Roosevelt's campaign for him.
Howe wangled enough free newspaper space to make up for
the lack of speeches by the candidate, who was running mainly
upon the issue of protecting the farmer from the wiles of the
commission merchant. In 1910 Franklin Roosevelt had won by
a 1140 plurality; this year, 1912, with Howe behind him and
Teddy's Bull Moose campaign confusing the entire electorate,
he was re-elected by 1701 votes.

Senator Roosevelt, serving his second term and supporting
such liberal legislation as came before that body, had by this
time discovered, like many another young Democrat throughout the land, a political hero. He was Woodrow Wilson, formerly a professor of history at Princeton University and now

Governor of New Jersey. He may have seemed chilly, even then, to some; but to Franklin Roosevelt he embodied all that was desirable in politics. The Progressivism of Uncle Teddy was so much balderdash as compared to Governor Wilson's conception of the New Freedom. Intellectually Wilson appealed to Roosevelt but an even greater, or more practical appeal, was the fact that Tammany was openly hostile to nomination of the New Jersey Governor.

Roosevelt went to the convention at Baltimore where Wilson was battling for the honor with Champ Clark, who had Tammany's blessing, and threw all his youthful weight behind Wilson. After Wilson became his party's choice Roosevelt worked for his election in New York.

That President Wilson, whom Tammany did its best to knife, thought highly indeed of his work is shown by the fact that he offered Roosevelt two enviable posts, each of which would have been considered a juicy plum by almost any politician. One was as Assistant Secretary of the Treasury under William Gibbs McAdoo; the other was as Collector of the Port of New York. He rejected both. Just why he wanted to get into the Navy Department is not known. Perhaps it was because he remembered that it was from this office that Uncle Teddy had stepped to glory; but, still, there was no war that would involve the United States discernible on the horizon in 1912. Perhaps it was because he always regretted he had not been able to attend Annapolis and this was the next best thing. At any rate, when Josephus Daniels, whom he had first met at the Baltimore convention, offered him the post of Assistant Secretary of the Navy, he accepted with alacrity, resigned from the Senate, and hurried to Washington.

Secretary Daniels had owned a liking for the urbane Roosevelt ever since he had read about his insurgency against Boss Murphy in 1910. Roosevelt, on the other hand, was able to see an element of greatness behind Daniels's shoestring tie and funny black felt hat. Although Roosevelt was a New Yorker and a Harvard man he felt none of the contempt for the North Carolina editor that Uncle Teddy had felt for Secretary John D. Long, whom he called a chocolate eclair when he was not patronizingly referring to him as a "perfect dear."

If Franklin Roosevelt had been an indifferent lawyer, both with Carter, Ledyard & Milburn and after establishing his own office with Harry S. Hooker and Langdon P. Marvin, it was mainly because his heart was not in his work. Almost from the day that he settled down in Aunty Bye's house in Washington with his growing family and began his daily visits to his desk in the State, War and Navy Building across the street from the White House, his heart was very much in his work. He had loved the Navy and ships since childhood; he had spent his allowances, while at Harvard, collecting books about the sea and prints of famous ships; he had cut his intellectual teeth on Admiral Mahan. Perhaps even more important, he had, up to this time, never had an executive job, never had the spending of money or the handling of men. It was a new experience. He loved it.

He took office in March, 1913, seventeen months before the European continent and the British Isles were plunged into war. Even before August, 1914, he was working for a greater Navy, with some success, especially in the matter of Congressional appropriations. The outbreak of war, with its potential threat to the United States, gave him a chance to go ahead. He kept things humming in his department. Faced by the inevitable red tape, with typical impatience, he slashed right and left, broke rules and got things done. His particular job was the supervision of navy yards, long a white elephant, and the purchase of supplies. He effected considerable savings as purchasing agent. Brought into close contact with the workers in the yards, he protected their rights and won their warm affection. He made scores of friends at this time. One who was attracted to him by his singular efficiency was young Joseph Patrick Kennedy, then Charles M. Schwab's bright young manager at the Fore River shipyards. Later Kennedy was to supply funds for Roosevelt's first Presidential campaign and become his ambassador to the Court of St. James's.

Franklin Roosevelt was a stanch advocate of a large and powerful Navy before America's entrance into the war. This is one policy, at least, in which his enemies cannot charge him with inconsistency.

Teddy had been a stormy petrel as Assistant Secretary of the

Navy, stirring up his "splendid little war" with Spain, but as soon as he could he left the office for the greater glory of a soldier's uniform. Interestingly enough Franklin Roosevelt, too, wanted to take a commission in the Navy rather than in the Army, but an attack of pneumonia, contracted aboard the ship that brought him back from a European tour of inspection, prevented that. He kept his office throughout the war, an indefatigable worker who accomplished much. Indeed, it was in the Navy Department, that Franklin Roosevelt formed the pattern of his later life.

But even with war approaching, politics must go on; especially in New York, where the Wilson Democrats had a score to settle with Tammany Hall. There was some talk by anti-Tammany leaders of nominating Franklin Roosevelt for Governor, but this did not materialize. He entered, instead, the primary for United States Senator. Tammany, insistent of holding New York, immediately threw James W. Gerard, President Wilson's Ambassador to Germany, into the fight. Roosevelt, although he showed surprising strength in the up-state districts, lost by seventy thousand votes. This was Franklin Roosevelt's first defeat at the polls. He had not resigned from the Navy Department, and after the primaries returned to his post.

As Assistant Secretary of the Navy Franklin Roosevelt matured both as man and politician. But he did not then, nor for many years, mature so greatly that he lost any of the magnificent ebullience that had endeared him to the up-state farmers or that had enabled him to laugh his way heartily through the campaign to keep blue-eyed Billy Sheehan out of the Senate.

Perhaps he was born to be a politician, for he had, from his Harvard days, an innate sense of the truth of the ancient maxim that the ends justify the means. As a *Crimson* editor he had found his campaign for fire escapes falling on unresponsive ears among the students. Knowing that an editorial which stirs up no excitement might as well not be written, he made up for the lack of response by writing "letters to the editor," which he duly printed. This allowed him to answer in another editorial (an old trick, but an effective one, as any editor knows) and made the issue seem more important than perhaps it was.

When he reached the Senate he tried a similar trick. He announced that he would oppose an anti-vivisection bill and thereupon was all but drowned by an avalanche of post cards, ostensibly from his constituents, demanding that he vote for the measure which he honestly thought a foolish one. As his mother later explained, the "happy idea" dawned on him that he might "organize a little unit whose function would be to distribute cards among the voters—but postals that would urge, just as persuasively, that he vote against the bill, rather than for it." Seeing to it that more of his own cards came back to him than those sent by the other side, he was "with a comparatively clear conscience, able to vote as his own good sense dictated!"

At the famous Baltimore convention he bought a quantity of Champ Clark buttons which he distributed to a bunch of hangers on and ward heelers. Thus falsely adorned he got them into the convention hall, safely past the Clark guards. When Champ Clark passed the majority vote and seemed on the way to the necessary two-thirds he turned his Clark-buttoned cohorts loose, shouting for Woodrow Wilson. It caused a pandemonium and stopped the voting long enough for William Jennings Bryan to marshal the weakening Wilson adherents and hold them. On the forty-third ballot Wilson won the majority and three ballots later the nomination.

Now as Assistant Secretary of the Navy in a country rapidly approaching war, realizing that his Chief could not keep the peace he had desired, Franklin Roosevelt (who had taken office on his eighth wedding anniversary) saw the necessity of drastic action, even if it meant utilizing another trick. In 1916 Congress, spurred on at last by Wilson, passed the three hundred twelve million dollar naval bill. Roosevelt was grateful, for he had been urging a greater Navy since he took office. But long before the bill was made law he began slashing red tape, placing war orders up and down the line, although he had absolutely no authority and the Navy no money to pay for the goods! Indeed, if America had not gone to war with Germany on Feb. 3, 1917, he and the Navy Department would have been in a precarious position as a result of his premature activity!

With the declaration of war he went to work with even

greater vigor. The very first thing he did was to contract for naval supplies, on a war basis, for the next entire year, cornering the market for the Navy before the Army had a chance to get going. The story is told that President Wilson called him to the White House, scolded him with a twinkle in his eye, and made him divide his supplies with the Army. Apocryphal or not, the anecdote was typical. Roosevelt is said to have ordered the construction of the five hundred thousand dollar Brooklyn Navy Yard cantonment by telephone and had it built and working before the contracts were awarded. It is a fact that he had orders out for forty million dollars worth of equipment—small-bore guns, ammunition, etc.,—several months before Congress made the necessary appropriation. It was his interest in a seemingly crack-pot inventor that brought the Navy around to accepting the Browne electrical submarine trap, once rejected by Admiral Sims, but which that officer later admitted was one of the most effective devices put in use during the war. It accounted for the loss of two hundred or more German submarines when the barrage was laid across the North Sea, from the Orkney Islands to the coast of Norway.

In July, 1918, aboard a new destroyer that accompanied a convoy of troop-filled liners, Assistant Secretary Roosevelt crossed the Atlantic to have a look at the military operations in Europe. He was met at Portsmouth by Vice-admiral Sims and the naval secretary to the First Lord of the Admiralty who was greatly impressed. Sir Eric Geddes saw him at the Admiralty; he lunched with Lord Balfour, was dined at the House of Commons, and received by King George, who had just received a letter from Uncle Teddy telling of the death behind the German lines of the older Roosevelt's son, Quentin.

Later he went to France for conferences with the French admiralty, and there he saw Clemenceau, President Poincaré, and the great Marshal Foch, with whom he discussed the mounting of huge naval guns on railway carriages to meet the German "Big Berthas." He spent a few days with the Marines in the combat area near Nancy, then went to Italy, after which he returned to France, visited the British front, and then examined Inverness and Invorgordon, the bases of the North Sea submarine barrage. He came back to America on the *Leviathan*.

During the voyage, which he had intended to end by resigning his post and taking a commission, he was stricken with a slight attack of pneumonia.

After the Armistice in 1918 Roosevelt was again sent to Europe on Navy business. Because he was still weak from effects of the pneumonia, and the influenza that he had contracted during the epidemic of that year, Eleanor went with him. But she was taken ill with pleurisy in London and he had to go on without her. He visited Belgium, then went to Paris where President Wilson was helping to set the terms of the peace. With Mrs. Roosevelt, now recovered, he returned with the Wilson party. Like President Wilson, Franklin Roosevelt firmly believed the League of Nations would be the salvation of the world, and bring about the end of wars and international hatred.

The Navy Department held Franklin until 1920. That was, of course, another Presidential year, and he was destined to be in the very thick of the fight. For the first place on the ticket the Democrats named James M. Cox, the Ohio newspaper publisher and Governor of that State. The second place went to the younger and far more colorful Franklin Roosevelt.

Governor Cox and Roosevelt visited Woodrow Wilson at the White House after their nomination and promised the sick and disheartened man that they would not desert his cause. The campaign that followed was fought, as promised, on the record of Woodrow Wilson's two terms as President and on the issue of the League of Nations, to which the Republicans and their candidate, Warren Gamaliel Harding, were firmly and noisily opposed.

Roosevelt toured the country in a special train and kept fighting until the very eve of the election. During this tour he made at least one thousand speeches, short or long, in behalf of the Democratic ticket and the policies of his party. But a war-weary world listened to Harding's promise of a return to "normalcy" and swept the Ohio editor, poker kit and all, into the White House that was at last evacuated by the dying and saddened Wilson. Franklin Roosevelt had suffered his second defeat at the polls.

Sometime during that year, as he crossed the continent,

Roosevelt conceived the notion of some day making a drive for the Presidency. But first there was work to do: there were five Roosevelt children to bring up. He resumed his law practice in New York and, thanks to the friendship of Van Laer Black, banker and publisher of *The Baltimore Sun,* he became Eastern district manager of the Fidelity & Deposit Company of Maryland. He did remarkably well at this business, and also had a lucrative law practice with a new partner, Basil O'Connor, with whom he became associated in 1924.

He had achieved the status of a man of importance: lawyer, banker, an Overseer of Harvard College. He knew people everywhere; in this country and in Europe. He was established, and he had had an amazingly good time in getting where he was. If the great political chance did not beckon, what did it matter? He could be a business man, and retire, some day, to Hyde Park. But he knew this was not in the stars. He had known too well the idealism of Woodrow Wilson not to want to see that great leader's conception of Democracy triumph.

IV

In August, 1921, Franklin Roosevelt and his family were having a glorious time at the cottage at Campobello Island. There was swimming in the warmer waters of Lake Glen Severn, the tiny land-locked pond near the beach across the island from the house. There was sailing on Roosevelt's little sloop, the *Vireo*. There were picnics and shore dinners on the rocks. There were camping trips up the rivers off the Bay of Fundy. The usual, gay and carefree summer life, far from the heat of the city and the cares of the law office.

After a picnic and a sail, which had been enlivened by landing on an island to fight a forest fire, the family arrived home about four in the afternoon. Mr. Roosevelt was tired; he had not been feeling well for several days. He thought a swim in the pond would do him good. After enjoying it with the children he crossed the beach and plunged into the cold waters of the bay. He then trotted the mile home. Still in his bathing suit, he sat on the porch to read his mail. He began to chatter, and then, feeling a chill, he went to bed.

In the morning he was worse. Mrs. Roosevelt decided not to go on a camping trip planned for the next day and sent the children off under the direction of her guest, Mrs. Louis Howe. Three days later Mr. Roosevelt's legs were paralyzed. The local doctor, summoned from the mainland, was puzzled. But he and Mrs. Roosevelt, who slept on a cot in her husband's room and nursed him day and night, feared that he had been stricken with infantile paralysis. They sent for an expert, and when he came at last he told them that they were right.

August, 1921, was a grim month for the Roosevelts. They did not know, from day to day, whether Franklin would live or die. After days of desperate anxiety the doctor said that he could be taken to New York. Although the year 1921 was not an auspicious year for politically ambitious Democrats, the realistic Louis Howe, uncertain how long the paralysis would last, was anxious to keep the news of Mr. Roosevelt's illness from the press. Quietly he obtained a private car, which was backed onto a siding at Eastport, Me. Then Mr. Roosevelt was taken, in the bottom of a motor boat, across the bay, and, with great secrecy, lifted through the window into the train. In New York he was taken from the car through the window, placed in an ambulance, and brought to the Presbyterian Hospital. He did not leave for his home on East Sixty-fifth Street until Christmas.

Louis Howe, whose entire time was now taken up as Mr. Roosevelt's political manager, for his law work and insurance business were regarded by both merely as an interim in a public career, came to live at the Roosevelt home. It worried Mrs. James Roosevelt no end to have him there, smoking incessantly, and always talking politics to her son. But politics were the breath of life to Franklin Roosevelt, who now bent every effort of his will towards recovery. He and Louis knew he would get better; they knew he would re-enter the lists. Although this was a sad period, it did give Franklin Roosevelt a chance to read. He read the history of his country, the history of his party, and, as a hobby, the history of the Navies of the world. He resumed his stamp-collecting. He had time to think, to study, and to plan. By spring, 1922, he had recovered so that he could sit on the floor and rough-house with his boys. That summer he was able to go to Hyde Park and within a year he could get about on crutches. He could devote time, now, to business, and he did.

In 1924 he learned about the benefits that other sufferers from infantile paralysis had obtained at Warm Springs, Georgia, and went there. The treatments did wonders for him; he learned to swim and to move himself better than he had ever hoped he would. All this meant that he could keep on going, do things, be active, and not have to retire from the life he loved so deeply—politics. It meant, too, that he could go back to the office to earn money; and he did, at the law and with the insurance company.

When he had first gone to Warm Springs he found the place badly run down, nothing more than a decrepit winter resort. Because he was greatly helped, other sufferers from polyomelitis began to come there, for he spread the word around. But there were no proper houses for invalids, nor other facilities. He undertook an obligation for the purchase of the site for a Warm Springs Foundation, contributed a great deal of his own money, and raised much more, for the erection of buildings. For himself he built a small house at the cost of six thousand nine hundred twenty dollars. By 1930 the Foundation took out a policy of five hundred thirty thousand dollars on his life to insure the completion of the endowment. After he became President, through the Birthday Balls, thousands of dollars have been raised, and the Foundation, which has done wonderful work for sufferers from infantile paralysis, has become one of America's favorite charities to which even those who blanch otherwise at the name of "that man in the White House" have given their pennies, dimes and dollars.

Warm Springs did wonders for Franklin Roosevelt but he did more for himself. His mother, whose influence over him cannot be denied, despaired of his ever being able to work or play again. His wife never lost faith in his own ability to rise above the wheel-chair. Louis Howe kept his mind working. But more than all the others, there was Franklin Roosevelt himself. His will power, his determination, and the self-reliance he had been taught as a child, all came to the fore. Then there was, too, the Roosevelt-Delano love of life, the gusto, the drive that he had in good quantity. He has never told, and perhaps never will tell, of the anguish he must have undergone, and the fear, and the despair, in those days of 1921 and 1922.

V

Franklin Delano Roosevelt could not have sat back, content with his law office and his banking business, and watched what was happening to his country under the corrupt Harding administration, without wanting to do something about it.

In 1920 he had attended the Democratic Convention at San Francisco hoping that the nomination would go to his old friend Al Smith, who had been floor leader at Albany the year he fought against Tammany Hall. It had gone, instead, to Governor Cox, with himself as the Ohioan's running mate. Then there had come the awful sickness and the three worst years of the desperate battle to regain his health. Now it was 1924, a Presidential year, and he was well enough not only to work but to get back, somewhat, into the political fray. He had to drag himself around on crutches, with two people to help him, but he had steeled himself against pity or laughter, and he was eager for the fight. He would go to battle for Al Smith.

The cruel heat of the summer burned down upon the pavements of New York, that had spawned Al Smith nine years before Roosevelt was born in the comfortable house at Hyde Park. It turned the old Madison Square Garden into a steaming chamber of torture. Braving the heat along with thousands of other hopeful Democrats, Franklin Roosevelt was carried into the building and onto the platform. There, in a polished and powerful speech, the Harvard aristocrat placed the name of the boy from the East Side into nomination. He did so effectively, for he believed in the integrity and decency of the man whom he described with the magnificent lines from Wordsworth:

> This is the Happy Warrior, this is he
> Whom every man in arms would wish to be.

But Roosevelt's Happy Warrior was a Roman Catholic seeking the highest office of the land in a year when the Ku Klux Klan was rampant. The rambunctious convention rejected

Smith, as it also did W. G. McAdoo, named John W. Davis, a corporation lawyer, and went home after many weary days. Calvin Coolidge was elected. Prosperity descended upon the land, the speakeasies were crowded, the newspapers lush with advertising, Wall Street boomed. Al Smith returned to Albany to do his work and wait for 1928.

During those four years Franklin Roosevelt labored for the Smith cause assiduously and ceaselessly. When the Democrats gathered again, this time at Houston, Texas, in 1928, he had so greatly improved his health that he now used only canes to get around with, and he had so held the Democrats that he could again nominate the Happy Warrior. This time there was no lengthy struggle. Al won the nomination easily and set out to annihilate Herbert Hoover. After the convention Roosevelt returned to New York, where he busied himself at the Eastern headquarters of his party. In September he went to Warm Springs, for even then the thought uppermost in his mind was his complete recovery. The doctors had told him if he stayed there he might some day walk without brace, or crutches, or even a cane.

The Democrats of New York State gathered at Syracuse that year to choose a candidate for Governor to succeed Al Smith, who, with the exception of one term, had been Governor continuously since 1918. It was a state convention of unusual significance. Not only did the party have no intention of losing the office after the remarkable record of Smith, but they had to choose a man who would certainly swing the state behind him. Smith was not even sure of carrying New York against Hoover. The party desperately needed a candidate of unusual calibre. But Roosevelt, before leaving for Georgia, had said he asked no part of it. He wanted to get well. The governorship could wait.

Whether he was playing the old political game of waiting for the office to be thrust upon him, or whether he truly meant what he said, he alone can answer. Eleanor Roosevelt, at least, was sure at the time that there was no guile in his heart. She certainly had no desire to see him return to public life, nor had his mother. But Al Smith, in his desperation, knew that his success, and his party's success, depended upon Roosevelt. There was no one else who could swing the state.

It was at this moment that Eleanor Roosevelt made her fateful telephone call, cleared the way to the White House for Franklin Roosevelt and wrecked Al Smith's career.

After a campaign which he took seriously, traveling the length of the state by train and automobile, a most appealing figure because of his physical handicap, he won the election by a plurality of a little more than twenty-five thousand votes. Al Smith lost his own State to Herbert Hoover by one hundred three thousand votes. It was a bitter blow.

VI

The Governorship of New York can be the jumping off place to the White House. Teddy Roosevelt made that eminence in two hops. Charles Evans Hughes would have made it if he had not stubbed his toe on California. No man who enters that office can be blind to its opportunities. If Al Smith had twice slipped as he tried the ambitious leap, there was no reason why Franklin Roosevelt should not try to make it safely. But there was no use in essaying it if, as Governor, he had not behind him the safe footing of an enviable record of achievement. This Franklin Roosevelt set out to secure.

The phrase the Happy Warrior that he bestowed on Al Smith might better have been saved for Franklin Roosevelt himself. If one saw him standing behind a desk there was no indication that he was lame. The swimming at Warm Springs had developed his shoulders until he looked far more the athlete than he had in Harvard. His face was ruddily healthy. The lines were not deep. He showed no signs of having suffered deeply. His smile was as infectious as ever. His laugh was as ready and as hearty. Undoubtedly he was happy, glad to get back into the swing of things, to be, as it were, at the helm again. When he was stricken he had said to his wife: "I'll beat this thing." He had.

Al Smith had left the State of New York in good order and its people accustomed to accomplishment in their behalf. He had done as much for the social progress of the state as any

Governor since De Witt Clinton, in the opinion of all except its most reactionary inhabitants. And he had done it in the face of a hostile Republican legislature. Indeed he had used the Republican opposition as a foil to his own political advancement. And now Franklin Delano Roosevelt, his personal choice for the office, was to take a page from the political primer of the Happy Warrior, who at this moment was comparing plus twenty-five thousand with minus one hundred three thousand and wondering just where he stood.

It would have been easier for Governor Roosevelt if he had succeeded a Republican governor or even an inefficient Democrat. Then he could have mounted a charger and with fanfares assailed a citadel of real or alleged corruption in the name of Reform. Instead he had to carry on with unfinished business. Among the issues he had inherited was that of water power which Al Smith, in his magnificent battles with the public utilities interests, had dramatized.

During his first term Roosevelt proposed the establishment of the huge state-owned water power plant on the St. Lawrence River and during his second term—he was re-elected in 1930— he was able to set up the St. Lawrence Water Power Authority, a victory which his resourceful predecessor had been unable to wangle from the Republican dominated legislature. Another issue that he seized upon, one which Al Smith had never appreciated or understood, was agriculture. However dull this may appear to some, the problem of the dairy and the truck farmer, especially the former, has been a serious one in New York for more than a century. To it Governor Roosevelt gave thought and towards it he took action. And when, in 1930, he campaigned for re-election against Charles H. Tuttle, the United States attorney for the southern district of New York, his interest in the farmers paid dividends. He won by the huge plurality of seven hundred twenty-five thousand votes, of which one hundred seventy-five thousand came from rural voters, a feat unprecedented for a Democrat.

In matters that may be summed up as Social Security he was active; as much constructive legislation was passed during his administration as during any similar period in the state's history. His administration, however, left his successor, Governor

Herbert Lehman, a treasury deficit of one hundred million dollars, when the latter took office in January, 1933.

Election day, 1930, made Franklin D. Roosevelt a national figure, a man to be watched, a presidential possibility. His victory over the able and eminent, if colorless, Tuttle was so tremendous—if he had lost New York city he would still have won! —that it became almost a foregone conclusion that he would be a candidate for the Presidency two years hence. If nothing occurred to mar his administration he would be away out in front of all other contenders for the nomination. Something very nearly did.

Franklin Roosevelt, having scored a touchdown in 1930, might easily have missed his try for the deciding goal. Few Governors ever faced a more delicate situation than he did in the winter of 1931 when a Republican sponsored investigating committee broke New York city, and its malodorous administration under the affable Jimmy Walker, wide open. Under the chairmanship of the Republican Senator Samuel H. Hofstadter and the investigations of former Judge Samuel Seabury, an anti-Tammany Democrat, the situation in New York city was exposed to the air. The smell was bad. It assailed the nostrils of the seven million residents of the five boroughs, who were less in a mood for forgiveness than they had been before the stock market crash of October, 1929, and the beginning of hard times.

Judge Seabury gave the city, state and nation a show such as had not been seen since the famous Lexow investigations that had helped so materially in pushing Teddy Roosevelt towards the White House. He painted a picture of municipal skulduggery, comedy, and scandal, that made the machinations of the Tweed Ring of Uncle Bob Roosevelt's day seem mild in comparison. Then, with a grand flourish, he handed the messy daub, all neatly framed with incontrovertible proof, to the man who would be President.

Although the reform elements in the state cried Wolf! and the press howled for a flock of new brooms, Governor Roosevelt, still smiling, remained silent. As a Democrat with no love for Tammany Hall and as a leading contender for the impending nomination for the Presidency, he naturally suspected that there was a Republican lurking in the woodpile. At least when the clamor began. But the Seabury investigation soon made it apparent that, whatever the original motives may have been, the situation could no longer be cavalierly dismissed as a political plot to stop Roosevelt.

Governor Roosevelt, who had been in no way responsible for the mess but who could not avoid it, as he heartily wished he could, held hearings on the charges brought against Sheriff Thomas M. Farley, who insisted that his fortunes had all come out of a "wonderful tin box" which he kept at his home. He removed the Sheriff, rendering at the time an opinion that holders of office should properly be held to a higher standard of honesty than was required of an ordinary citizen. Tammany frothed. Seabury pressed charges against Jimmy Walker, the mayor of New York, and every one asked what Roosevelt would do now.

While the newspapers of the entire nation had been filled with the scandal of New York, Governor Roosevelt had been laying his plans carefully. He had put Judge Samuel Rosenman, then his legal advisor, to work. He had his old and faithful friend, Louis Howe, busy on a state-wide organization. And he had taken on James Aloysius Farley, a building contractor and astute political seer, as his manager. He also had called in Professor Raymond Moley of Columbia University as an advisor. These five were the nucleus of his machine. Farley was the toughest and on his shoulder rested the greater part of the pre-convention labors.

On the eve of the convention at Chicago Governor Roosevelt sent the charges against Walker to that dapper young man to study and ponder and prepare his defense. Then managers Farley and Howe went off to Chicago, while Roosevelt remained in Albany. The fight these two were to put up was epic. Democratic conventions are always colorful. This was more so than most, for two strong men were battling for first place. Franklin D. Roosevelt was one. Alfred E. Smith was the other.

Since 1928 the relationship between the two men had become strained. There is no question but what Smith had become embittered after his defeat in that year, and yet the two men undoubtedly would have drifted apart sooner or later in any event. For, the truth is, they looked upon life differently. Smith had come up the hard way and, ironically, one seldom finds a liberal among his kind. Smith was the product of Tammany Hall, which is to politics what Wall Street is to Big Business. He was not fundamentally a reformer. His liberalism was not deep-dyed. Probably the two men had never been so closely drawn together as it seemed. At least the friendship had never been tested. Now it was to be.

At Chicago Howe and Farley made no apparent effort to woo Tammany, and so, on all the four ballots that were cast the Tammany delegates and those from Kings County (Brooklyn) voted solidly for Al Smith. The Roosevelt crowd could have won Tammany if they had been willing to make a deal. But they could not afford that kind of deal—not with the Seabury indictment in Jimmy Walker's inside pocket. And so they dealt with California and Texas, instead. The result was that Roosevelt wound up with 945 of 1,154 ballots cast. The Happy Warrior, his hopes of the Presidency blasted for the third time and by the very man who had given him his role, refused to release his 109½ votes, which would have made the nomination unanimous. Instead, after skulking in his tent, he started the short road to the Empire State Building and the Liberty League. The break was a sad one, but symbolic. Although none knew it then, at that convention the liberalism of the 1920's was strangled by the philosophy of the New Deal.

After the convention Governor Roosevelt called public hearings to let Mayor Walker answer the charges brought against him. His cross-examination of Jimmy Walker was inept, seemingly designed for the purpose of allowing him to reach the decision that the Mayor had been indiscreet but not criminally negligent enough for removal from office. The Mayor, however, saved him from this by resigning and sailing abroad on the *Manhattan* for a long vacation on the Riviera.

Franklin Delano Roosevelt gave the clue to the tone of his administration when he boarded an airplane with Mrs. Roosevelt and flew to Chicago. No other President-elect had ever dared to make such an unprecedented move. There he was greeted with tumultuous enthusiasm when he rode triumphantly from the airport to the platform at the stadium to accept his nomination. The speedy acceptance astounded every one. He told the cheering delegates, still amazed that a candidate should appear personally at a convention, that he was no worshipper of precedent and "foolish" tradition—if tradition stood in the way of social and economic regeneration of the country. He sprang to the defense of "the forgotten man." And he promised the people a "new deal."

Before his golden voice, before his shining phrases, and in the face of the depression he had done so little to avoid, Herbert Hoover did not stand a chance. He saw Republican progressives like Hiram Johnson, Bob La Follette, George W. Norris and Bronson Cutting desert the Republican banner. And on the morning after the election he saw that all but six of the forty-eight states had turned their backs on him, on his party, and the outworn economics they both represented. The people wanted the promised New Deal. Eight years later they still wanted it. And they wanted it from Franklin Delano Roosevelt and no one else.

<h1 style="text-align:center">VII</h1>

It is a cliché that posterity has to decide whether a man is really great. Posterity has conceded greatness, without much argument, to two Presidents of the United States: George Washington and Abraham Lincoln. With the latter Franklin Delano Roosevelt shared, at least before the "premeditated invasion" of the Philippines, the distinction of being simultaneously adored and hated with incredible passion. Already while living Roosevelt has been discussed almost as copiously as Lincoln, alive and dead; and it is conceded that only Washington and Lincoln had to cope with such tremendous problems as Roosevelt has had to face.

This tall, handsome, fluent man went to the White House on March 4, 1933. Even then many an observer, knowing that in reality the people had been more anxious to rid America of Herbert Hoover than to elect Franklin Roosevelt, believed with that great sage, Walter Lippmann, that "his mind is not clear, his purposes are not simple, his methods are not direct," and feared for the future of America in his hands. Eight years later some people still feared. But after Pearl Harbor they were able to put aside that fear with amazing speed and unity.

Yet, when he took office in the midst of the worst depression that this nation has ever known, his actions, if nothing else, were clear, simple and direct. In that grim moment the people wanted action. He gave it to them. The first thing he did was to order a banking holiday throughout the nation. Within a week he had declared a national emergency and received from Congress almost unlimited power over banking transactions. Within the next one hundred days he—born and bred a hard money man—took the country off the gold standard; he cut the pay of one million government employes and put through thereby a 25 per cent reduction in government expenditures; he established Federal aid for the unemployed; he approved a law permitting the sale of light wines and beer; he established the Agricultural Adjustment Administration for the control of agriculture; and he set up the Tennessee Valley Authority for conservation, military and electric power purposes.

The swiftness of his action, the dramatic qualities of his utterances, overwhelmed the constitutional and economic fallacies that lay within some of these acts. But they lifted the people out of the slough of despond. Not by any means did all these measures spring from his own fertile mind. There was the Brain Trust to guide him, a group of college professors for the most part, like Raymond Moley. But he gave to these theories, wise or foolish, legal or unconstitutional, the drive, the color, that was needed.

Later, of course, the Court trimmed some, emasculated others; many a New Deal "brain truster" went by the board; but month by month, as the fight went on, those who were willing to see it could watch the New Deal taking a definite shape. Mr. Roosevelt himself has termed this period "the continuing struggle for Liberalism," and perhaps no better description exists. Under this same heading he has placed the purges that marked the inner strife of the Democratic party, which, seemingly, he was willing to preserve only so long as it remained faithful to those liberal principles which he, as its leader espoused.

It became obvious, as the New Deal progressed, and Franklin

D. Roosevelt scored, in 1936, the most sweeping victory in American politics since the second election of James Monroe more than one hundred years before, that here was a man of tremendous stature. He could not be dismissed as a country squire in the White House. By one swift action after another he had done things. Many of them caused fear and trembling in Wall Street and the cry went up that Roosevelt was a "traitor to his class." If he had been an Oyster Bay Roosevelt the charge might more easily have been justified, but the one thing that stands out, to anyone who looks at the Roosevelt Family whole, is that he could not be a traitor to his class, for he had none.

It was his own kinsman, Joseph Alsop, who first pointed this out. In an article he (and his columnar partner, Robert Kintner) wrote for *Life* magazine Mr. Alsop makes his point: "The accident of James Roosevelt's age caused the President to be brought up in the atmosphere of the pre-Civil War American rich. And these once self-confident merchants, entrepreneurs, and country gentlemen found themselves hopelessly adrift in the booming industrial post-Civil War America. Some, like the President's half-brother, Rosey, managed to accommodate themselves comfortably to the new era. Others failed, taking refuge in cold withdrawal like Henry Adams or fleeing to Europe like Henry James or simply declining into a depressing shabby gentility. But as a class, an organized group with certain habits and privileges in common they were quite overwhelmed by the big-business age.

"Being overwhelmed rarely promoted acquiescence and it is only natural that Franklin Roosevelt never wholly accommodated himself to the big-business *Zeitgeist*. Then, too, the President passed most of his youth with older people, was not sent to Groton until two years after his form-mates, and had a mother so devoted she actually moved to Boston to be near him at Harvard. Precocious, an only child, starting after the crowd, he got on poorly with the sons of the rich with whom he was educated. Finally he married a woman who has always disliked the more luxurious shows and fleshpots. *Thus he was in some sense cut off from the new world in which the world of his father had disappeared; being cut off, his mind was liberated and being liberated he struck out on his own course.*"

This course led him to some strange companions for a politician: the wizened Howe, now dead; bluff Jim Farley, now driven from politics; Raymond Moley, Rex Tugwell, Felix Frankfurter, Henry Wallace, Harry Hopkins, Tommy Corcoran, Ben Cohen, Joe Kennedy, Robert H. Jackson, to name but a few. As many of his speeches are compounded of the thoughts and phrases of several contributors, so was the New Deal compounded of the thoughts of many. But the speeches, when they roll through the microphone to the fireside, are the speeches of one man—Franklin Roosevelt. So was the New Deal. And the New Deal, in essence, was a struggle for security for a self-ruled people, the extension of that security he knew as a boy, which he has always had, but which he has never had any reason to believe should belong peculiarly to him or his class.

This same dream of security has motivated his foreign as well as his domestic policy. His bringing about of the abrogation of the Platt amendment, thus ending America's assumed right to interfere in Cuba; his withdrawal of the marines from Haiti, his bill guaranteeing the future independence of the Philippines—all these were consistent. So was his warning to the world that he would not stand idly by if Canada should be attacked; his backing of Secretary Hull's trade treaties; his withdrawal of the American ambassador from Nazi Germany after the Hitler-led pogroms; his appeals to Hitler and Mussolini asking them to pledge their nations to ten years of peace; and finally his call for the amendment of the neutrality act—these, too, were consistent.

It was, fundamentally, in the name of security that he called for fifty thousand war planes in 1940, that he asked for a two-ocean Navy, that he began to build up the nation's defenses until he had spent twenty-eight billion dollars for that purpose. It was for this purpose that he put through the lend-lease bill after arranging the trade of over-age destroyers in return for the right to put up defenses on British territory.

And so, in 1940, he again went before the country. And the country answered by ordering him back to the Presidency for another four years. In spite of the ineptitude of some of his own politics, in spite of the great financial machine that was built to crush him, in spite of everything that could be said against his policies, the majority of the people gave him a gift never before given to any man.

During his first eight years in office President Roosevelt won most of his major battles. He entered his administration with a Democratic Congress and, in spite of the efforts of the opposition, his party was able to remain at the top throughout his administration. Upon some occasions, of course, he was forced to compromise, but upon only one notable occasion was he defeated by the legislature. That was when he attempted to liberalize the Supreme Court, which had defeated more New Deal measures than the legislative branch had done. He sought to bring about this liberalization, or modernization, or, as his opponents put it, his attempt to "pack" the court, through reorganization of the entire Federal judiciary. His efforts set off a Congressional battle more bitter than any the nation had known since the fight against the League of Nations.

President Roosevelt lost the battle but he won the campaign. Defeated by Congress he fought the Court for interpretation of the Constitution as a living document. Later, through death and resignation, he found it possible to appoint a Chief Justice, and more justices of his own social and economic beliefs, than any president in recent history.

This fight came in his second term. It gave the "economic royalists"—to use a phrase as lasting, perhaps, as "new deal," "forgotten man," "good neighbor," "one-third of a nation"— a chance they had avidly been waiting. They poured scornful words upon his smiling head. Perhaps if he had broached this subject earlier they might have driven him from office. But it is doubtful, and to suggest it is, at best useless speculation. In 1936 he carried every State but Maine and Vermont—an electoral vote of five hundred and twenty-three to eight. By the time the 1940 election for a third term came along the Supreme Court was a dead issue. And then, with war clouds growing daily nearer, he carried four hundred and forty-nine votes to the Electoral College, while Wendell Willkie, a far stronger opponent than poor Alf Landon had been, carried only eighty-two.

VIII

When Franklin Roosevelt was a small lad at Hyde Park, and Benjamin Harrison was President, the man in the White House could lead almost as leisurely a life as any squire on his Hudson River estate. That estimable gentleman was seldom at his desk after luncheon, but spent his time if the weather was good roaming the countryside with his wife's niece, or, if the weather was inclement, playing billiards with his youthful friends. By the time Teddy Roosevelt had come along, for all his advocacy of the strenuous life he did not have to put in an eight-hour day at Government business; after one o'clock he would set aside his papers and, until dinner time, would wrestle, or learn jujitsu, or play with the medicine ball with his cronies, or picnic on Rock Creek, or ride horseback with his Army friends. Even when Big Business was at its zenith, in those safe, calm days of the Coolidge administration, the President could—and did— forget even the gyrations of the stock market as he slept away the afternoon hours on his couch!

But the days were hectic and the nights sleepless for all manner of people when Franklin Roosevelt took over. He has kept up the fast pace ever since, through the days of depression and recovery, through two strenuous campaigns, and through the grim months of the second European war. Perhaps not since the time of the conscientious John Quincy Adams, who confided to his diary his distaste for the irksomeness of office, has any occupant of the White House put in longer hours there than Franklin Roosevelt. His physical handicap—he still has to wear a steel brace—has made it necessary for him to follow a reasonably rigid routine almost daily, which has varied only in intensity since he originated it in the winter of 1933.

When, in that year, he became the new occupant of the White House he knew that he would be pretty much of a prisoner. Both he and Mrs. Roosevelt set out to make the old place as homelike as possible. They succeeded; and no place better expresses the Rooseveltian atmosphere than his bedroom on the second floor where invariably his working day begins.

President Roosevelt awakens in a room that is as much his own domain as his cottage at Hyde Park is his house. The walls, covered with pictures and nautical prints, surround a marble-mantled fireplace on which rests his whimsical collection of some thirty china pigs, which creep up like steps on either side until they reach a climax in a lusty porker five and one-half inches high. Several wooden and brass donkeys, symbols of the Democratic Party, are also on the broad shelf on which stand framed photographs of his mother and father and some old friends. In a corner of the room—the "family corner," as the President calls it—hangs a pictorial record of his own life and pictures of his relatives. In another corner is displayed the treasured tail of Gloster, James Roosevelt's prize trotting horse.

Like most people with Yankee antecedents the President is a "saver," as piles of books and magazines cluttering up the hall outside the bedroom testify. Since childhood he has collected stamps. Nobody knows how valuable his collection is, but it is large. He keeps about sixty albums at the White House and as many, or more, at Hyde Park. At one time he spent several hours each week, personally soaking the stamps from their covers and hinging them in the big books. Another favorite hobby is the collection of Christmas cards, of which he has about three thousand selected from his annual haul and filed away.

When, around 9 o'clock, the President awakens, he has his breakfast in bed. At this meal he begins his day, conferring with Dr. Ross McIntyre, his physician, and his secretaries and aids. Miss Marguerite LeHand, his personal secretary, and Marvin McIntyre, his chief official secretary, almost always attend these bedside meetings. The conference usually starts with General Watson, who has charge of appointments, telling a funny story. Then they get down to the serious business of planning the day: whom the President will see and when, and such routine matters.

After a breakfast of coffee, eggs and toast, the President works and reads in his room until about 10:30 or 11 o'clock, by which time he has shaved and dressed and is ready to go in his wheel chair down the long corridor from his East Wing bedroom to his office in the West Wing. There he stays until late afternoon. He sees an average of a visitor every fifteen minutes. Luncheon, an office affair, usually consists of salad or an omelette or a soufflé, and if the meal is not shared with visitors, such as Secretary of the Treasury Henry L. Morgenthau, Jr., or some other high official, a member of his family is likely to be on hand. Tea is served at this simple meal, which may last for an hour.

One superlative nobody can deny to President Roosevelt. He has been the most accessible of Presidents. All the others, even Wilson, even the news-making Teddy, made little of their relations with the newspapermen in Washington. Roosevelt has them (if not their publishers!) in the palm of his hand, because, on the whole, he has had the intelligence to treat them fairly, and give them "the breaks." In addition to his regular press conferences, which he holds on Tuesdays and Fridays, he frequently sees the men on other days when big news is breaking. Only once did he fail to take them into his confidence upon an occasion of great news. That was at the time of his memorable meeting with Winston Churchill on the deck of a warship at sea. No reporter was taken to cover that.

His willingness to give time to the press, which has by no means always treated him fairly, is all the more astounding because he receives a volume of visitors that would lacerate any other's nervous system. His ability to meet people and do a tremendous amount of work stems from the time that he was stricken. He then thought he should resign from his banking business. His directors refused, and when he returned they soon found that he was doing far more work, and accomplishing a great deal more, than when he was free to get about as he pleased. There are days, now, when he receives a new caller every fifteen minutes. What keeps his secretaries on edge is the expansiveness of the man—he enjoys seeing all the appalling host, he likes them, and he loves to talk so greatly that the conscientious ones among them, remembering they have been warned to stay but fifteen minutes, have difficulty breaking away. Since the war, with its increased pressure, the number of visitors has, of course, been materially cut down.

After nine years he enjoys heartily every detail of his job, every self-imposed task. Perhaps his tendency to self-imposition is his worst weakness as an executive. He hates to delegate authority. He must be the boss, and do things by himself.

Somehow, despite his physical incapacities, he has found the strength. Since the outbreak of war, however, he has been willing to delegate some really great authority, as his selection early in 1942 of Donald Nelson, with almost dictatorial powers, to run the war production of the country.

Another superlative that is his alone is his great understanding of mass psychology. Exactly how or where he learned it, it is not easy to say. But somewhere along the political road he acquired his seemingly inexplicable charm for the common man. It is not based on an intellectual appreciation for his leadership entirely, although that may have some bearing on it. Nor is it entirely because of his golden voice that people—the mass of people—like him so well. Wherever the answer lies, this man whose voice is known by millions, has learned somehow the priceless gift of taking the world into his confidence, talking to it, saying what he wants to say so it can be understood, and getting the response he seeks. A "fireside chat," spoken from the White House over the radio, has more effect upon the people, and hence upon Congress, than a press one hundred per cent behind the President.

As a rule Mr. Roosevelt's office day ends at about 5:30 in the afternoon. At that hour he has a massage, or a swim in the small pool in the White House. Then he will go to his second-floor study where, if there are guests for dinner, the more favored ones will be asked to join him for a cocktail. He is proud of his old-fashioneds and his martinis, which he mixes himself while recalling, perhaps, how, when he was a young man and a member of the Racquet Club in New York, he invented the Roosevelt Special—one part benedictine and four parts gin. He no longer belongs to the Racquet Club and no longer mixes Roosevelt Specials.

Cocktails finished, the President goes down to dinner, joining the less favored guests who, sans cocktails of any kind, have been waiting for him in the Red Room. Dinner is a pleasant meal, but nothing special. It is prepared by Mrs. Nesbit, a Hyde Park widow, whom Mrs. Roosevelt brought to the White House when the Roosevelts first moved in. She tries to please him with soup, meat or fish, salad, desert or cheese. Mr. Roosevelt, no gourmet, is particularly fond of game and terrapin, and he likes to top off a meal with some snappy cheese from upper New York State. American wines are sometimes served at dinner.

In the evening his favorite diversion is a moving picture. Before the war he used to attend showings several nights a week in the second floor hall of the White House, a wide, comfortable, and book-lined room. The audience watched informally, seated in comfortable chairs, with the President in the first row, adding to his own enjoyment, if not his guests', by a running comment of criticism. When his mother was alive he loved to shock her and her elderly friends by his remarks, often bordering on the ribald. She would look at him as if he were a naughty boy, but say nothing, really enjoying her son's little touch of exhibitionism.

Newsreels and Walt Disney cartoons are the President's favorites. Sometimes, when the picture is poor, he will leave in the middle, go to his oval study down the hall, shut himself in, and work—on affairs of State or his stamp collection. This room, like his bedroom, is covered with naval prints and scenes of early New York history. His desk, a large one, is littered with animal figures, a *Bible,* the *World Almanac,* Bartlett's *Familiar Quotations,* and a Funk & Wagnalls *Standard Dictionary.* He keeps a box of cigars for guests, but never smokes them himself. He sticks to Camel cigarettes, which he puffs in a long ivory holder.

Proscribed to so rigid a regime Mr. Roosevelt, by nature an active man, is apt to get restive and might long ago have cracked under the strain were it not for his week-ends. During the first year of the New Deal he found that Herbert Hoover had sold the Presidential yacht *Mayflower* and so he requisitioned a former Coast Guard patrol boat, which he named the *Potomac.* With his friends—Justice Samuel I. Rosenman, of the New York Supreme Court, his "literary advisor," or Archibald MacLeish, Librarian of Congress, or Harry Hopkins, his closest friend who lives at the White House—he will spend Saturday and Sunday (for he believes in a Presidential five-day week) cruising on the calm Potomac River. He will do paper work on these trips, prepare an important speech, read, loaf, fish, talk, and sleep.

President Roosevelt has always craved action. Possessed of an

active, even restless, mind, he often has awakened at night and
called some cabinet member, Secretaries Knox or Hull or Stim-
son, on the telephone by his bedside. It is his standing rule that
his staff or department heads call him, at any hour of the night,
if startling news develops. When the Germans marched into
Poland he was awakened and sat up in bed, listening to reports,
until 2 A.M. And when the treachery of the attack on Pearl Harbor was committed he went into dynamic and decisive action.
Even as the bulletins came pouring into the White House, telling of the disaster, he issued orders with clipped words to the
Army and the Navy and started the American war machine.
That night he met with the Cabinet and with Congressional
leaders, and when they had left him, and the lights of Washington were dimmed in the capital's first semi-blackout, he worked
into the small hours, forming the message to Congress that sent
his country into war for the second time in twenty-four years.

Of all places, he still loves most "the farm"—as, not without
justice, he calls Hyde Park. He will leave the White House
on Thursday evening, or Friday, board his private Pullman
on his special eight-car train, accompanied by secretaries, secret
service men, reporters, photographers, and guests in the other
cars, and arrive there the next morning. At Hyde Park, even
more than his father before him he likes to act the country
squire. He loves the trees and lawns and roads of the estate
which today consists of more than one thousand acres. The
trees are his special delight and he has planted many in what
he calls his reforestation project. When he built his cottage
several years ago he changed the plans to avoid uprooting a
tree. Nothing pleases him more than to drive his own car, a
Ford which is operated entirely manually, up and down the
lanes of the estate.

Much work, of course, is done at Hyde Park, and many important announcements have been handed to the press at the
place. Before her death his mother was usually there, for it was
still her home. Now it is his alone, and when he retires from
the Presidency he will go there to live. After his mother's death
he put the two New York town houses on the market. In Hyde
Park he votes, mingles with the town folk when he can, studies
Dutchess County history. There, of course, he has built the

Franklin D. Roosevelt Library, which he has given to the Government as a repository for all his papers, the record of the New Deal.

IX

When Franklin Delano Roosevelt first went to the White House the crowds sang "Happy Days Are Here Again!", there was gay and marching music, and the slogan was "The only thing we have to fear is fear itself." The landslide roar of democracy echoed behind him.

Eight years of swift-moving history passed. There had been no revolution in the United States. At least there had been no bloody revolution. There was no Hitler here, as there was in Germany; nor a Mussolini, as in unhappy Italy; nor a wavering Chamberlain, as in fearful Britain. To a great extent the depression had been licked. There was a new order. The rights of man had been protected and extended. But the battle was not over. Four years before he had told the people, "We have only just begun to fight!"

The man himself was older. The lines in the familiar, the beloved and the hated, face were deeper. The light hair was greyer. But the blue eyes were still keen; the mouth was still ready for smiling. The friendly voice had not grown harsh.

But for all the gains—laws protecting labor, restraining the greedy, making social security more than a phrase—the atmosphere of crisis, which had hung heavily over the administration from the beginning, had deepened as time marched on.

The borders of the United States, where he had sought to house and clothe and feed the people better than they had been able to house and clothe and feed themselves, had widened. They stretched half way across the Atlantic, half way across the Pacific. Munich had become more than a city's name. It was a turning point, not only for the European, but for the worker on a Kansas farm, the canner in the Alaska factory, the W. P. A. worker in the parks of New York.

All this the American people knew and they turned to this man once again. Those who did not turn to him turned to another and, as it came out, he had nothing to offer them that Franklin Roosevelt had not already offered. Whatever the words used to describe it, this thing was the same, and all the words meant one thing: Security.

The smile did not go, the laughter did not disappear, the old cocky way of tossing his head before answering a question was not forgotten. But there was a change. The firm mouth became a thinner line. The words it spoke often made reference to the country's past, to precedent, and less to some brave new world of the future. The roots went deeper into the Hyde Park—the American—soil. Once, sitting in his oval study with some visitors, he gazed out of the window silently across the White House park.

"You know," he said, "this old building gives me the creeps sometimes. This is the same room from which Lincoln looked out and saw the lights of the Confederate Army's campfires burning across the Potomac River."

That night, perhaps at the same moment, bombers were over the English channel, fires were burning in the ruins of London streets.

The end of his second term approached with the great question in everyone's mind: Should the President of the United States kick over one of the great precedents, challenge an unwritten law, and ask for four more years?

Who can say, at this time, what made him answer, "of course." Did he believe he alone could lead? Was it vanity, or vanity sublimated into patriotism? In a world made ruinous by dictators, the leader of the Democratic party and the leader of the American democracy that had twice looked to him for that leadership. He went before the country at a time when, by all precedents, he should have stepped aside, and asked that which had never been given another man. In ordinary circumstances the gift would have been withheld, for the cycle of politics had reached the point at which it was the turn of those who had been out of office eight years to return to power.

But there was a war in Europe and the job at home had not been finished. He asked the unaskable and, although there were millions who fought to keep it from him, there were millions more who knew no other man who could take his place.

These millions marched to the polls to cast their vote in what many honestly believed might be the last free election ever held. Some marched to vote against what they feared was the end of the American way of life. More millions marched to vote to extend the promise of the New Deal, to them more nearly an American way of life than any other that they had ever known.

That November night, when all the words had ended—the clear fighting words with their familiar intonation and the husky words of his opponent—when in every hamlet in the land the votes were being counted and the wires hummed with the news, and the radios screamed forth the crescendant verdict, one man sat alone in a library in an old house in Hyde Park.

The verdict came. The precedent had been broken. In the moment of great crisis Franklin Delano Roosevelt became the first man thrice-chosen to lead the American people.

He sat alone. There was no sign of exultation on his face. The lines were deep beneath the greying, thinning hair. None but himself knows what he thought of then. Did he hear the feet of marching men in Europe? Did he hear the crash of bombs? Did he hear the sough of the torpedoes? And the sly chuckle of the war lords of Japan?

Did he think of old Isaac Roosevelt leaving New York when the British came, abandoning his sugar house and his handsome home, taking his side with the Patriots? Or of the Little One, perhaps, tramping the forest more than three centuries ago? Or of some doughty Delano turning his ship to the Horn?

For the roots of this man, his Dutch and Yankee roots, went as deep as any could go into the American soil. Since the days when the *Mayflower* anchored in Provincetown Harbor some ancestor of this man now sitting by the radio and the ticker in a house of memories had known and loved the soil and trees and streets and air of this country. Seven generations of revolutionaries and immigrants were behind him as he sat there, above the calm unruffled Hudson, above the green acres in the solid, comfortable house . . .

For seven generations and more to come, it is safe to assume, historians will cope with the problem of placing in history this most amazing of all Roosevelts. They will not forget the almost incredible love that millions have had for him, nor the deep and bitter hatred his name has engendered. Had he stepped

from the White House at the close of 1940, his two terms of
social reform (or revolution, if you will) were of such stirring
significance that they would have been the subject of discussion
for all time. The fact that for the first time in history he dared
seek a third term alone was sufficient cause to make him a
marked man in the annals of democratic history. But soon after
his third victory, that which an uneasy world had long feared
came to pass. Whatever Franklin Roosevelt's stature may have
been during the eight years of the New Deal, it increased meas-
urably in the early morning of December 7, 1941, when the sky
over Pearl Harbor was darkened with the armada of Japan.

At that moment, when the bombs dropped with all their
destructive fury on the Pacific outpost of the United States, he
was no longer merely President of the United States, but the
trusted leader of a people suddenly shocked into unity. First
generation Americans, who had known his largess through lean
years, and eighth generation Americans, who had long looked
with cold eyes upon his figure, became almost immediately
united. The bitter, squabbling words were silenced in the
echoes of the bombs. People of every class suddenly found a
new faith. They turned to this dynamic man, this man of such
magnificent strength, and bade him lead them into war.

Perhaps few of the things he had said ever were uttered with
deeper honesty than his oft-repeated phrase, "I hate war."

But he had warned, repeatedly, that mere hatred of war was
not enough in a world threatened with destruction. One can
hate war, and yet enter it willingly if that for which one is
forced to fight is something one loves above all else. And what
Franklin Delano Roosevelt loves most is democratic decency.
To maintain, or rescue, democratic decency this man, who already had lived as full a life as any man, was willing, even
eager, to undertake the tremendous task of running the biggest
war the world has ever known. Almost exactly thirteen months
after his third election and within a few weeks of his sixtieth
birthday, this war came. Ten years after his first crusading
campaign—when the bands played "Happy Days are Here
Again!" and the great majority of Americans turned with a will
to the calmly confident candidate—everything that he had battled for in the intervening years seemed faced with annihila-

tion: peace and prosperity, good neighborliness, democratic decency: all were threatened.

A lesser man would have trembled at the prospect, fled the fight. But not Franklin Roosevelt. He was sixty years old on January 30, 1942, and that day, when he might have been enjoying the winter landscape of the Hudson shores from the peaceful fireside of his old home, he was instead seated at his desk in the White House. There, at the most important desk in the entire world, the same spirit that had marked him in the grim crisis of 1933 gripped him again. Now it was not just a Nation that had to be saved from its own folly. It was a World. Above his desk there was a big map—a map with lines traced from Mozhaisk to Singapore, from Corregidor to the West African coast. On that tremendous front men were dying that day, as men have always died, for those nameless things that have always meant more than life. Calmly and with almost cheerful confidence he gazed at the map of the world, ready to fight as long as he is called upon to do so, to bring its people back to sanity, and decency, and peace.

Bibliography

The following books, magazines and newspapers have been freely used for facts and background in the writing of this book, and thanks are duly made to the various authors and publishers.

Wilbur C. Abbott: New York in the Revolution. 1929.

Charles Francis Adams: Three Episodes of Massachusetts History. 1892.

James Truslow Adams: The History of New England; 3 vols. 1927.

Walter S. Allerton: A History of the Allerton Family. 1900.

Joseph Alsop and Robert Kintner: Article in Life Magazine; Sept. 9, 1940.

A. A. Aspinwall: Aspinwall Genealogy. 1901.

J. S. Barbour: A History of William Patterson and the Darien Company. 1907.

"Walter Barrett" (pseudonym for J. A. Scoville): The Old Merchants of New York City. 5 volumes. 1885.

Moses Yale Beach: Wealth and Pedigree of the Wealthy Citizens of New York. 1842.

Carl L. Becker: History of the Political Parties in the Province of New York: 1760–1776.

Thomas Beer: Hanna. 1928.

Ruby Black: Eleanor Roosevelt: A Biography. 1940.

William Bradford: History of Plymouth Plantation. Commonwealth Edition. 1899.

Joseph G. B. Bullock: A History and Genealogy of the Families of Bulloch and Stobo. 1911.

Isabel MacBeath Calder: The New Haven Colony. 1934.

John Chamberlain: Farewell to Reform.

W. M. Clemens: The Ancestry of Theodore Roosevelt: A Genealogical Record. 1914.

Henry Clews: Fifty Years in Wall Street. 1908.

Anna Roosevelt Cowles, Editor: Letters from Theodore Roosevelt to Anna Roosevelt Cowles, 1870–1918. 1924.

H. W. Cushman: A History and Biographical Genealogy of the Cushmans. 1855.

Henry Barton Dawson, editor: New York City During the American Revolution. 1861.

Armand de Bahault: Les Origines de New York: Claes Rooswelt. Vol. 28. 1898.

Joel Andrews Delano: The Genealogy, History and Alliances of the American House of Delano. 1889.

Chauncey M. Depew: My Memoirs of Eighty Years. 1922.

Rev. de Saintagne, etc.: Genealogie de la Familie Rooswelt.

Bernard De Voto, Editor: Mark Twain in Eruption. 1940.

The Dictionary of American Biography.

Dutchess County Historical Society: Year Book. 1931, etc.

Stephen Fiske: Offhand Portraits of Famous New Yorkers. 1884.

Alexander C. Flick: Loyalism in New York During the American Revolution. 1909.

Fortune Magazine. Especially Sept. 1931, and Oct. 1932.

Anne Grant: Memoirs of an American Lady. 1808.

Margherita Hamm: Famous Families of New York. 1902.

The Historical Bulletin: Roosevelt, Bulloch and Allied Families. Vol. vii. 1906.

Geoffrey Hellman: Article in Life Magazine. January 20, 1941.

R. R. Hoes: President (Theodore) Roosevelt's Old Ulster Ancestry: Olde Ulster. Vol. 1; pp. 102–104. 1905.

Philip Hone: The Diary of Philip Hone (edited by Allan Nevins). 1936.

Franklyn Howland: A Brief Genealogical and Biographical

History of Arthur, Henry, and John Howland and their Descendants. 1885.

J. H. Innes: New Amsterdam and Its People: Studies Social and Topographical of the Town Under Dutch and Early English Rule. 1902.

G. P. Insh: Papers Relating to the Ships and Voyages of the Company Trading to Africa and the Indies. 1924.

Alvin Page Johnson: Franklin D. Roosevelt's Colonial Ancestors: Their Part in the Making of American History. 1933.

Judge Thomas Jones: History of New York During the Revolution. (Edited by E. F. de Lancey.) 1879.

Matthew Josephson: The Robber Barons. 1934. The President Makers: the Culture of Politics and Leadership in an Age of Enlightenment, 1896-1919. 1940.

King's Handbook of New York.

Life Magazine: Various Articles.

Ernest K. Lindley: Franklin D. Roosevelt. 1934.

Mrs. E. Fries Lumis: The Queens of American Society. n.d.

Gustavus Myers: History of the Great American Fortunes. History of Tammany Hall.

Walter Millis: The Martial Spirit.

William M. MacBean, editor: Biographical Register of the St. Andrew's Society of the State of New York; 1756–1806. 1902.

Ward McAllister: Society as I Have Found It. 1890.

New York Herald: Files.

New York Times: Files.

New York Tribune: Files.

New York World: Files.

Harvey O'Connor: The Astors. 1941.

Bellamy Partridge: An Imperial Saga: The Roosevelt Family in America. 1936.

Henry F. Pringle: Theodore Roosevelt: A Biography. 1931.

The Real Estate Directory of Manhattan. 1940.

Corinne Roosevelt Robinson: My Brother Theodore Roosevelt. 1921.

Franklin Delano Roosevelt, editor: Records of the Town of Hyde Park, Dutchess County. 1928.

Hall Roosevelt, in collaboration with Samuel Duff McCoy: Odyssey of an American Family: An Account of the Roosevelts and Their Kin as Travelers, 1613–1938. 1939.

Mrs. James Roosevelt: My Boy Franklin. 1933.

Selections from the Correspondence of Theodore Roosevelt and Henry Cabot Lodge, 1884–1918. 1925.

Lorenzo Sabine: Biographical Sketches of the Loyalists in the ,American Revolution. 2 vols. 1864.

St. Nicholas Society of New York: Genealogical Record. 1905.

Karl Schriftgiesser: Families. 1940.

George W. Schuyler: Philip Schuyler and His Family. 1885.

J. A. Scoville: See "Walter Barrett."

F. M. Smith: Roosevelt Arms and Family History. 1909.

I. N. P. Stokes: The Iconography of Manhattan Island.

Maria Longworth Storer: Theodore Roosevelt, the Child. 1925.

Roland G. Usher: The Pilgrims and Their History. 1918.

Hendrick W. Van Loon: The Life and Times of Peter Stuyvesant. 1928.

Mrs. Schuyler van Rensselaer: History of the City of New York in the Seventeenth Century. 1909.

Dingman Versteeg, Editor: New Netherland Register. 1908.

O. G. Villard: Prophets True and False. 1928.

Dixon Wecter: The Saga of American Society. 1937.

Don Wharton: The Roosevelt Omnibus. 1934.

C. B. Whittlesey: The Roosevelt Genealogy, 1642–1902. 1902.

Lyman Horace Weeks: Prominent Families of New York. 1897.

James Grant Wilson, editor: The Memorial History of New York. 1893.

INDEX

Index